SUSTAINABLE DEVELOPMENT
THE UK STRATEGY

WITHDRAWN

Presented to Parliament by the Secretaries of State for the Environment and for Foreign and Commonwealth Affairs, the
Chancellor of the Exchequer, the President of the Board of Trade, the Secretaries of State for Transport , Defence,
National Heritage and Employment, the Chancellor of the Duchy of Lancaster, the Secretaries of State for Scotland,
Northern Ireland, Education and Health, the Minister for Agriculture, Fisheries and Food, the Secretary of State for
Wales and the Minister for Overseas Development by Command of Her Majesty.
January 1994.

N 0074205 8

Cm 2426

£22.00 net

FOREWORD

BY THE PRIME MINISTER

At Rio, leaders and representatives from over 150 states, developed and developing countries alike, adopted a declaration committing themselves to make future development sustainable – not to turn their backs on growth, but to ensure that the price of growth did not become an intolerable bill for future generations.

This document looks at the challenges the UK will face over the next 20 years if it is to achieve that goal. There are some areas where considerable progress has already been made, others where the debate is only just starting. The document sets out a future agenda – not just for Government but for business, for organisations and for individual men and women.

It has already been the subject of extensive consultation – but we will need to go much wider than Government if we are to take it forward successfully. I am appointing a Panel of people of great expertise on environmental, scientific and business matters to advise the Government on future developments. The Secretary of State for the Environment will also bring together regularly representatives of interested groups in a UK Round Table on Sustainable Development.

Sustainable development is difficult to define. But the goal of sustainable development can guide future policy. We need a hard-headed approach to sustainability based on good science and robust economics. We also need to be sensitive to the intangibles that cannot be reduced to scientific imperatives and the narrow language of economics.

Making the choices necessary to deliver sustainable development requires a national and international debate. This Strategy is the starting point for that debate in the UK and the UK's contribution to the wider international debate.

John Major

INTRODUCTION

BY THE SECRETARY OF STATE FOR THE ENVIRONMENT

Man has grown used to living as conqueror. So sure are we of our title to the planet that we have long taken it for granted. Science, which has enabled us to discover the intricacies and the wonders of our world, has not led us to treasure it. Instead it has fed our desire to dominate all things. Disease must be eradicated, weeds destroyed, pests eliminated. Roads and railways could blast their way through mountain ranges, dams hold back mighty rivers, and bulldozers turn forests into pasture. There seemed no limit to what man could do.

Then science began to show the measure of our human weakness. As population grew exponentially and development spread ever more widely the effect we have upon the planet became a matter of increasing concern. Our successes were themselves the cause of many of our new fears. Healthier, well-nourished people lived longer; fewer children died; more and more survived to be parents themselves. We began to see that growth and development demanded a price, and that price was increasing beyond our ability to pay. Effects we could ignore when they were confined to the actions of a few, became intolerable when they were spread more and more widely.

What is now seen as a matter of global concern was heralded in the industrial areas of the rich world. Not much smoke and a vast amount of sky seemed of no account. A lot of smoke, pushed out by a lot of people in a concentrated area, made cities impossibly fog-bound and increasingly unhealthy.

Britain began to learn that lesson a hundred years ago when our pea-soupers were famed throughout Europe. The London fog was the stuff of many a novel and the cause of an untold number of deaths. Indeed, the phrase "acid rain" was coined by Britain's first Chief Alkali Inspector, Angus Smith, in the 19th century. Finally, in the 1950s, fogs led to the Clean Air Acts which mark the beginning of modern environmental legislation. London led the way with a law which has improved our cities and enabled us to restore our great buildings. Westminster Abbey and the Houses of Parliament can now be seen in their original colours for the first time – at the same time. For hundreds of years we had accepted the growth of pollution and only when it became utterly intolerable did we take effective action against it. Now we are seeing how much it has deprived us.

As the fish come back to our rivers and the wild flowers to the unsprayed margins of more and more of our fields we learn just how much we have lost. Like a former smoker recovering his sense of smell, we have begun to rediscover a richness in the world which we had all but forgotten.

Yet we cannot allow our proper concern to blind us to mankind's need to change and develop. A society which does not grow is one which cannot satisfy some of our basic human needs. "Growth is the only evidence of life": Newman's quotation warns us against suggesting that we could promote the shrinking economy as a basis for sustainability. Economic development is just as important a concept as environmental protection, and we must find ways of achieving both together.

The question however is, do we have to wait until disaster overwhelms us before we make the radical changes necessary to protect our world for future generations? That is the vital challenge of sustainable development. If we act now there is much that can be saved which will otherwise disappear forever.

We need a sense of urgency as well as a realisation of the need for global involvement. Urgency because time is running out. And global involvement because without it the efforts of individual nations will be undermined by those who refuse to shoulder their proper burdens.

The United Kingdom is determined to make sustainable development the touchstone of its policies. We recognise that this means a change of attitudes throughout the nation. That change cannot be achieved overnight, but that gives no grounds for defeatism – it should instead act as a spur to action.

This document is only the beginning. Year by year we shall need to revise and refine our policies so that our economy can grow in a way which does not cheat on our children.

SUMMARY

SECTION I: INTRODUCTION AND PRINCIPLES

- **Most societies want to achieve economic development to secure higher standards of living, now and for future generations.**
- **They also seek to protect and enhance their environment, now and for their children.**

"Sustainable development" tries to reconcile these two objectives. A widely quoted definition of this concept is "development that meets the needs of the present without compromising the ability of future generations to meet their own needs"[1].

2 The UK was one of the first countries to industrialise, and it has had long experience of the problems that economic development can bring for the environment in terms of resource depletion, pollution, congestion and degradation of the urban and rural environment. As awareness of these problems grew, the UK was also among the first to find ways of tackling them and to develop policies for restoring air and water quality, for reclamation of derelict land and for better planning of towns and countryside. As a major trading nation, the UK has also had long experience of the way in which its trade and investment overseas affect development and the environment in other parts of the world.

3 In September 1990, the Government published a comprehensive strategy for the environment in the UK in the White Paper *This Common Inheritance*[2]. This included many specific targets and objectives for policies in different areas, and progress on these, together with new commitments, have been reported annually since then in the update reports published in September 1991[3] and October 1992[4]. These reports have been a practical expression of the objective of bringing sustainable development to bear in all areas of policy and in all sectors of society. A further White Paper will report on progress in 1993.

The Earth Summit

4 Many other countries have also been trying to relate the concept of sustainable development to their national policy-making and it has become a subject of growing international concern. This concern culminated in the UN Conference on Environment and Development (the Earth Summit) held in Rio de Janeiro in 1992.

5 The main products of the Earth Summit were:
- **Agenda 21**: a comprehensive programme of action needed throughout the world to achieve a more sustainable pattern of development for the next century;
- the **Climate Change Convention**: an agreement between countries establishing a framework for action to reduce the risks of global warming by limiting the emission of so-called "greenhouse gases";
- the **Biodiversity Convention**: an agreement between countries about how to protect the diversity of species and habitats in the world;
- **a statement of principles** for the management, conservation and sustainable development of all the world's forests.

6 International machinery was also established to follow up these agreements. A new UN Commission on Sustainable Development (CSD) was set up to monitor progress on Agenda 21, and had its first meeting in New York in June 1993. Each of the Conventions will have a Conference of the Parties to monitor progress against commitments made and review the need for further action. The CSD will monitor implementation of the forest principles.

7 An important recommendation of the Earth Summit was that individual countries should prepare strategies and action plans to implement their parts of these agreements. The UK believes that effective national strategies of this kind, containing real commitments and targets and substantive measures to achieve them, are essential in order to make progress on the problems affecting the environment of the whole world. The UK Government has accordingly prepared a separate document on each of the four "Rio" agreements. All four are being published simultaneously as a coordinated follow-up to the Summit. The UK will also be working closely with its European and other international partners to carry forward the achievements of the Summit.

8 Agenda 21 placed great emphasis on the need for all sectors of society to participate in the formation of effective national strategies for sustainable development. The Government has consulted widely in the preparation of this Strategy, using written consultations, seminars, round table discussions and other contacts. Annex III summarises the written responses to the Government's consultation paper on the Strategy. The Strategy set out here is the Government's strategy, but it identifies the part that will need to be played by other bodies – local government, business, the voluntary sector, individual citizens – and it seeks their active participation.

The structure of the Strategy

9 The Strategy builds directly on the material already set out in the 1990 White Paper and its two successors. But it is structured in a different way to emphasise some of the key elements of sustainable development; it looks 20 years ahead at current trends and emerging problems; and it examines new arrangements and processes for carrying forward sustainable development in the different sectors of society in the future.

10 Section 1 considers the principles of sustainable development. Section 2 then goes on to review the state of the UK environment and to identify key trends and likely pressure points over the next 20 years. Section 3 reviews the major sectors of the economy and identifies where the objectives of sustainability may require new policy developments in the years ahead, and also where the challenge of securing environmental improvements may provide market opportunities and growth points for particular sectors of the economy.

11 Finally, Section 4 discusses how action by central and local government, by business and industry, by voluntary bodies, and by individual people can best help. Sustainable development cannot be achieved simply or solely by Governments adopting appropriate policies, important though these are. The decisions and actions of other agencies in society are equally important. And the decisions, choices and behaviour of individuals in their homes and working lives are perhaps the most significant of all. The most important part of the Sustainable Development Strategy will, therefore, lie in the way it is carried forward, and in the arrangements proposed for developing a fruitful partnership between all the different sectors of society in the cause of sustainable development.

The principles of sustainable development

12 The Strategy first reviews the basic aims and principles underlying sustainable development. Sustainable development does not mean having less economic development: on the contrary, a healthy economy is better able to generate the resources to meet people's needs, and new investment and environmental improvement often go hand in hand. Nor does it mean that every aspect of the present environment should be preserved at all costs. What it requires is that decisions throughout society are taken with proper regard to their environmental impact.

13 Historically, human health has been a primary consideration in environment policy and must always remain so. In the UK, acute health problems are now rarely the result of environmental causes, and attention has shifted to the health implications of long-term, low-level exposure to

environmental pollution. Cause and effect are harder to assess here and extensive studies may be needed in such cases to establish what the dangers are.

14 A parallel concern has been to conserve natural resources. The motive here is often to protect resources that are of economic value (such as land, fish stocks, and a diversity of species). But there is also a desire to protect resources, such as landscape and wildlife, that people value for their own sake. In the present age, concern extends beyond the immediate environment to global issues – such as protection of the oceans and great forests of the world, of the stratospheric ozone layer, and of the world's climate.

15 Because in many ways the environment is shared, collective action is necessary. There are certain specific principles to take into account in pursuing this:
- Decisions should be based on the best possible scientific information and analysis of risks.
- Where there is uncertainty and potentially serious risks exist, precautionary action may be necessary.
- Ecological impacts must be considered, particularly where resources are non-renewable or effects may be irreversible.
- Cost implications should be brought home directly to the people responsible – the "polluter pays" principle.

Judgements have to be made about the weight to be put on these factors in particular cases. Sometimes environmental costs have to be accepted as the price of economic development, but on other occasions a site, or an ecosystem, or some other aspect of the environment, has to be regarded as so valuable that it should be protected from exploitation.

16 In policy-making, proper tools of analysis have to be applied. An important objective is to develop better indicators and natural resource accounting which will over time give some better measure of the benefits and damage to the environment associated with economic change.

SECTION 2: ENVIRONMENTAL MEDIA AND RESOURCES

17 Human beings are now the main cause of change in the world environment. The rapid increase in world population, in consumption of resources and in the production of wastes and pollution have profound effects on the world and its natural systems. Further increases in population and in consumption could cause critical problems for the environment and hence mankind itself unless development is wisely guided.

18 This Section of the Strategy reviews issues of population,

resources and the state of the environment for the UK, and seeks to identify those issues and trends which may be particularly important over the next 20 years.

19 The UK pioneered pollution control and has strong regulatory agencies. They have recently developed a system of integrated pollution control that considers the effects of an industrial process on air, land and water together. This is to be taken further with the creation of a single agency for England and Wales and a single agency for Scotland.

Population

20 The population of the UK in 1992 was 57.6 million. Present projections of birth rates and migration trends suggest that the population might increase by 6% to about 61 million in 2012 and might stabilise thereafter at about 62 million (8% above present levels) around the year 2030.

21 The UK's rate of population increase is slow by comparison with that of many developing countries and compared with earlier periods of the UK's history. But the density of the population (235 persons per sq km) is already one of the highest among countries of the world. The density in the South East of England (746 persons per sq km) is much higher still, and this region has one of the most rapidly growing populations through internal migration, along with East Anglia and South West England. In contrast, the density of population in Scotland (66 persons per sq km) is among the lowest in Europe.

22 Moreover, although the overall population is not increasing rapidly, the number of households is increasing more rapidly as people choose to live in smaller groupings or separately. On present projections, the number of households in the UK is projected to increase by 14% to 26 million by 2012. This leads not only to increased pressures on the housing stock and on land for development, but also to increased consumption of many goods and services which tend to be used by households rather than individuals.

23 The standard of living is also increasing. Over the last 20 years, the economy has grown in real terms by around a half, and broadly similar growth rates are projected for the future.

24 The Government believes that couples should make their own decisions about how many children to have, although family planning services should be widely available. The upshot of all these individual decisions, together with continued economic growth, is expected to be:
- a slowing down of population growth, with population stabilisation in the first half of the next century;

- a projected 14% increase in household numbers.

This represents further potential pressures on land, water, energy and other natural resources required for housing, food, employment and transport. It is, therefore, all the more important to make good use of the UK's natural resources. Land must be carefully used, which will mean high densities of development in some areas, and derelict or contaminated land will have to come back into beneficial use. Other natural resources will have to be husbanded carefully and efficiently, minimising waste, and reusing or recycling materials wherever this is economical.

Global atmosphere

25 Emissions of carbon dioxide (CO_2) and other greenhouse gases may result in warming of the earth's surface and consequent changes in climate and rises in sea level. This will be one of the major problems for the whole world over the next 20 years and beyond if improved scientific understanding of climate change confirms present estimates. The UK is, therefore, supporting a wide range of research into the extent and possible effects of climate change.

26 The UK has committed itself under the Framework Convention on Climate Change to take measures aimed at returning emissions of CO_2 and other greenhouse gases to 1990 levels by the year 2000. But the current Convention measures will need to be reviewed in the light of further scientific evidence and it may be necessary to identify targets and measures for the years beyond 2000. The UK *Climate Change Programme*[5] identifies some of the options for further measures to contribute towards a sustainable international approach to greenhouse gas emissions into the next century, if these do prove necessary.

27 The production of substances which deplete the ozone layer, such as chlorofluorocarbons (CFCs), may allow harmful ultraviolet rays, which can cause skin cancer and crop failure, to penetrate to the earth's surface. The UK has played an active part in negotiating the Montreal Protocol on Substances that Deplete the Ozone Layer and its subsequent revisions, and is vigorously pursuing its own obligations under those agreements and related EC Regulations. The production and supply of new halons and CFCs in the UK will have been phased out by the beginning of 1994 and 1995 respectively, and arrangements made to recycle existing materials wherever possible rather than releasing them to the atmosphere. The UK is also playing an active part in bilateral and multilateral efforts to assist developing countries to phase out their production and use of these substances.

Air quality

28 The quality of the atmosphere in towns and cities in the UK has improved greatly. The regulation of industrial emissions and domestic smoke control policies, coupled with the steady replacement of coal by cleaner domestic fuels, have been the main causes of these improvements. However, pollution from vehicles is now becoming the major problem for urban air quality. Emissions of nitrogen oxides (NO_x) from road transport have more than doubled over the last 20 years. The new generation of cleaner vehicles (fitted with catalytic converters) which are now coming onto the roads will help. By 2012, NO_x emissions overall are expected to have fallen by between a quarter and a third from 1991 levels. By then, however, on current projections of traffic growth, the benefits of recent improvements in emissions will be counterbalanced by the number of vehicles and volume of traffic. But the UK is actively participating in EC-wide discussions to bring further significant improvements in vehicle emission standards.

29 Acid rain can harm vegetation, aquatic life and buildings, including historic monuments. Man-made sulphur emissions are the principal source of acid rain in most parts of Europe, and have contributed significantly to acidification of freshwaters and soils in many areas. Historically, the UK has put out relatively high levels of sulphur, because of early industrialisation and reliance on coal. However, UK emissions of sulphur have declined by nearly a half since the 1960s. Furthermore, reductions of 80% compared with 1980 are likely to be achieved by 2010–2015, following shifts in fuel use and the extension of clean technologies. Following these reductions, some waters are already becoming measurably less acidic – to the benefit of their fish and plant life. This is the case in the UK, for example, in sensitive Northern and Western parts. Further international agreements are expected in 1994 on the reduction of sulphur emissions. By 2012, sulphur emissions are expected to have fallen to levels at least closely approaching long-term sustainability.

Freshwater

30 Most of the UK has an abundance of water. However, East Anglia and South East England have only modest rainfall, leading to considerable pressure on water resources from the high density of population and the growing demands for water for domestic and leisure purposes as living standards rise.

31 Between 1992 and 2012, demand for public water supply is likely to have risen by around 10% in England and Wales, with the greatest need for additional resources likely in the Anglian, Thames, Wessex and Southern regions of the National Rivers Authority (NRA). Unless these trends are halted, these areas will need extra surface and groundwater sources, or to have substantial amounts of water transferred from other parts of the country. Both these alternatives could have environmental disadvantages, and this is, therefore, a key issue for sustainability. In Scotland and Northern Ireland, projected demand will be met from existing resources.

32 The approach of the Government, the Director General of Water Services, and the NRA is that, to the extent that it is economic to do so, the need for major new water resource schemes should be deferred through selective metering in areas of shortage and measures to restrict leakage.

33 In England and Wales, 99% of dwellings receive their water from public supplies. These supplies are rarely interrupted, are generally of high quality and do not present risks to health. Of the 3.7 million tests of drinking water, 98.7% showed compliance with the statutory water quality standards which incorporate EC requirements which in most cases are far higher than is necessary to safeguard health. Further improvements are in hand to refurbish supply systems and improve water quality. For the future, the reduction of lead in drinking water is a high priority, particularly from lead pipes in houses.

34 Freshwater quality is relatively good compared with elsewhere in Europe: 95% of rivers and canals in the UK are of good or fair quality. Major pollution incidents from sewage and agriculture are reducing rapidly. But a small proportion of rivers continue to be affected by severe industrial pollution. Present policies are directed towards cleaning up point source discharges by industry, agriculture, and water companies before release to rivers or coastal waters takes place, and towards taking positive measures to minimise diffuse pollution, for example through codes of practice and advice to farmers.

35 The protection of groundwater must also be a high priority over the next 20 years, because of the time it can take for pollutants to reach groundwater and the difficulty of cleaning it up once polluted. Pollution from nitrate and pesticides, and by leaching from waste disposal sites and land contaminated in former uses, is an actual or potential problem in some locations. Changes in agricultural practice and land usage are tending to contain nitrate pollution. However, intensification of agriculture (maximising production by increasing crop yields on the minimum area of land) can still cause problems in some localities. Some measures have been taken, or are in hand, to moderate threats, for example from storage of contaminating materials. The NRA has recently put in place a comprehensive policy on groundwater protection to guide its regulatory activities; this also should be taken into account by others including those who design and decide on new developments.

The sea

36 Marine water quality around the UK is generally good, with the exception of certain specific areas (mainly estuaries adjoining industrialised zones), and input from human activities are declining. Long-standing controls over pollution have recently been improved and international machinery is in place to ensure that over the next 20 years, land-based developments will be consistent with maintaining the marine environment. No significant problems are expected to arise from dumping waste at sea, since only very limited categories of wastes will be permitted to be dumped in future.

37 The level of demand for marine aggregates may raise difficult decisions over the next 20 years, depending on demand and other sources of supply. New offshore developments for oil and gas are carefully regulated, although difficult questions will arise as existing wells approach the end of their life. Levels of fish stocks depend not only on the quality of the marine environment but also on fishing practices. More powerful fishing vessels and improved technology are now putting many fish stocks under severe pressure. And as leisure activities grow, there could be increased pressures over the next 20 years on particular coastal zones, although bathing water quality around the coast does not present any significant health hazard.

Soil

38 The nature of the land and the quality of soil vary considerably throughout the UK. Soil is a vital, limited resource and needs to be managed and used in a way which sustains its functions.

39 The threats to soil come from erosion, irreversible decline in organic matter, increase in acidity and urban development. Pollution in the atmosphere, agricultural practices and contamination from industrial plants or from wastes can all affect soil quality. Fortunately, these problems are not widespread in the UK, although there are particular concerns in some areas.

40 Many industrial processes can contaminate land, and often the damage remains long after the plants concerned have closed down. Recent estimates suggest that as much as 100,000 to 200,000 hectares of land might be affected. It is important to stop this happening on a similar scale in the future, and to bring back as much contaminated land as possible into a usable state. This can help reduce pressures for development of green field sites. The Government is conducting a review of public bodies' powers and duties to deal with contaminated land and the Royal Commission on Environmental Pollution is currently examining the technical

and scientific issues to advise on proper management of the soil for the future.

Land use

41 Agriculture occupies 77% of the UK land, and forestry about 10%. The rest is mainly urban land, on which around three-quarters of the UK population live. The increasing pressures for housing and development require even greater care in optimising the use of finite land resources. If these pressures were unrestrained, the urban area could increase in some English counties by over 15% by 2001, compared with 1981, and still further by 2012. In principle, the free market in land should operate to achieve an efficient basic allocation of land between competing uses, but the land market is an imperfect one in various ways. Successive Governments have thought it necessary to intervene, for example, through the land use planning system and grants for restoration of derelict land. The planning system, in particular, has been a powerful instrument for protecting those aspects of the environment whose value is not adequately reflected through a free market.

42 Over the past 20 years, the UK has achieved a great deal in the conservation of wildlife, habitats and biodiversity; of hedgerows, trees and forests; of the coastline and other areas of outstanding natural beauty; and of urban parks and the Green Belts surrounding major cities. But although the demand to give continued protection to these features of the environment is as strong as ever, the countervailing pressures caused by population growth, household formation and demand for transport are no less strong. Land use will continue to be one of the most sensitive pressure points.

Minerals

43 Minerals are important natural resources which are essential in the production of many goods and services. There are large reserves of many useful minerals in the UK, but it is, nevertheless, crucially important to ensure that they are used efficiently and to recycle and minimise waste wherever possible.

44 The UK exports some minerals, including crude petroleum, gas and coal. The value of mineral exports was £4.9 billion in 1992. A wide range of minerals is imported, the most significant being crude petroleum, coal, natural gas, and some metals. Imports were valued at £5.9 billion in 1992. For aggregates, the trade is very small – less than 1% of total UK production and consumption over the period since 1985.

45 Within the UK, demand for aggregates (sand and gravel, and crushed rock) used in the construction industry is projected to increase sharply over the next 20 years. Some of this can be met through increased recycling, but new extraction sites will be needed. It is likely to be increasingly difficult to identify extraction sites which are environmentally acceptable.

46 The UK has substantial reserves of coal, oil and gas. Production from opencast mines rose during the 1980s but has since fallen back. Production from deep mines has been falling and no new planning permissions have been given in recent years for any major deep mines.

Wildlife and habitats

47 UK wildlife and habitats are strongly influenced by its geographical location as temperate off-shore islands on the North Eastern Atlantic edge of Europe. In global terms, the UK is not particularly rich in species. For example, it has only 210 of the 9,881 species of breeding birds in the world. However, the UK's range of habitats is unique, with many special characteristics such as extensive rocky coasts and estuaries and the extensive raised bog and mires and upland heaths.

48 Human activities have affected almost every corner of the UK and have produced a tapestry of landscapes which people value very highly. These semi-natural landscapes provide habitats for an abundance of species which might not have flourished in a wholly natural environment. Nevertheless, the rapid development of settlements and transport infrastructure, intensive agricultural production, and air and water pollution have contributed to a loss of biodiversity over the last 50 years, especially in lowland areas. At the same time, there have been increases in some sea-bird populations, a recovery in bird of prey numbers and a few successful re-establishments.

49 The planning system and measures to control pollution are important in countering decline in biodiversity. More direct protection of species and habitats is provided through statutory designation of protected areas. Beneficial ownership of such areas by public and voluntary bodies is helpful. In addition, there has been a substantial increase in publicly funded schemes to encourage measures to safeguard and enhance areas of landscape interest; this process has been significantly advanced by the 1992 reform of the Common Agricultural Policy. The *Biodiversity Action Plan*[6] sets out the position in detail.

SECTION 3: ECONOMIC DEVELOPMENT AND SUSTAINABILITY

50 Conventional measures of economic growth do not take into account the impact of that growth on the environment and the loss of some natural resources. Nonetheless, as measured, the UK economy has grown by about a half over the last 20 years, and a number of future projections contain a mid-range assumption that there may be 60% growth or thereabouts over the next 20 years.

51 Different sectors of the economy have had different growth paths and this divergence may be expected to continue. Particularly significant from the point of view of sustainable development are:

● **agriculture:** modern farming methods have led to substantially increased production over the past 50 years but at the price of additional pressures on the environment;

● **forestry:** the UK's forest cover had fallen to only 5% by the beginning of this century; this has been increased to 10%;

● **fisheries:** improved fishing technology is putting many stocks under serious pressure;

● **minerals extraction:** demands for some minerals have been increasing over the last few decades, and are expected to continue to increase over the next 20 years; this is particularly the case for aggregates, and it is likely to be increasingly difficult to identify extraction sites which are environmentally acceptable;

● **energy:** increased efficiency of energy use throughout the economy has facilitated economic growth over the last 20 years, and energy production has shifted to much less polluting technologies; however, increased demand over the next 20 years could lead to increased environmental pressure;

● **manufacturing and services:** a significant shift from heavy industry towards more advanced technology and provision of services has lessened some pressures on the environment, but it will always be necessary for industry to handle responsibly issues of resource depletion, pollution, emissions and waste;

● **waste:** large quantities of waste arise as an undesirable by-product of production, packaging and consumption, with threats to soil and water quality if it is not properly managed;

● **development and construction:** the increase in households coupled with increased economic activity will put increasing pressures on finite land resources, particularly in the South of the country;

● **transport:** increasing demands for mobility, mainly in road traffic, are placing increasing pressures on the environment in town and country, and giving rise to problems of pollution and CO_2 emissions;

● **leisure:** the demands for new forms of recreation and other leisure activity represent a strongly growing pressure on the environment.

Agriculture

52 The rapid growth in productivity over the last 50 years has brought substantial economic benefits. The challenge for the future is to build on this success and to continue to produce an adequate supply of good quality food and non-food products while paying greater attention to the methods of production and their effects on natural resources and the environment.

53 Because agriculture is the major land user in the UK, its environmental effects can be very significant. The drive for increased food production since the Second World War has had a substantial effect on the rural environment and the appearance of the countryside. The high level of agricultural support under the Common Agricultural Policy (CAP) has stimulated further intensification of production, with consequent adverse effects on the environment, including additional habitat loss and problems of water pollution in some areas, particularly from nitrates and farm wastes. The 1992 CAP reform package marked an important change of emphasis, with a reduction in EC support prices and a new requirement on all member states to introduce measures to encourage environmentally friendly farming. The full effects of these reforms are still to be seen.

54 The Government will continue to work for further reductions in levels of support and the full integration of environmental considerations into the CAP, and to encourage an internationally competitive and environmentally sensitive UK agriculture, to protect the best and most versatile agricultural land from development and to minimise the use of pesticides and the environmental impact of agricultural wastes. Research and monitoring will make a crucial contribution to the development of the Government's policies.

55 UK Government policies are now aimed at further reducing the level of commodity support under the CAP and at integrating environmental considerations into CAP and into agricultural policies generally. This will include maintaining and further developing measures to:
- promote environmentally friendly farming, the conservation of wildlife and habitats and the protection and restoration of threatened landscapes;
- reduce pollution from agricultural inputs and waste;
- minimise the use of pesticides;
- conserve non-renewable resources.

56 Monitoring the environmental impact of agriculture will play an important part in developing future policy and helping to ensure the long-term sustainability of agriculture.

Forestry

57 The policies of successive governments over the past 70 years have increased forest cover from 5% to 10%. The main strands of present policies are aimed at the protection of the very few surviving ancient and semi-natural woodlands, the sustainable management of all existing woodlands and forests, and a steady expansion of tree cover in harmony with the environment. The *Forestry Programme*[7] gives more details.

Fisheries

58 Sustainable fishing involves securing the survival of the fishing industry by ensuring that fish stocks are not over-exploited. Fishing methods should be adapted to protect biodiversity, to avoid inadvertent capture of non-target species and to prevent damage to the marine environment. Both inland and marine fish farming need to be carried out in such a way that they do not have adverse effects on natural resources and on the environment. Within the EC, sea fishing is controlled through the Common Fisheries Policy (CFP). This includes measures to conserve and rebuild fish stocks and to protect the wider marine ecosystem. However, many fish stocks in EC waters are still over-exploited as indeed is the case elsewhere in the world.

59 The Government will continue to work within the EC for policies based on scientific advice to promote the conservation and renewal of fish stocks and to minimise damage to the wider marine environment. Research will help to improve understanding of the factors affecting fish stocks and to minimise the adverse environmental effects of fishing and fish farming.

Minerals extraction

60 With increasing demands for some minerals, the key issues for sustainability in this sector are:
- to encourage prudent stewardship of mineral resources, while maintaining necessary supplies;
- to reduce the environmental impacts of minerals provision both during minerals extraction and when restoration has been achieved.

61 There are substantial tasks ahead; in particular, the Government will:
- continue its programme of revising and expanding Minerals Planning Guidance Notes to reflect the principles of sustainable development;
- continue research on the availability of mineral resources and the environmental costs and benefits of using different sources;

● encourage sound environmental practice, including the restoration of sites;

● promote more efficient use of mineral resources in general, for example encouraging recycling of materials, and substitution of alternative materials where appropriate.

Energy supply

62 Modern societies are critically dependent on the supply of energy. The way in which energy is produced, supplied and consumed is one of the major ways in which human activity affects the environment.

63 Energy supply remains dominated by fossil fuels. There are vast reserves throughout the world although, in the longer term, supply constraints could lead to higher prices. Meanwhile, it remains important to continue to reduce the pollution and CO_2 emissions from energy production and distribution in the light of improved scientific and economic analysis of their impact, by improving the efficiency with which energy is produced, supplied and consumed in the economy.

64 Realising energy efficiency improvements is a vital mechanism, with potential for reducing CO_2 emissions and combating global warming. The Strategy contains details of current Government initiatives and proposals for achieving greater energy efficiency and anticipated economic and environmental benefits.

65 The energy supply industries also need to be fully involved in promoting energy efficiency. Energy markets should operate within frameworks which do not undermine efforts to improve energy efficiency. Consumers are not interested in the amount of energy supplied to them as such, only in the services it provides such as comfortable living and working temperatures, lighting levels, mechanical operations and transport. The development of competitive markets in energy supply has already given some encouragement to these industries to improve their services to consumers rather than to increase the quantity of energy they supply. The setting up of the Energy Saving Trust and recent changes in the price control formulae for gas and electricity are welcome steps in this direction and progress will be kept under review.

66 Over the coming decades, there will be continuing debate about the proportions of energy being produced from different fuel sources (coal, oil, gas, nuclear, renewables). Questions will continue over the use of particular fuels and their advantages and disadvantages. Government policy is that these questions will be resolved through the operation of the market, guided by price signals which take proper account of the different costs and benefits. The Government intends to review the prospects of nuclear power. Radioactive waste will be managed in such a way as to ensure the continued safety of present and future generations. New and renewable energy technologies have the potential to make a significant contribution to UK energy supply in the next century.

Manufacturing and services

67 Industry is the major creator of wealth. But it has an impact on the environment through resource depletion, emissions and waste. Industry and the service sector also have many opportunities for achieving economic advances alongside environmental improvements: through new techniques and better design, new management practices, energy efficiency and so on. Firms have repeatedly demonstrated innovation, and over the next 20 years this will be a priority. Often innovation is most fertile in small firms, and it will be important to build on the work already being done to get environmental messages across to small firms.

68 Ideally, the manufacturing and service sectors will pursue environmentally friendly practices with the minimum of Government regulation. The Government, working with the EC, must establish the right conditions for adherence to and investment in good environmental practice by business. Industry can promote voluntary schemes; consumers can demand more sustainable products. There is scope for the use of market-based instruments as well as regulation.

69 Government must concentrate on:
● protecting or maintaining essential environmental standards by regulation, if necessary, although the preferred mechanism is the more efficient economic instrument;
● promoting environmental management and such schemes as BS 7750, Eco-Management and Audit, and Responsible Care in the chemicals industry;
● raising consumer awareness through measures such as eco-labelling and environmental reporting;
● encouraging energy efficiency in the workplace;
● encouraging the development of new products and processes to increase efficiency and minimise pollution and waste;
● encouraging the development of new technologies to assist in more effective, efficient and innovative pollution prevention.

70 The influence of the financial sector can be important in encouraging environmentally friendly investment and in considering the best way of providing for financial consequences and liabilities arising from past and present pollution. Systems of environmental accounting and reporting and the growth of "ethical investment" schemes are encouraging new developments.

Biotechnology

71 Biotechnology involves the use of living organisms for manufacturing and services purposes. Traditional biotechnology has already produced considerable benefits, and the advent of modern biotechnology, involving the use of genetically modified organisms, promises many potential benefits including products to improve the environment and human health. But, in accordance with the precautionary principle, biotechnology is regulated to ensure adequate safeguards for environmental safety. The Government has introduced new legislation, set up extensive research programmes, and established expert committees to advise on risks and regulation. As trade in modern biotechnological products grows, international collaboration will be essential.

Chemicals

72 Chemicals are a vital part of a modern economy and the number produced has increased rapidly over the last 20 years. It is clearly important to know whether exposure to chemicals can be harmful to human health or the environment and to take action to reduce the risks when necessary. New chemicals placed on the market for the first time are subject to mandatory testing and a notification requirement under EC legislation, and similar procedures are being introduced for chemicals already on the market.

73 Increased understanding of the biological activity of chemicals at the molecular level is helping chemical manufacturers to design new chemicals which are less hazardous and less persistent in the environment. This new knowledge, and the extensive testing and assessment programmes under way internationally, will help to ensure that chemicals are better managed in the future. It is vital that this knowledge and expertise is passed on to developing countries to avoid repeating past mistakes and to ensure that chemicals are used sustainably for the benefit of mankind.

Waste

74 Large quantities of waste arise as an undesirable by-product of modern production, packaging and consumption, with threats to soil, air and water quality if the waste is not properly managed. The aim must be to minimise the amount of waste produced and to make best use of the waste which is produced. In this way, loss of valuable raw materials and the land which is required for disposal can both be minimised.

75 Everyone has a part to play in securing a more sustainable approach to waste management. Business, in particular, can make a significant contribution by taking greater responsibility for what happens to the waste it generates. There is a hierarchy of waste management options:
● reduction;
● reuse;
● recovery (including recycling and energy recovery);
● disposal without energy recovery by incineration or landfill.

Current waste management practice is tilted too far towards the last option. However, truly sustainable choices are complex. They are restricted by technological possibilities and the balance of benefits against financial costs of the overall best environmental option. In some cases, the environmental costs of recycling waste, in terms of energy consumption and emissions, are higher than for disposal.

76 A legal framework to encourage recycling and to control pollution already exists. In particular, the major industrial processes are required by law to employ the best practicable environmental option under integrated pollution control. However, the Government is considering what further measures, including economic instruments such as a landfill levy, are needed to apply the polluter pays principle to encourage less waste production and more recycling. The Government will also continue to fund research and advice in these areas, as well as providing financial support for minimisation, recycling, and energy from waste initiatives. Specific problems will include the disposal of sewage sludge which can no longer be dumped at sea and the disposal of hazardous waste.

Development and construction

77 Over the next 20 years, economic growth and the projected 14% increase in the number of households will bring new pressures for development. The challenge will be to balance the need for some development against the environmental constraints on the use of land. This requires a strategy to:
● promote attractive and convenient urban areas, in which people will want to live and work;
● encourage new development in locations that are likely to minimise energy consumption;
● encourage the regeneration of urban land and buildings, and the restoration to use for development or open space of derelict and contaminated land;
● integrate the development which is necessary to sustain the rural economy with the protection of the countryside for its landscape, wildlife, agricultural, forestry, recreational

and natural resource value;

● promote an understanding of sustainable development among all those who have an interest in the development process.

78 The construction sector is a major user of natural resources. Its products, in the form of buildings and civil engineering, contribute in a major way to economic development and the quality of life. Decisions taken today on the design of buildings and structures will have an impact on the environment well into the next century.

79 The Government is working with the construction industry to encourage various ways of reducing the environmental impact of buildings. Appropriate design can enable flexibility of use and thus help to prolong the productive lifetime of buildings; it can also be used with environmental assessment methodologies and can help to identify ways to minimise the adverse environmental effects of a building and its site and to reduce energy consumption (and thus CO_2 emissions). Minimisation of waste in the construction process, together with the use of sustainable resources and reuse and recycling of materials, reduces the need for landfill and for the extraction and production of raw materials.

Transport

80 Travel and traffic have grown very rapidly over the last 40 years and are still doing so today. Overall, passenger travel has more than trebled with all the growth occurring in private car usage. Freight movements have increased similarly.

81 The vast bulk of transport growth has been in road transport, reflecting a strong demand from those who want to drive for work and leisure. But there is growing concern about the environmental costs of this growth in terms of congestion, air pollution, noise, disturbance to communities, and demand for land in sensitive areas. Over the next 20 years, increased demand for movement is projected as the economy grows, but with increased resistance to the environmental damage caused by road traffic.

82 Transport derives from the requirements of other activities for access to markets and facilities. It influences costs and decisions elsewhere in the economy. Any measures which are taken to address environmental impacts need to take account of the potential economic consequences and of the need to maintain, so far as possible, the access and choice which industry and individuals require.

83 The main goal for sustainable development in the transport sector must be to meet the economic and social needs for access to facilities with less need for travel and in ways which do not place unacceptable burdens on the environment. This requires policies which will:

● influence the rate of traffic growth;
● provide a framework for individual choice in transport which enables environmental objectives to be met;
● increase the economic efficiency of transport decisions;
● improve the design of vehicles to minimise pollution and CO_2 emissions.

84 Among the measures available to further these goals are:

● ensuring transport costs reflect the wider costs of transport decisions for the economy and the environment which are not currently priced, and so make transport decisions more efficient;
● land use policies which will enable people and business to take advantage of locations which meet their needs for access with less use of transport or with the use of less polluting means of transport;
● market measures or regulation to improve the environmental performance of transport;
● policies and programmes to promote use of public transport instead of the car, and rail and water to transport freight instead of roads, where these can meet the needs for transport efficiently.

Leisure

85 Leisure activities, including tourism, sport and active recreation, play a major part in most people's lives. There has been a marked growth in the scale and diversity of demands in recent years and this is likely to continue. Furthermore, leisure is now a major contributor to the economy, both nationally and in a number of areas.

86 Leisure has an almost unique relationship with the environment because so many leisure activities depend directly on the conservation of natural resources. Leisure activities often contribute directly to the maintenance of especially valued parts of the environment, whilst enhancing the quality of life and people's appreciation of the environment and support for its conservation.

87 However, leisure activities also affect the environment, sometimes adversely. Pressure of numbers can damage sensitive locations, whilst associated impacts include the growth of traffic and proposals for inappropriate development, disturbance and noise, and occasionally conflicts with the local community. Both the leisure industries and the public must become more aware of the consequences of their activities and of the close relationship between the pursuit of leisure and the conservation of the environment.

The Government already supports and encourages sustainable leisure, including practical measures such as local visitor management initiatives. However, both the Government and its agencies need to monitor impacts, provide guidance and consider how far the framework of voluntary restraint, regulation and economic incentives should respond to future developments.

SECTION 4 : PUTTING SUSTAINABILITY INTO PRACTICE

88 The pursuit of a more sustainable economy involves all sectors of the community: central and local government, industry, voluntary bodies and individuals. In preparing this Strategy, the Government has consulted widely with business groups, local authorities, academic institutions and non-governmental organisations. The UK also contributes as a member of the international community towards sustainable development worldwide.

International

89 The Government is committed to pursuing sustainable development for the UK in a way which promotes the sustainable development of the world as a whole, and takes account of potential impacts, direct or indirect, on other countries. The UK works with individual countries and international organisations to develop the right economic and institutional framework to achieve this.

90 The Government recognises the importance of encouraging sustainable economic growth in developing countries and countries in transition. The UK is a major source of private sector capital and technology, and these flows are likely to expand as international trade and investment regulations are liberalised. The UK's aid programme (supplemented by measures to alleviate the debt burden on the poorest countries) plays an important role and is broadly in line with the aims of Agenda 21. Since the Earth Summit, the Government has pursued further initiatives to help developing countries: the Global Technology Partnership Initiative, Partnerships for Change, and the Darwin Initiative for the Survival of Species. Non-governmental organisations too, both UK-based and local, make a valuable contribution in delivering support at an appropriate level.

91 Within the EC, the UK played a leading role in the development of the Fifth Environmental Action Programme. This Programme is linked closely to the principles and themes of Agenda 21 and the UK Government will be seeking to ensure that these principles are put into practice within the EC.

Central government

92 The Government must set the policy framework. It will continue to give particular attention to developing sustainable policies in the areas outlined earlier and promoting their adoption more generally at home and abroad.

93 The market is the most effective mechanism for maintaining the momentum of development, sharing its benefits, and for shaping its course towards sustainability; but it cannot give proper weight to environmental considerations unless the costs of environmental damage or the benefits of environmental improvement are built into the prices charged for goods and services.

94 Environmental quality objectives or targets have long played an important part in guiding policies for environmental improvement. Increasingly, it will be necessary to develop more specific environmental objectives or targets – for different media of the environment or different sectors of the economy as appropriate. These should be supported by sound science and cost benefit analysis. Environmental appraisal techniques should be applied to all policies that affect the environment. And a full range of indicators of environmental performance will be needed to enable progress or deterioration to be monitored.

95 The Government is committed to developing instruments which make markets work for the environment and channel development down sustainable paths. This will also help achieve another important objective: to reduce unnecessary and over-detailed regulation. Nevertheless, regulation will continue to play an important role in protecting the environment with increasing emphasis on more integrated approaches. But regulation which remains must be clear, fair and not excessive or economic activity will be unnecessarily hindered. One way of achieving this is through increased professionalism and efficiency of regulatory organisations and a reduction in the number of regulators with whom individual organisations must deal. The Government is committed to establishing Environment Agencies for England and Wales, and for Scotland, in pursuance of these goals.

96 In addition, the Government will give a clear lead in its application of sustainability and environmental principles to its own operations. The Government has already nominated "Green Ministers" in each Department and has a Cabinet Committee to consider environmental policy. It has also promoted the environmental appraisal of new policies and in 1994 will review the effectiveness of its measures for environmental appraisal of policies and programmes. All Departments have recently produced "green housekeeping"

strategies and will investigate environmental management systems by the end of 1994.

Local authorities

97 Councils have been in the forefront in developing the concept of sustainable development at a local level and applying their own versions of Agenda 21. Local government has set up its own Local Agenda 21 initiative to encourage this.

98 Local authorities have been active in developing new concepts of environmental management and audit to assist them in making their own operations more sustainable, and in mobilising their local communities. Central and local government are jointly devising a voluntary scheme for eco-management and audit in local government which should be in place by 1995.

Businesses

99 Many firms have voluntarily adopted environmental management practices. They are partly responding to the demands of the growing environmental marketplace but are also recognising that action to improve their environmental performance can increase competitiveness. Central government can help to promote this, but it must also set the right framework of regulation and economic instruments. The Government receives advice from industry through several channels and it values these. It proposes to review the way in which information is presented to smaller businesses – who may be less well informed about potential changes in the pipeline or potential market opportunities – to ensure that it is easy to comprehend and act on.

Voluntary bodies

100 The UK has a thriving voluntary sector and 10 of the largest environment and conservation groups have a combined membership of 4.5 million. The Government, where appropriate, supports this activity with grant aid and meets individuals from some of the leading groups in a consultative forum. It wants to encourage other voluntary groups to become involved in environmental issues but they may need more information, for example, on grants and sometimes practical suggestions. The Government has decided to review with representatives of the main environment groups whether new initiatives are required, especially to encourage and help smaller groups or those voluntary groups whose main activities have been outside the environmental field but which might become more involved.

Citizens

101 Sustainable development requires changes in lifestyle from everyone, such as limiting use of energy and of the car and exercising "green" criteria when buying goods and services. One of the most powerful influences on producers is that of the discriminating customer or private investor. Opinion polls show that the environment remains a major concern with members of the public but, in practice, people do not or cannot always make the changes in lifestyle that they say they are willing to make. As consumers, people will be helped by the eco-labelling scheme and, as citizens, by the programmes of central and local government and other organisations to publish information and invite discussion. The Government will also carry forward its new initiative – the Green Brigade – to involve children in environmental action, and is launching a voluntary scheme called Environment Watch. However, there may be more that could be done to encourage individual commitment, to give incentives or to remove obstacles in people's paths. The Government will look closely at this in 1994 and consult on what more might be done; a new proposal for a "Citizens' Environment Initiative" is outlined below (see 112).

Economic quantification

102 Better decisions about sustainability could be taken within government and in industry if the full economic costs of environmental considerations were taken into account. Research into environmental accounting is being promoted in many countries. There are major difficulties, however, including fundamental questions of methodology. The best hope in the short term lies in making better measurements of the quantities of environmental pollution or the use of resources, whether or not costs can be added. Nonetheless, the Government will take forward work on constructing environmental accounts for the UK.

Land use planning

103 The UK planning system has long existed to weigh the interests of economic development and environmental protection. The Government has been revising its planning guidance for local authorities to incorporate concepts of sustainability. For example, planning policy guidance now places greater emphasis on sustaining the viability and vitality of town centres. A current research project is looking at how well the guidance notes are being incorporated into individual plans and decisions in England and Wales. The Government proposes to build on this by further research into ways in which the principles of sustainable development can be applied by planning authorities, and the publication of a good practice guide.

Energy efficiency

104 The consumption of energy is one of the major issues of sustainability. It is important both to produce and consume available energy as efficiently as possible to minimise environmental impact. There are well established government programmes in the UK to promote energy efficiency in the different sectors of the economy and these will be developed further. New measures have also been taken recently to encourage the suppliers of gas and electricity to promote more efficient use of energy rather than to seek maximum sales. The Government sees this as an important new direction which it will monitor.

Science, engineering and technology

105 Much has been achieved in understanding the environment and how to exploit, manage and protect it. But there are vital roles for science, engineering and technology in pursuing economic development that goes fully with the grain of environmental protection. For example, engineering and technology not only provide cleaner industrial plant and catalytic converters in cars but, through biological and chemical advances, can also generate improvements in the treatment of waste waters and the development of new varieties of crop plants, which have built-in resistance to pests and diseases and thus require smaller applications of pesticides.

106 There are many challenges and opportunities, some requiring research at the very frontiers of knowledge. The Government will require those publicly funded bodies concerned with the promotion, support and conduct of science, engineering and technology to address in their programmes the issues of sustainable development and to consider measures to improve the dissemination of their findings. It will encourage similar approaches in the private and voluntary sectors and in European and wider international programmes.

107 Higher technology standards are also encouraged through pollution control policies: both by means of regulation, on the basis of the application of the best available techniques not entailing excessive cost (BATNEEC); and by economic instruments, which give firms incentives to adopt systems which give higher environmental standards at acceptable costs. The Government is reviewing the links it has with research institutions and private industry to ensure that new measures give as much long-term support as possible to improved technological development and application.

Working together

108 Sustainable development is already being promoted actively in many different ways in the UK at national and at local level, in business and in people's homes. But the Government believes that three new measures are desirable:

- the **Government's Panel on Sustainable Development** to give authoritative and independent advice;
- a **UK Round Table on Sustainable Development** to bring together representatives of the main sectors or groups;
- a **Citizens' Environment Initiative** to carry the message to individuals and local communities.

109 The Prime Minister is inviting a small group of individuals, with wide knowledge and practical experience, to advise the Government on strategic issues. They will keep in view general sustainability issues at home and abroad, identify major problems or opportunities likely to arise, monitor progress, and consider questions of priority. The Government will consult them on issues of major importance, and they will have access to all Ministers. They will meet about four times a year.

110 There is already more than one forum in which the Government discusses issues of environment policy with others, or from which it receives advice. These include those for local government, the voluntary sector, and business, and the Royal Commission on Environmental Pollution. The Government proposes to invite some of their members to meet together with Ministers twice a year in a UK Round Table on Sustainable Development, chaired by the Secretary of State for the Environment. The Round Table will discuss major issues of sustainable development between people who approach them from different positions and who have different responsibilities. Members will be able to compare notes on what is being done in different sectors, develop a better understanding of the problems faced by others, and see how far a common perspective might be developed. There will be further consultation about the details.

111 There is a key part to be played by individuals in developing a more sustainable world. They may act:

- **as green consumers or green householders:** saving energy, buying environmentally friendly goods, recycling or reusing materials, using cars less;
- **as volunteers:** in voluntary bodies and church groups, in fund raising, or in conservation projects;
- **at work:** supporting drives for energy saving, green purchasing, innovative techniques or technology;
- **as parents or others involved with children:** developing their interest in the environment or responding to their

concern;

- **as aware citizens:** becoming active in political parties or in local affairs, voting or simply exchanging views.

112 To encourage the growth of interest in the issues of sustainable development, the Government will stimulate a "Citizens' Environment Initiative" and will discuss proposals with voluntary bodies, local authorities, the churches and others. A year of activity could be planned, beginning with World Environment Day which the UK is to host on 3 June 1994. An umbrella committee might be set up to publicise ideas and advice. The Department of the Environment will fund a small secretariat, outside the Department.

113 The aim is to increase people's awareness of the part that their personal choices can play in delivering sustainable development and to enlist their support and commitment over the coming years.

REFERENCES AND FURTHER READING

1 *Our Common Future:* the report of the World Commission on Environment and Development (the "Brundtland Commission"). Oxford University Press, 1987. ISBN 0–19–282080–X.

2 *This Common Inheritance. Britain's Environmental Strategy.* Cm 1200. HMSO, 1990. ISBN 0–10–112002–8.

3 *This Common Inheritance. The First Year Report.* Cm 1655. HMSO, 1991. ISBN 0-10-116552-8.

4 *This Common Inheritance. The Second Year Report.* Cm 2068. HMSO, 1992. ISBN 0-10-120682-8.

5 *Climate Change: The UK Programme.* Cm 2427. HMSO, 1994. ISBN 0-10-124272-7.

6 *Biodiversity: The UK Action Plan.* Cm 2428. HMSO, 1994. ISBN 0-10-124282-4.

7 *Sustainable Forestry: The UK Programme.* Cm 2429. HMSO, 1994. ISBN 0-10-124292-1.

CONTENTS

SECTION	CHAPTER	PAGE
	LIST OF ILLUSTRATIONS	22
I	**INTRODUCTION AND PRINCIPLES**	
	1 Context and Scope	27
	2 Preparation of the Strategy	30
	3 Principles of Sustainable Development	33
2	**ENVIRONMENTAL MEDIA AND RESOURCES**	
	4 State of the Environment	37
	5 Population, Household Formation and Incomes	39
	6 Global Atmosphere	43
	7 Air Quality	49
	8 Freshwater	55
	9 The Sea	66
	10 Soil	73
	11 Land Use	79
	12 Minerals including Fossil Fuels	90
	13 Wildlife and Habitats	94
3	**ECONOMIC DEVELOPMENT AND SUSTAINABILITY**	
	14 Economic Activity	105
	15 Agriculture	106
	16 Forestry	113
	17 Fisheries	118
	18 Minerals Extraction	121
	19 Energy Supply	130
	20 Manufacturing and Services	135
	21 Biotechnology	140
	22 Chemicals	143
	23 Waste	148
	24 Development in Town and Country	158
	25 Construction of the Built Environment	165
	26 Transport	169
	27 Leisure	178
4	**PUTTING SUSTAINABILITY INTO PRACTICE**	
	28 International Context	189
	29 Central Government	197
	30 Local Government	200
	31 Voluntary Organisations	204
	32 Individual Awareness and Action	207
	33 Setting the Framework for the Private Sector	213
	34 Environmental Accounting and Indicators	218
	35 Land Use Planning System	221
	36 Energy Efficiency	226
	37 Science, Engineering and Technology	229
	38 Working Together	235
	ANNEXES	
	I Glossary	237
	II Abbreviations	245
	III Summary of Consultation Responses	249
	IV Technical Annex	257

LIST OF ILLUSTRATIONS

SECTION 1
INTRODUCTION AND PRINCIPLES

CHAPTER I

CONTEXT AND SCOPE

INTRODUCTION

1.1 The United Kingdom, as an early industrialised nation, has long experience of the uneasy relationship between economic development and protection of the environment. Economic development led to considerable prosperity, but industrialisation also brought disadvantages: uncontrolled exploitation and depletion of resources, pollution, congestion and poorly planned urbanisation. As awareness of these problems grew in the 19th century, the UK was among the first countries to look for ways to improve quality of life for everyone, and to preserve or restore a healthy and attractive environment.

1.2 These early efforts, however, were directed at specific perceived evils: the series of Public Health Acts, beginning in the 1840s, tried to deal with the problems of the unplanned growth of towns; the Alkali Acts of the 1850s onwards were aimed at gross air pollution; the first nature conservation legislation concerned itself with saving particular threatened birds and animals; and, in the 1890s, the National Trust's early actions attempted to protect specific cherished landscapes from urban development. These pioneering efforts were very valuable and, in their own terms, successful, but they focused on the most apparent problems rather than the underlying causes.

1.3 The beginnings of a more analytical approach, demanding a systematic consideration of causes as well as effects, can be seen in the development of a land use planning system in the 1930s and, in particular, in the 1947 Town and Country Planning Act which remains the foundation of the present system, and of many others which it has influenced and shaped around the world. However, it was another 40 years before nations considered it necessary to debate the need for a similarly comprehensive approach to the implications and impacts of decisions in fields broader than domestic land use planning.

1.4 The 1987 World Commission on Environment and Development brought the concept of sustainable development onto the international agenda. In 1992, it was the central theme of the UN Conference on Environment and Development (UNCED, popularly known as the "Earth Summit"). That conference called on governments to take action at national level and, in particular, to adopt strategies for sustainable development, building on their existing plans and policies.

1.5 This document is the UK Strategy for Sustainable Development, building directly upon the UK's environmental strategy (*This Common Inheritance*[1]) which was adopted in 1990. It also reflects the main themes of the EC Fifth Environmental Action Programme[2]. It looks afresh at the issues of environment and development in the light of the Earth Summit and its consequences. The Strategy looks ahead to the year 2012 – 20 years after the Summit – and longer term where this is possible and relevant. It is a Government document, although it has been prepared in consultation with many people and organisations outside central government (see chapter 2).

1.6 But it is not intended to be the last word. Sustainable development is, inevitably, a long-term process, although it is important to start thinking and acting now. Just as this Strategy has been preceded in the UK by many initiatives, so there will be a range of further programmes in the future building on this. The Strategy specifically commits the Government to further action, and involves industry, local government, researchers, voluntary groups and individuals in follow-up work.

INTERNATIONAL CONTEXT

1.7 The World Commission on Environment and Development, chaired by Mrs Gro Harlem Brundtland, published a report, *Our Common Future*[3], in 1987. This report has provided the most commonly used working definition of sustainable development, describing it as:

"development that meets the needs of the present without compromising the ability of future generations to meet their own needs."

1.8 The Brundtland Commission, however, wanted its report not to be seen as a "prediction of ever increasing environmental decay and hardship in a world of ever decreasing resources". Instead there remained "the possibility of a new era of economic growth, based on policies that sustain and expand the environmental resource base".

1.9 By the end of 1988, *Our Common Future* had received public backing from the leaders of over 50 nations, including the UK. The issues raised by the report were discussed at the UN General Assembly in 1989, leading to the passage of resolution 44/228, which called for a UN Conference on Environment and Development and established its terms of reference.

1.10 The Earth Summit was consequently held in Rio de Janeiro in June 1992. It was the first conference on the world's environmental future to be attended by heads of state and government. Over 120 world leaders attended the conference, and more than 150 countries were represented overall. Attendance was not confined to national governments; local authorities, businesses and non-governmental organisations (NGOs) played a key role both in preparation for, and in attendance at, the Summit.

1.11 The Earth Summit reached a number of important agreements, which together form a framework for further action. One of the statements agreed was the *Rio Declaration on Environment and Development*[4], which sets out 27 general principles for achieving sustainable development. To support this general declaration, the Summit adopted *Agenda 21*[5], a comprehensive action plan for the pursuit of sustainable development into the next century, with 40 chapters of detailed recommendations addressed to international agencies, national and local governments and NGOs.

1.12 Agenda 21 recommended the establishment of a new Commission on Sustainable Development (CSD) under the aegis of the UN to monitor progress. The CSD held its first meeting in New York in June 1993; the UK has been elected as one of its 53 members. Agenda 21 also called on governments to prepare national strategies for sustainable development, and to submit reports to the CSD on action to implement Agenda 21, on the problems faced and on any other relevant environment and development issues.

1.13 This Strategy is the UK's response to Agenda 21's call to national governments. A separate report on the Strategy is being sent to the CSD. The UK has also prepared a Climate Change Programme[6], a Biodiversity Action Plan[7] and a Forestry Programme[8]; this Strategy cross refers to these other documents where appropriate.

NATIONAL CONTEXT

1.14 The UK was one of the first countries to respond to the Brundtland Report, in July 1988. Its response, *A Perspective by the United Kingdom on the Report of the World Commission on Environment and Development*[9], states:

"There can be no quarrel with [the Brundtland principles] as a general definition. The key point is how to translate it into practice, how to measure it, and to assess progress towards its achievement. This is an area which needs to be tackled and on which international consensus is desirable in order to develop a consistent approach and agreement on what is being achieved."

1.15 In 1989, the Government produced a progress report on implementing sustainable development. This report, *Sustaining Our Common Future*[10], was a first attempt to set out policy aims and measures for the UK specifically directed towards achieving sustainable development.

1.16 The ideas in this report were taken up in 1990 in the UK's first comprehensive strategy: the White Paper on the Environment, *This Common Inheritance*:

"The Government therefore supports the principle of sustainable development. This means living on the earth's income rather than eroding its capital. It means keeping the consumption of renewable natural resources within the limits of their replenishment. It means handing down to successive generations not only man-made wealth (such as buildings, roads and railways) but also natural wealth, such as clean and adequate water supplies, good arable land, a wealth of wildlife and ample forests."[11]

1.17 The 1990 White Paper contained over 350 detailed commitments to action on the environment. Since then the Government has reported progress in anniversary White Paper reports in 1991[12] and 1992[13] and is doing so again in a further White Paper reporting on progress in 1993. The process includes separate national White Paper reports for Scotland, Wales and Northern Ireland. The Government also publishes statistical reports on the state of the environment. There is thus a solid basis in the UK for updating policy and monitoring its implementation.

SCOPE OF THE STRATEGY

1.18 This Strategy looks at the UK economy and the UK environment as a whole. There are not, therefore, separate chapters on England, Scotland, Wales and Northern Ireland, although there are references to geographical differences and similarities. However, the Strategy also looks wider than the UK's national boundaries, to begin to consider the effect this country has on other countries and on the global environment, and the effect others have on the UK.

1.19 Economic activity in one country can affect sustainability in other countries in a number of ways. The UK and other countries each have impacts at a global level: for example, the UK influences the global atmosphere through emissions of greenhouse gases and ozone-depleting substances. Deterioration in the quality of the global environment is a problem for all nations, and the Strategy describes how the UK approaches this through international cooperation. In important aspects the UK shares a common environment with other European countries; this Strategy takes account of policy and practice across Europe and, in particular, in the EC. The EC as a whole has been developing strategies for sustainable development, for example, through its Fifth Environmental Action Programme (see chapter 28).

1.20 Moreover, one country can also impact on other countries' economic development in a number of ways, either directly, through deliberate policy measures such as aid, or indirectly, through activities such as trade and investment. The Strategy considers UK policies and practices towards developing countries and areas such as Central and Eastern Europe and the former Soviet Union.

1.21 The Strategy also takes account of the UK's responsibilities towards its Dependent Territories, Sovereign Bases and Crown Dependencies. The Foreign and Commonwealth Office has overall responsibility for the administration and direct responsibility for the external relations of the UK's 14 Dependent Territories and two dependencies. The UK is encouraging the Dependent Territories to prepare their own strategies for sustainable development appropriate to their particular situations and several, including Hong Kong and St Helena, have already done so.

1.22 This document looks at the subject from three perspectives:
- the state of the environment (Section 2),
- economic development (Section 3), and
- types of policy response (Section 4).

Policies specific to different environmental media (such as policies on global warming or water quality) are reviewed in the appropriate chapters in Section 2. Similarly, environmental policies in the various economic sectors (such as agriculture or transport) are considered in the chapters in Section 3. Section 4 looks at policy responses more generally, and concludes with a chapter announcing proposals for new arrangements on "Working Together".

1.23 The remaining chapters in Section 1 provide background material on the preparation of the Strategy and a discussion of principles; an overview is set out in the Summary at the front of this document.

1.24 In summary, this Strategy sets out the situation in the UK, current policies which contribute to that situation, and plans and programmes which are designed to respond to it. It highlights key areas for future action and makes proposals for ways in which all sectors of society, individually or in partnership, can begin to work towards sustainable development following this first Strategy. It also seeks to set this information in the context of the UK's international role and response to Agenda 21.

REFERENCES AND FURTHER READING

1   *This Common Inheritance. Britain's Environmental Strategy.* Cm 1200. HMSO, 1990. ISBN 0–10–112002–8.

2   *Towards Sustainability: A European Community Programme of Policy and Action in relation to the Environment and Sustainable Development (The EC Fifth Environment Action Programme),* Commission of the EC. Official Publication of the EC, 1992 (Cm (92) 23/11 Final).

3   *Our Common Future (The Brundtland Report)* – Report of the 1987 World Commission on Environment and Development. Oxford University Press 1987. ISBN 0–19–282080–X.

4   *Rio Declaration on Environment and Development,* 1992. ISBN 9–21–100509–4.

5   *Agenda 21* – Action plan for the next century, endorsed at UNCED. Full text of Agenda 21 available from: Regional office for North America, UNDC Two Building, Room 0803, 2 United Nations Plaza, New York, NY 10017, USA.

6   *Climate Change: The UK Programme.* Cm 2427. HMSO, 1994. ISBN 0–10–124272–7.

7   *Biodiversity: The UK Action Plan.* Cm 2428. HMSO, 1994. ISBN 0–10–124282–4.

8   *Sustainable Forestry: The UK Programme.* Cm 2429. HMSO, 1994. ISBN 0–10–124292–1.

9   *A Perspective by the United Kingdom on the Report of the World Commission on Environment and Development,* July 1988.

10 *Sustaining Our Common Future.* Department of the Environment, 1989.

11 *This Common Inheritance (1990).* Para. 4.4.

12 *This Common Inheritance. The First Year Report.* Cm 1655. HMSO, 1991. ISBN 0–10–116552–8.

13 *This Common Inheritance. The Second Year Report.* Cm 2068. HMSO, 1992. ISBN 0–10–120682–8.

CHAPTER 2

PREPARATION OF THE STRATEGY

INTRODUCTION

2.1 Agenda 21 emphasises the importance of consultation and participation in the preparation of national sustainable development strategies. On this basis, the UK Government has engaged in extensive consultation on this Strategy. This chapter describes that process.

2.2 Sustainable development is relevant to the policy responsibilities of most Government Departments, and they have all been involved in the preparation of this Strategy. Many other organisations and individuals have also been involved, from initial negotiations at the Earth Summit in Rio, through consultation on the broad scope and content of the Strategy, to active participation in preparing draft text.

CONSULTATION – A NATIONAL DEBATE

2.3 The Government has consulted widely about the scope and content of the Strategy. Publishing the Second Year Report on *This Common Inheritance*[1] in October 1992, the Government called for a national debate on sustainable development. In November 1992, the Department of the Environment (DOE) issued an open letter inviting views on the nature of sustainable development and on the possible framework for the national Strategy. Similar letters were issued in Scotland, Wales and Northern Ireland. The DOE prepared a draft framework for the Strategy and discussed this with a number of non-governmental organisations (NGOs) and with representatives of EC member states and the European Commission.

2.4 A three day seminar on sustainable development was held at Green College, Oxford, in March 1993. This brought together about 100 representatives from environmental groups, business organisations, local authorities, academic and research institutions, and Government Departments. They looked at the general principles of sustainable development, the implications of the Earth Summit, the scope and content of the Sustainable Development Strategy, and policy areas central to sustainability. A summary of the proceedings was prepared and published by the Green College Centre for Environmental Policy and Understanding[2].

2.5 The Government prepared a consultation paper[3] giving a more detailed outline of the Strategy and setting out the main topics likely to be covered, which was published by the DOE in July 1993. The paper was circulated to over 6,000 organisations and individuals, and over 500 responses have been received. Responses were submitted by local authorities, a range of companies including multinationals and small businesses, voluntary groups with a wide variety of interests including both environment and development concerns, universities, professional institutions and individuals. Comments on the consultation paper ranged from thoughts on fundamental principles – such as the time frame for sustainable development, the international context, and the distinctions between development, economic growth, and sustainability – to specific points related to consultees' direct experience. A summary of the consultation responses is contained in Annex III.

2.6 The launch of the consultation paper led to a number of associated articles in both national and local press. These included a series run during the summer by the *Daily Telegraph* newspaper, with a questionnaire on attitudes and priorities for sustainable development which drew over 8,000 responses.

2.7 Government Departments have discussed chapters of the Strategy with NGOs and other interested parties. Nearly 40 meetings were held between July and October 1993 involving more than 100 different organisations. Proposals for the Strategy were also discussed by three consultative bodies – the Advisory Committee on Business and the Environment, the Central and Local Government Environment Forum, and the Voluntary Sector Environment Forum.

PARTICIPATION OUTSIDE CENTRAL GOVERNMENT

2.8 In the UK, the associations who represent different groups of local authorities have taken a strong and direct interest in sustainable development issues, and have discussed and commented on the Strategy at a number of stages. They have set up their own Local Agenda 21 committee to promote sustainable development. Many individual local authorities are already working to integrate sustainable development into their activities, and to raise awareness and provide information on sustainable development issues within their communities. Many of the UK NGOs have also shown considerable interest in these issues, setting up their own campaigns and participating in discussions with central and local government. Businesses, too, have taken part in the consultation process for the Strategy and, in many cases, are very interested in practical action to integrate sustainable principles into their working practices.

2.9 All these groups, as well as local communities, schools and colleges and individuals, have a major contribution to make to sustainable development, both in partnership and through specific individual action. These activities are discussed further in Section 4, which sets out proposals for involving all sectors of society and individuals in sustainable development issues.

CONCLUSION

2.10 Although the UK had a firm foundation for this Sustainable Development Strategy in the 1990 Environment White Paper[4] and other policies, the production of the Strategy has been a major task. Existing policies have been reviewed, updated and broadened in the light of concepts of sustainable development.

2.11 Consultations have been overlaid on the extensive arrangements that were already in place for Government Departments generally to sound out views on policies.

Nonetheless, the scope of this consultation exercise has been new, involving as it has a wider range of Departments and bodies in a single exercise. The Government has found the process instructive and hopes that others have too. Inevitably, in the time available, there were limits to what could be achieved, but the Government believes that the Strategy has benefited from the extensive consultations, and hopes that the process and this Strategy have stimulated a wider understanding of sustainable development and of the difficult issues that it raises. Chapter 38 outlines the way in which this process of consultation and participation will be taken forward.

REFERENCES AND FURTHER READING

[1] *This Common Inheritance. The Second Year Report.* Cm 2068. HMSO, 1992. ISBN 0–10–120682–8.

[2] *Sustainable Development Seminar, Green College, Oxford. 18–20 March 1993.* Green College Centre for Environmental Policy and Understanding, 1993.

[3] *UK Strategy for Sustainable Development. Consultation Paper.* DOE, 1993.

[4] *This Common Inheritance. Britain's Environmental Strategy.* Cm 1200. HMSO, 1990. ISBN 0–10–112002–8.

CHAPTER 3

PRINCIPLES OF SUSTAINABLE DEVELOPMENT

INTRODUCTION

3.1 Most societies aspire to achieve economic development to secure rising standards of living, both for themselves and for future generations. They also seek to protect and enhance their environment, now and for their children. Reconciling these two aspirations is at the heart of sustainable development. This chapter analyses the concept of sustainable development and sets out some of the basic principles which need to be applied in order to secure it.

3.2 The debate is often presented in terms of a conflict between economic activity and the environment, as if it is only possible to pursue one at the expense of the other. But this is mistaken: economic activity and the state of the environment both affect the quality of life. Often economic investment and environmental protection – or improvement – go hand in hand. What matters is that decisions throughout society are taken with proper regard to their environmental impact.

THE NEED FOR ECONOMIC DEVELOPMENT

3.3 Economic development is sought by societies not only to satisfy basic material needs, but also to provide the resources to improve the quality of life in other directions, meeting the demand for health care, education and a good environment.

3.4 Many forms of economic development make demands upon the environment: they use natural resources which are sometimes in limited supply, and generate by-products of pollution and waste.

3.5 But there are also many ways in which the right kind of economic activity can protect or enhance the environment. These include energy efficiency measures, improved technology and techniques of management, better product design and marketing, waste minimisation, environmentally friendly farming practices, making better use of land and buildings, and improved transport efficiency. The challenge of sustainable development is to promote ways of encouraging this kind of environmentally friendly economic activity, and of discouraging environmentally damaging activities.

CARING FOR THE ENVIRONMENT

3.6 There are several different reasons for caring about environmental quality.

3.7 Historically, in the UK and elsewhere, the motivation for much of the early environmental legislation was concern for the protection of health. That led to measures to curb air pollution, provide clean water, and minimise risks from waste disposal. Many of the major, obvious causes for concern about public health have largely been eradicated in the UK but health must always remain a fundamental consideration. Acute health incidents as a result of pollution are now comparatively rare, and public concern centres more on issues where cause and effect are harder to prove or disprove. For example, it is not easy to assess the possible effects on health of long-term exposure to low levels of pollutants, and extensive studies may be needed in such cases to establish what the dangers are.

3.8 A second concern is to conserve those common natural resources that have an economic value and which are in finite, or potentially finite, supply. These include land itself, stocks of fish in the sea, and the diversity of species that potentially offers opportunities for research and development.

3.9 Even where there are no market transactions involved, people value aspects of the environment – landscape, wildlife and habitats, and some of the built heritage – for their own sake and wish, so far as possible, to pass them on to later generations.

3.10 In the present age, these concerns have broadened beyond people's immediate environment to global issues, such as protection of the stratospheric ozone layer and the world's climate. With issues such as these, far more is at stake than health or aesthetic interests alone.

SOME SPECIFIC PRINCIPLES

3.11 Because the environment is shared, to a large extent its protection requires collective action. Decisions about economic development ought to take account of the costs of potential pollution and waste and the value of resources that are consumed and, conversely, of the value of any environmental improvements made. Often, however, it is difficult to establish what the environmental costs and benefits are or to ensure that they are taken into account. Where this is the case, the environment is in effect treated as a "free good", which can be damaged with impunity and whose enhancement secures no economic return. A key objective of environmental and sustainable development policy is to prevent this situation, by ensuring that environmental costs and benefits are properly and fully taken into account in public and private sector decisions. Partly to assist in this, a number of complementary or supporting principles have been developed in recent years, and are now widely applied in domestic and international environmental policy-making.

3.12 Primarily, the Government remains committed to basing action on fact, not fantasy, using the best **scientific**

information available; precipitate action on the basis of inadequate evidence is the wrong response[1]. However, when potential damage to the environment is both uncertain and significant, it is necessary to act on the basis of the **precautionary principle**. This was described in the 1990 White Paper in the following terms:

"Where there are significant risks of damage to the environment, the Government will be prepared to take precautionary action to limit the use of potentially dangerous materials or the spread of potentially dangerous pollutants, even where scientific knowledge is not conclusive, if the balance of likely costs and benefits justifies it".[2]

This interpretation of the principle is consistent with others in international usage, notably the *Rio Declaration* which sets out the "precautionary approach" thus: "Where there are threats of serious or irreversible damage, lack of full scientific certainty shall not be used as a reason for postponing cost-effective measures to prevent environmental degradation"[3]. This wording is a useful reminder that the principle can be applicable to all forms of environmental damage that might arise; nor should it apply only to the actions of government.

3.13 Ecological criteria have a central role to play. This may mean considering the ability of a habitat or ecosystem to sustain a population of a particular species – sometimes described as the **carrying capacity**, although different meanings are ascribed to that concept. The term is sometimes extended to refer to the capacity of the environment to absorb pollution or waste. The ozone layer provides an important example: if it were to deteriorate significantly, the earth could not sustain as many species and there would be a threat to human life, as well as a loss of many fauna and flora. A specific application in the context of pollution control is the calculation of the critical load of a pollutant that an ecosystem can absorb.

3.14 The total of human wealth cannot be measured only by man-made capital but must allow also for **natural environmental capital** and other aspects of the quality of life. That natural capital consists both of **renewable and non-renewable resources**. The challenge of sustainable development is to find ways of enhancing total wealth while using common natural resources prudently, so that renewable resources can be conserved and non-renewables used at a rate which considers the needs of future generations. In this it is especially important to consider whether there is a risk of **irreversible** environmental effects and, if so, how significant they may be.

3.15 Judgements have to be made about the weight to be put on these factors in particular cases. Sometimes environmental

costs have to be accepted as the price of economic development, but on other occasions a site, or an ecosystem, or some other aspect of the environment, has to be regarded as so valuable that it should be protected from exploitation. Such judgements should make a proper allowance for the interests of **future generations** and for the pressures that one society places upon the **global environment**.

3.16 Much environmental pollution and resource depletion occurs because the people responsible are not those who bear the consequences. If the polluter, or ultimately the consumer, is made to pay, then the costs of pollution, waste and the consumption of natural resources are brought into the calculations of the enterprise. Environmental policy in this field is therefore guided by the **"polluter pays" principle,** which was adopted by Organisation for Economic Co-operation and Development (OECD) countries as long ago as 1972. This requires that, when production processes threaten or cause damage to the environment, the cost of necessary environmental measures should be borne by the producer, and not by society at large, giving incentives to reduce the pollution. To the extent that those costs are passed on to the consumer, it can be said that the **user pays** and this may in turn reduce demand for the polluting activity.

TAKING THE RIGHT DECISIONS

3.17 Translating principles into practice is not easy. In the first place it requires **better information** about environmental impacts. Scientific understanding of the environment must constantly be taken forward, especially in areas where the issues are of critical importance. Better health-related indicators are needed, including greater understanding of the implications of different levels of exposure to pollutants. So, too, are better indicators of the state of the natural environment, and other information that would assist in putting appropriate values for environmental effects into assessments of new proposals.

3.18 Better information will enable environmental quality standards and targets for environmental improvement to be established and refined with more confidence. Without this, potential dangers can be underestimated or, conversely, scarce resources can be misused by imposing excessively high standards. Environmental quality objectives or targets have long played an important part in guiding policies for environmental improvement, whether for broad policy development and monitoring or for specific purposes, such as regulation or the design of economic instruments. Increasingly, it may be necessary to develop more specific environmental objectives or targets, for different environmental media or different sectors of the economy as appropriate.

3.19 In 1993, the Government announced support for the Medical Research Council's new Institute for Environment and Health which is aimed at improving understanding of relationships between environmental factors and health. The Government is also improving the quality and coverage of environmental information and indicators for monitoring purposes. A wide-ranging review of the state of the UK environment, drawing on existing data sources was published in 1992[4], and work is now being undertaken to identify gaps in its coverage and to extend its scope for future reviews. The Government is participating in international work on indicators. It will also continue to work on the underlying questions of environmental accounting (see chapter 34).

3.20 The second requirement is for **suitable mechanisms in the private sector** to ensure that this understanding and information is brought to bear on the decisions being taken, and brought fully into the decision-making, not just as an afterthought. This should be done, wherever possible, by market mechanisms, as a way of integrating environmental costs and benefits into firms' and individuals' behaviour.

3.21 The traditional way of reducing environmental damage has been to impose regulatory requirements, for example, the control of emissions by the pollution control authorities, or of land development through the planning system. But regulation may not always be the best way of achieving objectives, either from an environmental or an economic point of view. Regulations impose hidden costs which can lead to inefficiency and waste. The Government's general policy is to reduce and simplify regulations wherever appropriate. And in environmental policy, the commitment is to make use of economic instruments where possible, rather than regulation. Economic instruments seek to make environmental costs explicit and to ensure that people take account of them in making decisions. They can give a continuing incentive for innovation and the development of environmentally friendly techniques. Some regulatory regimes are always likely to be needed in the environmental field – but the quest for economic instruments as a real alternative will be actively pursued. A review of the scope for such instruments was published in November 1993[5].

3.22 The third requirement is for sound **techniques of analysis for public decisions** and standard setting, looking at environmental impacts alongside those of public expenditure, compliance costs for business, and so on. Environmental appraisal is not new in the UK. For example, the Treasury's "green book"[6] has long advocated that non-market impacts, including environmental impacts, should be taken into account in economic appraisal. More recently, the Government has issued a number of guidance documents on environmental assessment: on policy proposals in Government Departments[7], on major projects for development control[8], and on local authority development plans[9].

3.23 In principle, it should be possible through cost benefit analysis to place values upon any of the impacts made on the environment by economic development. In practice, it is not always possible to quantify the value of improvements or losses to the environment. Moreover, it is not always obvious what the environmental impact of a decision will be, even in physical terms.

3.24 Risk assessment can help when taking decisions or planning action under conditions of uncertainty. It should begin with the best available science to identify the hazards, the potential consequences and what might be done to mitigate the consequences under alternative options. It is, of course, essential that uncertainties in the science be clearly identified and given proper weight in the assessment.

CONCLUSION

3.25 There will continue to be discussion and debate in the UK and internationally about the principles of sustainable development, but in general terms these are now well established. Economic development is important to any society but the benefits of any development must be sufficient to outweigh the costs, including the environmental costs. There are key principles to be kept in mind when assessing those costs. Attention must now focus on how these principles can and should be applied in different sectors of the economy and by different people to promote development that enhances rather than detracts from the environment.

REFERENCES AND FURTHER READING

1 *This Common Inheritance. Britain's Environmental Strategy.* Cm 1200. HMSO, 1990. ISBN 0–10–112002–8.

2 Ibid. Paragraph 1.18.

3 *The Rio Declaration on Environment and Development.* 13 June 1992. Principle 15.

4 *The UK Environment.* Department of the Environment. HMSO, 1992. ISBN 0–11–752420–4.

5 *Making Markets Work for the Environment.* Department of the Environment. HMSO, 1993. ISBN 0–11–752852–8.

6 *Economic Appraisal in Central Government: A Technical Guide for Government Departments.* HM Treasury, 1991.

7 *Policy Appraisal and the Environment: A Guide for Government Departments.* Department of the Environment. HMSO, 1991 (published in fulfilment of an Environment White Paper Commitment).

8 *Environmental Assessment: A Guide to the Procedures.* HMSO, 1989.

9 *Environmental Appraisal of Development Plans: a Good Practice Guide.* HMSO. 1993.

SECTION 2
ENVIRONMENTAL MEDIA AND RESOURCES

CHAPTER 4

STATE OF THE ENVIRONMENT

SYNOPSIS

4.1 This Section of the Strategy sets out to review the state of the environment in the UK, and how it is likely to evolve over the next 20 years in the light of expected pressures and current policies.

4.2 Some trends are clearly identifiable now, others are more speculative, particularly towards the end of this period.

- Economic growth, coupled with increasing population and household numbers, means that pressures on the environment are likely to increase over the next 20 years.
- Further international measures may also be needed to control carbon dioxide and other greenhouse gas emissions beyond the present commitments to the year 2000.
- Emissions causing acid rain damage to soils and surface waters will decline considerably by 2012.
- The increase in road traffic is likely to have outweighed the benefits of cleaner cars currently being introduced, and further measures will be needed to maintain improvements in local air quality beyond 2012.
- In parts of the country, particularly in South and East England, the expected growth in demand for water over the next 20 years is unlikely to be met from existing developed resources. A combination of measures, including demand management, further improvements in the distribution system and the development of new resources is likely to be needed.
- Water quality, both freshwater and marine, is good except in some limited areas, and likely to improve as a result of investment in improvements in sewerage systems, measures already taken to improve control on discharges to water courses and on potential diffuse sources of pollution, and action to increase flows in low-flow rivers. However, groundwater quality is a potential cause for concern in some areas: policies may need to be further developed.
- Soil quality is not a problem in the UK generally; however, localised erosion and loss of soil organic matter in some areas may need to be addressed.
- There is likely to be increased demand for the development of rural or agricultural land for housing and other development, particularly in South Eastern and South West England; consumption is likely to increase, perhaps leading to increased imports of raw materials from other countries.
- The demand for aggregates for building is likely to increase sharply. Even with an increase in use of recycled materials, new extraction sites will be needed, but it is likely to be increasingly difficult to identify sites which are environmentally acceptable.

- Over the next 20 years, a package of measures will increasingly benefit UK wildlife. These include agri-environment measures under the EC Common Agricultural Policy, species recovery plans, new approaches to marine conservation and coastal protection and programmes for the regeneration and management of woodlands.

INFORMATION AND MONITORING

4.3 A considerable amount of information about the state of the environment in the UK is available; most of this information is already set out in other publications. Last year, the Government published a comprehensive new statistical report, *The UK Environment[1]*, to help to inform and stimulate public debate on environmental issues. However, gaps and weaknesses in current knowledge remain, owing to limitations in understanding of the mechanisms at work and the difficulty in making sufficiently accurate measurements, and because the resources available for extending the coverage of monitoring networks must, inevitably, be limited. As well as drawing on the information which is available, this Strategy highlights those areas where information is poor or absent, or where further research is needed, and identifies some priorities for filling those gaps. One particular priority which has been identified is the development of key environmental indicators. This is discussed in chapter 34.

4.4 One of the areas where quantification is particularly difficult to obtain is on the links between environment and health. While the acute effects of exposure to high levels of pollutants may be relatively obvious, and easy to measure – as, for example, with the effects of the poor air quality in British cities in the early 1950s, which caused large numbers of premature deaths – little is known about the possible effects of long-term, low-level contamination, and it is often very difficult to establish causation, let alone to quantify the impacts. However, risk to human health is one of the key criteria for judging the relative importance of sustainability issues, as discussed in chapter 3; this theme is picked up in this Section of the Strategy, where specific risks to human health are identified and discussed in the relevant chapters.

4.5 Most of the numerical information presented in this Section is in summary form. Annex IV gives further details about sources and reference documents, and comments, where appropriate, on the information presented in the main text.

FRAMEWORK OF POLLUTION CONTROL

4.6 The UK pioneered pollution control, being probably the first country in the world to introduce systematic controls over air pollution and waste disposal. Over the past 150 years, there have been various pollution control agencies concerned with air, land and water, but recently a more comprehensive and integrated approach has been developed.

Integrated Pollution Control

4.7 In many cases, a choice can be made whether a discharge should be directed to air, land or water, or indeed to more than one of them. The concept of the "best practicable environmental option" (BPEO) has been recognised for some time. This involves looking at each industrial process, and selecting a pattern of discharges which ensures the best overall outcome for the environment. To get closer to this, the main pollution inspectorates in England and Wales were brought together in 1987. They became Her Majesty's Inspectorate of Pollution (HMIP) and were given a remit to work towards an integrated approach to pollution control. Her Majesty's Industrial Pollution Inspectorate (HMIPI), and the Alkali and Radiochemical Inspectorate (ARCI), are the equivalent bodies for Scotland and Northern Ireland respectively.

4.8 HMIP, which is part of the Department of the Environment, brought together the former Industrial Air Pollution Inspectorate, the Radiochemical Inspectorate and the Hazardous Waste Inspectorate. HMIP also took on a new role in controlling certain discharges to water, and is the statutory pollution control authority in England and Wales for those industrial processes which discharge significant quantities of harmful non-radioactive waste. It regulates all the pollution discharges of these "scheduled" processes to all environmental media.

4.9 All discharges to the aquatic environment in England and Wales require the prior consent of the National Rivers Authority (NRA); these duties are carried out by the river purification authorities (RPAs) in Scotland and, in Northern Ireland, by that country's Department of the Environment. On land, local authorities have responsibility for waste regulation and disposal; waste regulation authorities deal with waste management licensing and inspection, while waste disposal authorities issue site licences for the disposal of controlled waste and deal with recycling schemes and targets.

Environment Agencies

4.10 The coordination and integration of pollution control will be enhanced by the creation of new Environment Agencies – public bodies with a board appointed by the Government. The pollution control functions of HMIP and the NRA, and local authorities' responsibility for regulating the handling and disposal of waste, will be brought together in a single body for England and Wales. In Scotland, a similar body will be formed as HMIPI and the RPAs are brought together. The integration of pollution enforcement functions in single agencies will simplify matters for industry and will lead to more effective control. The introduction of paving legislation to allow preparatory work on these agencies was announced in the Queen's Speech in November 1993.

Land use planning

4.11 The land use planning system is a key instrument for delivering land use and development objectives which are compatible with the aims of sustainable development. The system is based on the right of central and local government to control all development, including changes in the use of land. Decisions on most of the half million proposals each year which require a full planning application are taken by local authorities, although decisions on appeals against a local authority refusal are taken by central government. Central government may also call in certain planning applications for a direct decision where the application raises issues of regional or national importance.

REFERENCES AND FURTHER READING

1   *The UK Environment.* Department of the Environment. HMSO. 1992. ISBN 0–11–752420–4.

CHAPTER 5

POPULATION, HOUSEHOLD FORMATION AND INCOMES

SYNOPSIS

5.1 Population, economic activity and consumption are major influences on sustainability. UK population growth is expected to be fairly small over the next 20 years but, combined with falling household size, will result in a 14% increase in the number of households. Shifts in population within the UK are likely to lead to demands for new development in the already highly developed South East of England, increasing pressures on the existing infrastructure and for development of rural land. Meanwhile, population in some other areas may decline, leading to converse problems of run-down and dereliction. Effective planning policies will minimise adverse environmental impacts, reducing land take for housing and other development, and reducing the need to travel. Real increases in income over the next 20 years are likely to lead to rises in consumers' expenditure, increasing demands for both renewable and non-renewable resources. Economic growth will also increase opportunities for developing technical innovations which will contribute to environmental improvement.

5.2 The key issues for sustainability are:

- how to maintain or improve the quality of life, including environmental quality, as population levels and structure change;
- how to combine economic growth with minimisation of natural resource consumption, pollution and waste generation;
- how to balance the wishes of the individual and society through the planning system and in other ways.

INTRODUCTION

5.3 This chapter presents trends and projections for the main demographic and economic factors contributing to sustainability in the UK. People create the demand for goods and services which can cause environmental pressures. Increases in economic activity and in personal consumption can increase pollution levels and waste and use more renewable, and non-renewable, natural resources.

5.4 The Government does not seek to influence population numbers; it regards decisions about having children as being for individual couples to make. It is concerned with improving the well-being of individuals, ensuring that information and services are available for people to plan childbearing, and ensuring the welfare of dependent children.

POPULATION

Structure and changes

5.5 Of those countries with a population greater than 5 million, the UK has the 15th highest and 11th most dense population in the world[1] (235 persons/sq km). Densities are much higher in England (368 persons/sq km), particularly in South East England (746 persons/sq km). The UK population was almost 58 million in 1992, compared with 56 million in 1972 – an increase of 3%. By 2012, the UK population is projected to grow to around 61 million, and by another million over the following 10 years. The populations of England, Wales and Northern Ireland are forecast to grow over this period while Scotland's population is expected to fall (Figure 5.1). These projections depend, however, on a number of assumptions which are difficult to predict accurately.

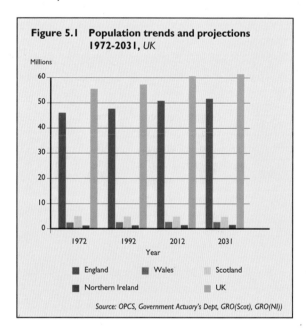

Figure 5.1   Population trends and projections 1972-2031, *UK*

Millions

| England | Wales | Scotland |
| Northern Ireland | UK |

Source: OPCS, Government Actuary's Dept, GRO(Scot), GRO(NI))

5.6 Future changes in the size of the UK population are expected to be determined principally by natural increase (that is, the number of births less the number of deaths). The number of births increased slowly during the 1980s, but is expected to show a decrease from the mid-1990s. The increase in life expectancy seen in the 20th century is expected to continue over the coming decades, leading to increasing numbers of the very elderly (aged 80 and over), who are heavy consumers of medical and social services and have special housing needs. However, because of the age structure of the population, the large generation born in the late 1940s will account for increasing numbers of deaths in

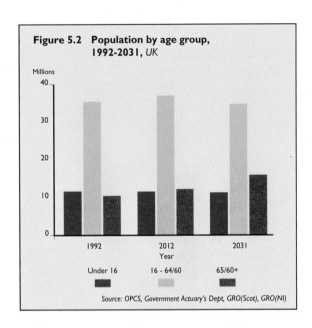

Figure 5.2   Population by age group, 1992-2031, *UK*

Millions

Source: OPCS, Government Actuary's Dept, GRO(Scot), GRO(NI)

the first decades of the next century, resulting in a peaking of population numbers by about 2030 at around 62 million. Thereafter, the population is expected to decline as a result of generally falling birth rates in the latter part of this century.

5.7 The population of those most likely to be available for work (that is, men aged 16–64 years and women aged 16–59 years), and hence most likely to form new households, stood at over 35 million in 1992. It is expected to reach 37 million by 2012 but fall back again to 35 million by 2032 (Figure 5.2). The population at pensionable age (that is, men aged 65 years and over and women aged 60 and over) has grown by nearly a fifth since 1972 to 10.5 million in 1992. It is expected to increase further over the next 40 years, reaching about 12 million by 2012 and 16 million by 2032. The increase in the elderly population, and the likelihood that people will live longer, will mean that houses lived in by the elderly will be released at a slower rate for use by others looking to form a household for the first time. This will in turn create increased demand for new housing (see chapter 11).

5.8 Over the last 20 years, people have been less inclined to marry, more inclined to cohabit and increasingly likely to divorce. There were 350,000 marriages in 1991, compared to 480,000 in 1972. Married people now account for about 47% of the UK population, compared to 50% in 1972. Over the same period, the number of divorced people has increased more than fivefold to over 2.5 million in 1992. There have also been relatively small increases in the number of single and widowed people. These changes have resulted in a 3.5 million increase between 1972 and 1992 in the number of households in the UK.

Migration

5.9 Net migration into and out of the UK is small by comparison with the overall population. There was a net outflow of people from the UK for much of the 1970s and early 1980s, averaging 43,000 per year (less than 0.1% of the total population) between 1973 and 1982. Conversely, in the mid-to-late 1980s, there was an average net inflow of about 40,000 people per year (again, less than 0.1% of the total population). Migration patterns are unlikely materially to affect the projections given in this chapter.

Regional population changes

5.10 Over the last 10 years, the largest changes in population growth have occurred in parts of South East and South West England (Figures 5.3.1 and 5.3.2). The growth in population over the next 20 years is expected to be greatest in East Anglia, South West and South East England, the East Midlands and Northern Ireland, with increases of between 8% and 14% by 2012. These increases will be particularly significant in the South East and parts of South West England where population density is already high. Smaller increases in population are expected to occur in parts of the Midlands and North East England. The increases will be fuelled not only by overall population growth but also by internal migration from areas such as Merseyside (whose population is expected to fall by up to 15%) and large parts of Central and South West Scotland. Regional development policies will need to take account of these expected changes to population levels and densities when assessing the future provision of housing and other development, leisure and other amenities, and transport infrastructure.

Household formation

5.11 The demographic changes discussed above mean that the average size of households is reducing and the number of households is growing at a faster rate than the overall population. Trends and projections for average household size in the UK are shown in Figure 5.4. Changes in household structure in England and Wales are shown in Figure 5.5. The number of single occupancy and lone parent households in England and Wales grew by over 70% between 1972 and 1992, and is forecast to grow by 40% between 1992 and 2012. Overall, by 2012, the number of households in the UK is projected to have increased by 14% to around 26 million.

5.12 Across England and Wales, the largest increases in household formation are forecast to occur in a diagonal band stretching from Somerset to Lincolnshire, where county-wide increases of more than 25% are forecast. If realised, these projected increases in population and household formation

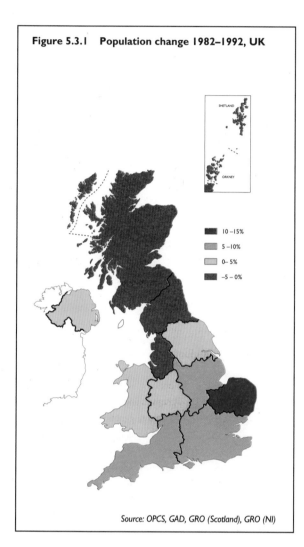

Figure 5.3.1   Population change 1982–1992, UK

SHETLAND

ORKNEY

■ 10 –15%
▨ 5 –10%
▨ 0– 5%
■ –5 – 0%

Source: OPCS, GAD, GRO (Scotland), GRO (NI)

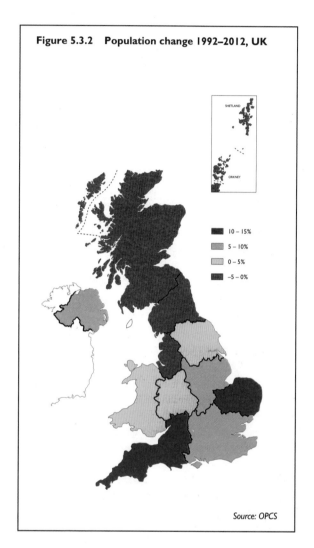

Figure 5.3.2   Population change 1992–2012, UK

SHETLAND

ORKNEY

■ 10 – 15%
▨ 5 – 10%
▨ 0 – 5%
■ –5 – 0%

Source: OPCS

will create demands for housing and the associated infrastructure of roads and sewage systems, and will increase pressures on natural resources such as land, water and fossil fuels. They also have implications for the formulation of planning policies (see chapter 35). In the South East, in particular, population and household increases are likely to lead to greater pressure for the development of land in an area where levels of urbanisation are already high, and much of the remaining land is protected by special designations. Conversely, the depopulation of areas such as Merseyside may give rise to areas of derelict and vacant land (see chapter 11).

INCOMES AND CONSUMPTION

5.13 Increasing population and household formation, coupled with rising living standards, are two of the main influences on consumption in the UK. Figure 5.6 shows how UK Gross Domestic Product (GDP) per head and consumers' expenditure per head have risen over the last 20

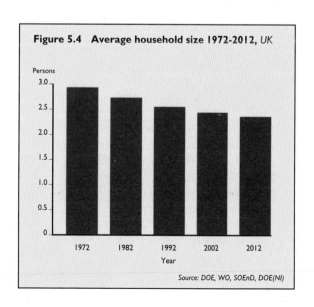

Figure 5.4   Average household size 1972-2012, *UK*

Persons

Year

Source: DOE, WO, SOEnD, DOE(NI)

years. Forecasts of future growth in national income are particularly uncertain. Over the last 20 years, GDP has grown by around a half, and over the past three decades it has nearly doubled. A simple extrapolation of these rates of change would, however, be an unreliable guide to the future. Growth in the economy over the past three decades has been affected by two major oil price rises in the 1970s and de-industrialisation in the 1980s; similar influences may not occur over the next 20 years.

5.14 Most of the GDP projections, however, have a "central" assumption of 2.25–2.5% growth per year, which means that GDP will have grown by around 60% in real terms by 2012. A growth rate of 2.5% per year would be needed to maintain the current rate of improvement in living standards.

5.15 Forecasts[2] show that output in all the main economic sectors is expected to increase (in real terms) in the two decades to 2010, but more rapidly in some than others. Manufacturing output is projected almost to double over this period, with the output of the electronics industry expected to grow by more than 150%. By 2010, the electronics sector is expected to be the largest of all the manufacturing industries in terms of output value. Rapid growth is also expected in the construction, hotels and catering and other private sector service industries.

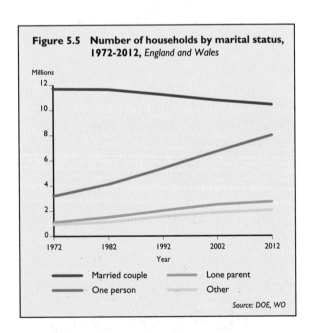

Figure 5.5 **Number of households by marital status, 1972-2012,** *England and Wales*

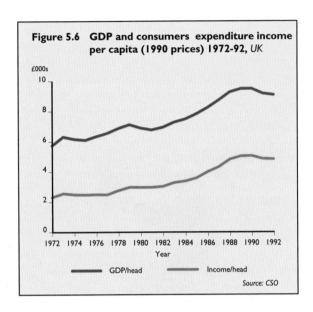

Figure 5.6 **GDP and consumers expenditure income per capita (1990 prices) 1972-92,** *UK*

Source: CSO

5.16 The increases in GDP in recent decades have enabled consumers to spend increasing amounts on durable, and non-durable, household and other goods. Reducing average household size has also tended to increase demand per head of population, since consumption of household appliances, furniture and Do It Yourself (DIY) goods tends to be related to households rather than individuals.

5.17 The projected increase in households over the next 20 years, together with improving housing standards, are likely to lead to increased consumer expenditure on housing related items. Expenditure on DIY goods is expected to treble in real terms between 1990 and 2010. Expenditure on major domestic appliances is expected to more than double during this period, and increases are also expected in expenditure on carpets, furniture and other household goods. These increases, if realised, are likely to lead to increased consumption by UK citizens of natural resources both from within the UK itself and from overseas. The rate of increase of resource use in future years may not, however, be as great as the increases in consumption, owing to changes in the resource intensity of production. In the last 20 years, for example, increases in energy use have been much less than the growth in overall GDP, owing to greater efficiency in energy use (stimulated in part by large increases in energy prices since 1973). It is possible, therefore, that resource use could even fall over the coming decades if resource prices increase.

REFERENCES AND FURTHER READING

1   *United Nations Demographic Yearbook 1991.*

2   *Britain in 2010: The Policy Studies Institute (PSI) Report.* J. Northcott et al. PSI Publishing, 1991.

CHAPTER 6

GLOBAL ATMOSPHERE

SYNOPSIS

6.1 Recent scientific progress has identified two threats to the global atmosphere caused by human activities. First, the increased emission of gases, such as carbon dioxide (CO_2), may result in a warming of the earth's surface and consequent changes in climate. Second, the production of substances which deplete the ozone layer, such as chlorofluorocarbons (CFCs), may allow harmful ultraviolet rays to penetrate to the earth's surface. Although scientific understanding is not yet certain, precautionary action is needed to confront these threats.

6.2 The key issues for sustainability are:
- to limit emissions of greenhouse gases which may contribute to enhanced global warming;
- to restrict emissions of substances which cause stratospheric ozone depletion.

GLOBAL CLIMATE CHANGE

6.3 Dealing with the threat of climate change is one of the best examples of the balances that need to be struck to achieve sustainable development. Industrial development has brought many benefits, such as better living conditions through the use of electricity and greater mobility through the use of cars. However, a consequence has been the release into the atmosphere of increasing amounts of greenhouse gases, such as CO_2 and methane, which could result in warming of the earth's surface.

6.4 There are many uncertainties in scientific understanding of climate change. For example, the climate has warmed by about 0.5°C over the past 150 years, but it is not yet possible to prove beyond doubt that this change is attributable to mankind's emissions of greenhouse gases. However, rapid progress is being made to improve scientific understanding. Present knowledge is summarised by the work of the Inter-Governmental Panel on Climate Change (IPCC), which includes the world's leading experts on climate change.

6.5 The IPCC's 1992 *Supplement*[1] to its 1990 *First Assessment Report*[2] confirmed that emissions of greenhouse gases from human activities are increasing the concentrations of these gases in the atmosphere, which may result in additional warming of the earth's surface. The Report also confirmed that average global temperature and sea level have increased over the last century. Much uncertainty remains but, using the best models available, IPCC estimates that if nothing is done to limit greenhouse gases, the global average temperature could increase by between 0.2°C and 0.5°C every decade over the next 100 years.

6.6 Although there is even more uncertainty about the complex effects of climate change, there is a strong possibility of adverse environmental consequences. IPCC estimates that an increase in temperature of about 0.3°C a decade could cause sea levels to rise by, on average, about 6 cm a decade. Climatic changes could alter the frequency and severity of storms and result in more frequent flooding. The 1991 report of the UK Climate Change Impacts Review Group[3] emphasised that the potential impacts of climate change in the UK could be substantial, and might include a 20 cm rise in sea level by 2030, and more hot spells, droughts and storms. Figure 6.1 shows areas of Britain which could be particularly vulnerable to accelerated sea level rise, and Figure 6.2 shows the trends in average annual temperatures in Central England and globally.

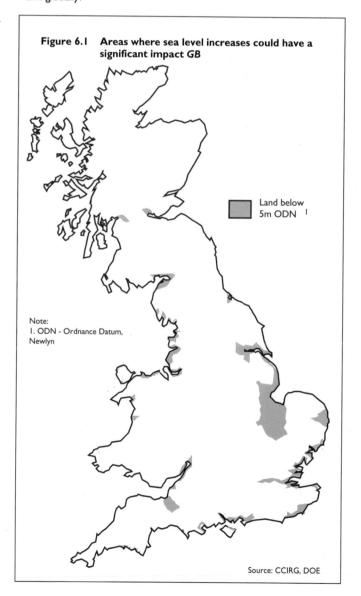

Figure 6.1   Areas where sea level increases could have a significant impact GB

Land below 5m ODN [1]

Note:
1. ODN - Ordnance Datum, Newlyn

Source: CCIRG, DOE

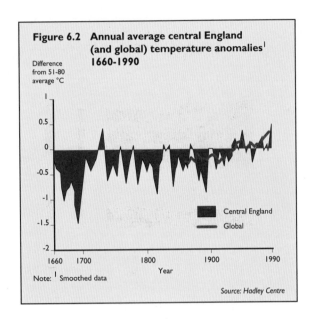

Figure 6.2   Annual average central England (and global) temperature anomalies[1] 1660-1990

Difference from 51-80 average °C

Central England

Global

Note: [1] Smoothed data

Source: Hadley Centre

6.7 The scientific priority is to reduce the uncertainties surrounding climate change. In November 1992, the IPCC undertook to provide by 1995 a *Second Assessment Report*, including the latest results of comparisons between new and improved climate models. The UK is supporting a wide range of research to improve understanding of climate change. An important part of this is the Hadley Centre for Climate Change Prediction and Research. Although uncertainties remain, the aim is to have, well before 2012, unequivocal evidence of the extent of human-induced climate change and reliable regional predictions of its effects. If the warming of the climate continues, there will come a time when it is so increased that only mankind's emissions can explain the change.

Framework Convention on Climate Change

6.8 The Framework Convention on Climate Change[4] ("the Convention") was signed by 153 countries, including the UK, in June 1992 at the Earth Summit in Rio and was the starting point for worldwide action to address the problem of climate change. Sustainable development is at the heart of the Convention's objective "to achieve stabilisation of greenhouse gas concentrations in the atmosphere at a level that would prevent dangerous anthropogenic interference with the climate system". However, defining exactly what degree of climate change may be sustainable within these terms is difficult.

6.9 To protect the world's climate for present and future generations, a "precautionary" approach was adopted in the Convention. In other words, the Convention parties concluded that the potential risks of climate change are sufficiently great to require action now, notwithstanding the scientific uncertainties if the balance of likely costs and benefits justifies it.

6.10 The Convention commits all parties to formulate, implement and regularly update national programmes containing measures to limit greenhouse gas emissions and to protect carbon sinks, such as forests. This crucially includes developing countries, whose total levels of emissions of CO_2 and other greenhouse gases are projected to overtake those from currently industrialised nations early in the next century.

6.11 The Convention commits developed country parties to give a lead in combatting climate change, by taking measures aimed at returning their emissions of CO_2 and other greenhouse gases to 1990 levels by the year 2000. It also commits some of them to providing new and additional resources to help developing countries meet their Convention commitments, and to assisting their development along sustainable lines, including through the transfer of new and energy efficient technologies.

UK Climate Change Programme

6.12 The UK ratified the Convention at the end of 1993. It has also produced the UK *Climate Change Programme*[5], published in parallel with this Strategy, which sets out how the UK intends to meet its Convention commitments. It details the action being taken to limit domestic greenhouse gas emissions and, through the UK aid programme, those of developing countries.

6.13 Before taking final decisions on the CO_2 programme, the Government initiated a wide-ranging public debate, issuing a consultation document and holding a major conference and several workshops. The result is a programme based on a partnership approach.

6.14 The programme starts from the premise that sustainable energy use is the responsibility not just of government, but of everyone. The Government's role is to provide the correct fiscal, regulatory and financial framework for the programme, and to ensure that advice and information are available on the actions that can be taken to make savings. But it is people in households and businesses who will make the decisions and take the actions that will lead to lower emissions. The Government is seeking help from all sectors, including asking business groups, trade associations and voluntary and consumer groups to act as channels of information and encouragement to such decision-makers.

6.15 As described in 6.11, the UK is committed to taking measures aimed at returning CO_2 and other greenhouse gas emissions to their 1990 levels by 2000. In 1990, this country was responsible for human-induced CO_2 emissions corresponding to an estimated 158 million tonnes of carbon (MtC), about 2.6% of world CO_2 emissions from fossil fuel combustion. Because it is not possible to predict future emissions with certainty, the Government has produced a range of scenarios in Energy Paper 59[6]. To provide a focus for the development of a programme of measures to meet the UK's Convention commitment, the Government has selected a representative scenario, roughly in the centre of the range. This shows the need to reduce projected emissions by about 10 MtC in 2000 to meet the Convention commitment.

6.16 Figures 6.3.1 and 6.3.2 show possible future trends in CO_2 emissions, based on central economic growth and low fuel price assumptions (see Annex IV). The largest contributor to the increasing trend in CO_2 emissions is the transport sector. Chapters 19 and 36 describe the measures to reduce emissions in the energy sector, which are aimed principally at encouraging greater efficiency of energy use. But the CO_2 programme also includes measures to achieve an increase in renewable energy capacity. Details of measures in the transport sector are included in chapter 26.

6.17 The *Climate Change Programme* also describes action to return emissions of other greenhouse gases, such as methane and nitrous oxide (N_2O), to 1990 levels by 2000. For example, by 2000, the methane programme should reduce emissions by about 10% from 1990 levels. The measures involve fiscal, regulatory, voluntary and planning policies. The Government will encourage emitters to adopt best practice where it is cost effective to limit emissions, including utilising methane for electricity generation wherever possible.

Beyond 2000

6.18 The UK recognises that the *Climate Change Programme* is only the start of the action likely to be needed to combat global warming in a sustainable way. Projections for emissions after 2000 are even more uncertain than those up to that year, but present IPCC estimates suggest that atmospheric concentrations of greenhouse gases could increase by 20% over the next 20 years.

6.19 Even if developed countries succeed in returning their emissions to 1990 levels by 2000, further international action may well be necessary. The current Convention measures will need to be reviewed in the light of the further scientific evidence that has been sought.

6.20 When the measures in the *Climate Change Programme* have been implemented, UK emissions of most greenhouse

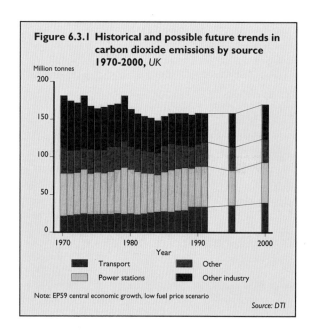

Figure 6.3.1 Historical and possible future trends in carbon dioxide emissions by source 1970-2000, *UK*

Note: EP59 central economic growth, low fuel price scenario

Source: DTI

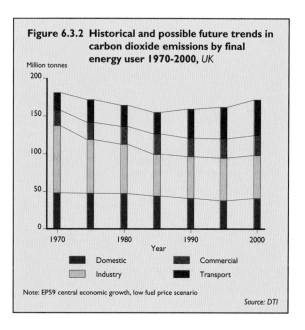

Figure 6.3.2 Historical and possible future trends in carbon dioxide emissions by final energy user 1970-2000, *UK*

Note: EP59 central economic growth, low fuel price scenario

Source: DTI

gases should decline beyond 2000. However, this may not be the case for CO_2, the most important greenhouse gas. Figure 6.4 shows a range of possible future scenarios for CO_2 emissions, reflecting different assumptions about economic growth and fuel prices (see Annex IV). The scenarios in Figure 6.4 do not take account of the measures in the CO_2 programme. It is important to begin thinking now about possible strategies for preventing such an increase. Some of the options, particularly in the energy, transport and forestry sectors are discussed in the *Climate Change Programme*.

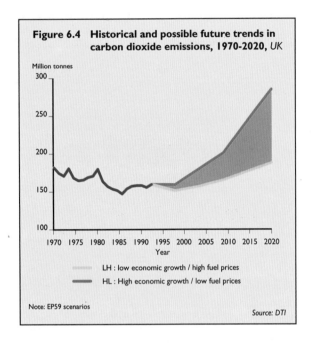

Figure 6.4 Historical and possible future trends in carbon dioxide emissions, 1970-2020, *UK*

Million tonnes

LH : low economic growth / high fuel prices
HL : High economic growth / low fuel prices

Note: EP59 scenarios

Source: DTI

6.21 The principal cause of the projected rise in CO_2 emissions after 2000 is the expected growth in emissions from the electricity generating and transport sectors. The challenge is to find means of producing electricity economically in ways that minimise carbon emissions, to continue to improve the efficiency with which energy is used, and to ensure that demands for access to goods and services can be met in ways that substantially reduce increases in travel. There would be wider environmental benefits from meeting these challenges, in addition to the effect on greenhouse gas emissions.

6.22 The UK programme will be reviewed and developed in the context of the international response. The IPCC will produce a *Second Assessment Report* in 1995 (see 6.7). The Convention provides for the present commitments to be reviewed at the first meeting of the Conference of Parties (probably in 1995), and again before the end of 1998. Those reviews will provide the context in which the Government considers further UK commitments.

STRATOSPHERIC OZONE DEPLETION

6.23 The depletion of the ozone layer shows how technological advances, such as using CFCs as coolants in refrigerators, can have unsustainable paybacks. The ozone layer protects the earth's surface from harmful ultraviolet rays, which can cause skin cancer and crop failure. Although the depletion recorded so far over the UK is unlikely to have any significant effect on human or animal health or on crop yields, action is needed now to respond to the global threat of ozone depletion.

6.24 The first clear sign of damage to the ozone layer was reported in 1985 by the British Antarctic Survey team who had been measuring ozone levels over the Antarctic since 1957. Since the late 1970s, they have observed that every southern spring, ozone destruction over the Antarctic covers an area as big as the United States and as deep as Mount Everest. In October 1987, when this "hole" was very severe, the total amount of ozone measured was less than half of its 1970 levels. In each year from 1989 to 1992 the ozone layer was again severely depleted. In 1993, ozone depletion began earlier than usual and the 1993 Antarctic ozone hole was the deepest ever recorded, with two thirds of the protective ozone shield being destroyed by early October. Research also shows that since 1979 the total annual amounts of ozone recorded over Antarctica have declined by some 5%.

6.25 Scientific research has increased knowledge of the complex processes of ozone depletion. The UK contributes to international research on the stratosphere and the effects of ozone depletion. When released in large quantities, many ozone-depleting chemicals do not break down in the lower atmosphere. Most are carried up to the upper atmosphere where they are eventually broken down by ultraviolet radiation, releasing chlorine or bromine which act as catalysts in the destruction of ozone. This is the principal cause of ozone depletion. In order to protect the ozone layer, it is necessary to reduce the amounts of chlorine and bromine in the atmosphere.

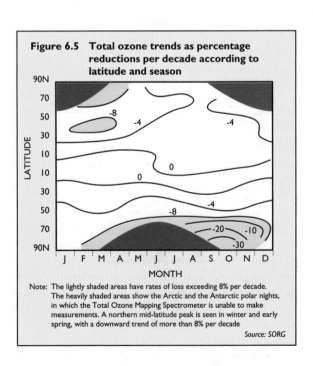

Figure 6.5 Total ozone trends as percentage reductions per decade according to latitude and season

LATITUDE

MONTH

Note: The lightly shaded areas have rates of loss exceeding 8% per decade. The heavily shaded areas show the Arctic and the Antarctic polar nights, in which the Total Ozone Mapping Spectrometer is unable to make measurements. A northern mid-latitude peak is seen in winter and early spring, with a downward trend of more than 8% per decade

Source: SORG

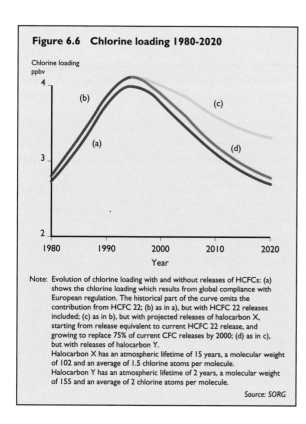

Figure 6.6   Chlorine loading 1980-2020

Chlorine loading ppbv

(b) (a) (c) (d)

1980   1990   2000   2010   2020

Year

Note: Evolution of chlorine loading with and without releases of HCFCs: (a) shows the chlorine loading which results from global compliance with European regulation. The historical part of the curve omits the contribution from HCFC 22; (b) as in a), but with HCFC 22 releases included; (c) as in b), but with projected releases of halocarbon X, starting from release equivalent to current HCFC 22 release, and growing to replace 75% of current CFC releases by 2000; (d) as in c), but with releases of halocarbon Y.
Halocarbon X has an atmospheric lifetime of 15 years, a molecular weight of 102 and an average of 1.5 chlorine atoms per molecule.
Halocarbon Y has an atmospheric lifetime of 2 years, a molecular weight of 155 and an average of 2 chlorine atoms per molecule.

Source: SORG

Table 6.1   Montreal Protocol and EC target reductions for ozone-depleting substances

Substance	New EU regulation (agreed by Ministers December 1993)	Montreal Protocol position (Nov 1992)
CFCs	85% cut by 1/1/1994 Phaseout by 1/1/1995*	75% cut by 1/1/1994 Phaseout by 1/1/1996*
Carbon tetrachloride	85% cut by 1/1/1994 Phaseout by 1/1/1995*	85% cut by 1/1/1994 Phaseout by 1/1/1996*
Halons	Phasout by 1/1/1994*	Phaseout by 1/1/1994*
1,1,1 trichloroethylene	50% cut by 1/1/1994 Phaseout by 1/1/1996*	50% cut by 1/1/1994 Phaseout by 1/1/1996*
Methyl bromide	Freeze at 1991 levels from 1/1/1995 25% cut by 1/1/1998	Freeze at 1991 levels from 1/1/1995
HCFCs	Freeze at 2.6% of CFC consumption + total HCFC consumption in 1989 35% cut - 2004 60% cut - 2007 80% cut - 2010 95% cut - 2013 Phaseout by 2015	Freeze at 3.1% of CFC consumption + total HCFC consumption in 1989 35% cut - 2004 65% cut - 2007 90% cut - 2010 99.5% cut - 2013 Phaseout by 2030

Note: * indicates provision for possible "essential use" exemption

Source: DOE

6.26 The atmosphere over the Antarctic in winter is isolated from the rest of the world by a natural circulation of wind called the polar vortex. During the winter, when it is cold and dark, polar stratospheric clouds (PSCs) form in the stratosphere. Inactive chlorine is converted on the surface of these clouds into forms that react with ozone in the presence of sunlight. Each spring, when the sun returns to Antarctica, ozone is rapidly destroyed. The hole disappears again when the Antarctic stratosphere warms up enough to disperse the PSCs and break up the winds which isolate it from the rest of the world. Ozone-rich air then flows in to replenish the ozone lost during the previous months.

6.27 Although ozone depletion occurs over the Arctic, meteorological conditions are very different to the Antarctic and a similar hole has not been formed so far. However, there is now increasing evidence from satellite and other observations that the ozone layer is thinning all over the world. Figure 6.5 shows the trends in ozone depletion as a function of latitude and season. The average depletion is estimated at 3% per decade over mid-latitudes in both hemispheres. Over northern mid-latitudes, this loss is about 8% per decade during late winter and early spring. Record low ozone values during the winters of 1992 and 1993 over Europe were associated with unusual and persistent weather patterns.

Montreal Protocol

6.28 The *Montreal Protocol on Substances that Deplete the Ozone Layer*[7] is the international response to this problem. It controls the production and consumption (defined as production plus imports minus exports) of the most significant ozone-depleting substances. Over 100 countries have signed the Protocol since it came into force on 1 January 1989. It has been revised twice since then – the 1990 *London Amendment*[8] and the 1992 *Copenhagen Amendment*[9]. The Protocol now covers CFCs, halons, carbon tetrachloride, 1,1,1 trichloroethane, hydrobromofluorocarbons (HBFCs), hydrochloroflurocarbons (HCFCs) and methyl bromide.

6.29 The Protocol is implemented in the EC by Regulations which are directly applicable in the law of each member state. A consolidating Regulation, which will also place controls on the substances added to the Protocol in Copenhagen, is under discussion. As with the controls on CFCs and carbon tetrachloride, these are likely to be tighter than the Protocol (see Table 6.1).

6.30 Figure 6.6 shows the effect of the Protocol and EC controls on chlorine and bromine loading between 1980 and 2020. The height of the peak of chlorine and bromine loading is relatively little affected by changes in emissions between now and 2000 because of time lags in the atmosphere, but the rate of decline from the peak after 2000 is dependent on emissions over the next decade. On the basis of the controls agreed at Copenhagen, chlorine and bromine in the atmosphere are expected to return to around today's level by 2012.

6.31 Controls on ozone-depleting substances which survive in the atmosphere for a long time, such as CFCs and halons, will halt their production very shortly. The controls on HCFCs and methyl bromide are likely to be tightened as environmentally friendly alternatives become more easily available. Reduction of chlorine and bromine loading must be achieved globally, however, and the UK will be pressing other Parties to the Protocol to tighten these controls as soon as technically possible.

The UK response

6.32 The UK will ensure that the controls are complied with fully and that users of ozone-depleting substances move as quickly as possible to alternatives that do not deplete the ozone layer. To this end, the UK Government has been running a publicity campaign to make users aware of the problem and the range of alternative solutions. The campaign stresses that the use of ozone-depleting HCFCs should be kept to a minimum and that, when CFCs are being replaced, HCFCs should be used only where there are no suitable less ozone-depleting alternatives available.

6.33 The UK is acting to control emissions of ozone-depleting substances. Under the Environmental Protection Act 1990[10], safe disposal or recovery of waste CFCs and other ozone-depleting substances is mandatory. The Government provides financial support to local authorities for CFC recycling, and has also supported probably the world's first halon bank run by the Halon Users' National Consortium. This aims to manage the UK installed bank of halons to minimise unnecessary use and to encourage recycling, and has enabled production of new halons to be stopped.

6.34 Developing countries, who will have more difficulty in implementing the Protocol, are allowed a 10 year "grace period" before they are required to start following the phase out schedules. The UK has contributed $7.2 million to a fund established to provide financial and technical cooperation, including technology transfer, to these countries.

6.35 The UK will be pressing for controls on methyl bromide and HCFCs to be tightened as appropriate when the Protocol is next reviewed. The Government will continue to press the international community to comply fully with the Protocol. The UK will urge countries which have not yet signed and ratified the amended Protocol to do so as quickly as possible, to ensure that ozone-depleting substances are phased out globally. The UK considers this to be a sustainable approach to the problem of ozone depletion.

REFERENCES AND FURTHER READING

1   *Climate Change 1992: the Supplementary Report to the IPCC's Scientific Assessment.* J.T. Houghton, B.A. Callender, and S.K. Varney (eds). Cambridge University Press, 1992..

2   *Climate Change: the IPCC Scientific Assessment.* J.T. Houghton, G.J. Jenkins, and J.J. Ephraums (eds). Cambridge University Press, 1990.

3   *The Potential Effects of Climate Change in the United Kingdom.* UK Climate Impacts Review Group. HMSO, 1991.

4   *Report of the Intergovernmental Negotiating Committee for a Framework Convention on Climate Change on the Work of the Second Part of its Fifth Session, held at New York from 30 April to 9 May 1992.*

5   *Climate Change: The UK Programme.* Cm 2427. HMSO, 1994. ISBN 0–10–124272–7.

6   *Energy Paper Number 59. Energy-Related Carbon Emissions: Possible Future Scenarios in the United Kingdom.* HMSO, 1992.

7   *Montreal Protocol on Substances that Deplete the Ozone Layer.* UNEP, 1987.

8   *Amendment to the Montreal Protocol on Substances that Deplete the Ozone Layer.* Cm 1576. Adopted at London, 1990. HMSO, 1990.

9   *Amendment to the Montreal Protocol on Substances that Deplete the Ozone Layer.* Cm 2367. Adopted at Copenhagen, 1992. HMSO, 1992.

10 Environmental Protection Act 1990. HMSO, 1990. ISBN 0–10–544390–5.

CHAPTER 7

AIR QUALITY

SYNOPSIS

7.1 Much has been achieved in combatting air pollution in recent years, but in order to continue to reduce the risk of adverse effects on natural ecosystems, human health and quality of life, in line with the objectives for sustainable development, further progress will be necessary in each of the main areas of air pollution: acid emissions, photochemical pollution and urban air quality.

7.2 The key issues for sustainability are:
- to ensure that the framework of international targets and programmes, based on critical loads development, operates effectively to limit acid emissions;
- to measure and control photochemical pollution;
- to manage local air quality, especially in urban areas, and in particular to ensure that all relevant sectors – industry, transport, local authorities and the general public – contribute.

INTRODUCTION

7.3 Good air quality is essential for human health and the well-being of the environment as a whole. Mankind's industrial, domestic and agricultural activities, notably fuel combustion, result in a wide range of emissions including sulphur dioxide (SO_2), smoke, oxides of nitrogen (NO_x), and volatile organic compounds (VOCs) into the atmosphere. These emissions are presently broadly comparable, on a global scale, to those derived from natural sources (mainly volcanoes, lightning, and organisms in soils and the oceans). However, in the industrialised regions of Europe, North America and Asia, man-made emissions predominate, to the detriment of air quality and with corresponding effects on health, ecosystems and building materials, for example.

7.4 There have been major changes in UK air quality since the 1970s. Widespread coal burning in the domestic sector has been all but eliminated with the move to cleaner fuels, such as gas and electricity, in the home. In the industrial sector, cleaner fuels, newer less polluting processes and the installation of abatement equipment on existing ones have all contributed to lower emissions. Urban smogs have now become a thing of the past. However, over the same period motor traffic has increased enormously, to the extent that vehicles are now the major source of most significant pollutants in major towns and cities.

7.5 Since the 1970s, there has also been increasing recognition of the international dimension in air quality issues; initial concerns were about the Europe-wide movement of acidic pollutants derived from sulphur and nitrogen oxides, but concern has been growing about the problem of photochemically-produced pollutants such as ozone, the main constituent of so-called "summer smogs".

7.6 Both the domestic and international dimensions of air quality problems will present considerable challenges to policy makers in the coming decades. Some progress has also been made in establishing the principles of sustainability in both international and national air quality management. The World Health Organisation's (WHO) target for air quality states that by the year 2000, air quality in all countries should be improved to a point at which recognised air pollutants do not pose a threat to public health. More progress will, however, be required to build on that objective to secure sustainability in air quality over the time frame of this Strategy. As background, this chapter outlines the UK's main air quality problems, with trends and forecasts for the main pollutants which cause them.

ACID DEPOSITION

7.7 Enhanced acid deposition, arising from man-made emissions of SO_2, NO_x and ammonia, causes concern in many parts of Europe and North America because it can add to the acidification of soils and freshwaters, adversely affecting vegetation and aquatic life in geologically sensitive areas. To assess the risk of possible harmful effects arising from increased acidification from depositions, the concept of "critical loads" is used. A critical load is the estimated level of deposition of one or more pollutants below which present knowledge indicates that there are no significant harmful effects on a specified, sensitive element of the environment. Critical loads for total acidity have been estimated, using chemical criteria, for soils and freshwaters in Britain. These estimates will be reviewed and updated to reduce uncertainties as more information becomes available. Acid depositions from man-made sources have probably exceeded these levels in some upland Northern and Western areas for many decades, coinciding with measurable biological changes over the last century or more in many fresh water bodies. Figure 7.1 gives a general indication of areas in which it is estimated that, in 1986–88, the dominant soil type was subject to acid depositions above its estimated critical load. It is clear that substantial reductions in man-made emissions will be needed in order to reduce the risks from further acidification, and measures to achieve these reductions are outlined in the following paragraphs.

7.8 In 1991, electricity generation was responsible for over 70% of SO_2 emissions in the UK, the rest emanating mainly from manufacturing industry. The main sources of NO_x emissions are road transport (51%) and electricity generation (26%). UK emissions of SO_2 have decreased by about 45% since 1970 and

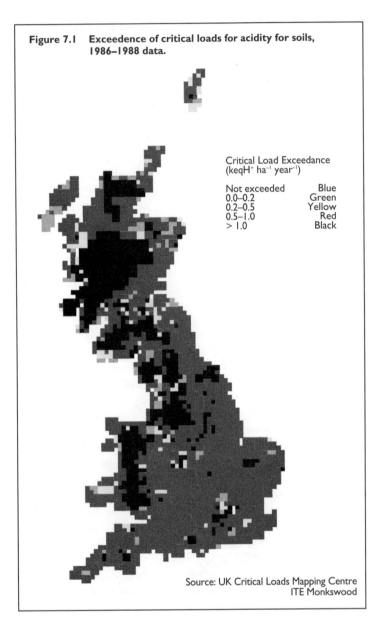

Figure 7.1 Exceedence of critical loads for acidity for soils, 1986–1988 data.

Critical Load Exceedance
($keqH^+ ha^{-1} year^{-1}$)

Not exceeded	Blue
0.0–0.2	Green
0.2–0.5	Yellow
0.5–1.0	Red
> 1.0	Black

Source: UK Critical Loads Mapping Centre
ITE Monkswood

to reducing SO_2 and NO_x emissions from existing large combustion plants (LCPs), which include power stations. Target SO_2 reductions are 20% by 1993, 40% by 1998 and 60% by 2003, taking 1980 as the baseline. Target NO_x reductions are 15% by 1993 and 30% by 1998. The UK expects to have more than met the 1993 targets for both SO_2 and NO_x. The LCPD is due for review in 1994. Under the NO_x Protocol to the UNECE Convention on Long Range Transboundary Air Pollution, the UK is committed to maintaining its 1994 emissions at their 1987 level. At the present time, the UK is projected to meet this target with 6% to spare.

7.10 Scenarios for future SO_2 emissions show a continuing decline over the period of this Strategy. Ultimately, reductions in emissions of about 80% compared with 1980 should be achievable by 2010–2015, following shifts in fuel use and the extension of clean technologies in the electricity supply and other industries. These reductions will result in considerably fewer areas where critical loads are exceeded, and will provide a basis for the approach to sustainability. The timing and scale of emission reductions in the context of ecosystem recovery is the subject of continuing research. Further international agreements on the reduction of SO_2 emissions are expected in 1994.

7.11 NO_x emissions are expected to peak in the early 1990s and then fall steadily beyond the year 2000 before reaching a minimum. The overall decrease to the year 2010 of between 22% and 36% from 1991 levels is due largely to the reduction in emissions from road transport as a result of the introduction of catalytic converters. Based on current traffic forecasts, NO_x emissions will increase again beyond 2010 as increasing traffic activity outweighs the benefits obtained from catalytic converters. By the year 2010, NO_x emissions from existing LCPs should be between 60% and 70% of their 1980 levels.

PHOTOCHEMICAL POLLUTION

7.12 Ground-level ozone occurs naturally but levels can be increased as a result of human activities. Ozone, a secondary pollutant, is formed by a complex series of reactions between NO_x and VOCs in the presence of sunlight; ground-level ozone is a different problem from the depletion of the ozone layer in the stratosphere, where ozone forms a layer which protects the earth from harmful ultraviolet radiation. At ground level, however, high concentrations of ozone can affect human health and can damage plants and crops. Evidence suggests that background ground-level ozone concentrations have doubled over the past 100 years to current levels of around 30 ppb (parts per billion) over the UK. Some 51% of VOC emissions in the UK currently arise

some lochs in Scotland are already showing signs of recovery from acidification. This reduction has largely occurred in the industry sector through the increased use of low-sulphur and sulphur-free fuels. Power station emissions have decreased by 13% since 1970. Total NO_x emissions remained relatively constant up to the mid-1980s but have risen steadily since then, reflecting the increasing emissions from road transport which have more than doubled since 1970.

7.9 Current policies, under the Environmental Protection Act (EPA) 1990[1] and Integrated Pollution Control (IPC), are aimed at achieving major reductions in SO_2 and NO_x emissions from the major point sources. Under the EC Large Combustion Plant Directive (LCPD)[2], the UK is committed

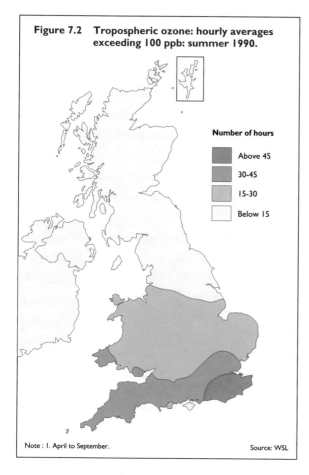

Figure 7.2 Tropospheric ozone: hourly averages exceeding 100 ppb: summer 1990.

Number of hours

- Above 45
- 30-45
- 15-30
- Below 15

Note : 1. April to September.   Source: WSL

from various industrial processes and solvent use, and 37% from road transport through exhaust emissions and evaporative losses of petrol.

7.13 Ozone episodes, in which concentrations rise substantially above background levels, occur in summer heat waves when there are long hours of bright sunlight, high temperatures and light winds. Once formed, ozone can persist for several days and can be transported long distances. Levels of ozone are therefore very dependent on the weather; for that reason, exceedences of indicators such as WHO guidelines can vary markedly from year to year, making the effect of abatement policies difficult to assess. Nonetheless, even in relatively cool summers, the WHO hourly guideline for ozone (76–100ppb) is widely exceeded, particularly in the South, where the contribution from European sources of ozone and its precursors adds to the production of ozone from UK sources. Figure 7.2 shows the extent of exceedences of the upper end of the WHO hourly guideline range in the UK in 1990. Exceedences of the 8-hour WHO guideline (50–60ppb) are even more widespread, of the order of 80 days per year at maximum. Critical levels for a series of plant species of varying ozone sensibility have been

proposed within the UNECE framework and many of these are also likely to be exceeded in the UK.

7.14 Photochemical pollution is an international issue, and the first steps toward the control of ozone levels in Europe were taken with the signing of the VOC Protocol in 1991. This requires a 30% reduction of VOC emissions in each country by 1999 on a 1988 base. There is recent evidence to suggest that, in the remoter parts of Europe including parts of the UK, ozone production is limited by the availability of NO_x. To reduce levels of ozone below WHO guidelines and UNECE critical levels, reductions of both VOCs and NO_x will be necessary. Studies of ozone formation and long range transport suggest that these international agreements should reduce peak hourly ozone levels by about 10–20ppb (10–20%); 8-hour running mean levels above 50ppb (the lower end of the WHO guideline) should reduce by about 10–20 days per year by 2000. There is, therefore, still a need for reductions in ozone levels before WHO guidelines and UNECE critical levels are achieved across the UK.

7.15 The basis for progress to sustainability in this area has, therefore, been laid. Critical levels have been identified and the main policy instruments are in place. Nevertheless, problems of measurement and control mean that securing sustainability in this area over a reasonable time frame will present significant challenges.

URBAN AIR QUALITY

7.16 Although there are significant air quality problems in rural areas, it is air pollution in urban areas that has historically been the principal focus of concern. The character of urban air pollution has changed over time, but the complexity of urban systems means that it inevitably has diverse origins and requires diverse responses. Nevertheless, the improvement in urban air quality in recent decades has been dramatic. In little over a generation, the urban smogs which led to 4,000 additional premature deaths in London during the winter of 1952 have been eliminated. This success has been attributed to the Clean Air Acts of 1956 and 1968 and the creation of smokeless zones which have considerably reduced the main source of this kind of problem, that is, smoke and SO_2 pollution from the widespread combustion of coal. But, as domestic and industrial pollution have receded, traffic-generated pollutants (NO_x, carbon monoxide (CO), particulates and VOCs) have steadily increased.

7.17 Figure 7.3 shows trends in UK air quality for smoke and SO_2. Average urban UK concentrations have decreased significantly since the Clean Air Acts and, as the areas subject

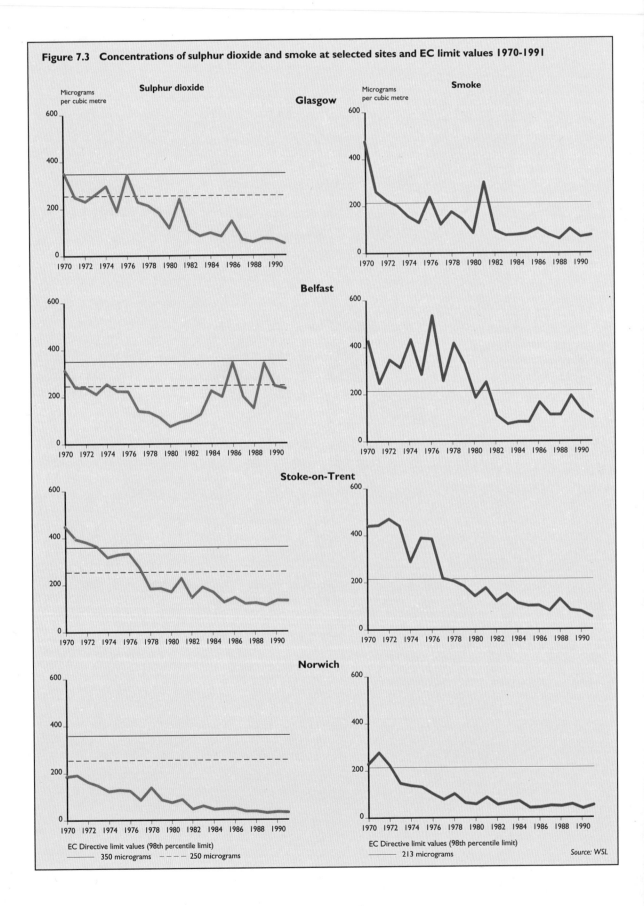

Figure 7.3   Concentrations of sulphur dioxide and smoke at selected sites and EC limit values 1970-1991

Sulphur dioxide

Smoke

Glasgow

Belfast

Stoke-on-Trent

Norwich

EC Directive limit values (98th percentile limit)
───── 350 micrograms   ─ ─ ─ 250 micrograms

EC Directive limit values (98th percentile limit)
───── 213 micrograms

Source: WSL

to smoke control increase, concentrations have decreased well below EC Directive Limit Values in most areas. Some exceptions remain, however, notably in Belfast and in a small number of areas in the North of England where solid fuels are still burned in significant quantities. Belfast does not have access to natural gas and there is still a great reliance on solid fuels for domestic heating; it is likely to remain at risk of breaching EC Directive Limit Values until gas is available. This risk is exacerbated in this and other areas where unauthorised smokeless fuels, some with high sulphur content, present an attractive alternative in view of their relative cheapness compared to authorised smokeless fuels. While there has been a widespread major reduction in SO_2 levels in towns and cities in the UK, peak hourly concentrations can occasionally exceed WHO guidelines for SO_2 both in coal burning areas and elsewhere, largely due to large point sources such as power stations.

7.18 The most significant feature of UK emissions of NO_x in the past two decades has been the estimated doubling or more of emissions from road transport since 1970. This has arisen largely from an increase in traffic activity, but there is also evidence that, in recent years, increasing engine efficiencies and reductions in CO and VOC emissions have been gained at the expense of increased NO_x emissions. These emission increases have been manifest in two recent large scale diffusion tube studies of nitrogen dioxide (NO_2) from 1986 to 1991. In a study in rural Wales, the average difference in NO_2 levels from 1986 to 1991 was 53% while, in a study over the whole UK, the difference was 35%.

7.19 Figure 7.4 shows historical and projected trends for CO, particulates and VOC emissions from road transport. The future patterns of both CO and VOC emissions from road transport are very similar to those of NO_x. They result from the beneficial effect of catalytic converters on petrol-run vehicle emissions, which would reach a minimum around 2010 but, as with NO_x emissions, would rise again beyond that date with the forecast increasing traffic activity. Particulate emissions arise mainly from diesel vehicles and, although increasingly stringent EC emission limits have been incorporated into the forecasts, their effects are nothing like as large as those of catalytic converters on petrol-engined cars. In the high traffic growth scenario, emissions of particulates in the UK in 2010 are forecast to be similar to those in 1991. Between now and 2010, the minimum level of emissions is only about 20% below the current level.

7.20 It is now well established that motor vehicles are the dominant source of NO_x concentrations, contributing 70% or more to levels in London and in other major urban areas. The EC Limit Value for NO_2 is not exceeded, but the Guide Value

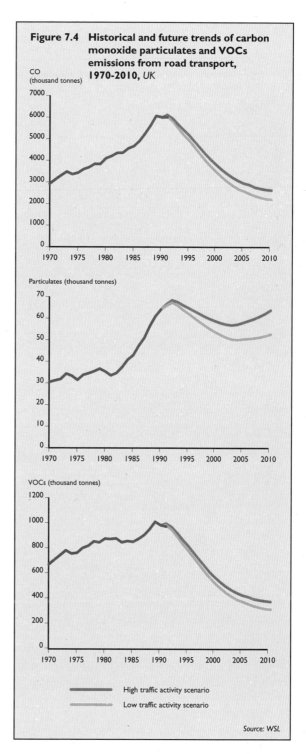

Figure 7.4 **Historical and future trends of carbon monoxide particulates and VOCs emissions from road transport, 1970-2010,** *UK*

CO (thousand tonnes)

Particulates (thousand tonnes)

VOCs (thousand tonnes)

High traffic activity scenario
Low traffic activity scenario

Source: WSL

is frequently exceeded, in these areas. The WHO hourly guideline is also frequently exceeded in major cities. The rising trend in NO_x emissions, in parallel to the increase in rural NO_2 concentrations, does not appear to have been accompanied by a similar increase in central urban NO_2 levels. Some locations show increases, but at most sites

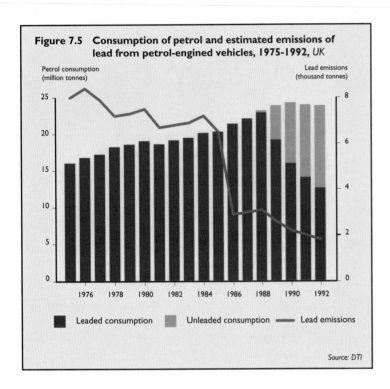

Figure 7.5 Consumption of petrol and estimated emissions of lead from petrol-engined vehicles, 1975-1992, *UK*

Petrol consumption
(million tonnes)

Lead emissions
(thousand tonnes)

■ Leaded consumption   ■ Unleaded consumption   ── Lead emissions

Source: DTI

effect and, consequently, it is prudent to continue to reduce ambient levels as much as possible. The largest source of ambient exposure to benzene is the combustion and distribution of petrol (leaded and unleaded petrols in the UK currently contain similar amounts of benzene). However, catalytic converters in the car fleet could reduce exhaust emissions of benzene by up to about 90%. Controls on evaporative and fugitive losses of petrol vapour during petrol distribution and sales and on board vehicles, which are currently being discussed within the EC, will also reduce ambient levels. The main source of butadiene exposure for most of the population appears to be motor vehicle exhausts, where butadiene is formed from the cracking of higher olefines in petrol. Butadiene is a suspected human carcinogen, and current estimates suggest that it may have a considerably higher unit risk factor than benzene. Butadiene is a reactive compound and emissions from petrol vehicles should be significantly reduced by catalytic converters. However, for both benzene and butadiene, care will be needed to assess the effect of cold-start and other inefficiencies of catalytic converters in practice, and the extent to which increasing traffic activity outweighs the benefits of the converters.

concentrations have remained broadly similar over the past five years or so. The introduction of catalytic converters should reduce concentrations, but doubts remain over the problems of cold starts and/or short journeys in urban areas which may lead to smaller reduction in episode levels of NO_2 than anticipated. However, recent studies of the mechanism of formation of episodic NO_2 levels, suggests that the benefits of NO_x reduction from catalytic converters and from reductions in traffic activity would be greater than anticipated. But the forecasts of national traffic activity indicate that the benefits of catalytic converters in urban areas will be outweighed by the increase in traffic by 2010 (see 7.11).

7.21 Similarly, if the forecasts of national emissions of particulates are reflected at the urban level, concentrations of urban particulates are unlikely to improve significantly in the time-scale considered here. This is potentially of some concern as recent studies in the USA and parts of Europe have demonstrated associations of airborne particulate levels with mortality and morbidity, at levels below the US National Ambient Air Quality Standard and similar to levels in some UK cities.

7.22 As well as their role in the formation of ground-level ozone, some VOCs exhibit toxic or carcinogenic properties. Two of the most important in the latter category are benzene and 1,3 butadiene. Benzene is a known human genotoxic carcinogen. As such, there is no recognised threshold for an

7.23 Historically, the principal source of atmospheric lead has been the use of lead additives in motor fuels. The contribution from this source has decreased substantially in the UK as a result of controls on the lead content of fuels and the availability of unleaded petrol. Estimated UK lead emissions from petrol-engined road vehicles have fallen from 8,000 tonnes in 1975 to 2,000 tonnes in 1992. Virtually all petrol stations in the UK now sell unleaded petrol, compared with only around 10% as recently as late 1988. Figure 7.5 shows that, assisted by the duty differential between leaded and unleaded petrol, the uptake of unleaded petrol in the UK had increased from virtually zero in 1987 to nearly 50% in May 1992, the largest increase for any European country. This had increased further to 54% by October 1993. Projections are that, by the end of the century, unleaded petrol will account for 90% of petrol sales and, by the year 2012, virtually all petrol-engined vehicles are projected to run on unleaded petrol, so that lead emissions from this source should fall to virtually zero.

7.24 Against this background, it will not be easy to achieve the progressive improvement in urban air quality and the improvement in the quality of life in urban areas which it can bring. Control strategies for particular pollutants, discussed in this chapter, will make a cumulative contribution, but if this objective is to be achieved, contributions must also come from improvements in vehicle emissions, in traffic limitation and in techniques of local air quality management.

REFERENCES AND FURTHER READING

1   Environmental Protection Act 1990. HMSO, 1990. ISBN 0–10–544390–5.

2   *EC Directive on large combustion plants. 88/609/EEC.* Official Journal of the European Communities L336, 24 November 1988.

CHAPTER 8

FRESHWATER

SYNOPSIS

8.1 The inland freshwaters of the UK are essential resources for a number of purposes. They are a vital and highly valued component of the UK environment and ecology. The biodiversity of an important aspect of the UK flora and fauna depends on maintaining their character and quality. These waters are also a vital economic resource for industry and agriculture, for use in production and as a medium for disposing of waste. High quality water supply is essential for human consumption; and large quantities are also used for disposal of human waste in the interests of both health and amenity. There are important potential conflicts between these different purposes and uses of water and the water environment.

8.2 The key areas for sustainability are:
- to ensure adequate water resources are available to meet consumers' needs;
- to manage and meet the demand for water from households, agriculture and industry;
- to ensure that the supply of drinking water is of sufficient quality;
- to sustain the aquatic environment;
- to manage the inevitable discharges of waste water;
- to control, as far as possible, pollution from diffuse sources;
- to enable the recreational use of water in harmony with these other concerns.

WATER RESOURCES AND SUPPLY

Existing resources and demands

8.3 Although, overall, the available water resources in the UK well exceed demand, the balance between them varies widely from region to region. Parts of the UK have long had to make arrangements to ensure that water can be reused between its falling as rain and its eventual mixing back into the sea. The UK pioneered river basin management, and arrangements are well-developed everywhere for the management of the water cycle in each catchment area, thus providing the mechanisms for resolving the conflicts that may arise between the different demands.

8.4 Water is drawn both from surface freshwater and from groundwater. Of total UK abstractions of about 34.5 megalitres per day in 1991, 51% was abstracted by water undertakers for public supply; direct abstractions by industry (including electricity suppliers) accounted for 47.6% of the total. Of the public supplies, about 70% comes from surface waters and 30% from groundwater. Surface water is used extensively in Wales, Scotland, Northern Ireland and the North and the West of England. Groundwater is of greater importance in South and East England.

8.5 Figure 8.1 illustrates this in broad terms for England and Wales by showing the theoretically available resources and the related demand for abstraction from them in each of the National Rivers Authority (NRA) regions. The availability of resources is measured by the availability of water from effective rainfall (total rainfall less transpiration by foliage) in a drought of a severity which could be expected to recur once in every 50 years. Figures 8.2 (Scotland) and 8.3 (England and Wales) show the present balance between existing developed resources and resources for public water supply (PWS) on a regional basis for Great Britain. (Developed resources are those that are readily available for abstraction.) In Northern Ireland, the demand and yield in the PWS in 1992 was 670 and 700 megalitres per day, respectively.

8.6 Although total abstractions from surface freshwater and groundwater in England and Wales have changed very little since 1980, there has been a steady increase in water withdrawn for PWS and a steady decline in water abstracted for industrial use. In Scotland, demand for unmetered PWS has also increased annually since 1986, but metered industrial demand has slightly increased. In Northern Ireland, consumption from PWS has increased annually by 6 megalitres per day over the past decade.

8.7 Many industrial and agricultural abstractions, such as those for hydro-electric power, by electricity generating companies for cooling purposes, or for fish farming, do not consume water resources; virtually all the water abstracted is later discharged

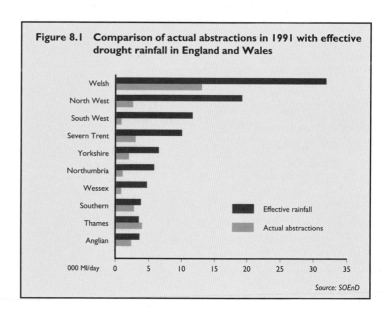

Figure 8.1   Comparison of actual abstractions in 1991 with effective drought rainfall in England and Wales

Source: SOEnD

Table 8.1 Estimated consumption of groundwater and non-tidal surface water abstracted 1991

	Public water supply	Spray irrigation	Other agriculture	Evaporativv cooling in ESI	Industrial cooling other uses	Total
Anglian	1,801	235	20	0	0	2,056
Northumbrian	982	0	0	0	0	983
North West	1,898	4	3	0	411	2,316
Severn Trent	2,439	52	14	0	249	2,755
Southern	1,242	10	6	0	0	1,259
South West	577	3	30	0	124	733
Thames	3,915	20	14	0	0	3,948
Welsh	2,574	7	17	0	4,,262	6,860
Wessex	718	8	23	0	0	748
Yorkshire	1,416	26	7	0	126	1,575
Total	1,756	365	134	0	5,172	23,233

Source: NRA

Table 8.2 Public water supply, baseline average demand projections to 2010 and surplus resources in 2021 as a percentage of average demand England and Wales

Region	1990 demand Ml/day	Baseline 2021 demand projection Ml/day	Change in demand 1990-2021 %	Surplus resources in 2021[1]
Anglian	1820	2589	42	-4
Northumbrian	1082	1301	20	62
North West	2574	2317	-10	24
Severn Trent	2421	2649	9	13
Southern	1408	1736	23	0
South West	493	687	39	11
Thames	4024	5076	26	1
Welsh	1182	1281	8	25
Wessex	904	1307	45	0
Yorkshire	1430	1583	11	15

Note: [1] Assumes all present resources available together with schemes identified in National Rivers Authority s 5143 Report

Source: NRA

back to surface waters. In contrast, uses such as spray irrigation represent a loss to water resources. Table 8.1 categorises by purpose, for England and Wales, the estimated consumption of surface freshwater and groundwater abstracted in 1991.

8.8 There remains some uncertainty over the effects of climate change on water resources over the next few decades. Recent events have not been outside previously recorded limits, although it is not clear whether the pattern of incidence may be changing. But the incidence of prolonged droughts affecting water supplies is even more uncertain. Climate change scenarios from global models are being fed into regional hydrological models to assess the implications for water resources. Further research is also required to improve estimates of seasonal changes in temperature, rainfall

and evaporation and the effect on supplies. Although climate changes are likely to occur slowly, potential problems need continuing review, since major water supply sources can take at least a decade to develop.

Future resources and demands

8.9 The main issues to be resolved in ensuring the future sustainable use of UK water resources are:

● the experience of the well below average rainfall in South and East England in the winters of 1988–92 has shown that the present margin between developed resources and demand may be uncomfortably narrow; action may be needed to give greater assurance of supplies;

● there is a mismatch between the areas where water is

available and the areas where the main growth in future demand (at least to 2012) is likely to occur; action may be needed to resolve this;

● over-abstraction, often for public water supply, has led to unacceptably low flows in some rivers in England and Wales, thereby damaging wildlife habitats and having an adverse impact on water quality and recreational and amenity value; action is needed to redress this legacy.

Any such action will have to be both cost-effective and compatible with maintaining (or improving) the existing quality of surface waters and groundwater and the aquatic environment.

8.10 For England and Wales, the NRA has a duty, under Section 188 of the Water Resources Act 1991[1], to collate and publish information from which assessments can be made of the actual and prospective demands for, and resources of, water. It expects to publish, early in 1994, its National Water Resources Development Strategy. Based on the work for this, Figure 8.4 shows the projections (for England and Wales) for public water supply demand to the year 2021, with the upper and lower bounds around the baseline estimate that has been adopted. Table 8.2 shows, region by region, the predicted surplus or shortfall in resources over the next 30 years. The projected rate of increase over the next 30 years is highest in the South and East of England. The main factors influencing demand are population growth, consumption per person, losses from the mains supply system and at consumers' premises, and the level of economic activity.

8.11 It is difficult to make long term forecasts of demand for commercial and industrial purposes. Recent trends in demand in England and Wales reveal a general decline in water abstracted for industry and general agricultural purposes, and an increase in demand for abstractions for spray irrigation, fish farming and hydro-electric power. It is uncertain whether either of these trends will continue.

8.12 In Scotland, the situation is simpler: there is no reason to think that demand in any of the major groups of catchments is likely to grow beyond the capability to develop new water resources to meet it. Nevertheless, in certain localities (particularly those where irrigation is practised on a large scale), demand for abstraction may run ahead of the ability of the available resources to meet it. Legislation already provides for the introduction, where and when necessary, of controls over abstraction for commercial, agricultural and horticultural irrigation. The Government is considering the outcome of consultation on proposals to broaden these selective powers to cover all forms of abstraction. The Department of the Environment for Northern Ireland has powers to make regulations to license water abstraction, and

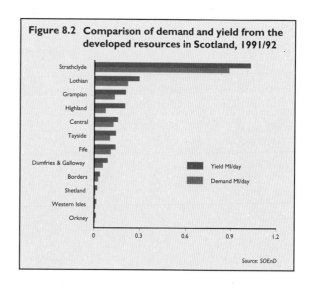

Figure 8.2 Comparison of demand and yield from the developed resources in Scotland, 1991/92

Source: SOEnD

a consultation paper is being prepared seeking views, among other matters, on the need to introduce such controls.

8.13 The framework within which the UK must establish a policy for the sustainable use of water resources up to 2012 and beyond is, therefore, a general abundance of water

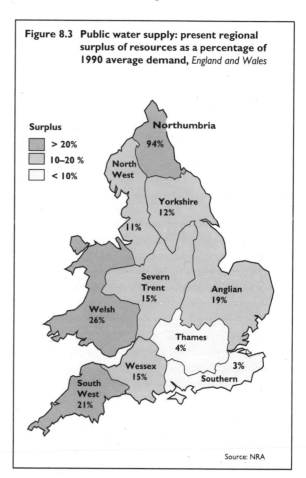

Figure 8.3 Public water supply: present regional surplus of resources as a percentage of 1990 average demand, *England and Wales*

Source: NRA

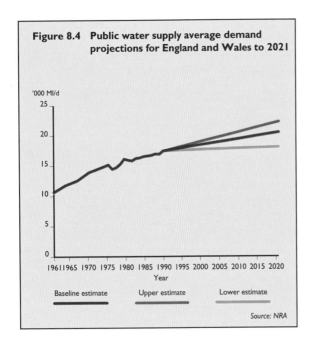

Figure 8.4 Public water supply average demand projections for England and Wales to 2021

'000 Ml/d

Year

Baseline estimate   Upper estimate   Lower estimate

Source: NRA

resources (even given general growth in domestic demand and for certain agricultural and industrial purposes), but with local or regional deficiencies in various areas and for various periods.

8.14 Major new supply infrastructure (whether in the form of new reservoirs, new groundwater abstractions – where feasible – or interregional transfers) is not the only answer to these regional imbalances. Such measures not only have significant costs but can also have serious environmental implications: new reservoirs lead to major changes in landscapes (although they can also offer new recreational possibilities and can enhance the visual amenity of the area if they are well located and designed); in the regions where demand is likely to exceed supply, there is little scope for new groundwater abstractions without creating (or worsening) low-flow problems in rivers; transfers of water between catchments with markedly different chemical characteristics can cause problems. In some cases, the costs and benefits of cutting waste or reducing demand are likely to be more attractive in economic and environmental terms as a first step to meet demand. The Government has assessed these possibilities in the 1992 consultation paper, *Using Water Wisely*[2]. This document reviewed the question of water shortages, looked at options for metering (most domestic consumers pay a flat rate regardless of consumption), and for saving and recycling water in the home and elsewhere; it considered the scope for a better match of supply and demand.

8.15 Maintaining and improving the yield of the existing developed resources will therefore require:

- **Demand management:** The consultation paper *Using Water Wisely* indicated that a better match of supply and demand could be achieved most readily through the use of economic instruments (including improved abstraction charges) and water metering on a selective basis. Current abstraction charges under the Water Resources Act 1991 are permitted by that Act to do no more than recover the costs of the NRA in administering the abstraction licensing system and in managing and supporting flows in certain rivers. A different basis of charging might bring greater efficiency in water use. Metering trials in England and Wales have taken place over some four years. The introduction of metering to an area, although not without significant cost, and accompanied by a suitable tariff, encourages customers to economise in their use of water. The overall reduction in demand is likely to be about 11%, but can be as high as 20% at times of peak demand. However, the full benefit of these reductions is often only realised if they offset the need to develop additional resources.

- **Day-to-day management measures:** A significant proportion of water put into public supply does not get used effectively: the distribution system and occupiers' piping loses it through leaks. In some cases, these losses could be in excess of 25% of the water put into supply. Improvements to the water undertakers' distribution systems are in hand as part of general improvements to the PWS at a cost in the current decade of £2,000 million. These improvements, and a swifter response to leaks in general, will make much more water available for effective use. Leaks in consumers' piping are legally the responsibility of the consumer. The metering trials have shown that substantial amounts of water are currently lost to effective use through leaks in these connection pipes. Pipe replacement, connected with the installation of meters, may reduce these leaks, as well as making it easier to detect leaks both in mains and connection pipes. There may also be scope for looking at the rules applying to flows into, and out of, some reservoirs, in order to make the best use of existing infrastructure. Recent research projects, part funded by HM Inspectorate of Pollution (HMIP) and the NRA, have shown how good industrial management practice can minimise both the use of clean water and the consequent production of waste, often at minimal cost. HMIP are extending this research.

- **Control of pollution:** There is always the risk of loss of existing or future resources due to pollution. Action has been taken to control the effects of increasing nitrate levels by groundwater protection schemes and the designation of Nitrate Sensitive Areas. Action in implementing the EC Urban Waste Water Treatment (UWWT) Directive[3] and the Nitrates Directive[4] will also safeguard and improve existing sources. Some sources of high nitrate levels have been removed from public supply, or supplied with additional treatment facilities. Research has been carried out on the toxicity levels of various pollutants, including agricultural pesticides and fertilizers, chemical spillage and mine discharges. Further research is necessary on the effects of existing and new pollutants, to protect groundwater and surface water supplies.

8.16 Even with all these measures, however, it is possible that there will be a need to provide new resources for PWS. The approach should be that new resources should be provided only when the alternatives have been utilised to the extent that is practicable and economic (with environmental considerations being given proper weight in the decisions). Where new reservoirs or transfer schemes are needed, the sites and designs will also need to take environmental considerations fully into account.

Quality of drinking water supplies

8.17 A new legal framework for drinking water quality in England and Wales was established in 1989. The regulatory body is the Drinking Water Inspectorate (DWI) in England and Wales, set up under provisions in the 1989 Water Act[5]. Different arrangements have a similar purpose in Scotland and Northern Ireland. Regulations made in 1989, implementing the EC Drinking Water Directive[6], set detailed quality standards for public water supplies; similar regulations covering private water supplies came into force in 1992. The European Commission is expected to bring forward in 1994 proposals for a revision of the EC Drinking Water Directive, which accounts for a large proportion of UK requirements on drinking water.

8.18 The DWI Report[7] covering water quality in 1992 confirmed that public supplies of drinking water in England and Wales are of very high quality, with 98.7% of the 3.7 million tests carried out showing that the samples complied with the regulatory standards. In Scotland, 262,000 tests on water from consumers' taps in 1992 showed that 98.4% complied with the regulatory standards. In Northern Ireland, the quality of public supplies of drinking water is also high, with 99% of water quality tests in 1992 complying with regulatory standards. In the light of the commitments made by the water undertakers, and the extensive work in hand to implement these commitments, an even better level of performance is expected in the UK by 1995. The DWI and the Scottish Office have reviewed and, where possible, accelerated programmes to improve water quality. These very high standards of drinking water can be expected to be maintained into the next century.

8.19 The main matters of continuing concern on drinking water quality are lead, nitrate, pesticides, and cryptosporidium.

8.20 The ingestion of lead in significant quantities, particularly by foetuses in the womb and bottle-fed babies, reduces intellectual performance. The World Health Organisation's (WHO) revised guideline on lead is 10 micrograms per litre as an average ingestion over a period of time. This is much below the current UK ceiling of 50 micrograms per litre in an unflushed sample, and the EC ceiling of 50 micrograms per litre in a flushed sample. There is very little lead in water as it leaves the treatment works; where lead is found in tap water, this is usually because it has been in contact with lead pipes, often in the domestic plumbing system. Dosing plant is being installed in risk areas to reduce lead levels in water. This should normally achieve levels of 25–30 micrograms per litre. Water undertakers are also gradually replacing their piping in risk areas. Thereafter, a better performance will not be achievable unless householders' lead piping is replaced. The standard for lead will be a particular focus of discussion in the revision of the EC Drinking Water Directive and, in the UK, action to reduce ingestion through water supply can be expected to continue and greatly to reduce the problem over the next 20 years.

8.21 Recent scientific and medical research on nitrates has been reassuring. The risk of methaemoglobinaemia ("blue baby" syndrome) is very small, even at levels considerably in excess of the EC absolute limit of 50 milligrams per litre. This is supported by the great rarity of the condition in the UK, as in other developed countries. The WHO has recently proposed a guideline (for average ingestion over a period of time) of 50 milligrams per litre, to meet the range of circumstances found across the world. The Government is urging the EC to take account of the WHO advice in the current review of the Drinking Water Directive. Where there is risk of exceeding the EC ceiling, water is treated to reduce nitrate levels and the Government is introducing measures to reduce the amount of leaching from agriculture.

8.22 Where pesticide levels exceed the EC ceiling of 0.1 micrograms per litre on a continuing basis, water companies are in the process of installing treatment to meet the standard. The revised WHO guidelines which, unlike the EC limit, are based on health-related standards, propose specific limits (as an average ingestion) for 34 specific pesticide substances in common use: the numerical value is based on assessment of the scientific and medical risks of the substance concerned. The Government believes that, to avoid wasteful expenditure on treatment, or unnecessary restrictions aimed at resource protection, the pesticide standards of any revised drinking water directive should be consistent with the WHO's revised guidelines.

8.23 Cryptosporidium is an animal parasite which has probably always been present in surface waters in areas where animals are present. It has recently been discovered that it can be transmitted by water and so can cause serious dysenteric symptoms which are of particular concern to those with reduced resistance to disease. To provide a surer foundation for formulating policy and standards, more knowledge is needed of the organism, the medical risk that it presents, its incidence in the environment, the means by which it gets into surface water, the extent to which drinking water is a route of human infection, and the most effective means of treating drinking water supplies.

THE FRESHWATER ENVIRONMENT

Low-flow rivers

8.24 Society is increasingly conscious of the amenity value of rivers and other water bodies: they are valued aesthetically, for fishing and other leisure purposes, and for their distinct flora and fauna. Where they, and the aquifers which feed them, are used for water supply and irrigation, there may be conflicts with amenity considerations and between the different supply purposes concerned. Lower flows may also limit the extent to which particular water bodies absorb waste water discharges and agricultural run-off. Where low flows are the result of chronically lower rainfall, some may wish action to be taken to sustain earlier flows.

8.25 The NRA has given considerable attention to the problem of unacceptably low flows in some rivers. Problems are often caused by excessive abstractions dating from before the Water Resources Act 1963[8], which gave existing abstractors the right to a licence to cover their existing, or legally authorised, level of abstraction without having to show that the abstraction was compatible with acceptable river flows (as was thereafter required for new abstractions). The most direct approach in these cases is to reduce or revoke the abstraction licences causing the problem. However, alternative sources may need to be found and the NRA may also be liable to compensate the licence holder. Technical solutions include the lining of river beds (which is not without environmental problems), and recycling water within the river system by pumping from downstream reaches to augment headwaters.

8.26 The NRA already has a programme of action completed or in hand on 14 rivers, and a further 21 are being investigated. In some cases substantial works costing several million pounds may be required. The NRA will also seek to improve other rivers if the environmental need is demonstrated. It will continue to regulate groundwater and surface water abstraction through the use of abstraction licensing controls. This is particularly important in those catchments where demand is already at or near to the

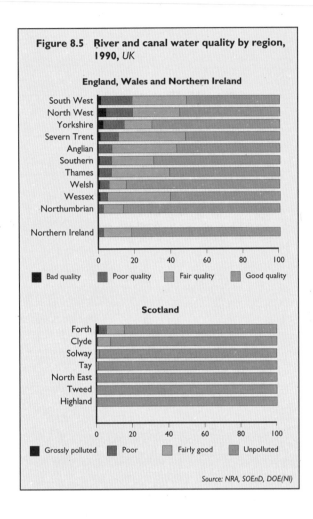

Figure 8.5 **River and canal water quality by region, 1990,** *UK*

maximum sustainable. By these means, a significant improvement for rivers suffering from low flows can be expected by 2012.

Freshwater quality

8.27 The quality of freshwater in the UK is influenced by a variety of factors: directly, by discharges from sewage works and agricultural and industrial installations, or from pollution incidents such as spillages; and indirectly, from run-off and from leaching of contaminants from soil or rocks. Water quality, particularly in lakes and reservoirs, can be influenced by surrounding vegetation and soil, and by deposition from pollutants in the air (in particular "acid rain" – see chapter 7). Other major influences on water quality are the weather (in the form of floods or droughts) and water abstractions.

8.28 The effects of industry's activities depend on the extent to which it uses watercourses for the controlled discharge of waste water; the type of industries and the nature and quantity of the substances that are allowed to be discharged;

the efficiency of collecting systems for sewage and the level of treatment provided. Changes in industrial practices, including farming methods, are also important since they can affect the level of indirect discharges. In addition, there is a legacy of past industrial activity, such as pollution from contaminated land and abandoned mines. The way in which these factors influence freshwater quality depends on the nature of the receiving waters. Where there is adequate dilution and dispersion, surface waters can more readily assimilate inputs provided that total quantities are not excessive.

Current freshwater quality

8.29 Recent river quality surveys have shown that the great majority of watercourses in the UK are of good or fair quality, that is, they support at least reasonably good coarse fisheries,

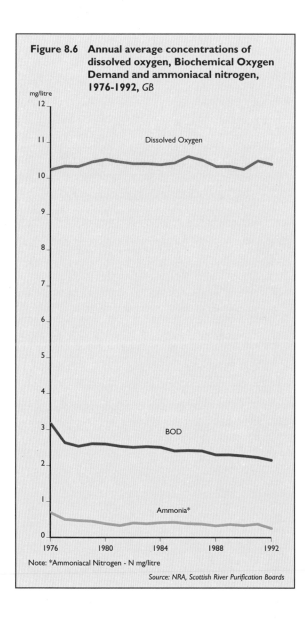

Figure 8.6 **Annual average concentrations of dissolved oxygen, Biochemical Oxygen Demand and ammoniacal nitrogen, 1976-1992**, *GB*

Note: *Ammoniacal Nitrogen - N mg/litre

Source: NRA, Scottish River Purification Boards

have moderate or high amenity value, and are generally appropriate for abstraction for treatment as drinking water. In 1990, as Figure 8.5 shows, 95% of UK freshwater rivers and canals were classified as good or fair quality.

8.30 For England and Wales, data from 1980, 1985 and 1990 suggest that there was a small deterioration in the best quality rivers over that period. However, the 1990 survey was based on data collected in the period 1988–90, and could not reflect the benefits of recent investment by the waste water industry. There may also have been an effect from the lower flows resulting from the low rainfall in the winters of 1988–92. NRA monitoring is already suggesting that there are signs of improvement in 1991 and 1992. Figure 8.6 (based on parallel monitoring data) illustrates the improvements in annual average concentrations in Britain of three major indicators of overall river quality – dissolved oxygen (where the greater the amount present, the better is the water quality), biochemical oxygen demand (BOD) and ammonia (where the smaller the amount present, the better is the water quality). In Scotland, more than 99% of rivers, lochs and canals were classified in 1990 as good or fair quality, and there has been continuing improvement in river quality since the first survey in 1968.

8.31 More information is needed on the quality of groundwater. It is particularly vulnerable to diffuse contamination, by nitrates and pesticides from farming, landfill sites and other activities, which is harder to reduce than pollution from point sources. Once contaminated, it may take many years before the groundwater recovers, even when the source of the pollution has been removed.

Improvement and preventative measures

8.32 The NRA has responsibility for controlling pollution in England and Wales in respect of inland waters (including groundwater) as well as estuarine and coastal waters. Similar controls are exercised by the Scottish river purification authorities and by the Environment Service of the Department of the Environment for Northern Ireland. Any discharges (for example, by sewage treatment works or industry) must be authorised by the relevant authority, through the system of discharge consents. These may impose conditions on the quality and quantity of the discharge, so that the quality of water can be maintained. The standards imposed through these systems include those necessary to meet the requirements of EC Directives for the protection and improvement of water quality.

8.33 Local water quality targets have hitherto been provided by the informal system of river quality objectives (RQOs). These will remain until they are gradually replaced in England

and Wales by statutory water quality objectives (WQOs) under the provisions of the Water Resources Act 1991. WQOs will provide a broad and stable framework, maintaining and, where the cost can be justified and is affordable, progressively improving water quality over the next 20 years.

8.34 Discharges from the most potentially polluting processes are subject to the system of integrated pollution control (IPC), operated by HMIP in England and Wales, and by HMIPI and river purification authorities in Scotland. IPC allows the overall impact on the environment to be minimised. A precautionary approach based on the principle of best available techniques not entailing excessive cost (BATNEEC) is applied.

8.35 Pollution from diffuse sources, such as farming activity and accidental spillages, is not amenable to such controls. Regulators have previously relied on the deterrent effect of the threat of prosecutions and other enforcement activity. Increasingly, however, a more positive approach based on prevention is being adopted. For example, a *Code of Good Agricultural Practice for the Protection of Water*[9] has been issued, and farmers are being strongly encouraged to prepare farm waste management plans. In addition, the Government has set minimum statutory standards for the construction of farm waste stores. The Government and regulatory authorities are active in improving the performance of all those responsible for activities liable to lead to diffuse pollution or accidental spillages. These measures are already proving their value in containing and reversing trends in major pollution incidents.

Threats to freshwater quality

8.36 A number of aspects of freshwater quality can be expected to require continued attention over the next 20 years.

Groundwater

8.37 As in many countries, the development of policy and practice to protect groundwater has tended to lag behind that relating to the protection of surface waters. Nevertheless, in December 1992, the NRA published *Policy and Practice for the Protection of Groundwater*[10]. The document aims to provide a comprehensive framework to preserve this vital resource; to identify the vulnerability of individual areas of groundwater; and to define non-statutory source protection zones around abstraction points. One of the principal aims is to provide information to land use planners and others to enable development decisions to be taken in such a way as to minimise possible threats to groundwater quality in the future. The protection of groundwater can be expected to be the subject of considerable research and policy development in the period up to 2012.

Treatment works discharges

8.38 Discharges from sewage treatment works into rivers can be a significant cause of poor water quality. However, in England and Wales, there has been a major, sharp improvement since 1986 in the compliance by sewage works with the standards required. Similar steady improvements have been taking place in Scotland.

8.39 Further improvements will flow from the UWWT Directive. All larger sewerage systems fall within the scope of this significant measure, which sets standards for sewage discharges to inland, estuarine and coastal waters, depending on the size and location of the discharge and the nature of the receiving waters. It has been estimated that improvements to

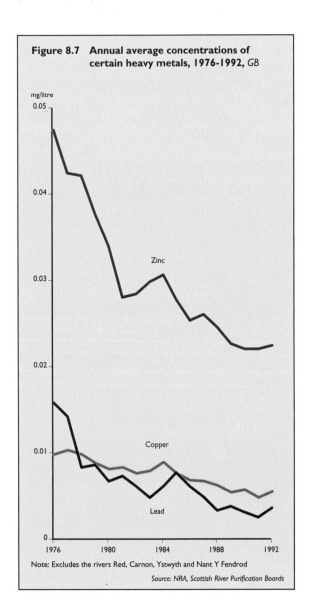

Figure 8.7   Annual average concentrations of certain heavy metals, 1976-1992, *GB*

mg/litre

Zinc

Copper

Lead

Note: Excludes the rivers Red, Carnon, Ystwyth and Nant Y Fendrod

Source: NRA, Scottish River Purification Boards

the systems for the collection, treatment and discharge of sewage in order to implement this Directive may cost as much as £10,000 million.

Dangerous substances

8.40 The UK has developed the "Red List"[11] of the most dangerous substances in water, scientifically selected for their persistent, toxic and bioaccumulative characteristics. The 23 substances on the list are considered to pose the greatest threat to sensitive aquatic life, and include heavy metals and organic compounds such as pesticides. The Red List is the basis for defining "special category effluents" for control under the Water Industry Act 1991[12], the list of prescribed substances to water under the Environmental Protection Act 1990 and the arrangements for IPC operated by HMIP. Twelve of the Red List substances are also EC List I substances, in that they are subject to Environmental Quality Objectives under Dangerous Substances Directives, which are enforced as Environmental Quality Standards (EQSs) in the UK. Regulations for a further eight such EQSs are being prepared.

8.41 Concentrations of dangerous substances in the aquatic environment are generally very low, and may fall below the limit of detection of current analytical techniques. Where they have been detected, they are normally well within environmental quality standards introduced under EC Dangerous Substances Directives. Figure 8.7 shows the annual average concentrations in 200 or so rivers in Britain of three heavy metals: zinc, copper and lead. In all three cases there were significant reductions between 1976 and 1991.

Eutrophication

8.42 Eutrophication is a complex phenomenon controlled by a number of factors. These include the presence of nutrients in sufficient quantity to support sustained algal and macrophyte growth. The nutrient which controls the production of these in most freshwater is phosphorus and, in most saline waters, nitrate. Although UK waters are largely free from eutrophication, there must be concern about nitrate leaching to surface freshwaters since much freshwater ends up in the sea.

8.43 A great deal of work is already under way to identify the extent of such effects and to establish appropriate remedial measures. Continuing research is needed, however, because the presence of either substance in the appropriate quantities does not necessarily lead to sustained algal and macrophyte blooms, and there is the risk of targeting remedial resources where they are not needed.

8.44 The EC UWWT and Nitrates Directives both require action to be taken where waters are eutrophic, or may become so if protective action is not taken.

8.45 About 75% of phosphate in rivers comes from domestic sewage and about 20% from agriculture. Levels of orthophosphate in the Severn Trent, Anglian and Thames regions are significantly above the national average. In general, however, problems of eutrophication are not widespread.

8.46 The main source of nitrate in water is agriculture, although sewage discharges are also a factor. Current nitrate levels in groundwater can result from agricultural practices many years ago. In many areas of Britain, levels of nitrate have been low over the last decade and are stable or falling in most areas. There are, however, signs in some areas of rising trends, and cases of high levels are found more frequently in some regions (such as Anglian and Severn Trent) than others. There are also some indications of rising levels of nitrate in groundwater.

8.47 The Government's policy is to minimise nitrate loss in general and, in particular, to lower nitrate leaching from agriculture by the promotion of good practice, backed up by regulations where appropriate. In the areas where nitrate leaching is known to cause pollution, regulatory schemes will be used, in conjunction with payment schemes, to achieve a more marked impact. It is recognised, however, that in many cases hydrogeological factors mean that the effect in terms of reduced nitrate concentrations will not occur quickly. The payment scheme approach is used in the Nitrate Sensitive Areas, where farmers undertake voluntarily to follow practices going beyond good agricultural practice in order to reduce nitrate leaching. Following an earlier pilot exercise, the Ministry of Agriculture, Fisheries and Food (MAFF) plan to designate further areas in respect of up to 28 groundwater sources. The regulatory approach is incorporated in the EC Nitrate Directive of 1991, but which requires action by deadlines up to the end of the century. The Directive requires EC member states to identify waters which are, or are likely to be, polluted by nitrate. Regulations affecting farming practices will come into effect within the areas of land which drain into those polluted waters, whether surface waters or groundwaters.

8.48 There is a need for greater understanding of the threat presented by nitrate to the aquatic environment, in both fresh and marine waters, and of the significance in this context of the limit of 50 milligrams per litre derived from drinking water standards.

Pesticides

8.49 In 1986, a statutory system of controls over pesticides was established. This requires that, before a pesticide is approved for use, it must be considered by the independent Advisory Committee on Pesticides (ACP), and must be judged to pose no unacceptable risks to workers, consumers or the environment. Products approved before 1986 are undergoing review of their status. The UK programme is being integrated with the EC programmes now required under the EC Agricultural Pesticides Directive. The major uses of dieldrin were banned in 1985, with a total ban after 1989. It is still being detected, although in much smaller quantities. There also appears to be a reducing trend in the concentrations of lindane. Other pesticides are also detected, usually at or near the limits of detection. The pesticides most commonly found in surface waters are the triazine herbicides, atrazine and simazine, which come mainly from non-agricultural use. To help meet the requirements of the Drinking Water Directive, approvals for the non-agricultural uses of these pesticides were withdrawn at the end of August 1993. The ACP confirmed that the levels of atrazine and simazine found in water in the UK do not endanger the health of consumers or the environment. Withdrawal of approvals should lead to a decline in concentrations found in water courses.

8.50 More knowledge of the impact of different pesticides on aquatic environments is desirable.

Acidification
8.51 Pollutants deposited from the air (in particular, deposition of acids or substances which can form acids) have adverse effects on freshwater quality, especially in lakes and reservoirs. The burning of fossil fuels has become a major contributory factor in the scale and rate at which waters have become acidified. Acidification is likely to decrease as sulphur emissions, and thus sulphur depositions, are expected to reduce, although some sensitive areas will remain at risk into the 21st century. However, with current planned reductions in sulphur dioxide (SO_2), it is estimated that, by 2005, sulphur depositions will exceed freshwater critical loads in only 7% of Britain (see chapter 7).

Environmental impacts of sewage sludge
8.52 Sewage sludge is an inevitable product of sewage treatment. It consists mainly of biodegradable organic matter and inert rock and soil particles, with trace concentrations of a wide range of metals and other potentially contaminating substances arising from domestic and industrial discharges to sewers and aerial deposition on surfaces which drain to sewers. It is these potentially contaminating substances which determine the sustainability of the use of sewage sludge as a fertilizer and soil conditioner, and influence the choice between disposal by incineration or landfilling. At the Third North Sea Conference in 1990, the UK agreed to ban the dumping of sewage sludge at sea. This commitment was incorporated into the UWWT Directive. These provisions, together with the requirements to treat more sewage and to raise standards of treatment, will increase substantially the quantity of sewage sludge to be recycled or disposed of by land-based methods.

8.53 Almost half of the sewage sludge produced is currently used on agricultural land. It is subject to controls which, among other things, limit the addition of heavy metals to soils to safeguard human and animal health and the productivity of the soil. Because the addition of heavy metals to soils is largely an irreversible process, the limits are precautionary, derived from comprehensive research and subject to periodic review as scientific knowledge advances. The sustainability of the agricultural use of sewage sludge is also maintained through controls on contaminating discharges of trade effluents. A recent survey for the Department of the Environment (DOE) has shown a dramatic reduction in the concentration of heavy metals in sewage sludge over the last decade. Together with the water industry, the DOE is funding research into the contribution of heavy metal contaminants from domestic plumbing systems, household products and other diffuse sources which cannot be limited by trade effluent controls.

CONCLUSIONS
8.54 Surface freshwater and groundwater resources are subject to many competing and interrelated demands. Although long term demand for water is difficult to predict, the UK remains likely to have adequate overall water resources in the foreseeable future. However, steadily increasing demand, and regional and seasonal deficiencies in supply, require attention.

8.55 Policies for regulation and planning need to cover matters of conservation, demand management and the development and protection of new resources. These are being addressed by the regulatory authorities, water companies in England and Wales, and water and sewerage authorities in Scotland. Immediate steps relate to abstraction control, conservation and new resources. For the longer term, the NRA is developing a national water resources development strategy. The Government is supporting that action, and will keep under review the way in which all concerned work together to ensure adequate supplies.

8.56 Over the next 20 years a number of important factors will help to maintain and improve freshwater quality. The establishment of independent environmental regulators, in the form of the NRA, river purification authorities, and DWI, has already led to a tighter regulatory regime. Further progress will take place through domestic statutory controls on all forms of water pollution, the implementation of EC Directives and action to meet other international commitments.

8.57 The water industry already has major investment programmes in hand following privatisation in 1989. Of the £35,000 million planned to be spent in the years up to the end of the century, approximately half is directed to maintaining and improving sewage treatment and disposal systems. This includes improvements to sewage treatment works, and increased capacity in sewerage systems designed to improve unsatisfactory overflows.

8.58 Further investment programmes are already planned and major improvements will flow from the implementation of the UWWT Directive. As a result of the regulators' activities, the large programmes already in hand, and the UWWT Directive, the UK will be embarking on a significant programme of renewal and upgrading of its sewerage infrastructure.

8.59 There is a direct connection between freshwater quality and the level and type of economic activity in the UK. Whilst this does not currently restrict the rate of economic growth, there is no cause for complacency, since some types of pollution are insidious, difficult to monitor and to rectify. In some cases, there is a need for further research to identify the nature of the problem and the available options. The Government already sponsors work on groundwater quality, eutrophication, pesticides and nitrate leaching. Additional work in these areas would be useful.

8.60 The UK also needs to address the problem of cost. Where financial resources are limited, it is important that expenditure to improve the environment is prioritised and targeted, so that the best use is made of available resources. Balancing conflicting demands for resources is never easy and, in the case of water quality, the Government has encouraged regulators and water companies to engage in consultative exercises in an attempt to gauge public opinion.

8.61 Overall, in view of the substantial planned investment and the continuing rigour of regulatory enforcement, the Government considers that present policies are sustainable. However, water resources and quality are of such importance to the UK population that issues such as adequacy of water supplies, drinking water quality, groundwater protection, river quality, and the presence in the aquatic environment of dangerous substances must remain under close scrutiny.

REFERENCES AND FURTHER READING

1 Water Resources Act 1991, chapter 57. HMSO, 1991. ISBN 0–10–545791–4.

2 *Using Water Wisely.* Consultation paper and *Wise Up on Water* leaflet. Department of the Environment, 1992.

3 *Urban Waste Water Treatment Directive.* 91/271/EEC. Official Journal of the European Communities L135, 30 May 1993.

4 *Nitrates Directive.* 91/676/EEC. Official Journal of the European Communities L375, 12 December 1991.

5 Water Act 1989, chapter 15. HMSO, 1989. ISBN 0–1–541589–8.

6 *Drinking Water Directive.* 80/778/EEC. Official Journal of the European Communities L229, 15 July 1980.

7 *Drinking Water 1992: A Report by the Chief Inspector, Drinking Water Inspectorate.* DOE/Welsh Office. HMSO, 1993. ISBN 0–11–752853–6.

8 Water Resources Act 1963, chapter 38. HMSO, 1963.

9 *Code of Good Agricultural Practice for the Protection of Water.* MAFF Publications, 1991.

10 *Policy and Practice for the Protection of Groundwater.* NRA, 1992. ISBN 1–87–316037–2.

11 *Agreed "Red List" of Dangerous Substances Confirmed by Lord Caithness.* DOE Press Release No. 194, April 1989.

12 Water Industry Act 1991, chapter 56. HMSO, 1991. ISBN 0–10–545691–8.

CHAPTER 9

THE SEA

SYNOPSIS

9.1 Marine water quality around the UK, with the exception of certain specific areas, is generally good. In particular, bathing water quality around the coast does not present any significant health hazard. Inputs to the sea from anthropogenic sources are generally declining, and the international machinery is in place to ensure that, over the next 20 years, land-based developments will be consistent with maintaining the marine environment. No significant problems are expected to arise from dumping waste at sea, since only very limited categories will be permitted to be dumped. The level of demand for marine aggregates may lead to difficult decisions during the next 20 years, depending on decisions on land-based sources of aggregates, the possibility of recycling and the demands of the construction industry. New offshore developments for oil and gas are carefully regulated although, as existing wells approach the end of their life, there could be a greater volume of oil discharges; and decisions will be needed about whether this is acceptable. Levels of fish stocks depend not only on the quality of the marine environment but on fishing practices. More powerful fishing vessels and improved technology are now putting many fish stocks under severe pressure. And, as leisure activities grow, there could be increased pressures over the next 20 years on particular coastal zones.

9.2 The key issues for sustainability are:
- to continue to control anthropogenic inputs to the sea;
- to manage the fishing industry to prevent over-exploitation of fish stocks.

INTRODUCTION

9.3 Although the quality of the marine environment is affected by many natural factors, a wide range of human activities also affect the sea and thus raise questions about how sustainable they are.

Land-based activities

9.4 Mankind's activities on land affect the marine environment when discharges or emissions from the land reach the sea. These can be either direct, through pipelines from coastal sewage treatment work or factories, or indirect, through rivers and streams. All such inputs can come from point sources, which are controlled by discharge consents, or from diffuse sources, which depend upon control or influence on the general activity giving rise to the inputs.

9.5 Emissions to the atmosphere can also result in deposits on the sea; again, both point sources (for example, power stations) and diffuse sources (for example, motor vehicle exhausts) are involved.

9.6 The impact of the discharges and emissions can come from their chemical content (which is of particular concern where the chemicals are toxic, persistent and liable to bioaccumulate), biological content (which may affect either the leisure use of water or shellfisheries), quantity (which can determine whether they have a significant effect on the receiving water) or energy content (either their temperature as, for example, with electricity generating stations, or their radioactivity as, for example, with discharges from British Nuclear Fuels Ltd's Sellafield plant).

Navigation

9.7 The carriage of people and goods by sea is essential to a country like the UK which consists of islands; in all aspects of navigation, the location of the UK beside and across shipping lanes serving much of North West Europe means that the impact of shipping comes from more than just the traffic serving this country. Key impacts on wildlife are the result of operational discharges and emissions, marine accidents, and clearing approach channels, anchorages and moorings; and the discharge of ballast waters taken on elsewhere could lead to the possible introduction of non-native species.

Fisheries

9.8 The removal from the marine environment of catches of fish and shellfish can have significance for the populations of those species. By-catches, and the impact of fishing gear on the sea-bed, can also have impacts on other species.

9.9 Both fin-fish (mainly salmon) and shellfish farming continue to raise issues of concern. These include the siting and appearance of fish farms, possible localised pollution, the introduction of chemicals and antibiotics, the introduction, and possible escape, of non-native species, diseases and parasites, and predator control (see chapter 17).

Dredging and dumping

9.10 The removal of spoil to maintain shipping channels and river flows leads, inevitably, to disturbance, both of those specific environments and of the environment where the spoil is dumped. In the case of fine grained spoil, a wider environment can be affected. Where the spoil contains potential pollutants, their remobilisation may be harmful; likewise, the extraction of aggregates from the sea-bed can have effects as significant for the marine environment as the extraction of gravel and sand from land sites can for land environments.

Offshore installations

9.11 The development of an important oil and gas extraction industry offshore has introduced a new source of possible impacts on the environment: seismic testing, discharges of cuttings from drillings, chemicals discharged from the rigs, the installation of pipelines, mooring arrangements and accidental spills can affect both the sea itself and the sea-bed. The decommissioning and disposal of obsolete installations and pipelines also have environmental implications.

Seaweed harvesting

9.12 There is an increasing interest in the commercial harvesting of both kelp and maerl. Removal of large quantities of these seaweeds can affect a wide range of associated organisms. The removal of kelp may, additionally, affect local availability and turnover of organic material, and have some effect on wave action on low-lying coasts and the ability of coasts to withstand storms.

Recreation

9.13 As well as the impacts resulting from the introduction of substances into, or their removal from, the sea, the rapid development of recreational activities beside, on, in and under the sea has important effects, particularly where these activities are competing with wildlife (see chapter 27).

Effects of human activities

9.14 Each of these activities is important in itself. Their impact in combination is even more important. And there is an overriding effect of development in taking land and changing patterns of use. No single form of unified regulation is possible for such a wide range of activities. It is essential for all the regulatory bodies concerned to take account of the way in which their decisions will interact with the decisions of others involved. A continuing question in seeking a strategy for sustainability is, therefore, whether these links in information-gathering and decision-making are being adequately maintained.

9.15 Marine water quality around the UK, with the exception of certain specific inshore zones and industrialised estuaries, is generally good. This is mainly because the majority of substances discharged are substantially diluted and dissipated or degraded naturally; they do not, therefore, cause pollution, although concentrations of these substances would be harmful.

9.16 International agreements require the states concerned to cooperate in preparing assessments of the marine environment in the whole of the North East Atlantic. Such an assessment has been prepared for the North Sea; it draws attention to certain specific issues of concern and makes recommendations for action. A similar assessment of the Irish Sea is planned by the Governments of the UK and the Republic of Ireland as part of this general programme.

DIRECT, RIVERINE AND ATMOSPHERIC CONTAMINANT INPUTS

Recent developments

9.17 Table 9.1 shows changes in selected direct and riverine inputs from the UK to marine waters since 1985. It is difficult to estimate such inputs, not least because many of them are near the limits of detection. The figures shown are upper estimates, based on the assumption that the concentration is equal to the level of detection – the actual figures are probably substantially smaller. There have been significant reductions in the inputs of mercury, copper and lead, reduced inputs of cadmium and orthophosphate, relatively little change in inputs of nitrogen and increased inputs of zinc. The reductions which have been achieved reflect tighter controls on discharges of effluents into rivers and estuaries, the removal of old plant and better treatment of sewage that is discharged into rivers and estuaries.

Table 9.1	Direct and riverine inputs[1] from the UK to saline waters around the UK, 1985-1991			
	1985	**1988**	**1990**	**1991**
Metals (tonnes)				
Cadmium	79.9	65.9	63.6	63
Mercury	27.0	19.9	11.8	10.6
Copper	1,275	893	849	718
Lead	1,660	633	667	655
Zinc	3,630	3,168	3,920	3,800
Nutrients (thousand tonnes)				
Total nitrogen	319	..	313	322
Orthophosphate	58	..	38	36
Organic compounds (kg)				
Lindane	1,560	1,420	779	910
Note: 1. upper estimates	.. = not available			
				Source: DOE

9.18 Inputs of potential pollutants are likely to continue to decline through further improvements in control in the light of the Government's target of reducing inputs of Red List[1] substances by 50% between 1985 and 1995. The manufacture and sale of polychlorinated biphenyls (PCBs) has been completely prohibited since 1986, and their use is only permitted in a limited range of equipment already in use. It is

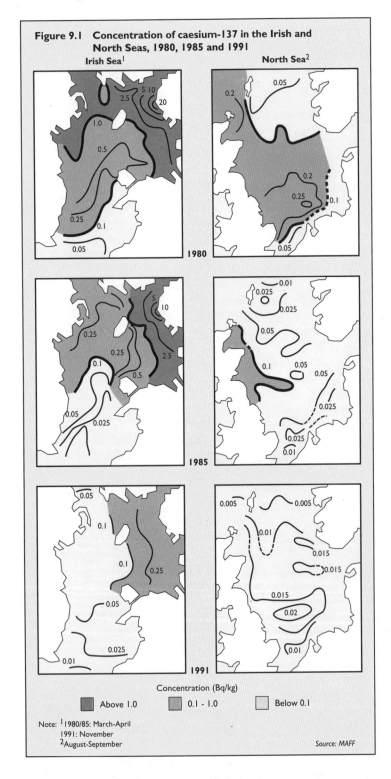

Figure 9.1 Concentration of caesium-137 in the Irish and North Seas, 1980, 1985 and 1991

Irish Sea[1]   North Sea[2]

1980

1985

1991

Concentration (Bq/kg)

- ■ Above 1.0
- ■ 0.1 - 1.0
- □ Below 0.1

Note: [1]1980/85: March-April
1991: November
[2]August-September

Source: MAFF

become new sources of pollution as existing precautions cease and there is no obvious person to take over responsibility.

9.19 Sewage treatment will also continue to improve with large scale expenditure in new sewerage and sewage-treatment infrastructure (see chapter 8).

9.20 Discharges of radioactive substances (mainly low-level liquid waste in water used by nuclear establishments) have been falling in recent years, with improvements in technology and the application of the requirement to use the best practicable means (including the best available techniques) to keep discharges as low as reasonably achievable. For example, radiologically significant discharges from Sellafield are currently around 1% of the levels in the late 1970s (see chapter 19). Reductions in discharges are reflected in reducing marine concentrations. Figure 9.1 shows the consequential reductions in concentrations of caesium-137 in the Irish and North Seas since 1980.

9.21 There have also been significant atmospheric inputs of potential pollutants (such as heavy metals and nitrogen compounds), but estimates of these are subject to considerable uncertainties and no data capable of identifying trends are available.

Impact of nutrient discharges

9.22 Among the contaminants discharged from land are nutrients – mainly compounds of nitrogen and phosphorus. The cycling of nutrients between land and water and within the

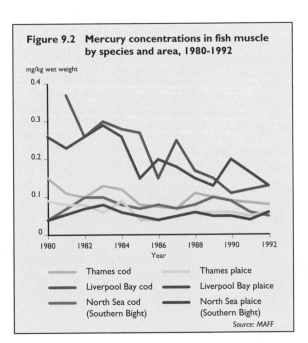

Figure 9.2 Mercury concentrations in fish muscle by species and area, 1980-1992

mg/kg wet weight

- ——— Thames cod
- ——— Thames plaice
- ——— Liverpool Bay cod
- ——— Liverpool Bay plaice
- ——— North Sea cod (Southern Bight)
- ——— North Sea plaice (Southern Bight)

Source: MAFF

planned to destroy remaining PCBs by, at the latest, 1999. The most significant problems are likely to be over land-based sites which cease to be used for economic purposes (such as closed mines and disused factories); there is a risk that these may

Table 9.2		Average concentrations of heavy metals[1] in fish muscle by species and area, 1980-1992										mg/kg wet weight		
			1980	1981	1982	1983	1984	1985	1986	1987	1988	1989	1990	1991	1992
Thames	Cod	Mercury	0.15	0.11	0.1	0.13	0.12	0.08	..	0.07	0.11	..	0.09	..	0.08
		Copper	0.2	0.2	..	..	..	0.2	..	0.3	0.2	..	0.1	..	0.2
		Zinc	4.0	3.3	..	..	..	3.5	..	3.3	4.2	..	3.5	..	3.6
	Plaice	Mercury	0.09	0.08	0.08	0.06	0.09	0.04	0.04	..	0.06	..	0.06	0.05	0.06
		Copper	0.4	0.3	..	..	..	0.2	0.3	..	0.2	..	0.2	0.2	0.1
		Zinc	6.2	7.0	..	..	..	5.5	5.6	..	4.9	..	4.3	5.1	3.8
Liverpool Bay	Cod	Mercury	..	0.37	0.26	0.30	0.28	0.27	0.15	0.25	0.17	0.15	0.11	..	0.13
		Copper	0.3	0.4	..	..	..	0.2	0.2	0.2	0.3	0.1	0.2	..	0.3
		Zinc	3.7	3.6	..	..	..	3.6	3.5	3.2	3.2	3.2	3.1	..	3.7
	Plaice	Mercury	0.26	0.23	0.26	0.29	0.26	0.15	0.2	0.18	0.15	0.13	0.2	..	0.13
		Copper	0.2	0.6	..	..	..	0.3	0.3	0.2	0.3	0.3	0.1	..	0.2
		Zinc	6.3	6.0	..	..	..	5.4	5.1	4.4	4.4	4.0	3.9	..	4.7
North Sea (Southern Bight)	Cod	Mercury	0.04	..	0.10	0.10	0.08	0.07	0.08	0.07	0.08	0.1	0.09	0.06	0.05
		Copper	0.3	..	..	..	..	0.3	0.2	0.2	0.2	0.2	0.2	0.2	0.2
		Zinc	3.6	..	..	..	..	3.3	3.1	3.5	3.3	3.3	3.5	3.2	3.7
	Plaice	Mercury	0.04	..	0.07	0.08	0.06	0.05	0.04	0.05	0.06	0.05	0.05	0.04	0.06
		Copper	0.2	..	..	..	..	0.3	0.2	0.2	0.3	0.3	0.2	0.3	0.2
		Zinc	6.6	..	..	..	..	4.1	4.0	4.4	4.5	3.8	3.7	4.9	3.8

Note: 1 Concentrations of lead and cadmium are no longer analysed as previous work has shown that levels are very low and fall below the limits of detection using routine methods of analysis

.. = not available

Source: MAFF

sea is a natural feature, but mankind's activities have, in many cases, increased the flows. Sewage discharges can concentrate, in a single point, discharge material which would otherwise have been discharged over a much larger area on land, and thus affected the sea (if at all) only over a very different timescale. The phasing-out of dumping of sewage sludge at sea, and the improvements in sewage treatment prior to discharge, should reduce the inputs of nutrients from this source. High levels of usage of nitrogen fertilisers can increase the run-off to the sea – although the processes involved are complex and their overall impact difficult to predict; the time and method of application, and the type of crop and soil, will all have an important effect.

9.23 Enhanced levels of nutrients may have, in certain conditions, the adverse impact of unusual growths of algae in the sea. In some cases, the bloom that is stimulated involves a species that can be toxic to people or marine life. Others can result in reduced oxygen levels as they decay, which can, equally, have serious effects on other marine life, particularly on sea-bed flora and fauna. The blooms themselves can have unwelcome impacts on coasts and waters, blanketing them with thick layers of scum. The precise link, however, between enhanced nutrient inputs and algal blooms is not clear; only certain areas (such as the German Bight) are affected under certain conditions (for example, during warm, calm summers). Such algal blooms are not new: records of them go back over a century. Concern over algal blooms will mean that, over the next 20 years, continuing attention will have to

be given to understanding the links between them and inputs of nutrients from agriculture, industry and sewage.

Trends in the condition of fish and shellfish

9.24 The Ministry of Agriculture, Fisheries and Food (MAFF) and the Scottish Office carry out routine shellfish monitoring to alert public health authorities if algal toxin levels approach concentrations in shellfish which could affect human health. Measurements of heavy metal concentrations in fish and shellfish indicate that there is no significant risk to human health from present concentrations. Table 9.2 shows average concentrations of heavy metals in fish in selected areas over the last 13 years. These tend to vary appreciably from year to year, but are generally very low in comparison with accepted environmental standards. Concentrations of cadmium and lead are no longer analysed, since levels are very low and fall below the limits of detection using routine methods of analysis. Figure 9.2 illustrates the trend in environmental quality standards with regard to mercury concentrations in fish in three separate areas – the Thames estuary, Liverpool Bay and in the North Sea. Concentrations of mercury in Liverpool Bay have declined significantly over the decade, from a relatively high level in the early 1980s. Following a marked decline in concentrations in the 1970s, there has been only a marginal further decrease in levels in the Thames estuary, and little or no detectable change in the North Sea.

9.25 The incidence of disease in fish is also an indicator of environmental stress. All studies since 1989 have been carried out using internationally standardised sampling and recording procedures. Although these studies have shown variations in disease prevalence between areas, there is no clear evidence of a link between diseases and pollution in UK coastal waters: it cannot yet be ruled out, however, as a contributing factor. Inadequately treated sewage effluent, or discharges through improperly sited outfalls, can affect the microbiological conditions of shellfish and their consequent marketability as a safe and nutritious food. To guard against this, shellfishing is closely monitored and regulated, and the impact on shellfishing is considered in decisions on sewage discharge consents and siting.

The way ahead

9.26 Although inputs of persistent substances (such as heavy metals) are generally declining, it does not necessarily follow that concentrations will also decline. The level of concentrations will depend on the combination of the rate of input and the fate of these substances in the sea. Settlement to sediment often leads to the effective elimination of substances from the sea itself. That process may, however, be reversed, and the substance again released to the water column, if the sediment is disturbed. To guard against longer-term problems for human health and the health and diversity of marine life, the effect of potentially polluting substances is monitored by looking at trends in the condition of fish and shellfish and in the heavy metal and organic contaminant concentrations in both living creatures and sediments.

9.27 The focus for further work on the effects on the marine environment of land-based activities will be the Oslo and Paris Conventions and their Commissions and – when the 1992 Convention for the Protection of the Marine Environment of the North East Atlantic[2] comes into force – the new unified Commission that will replace them. A comprehensive assessment of the Quality Status of the North Sea has been prepared. Similar assessments of the other areas of the North East Atlantic, including the Irish Sea, are intended over the period to 2000 (see 9.16). The overall aim of the Conventions is to prevent any further erosion of the quality of the marine environment and, where appropriate, to reverse past trends. Suitable procedures are in place, therefore, to ensure that land-based developments over the next 20 years will be consistent with maintaining the marine environment. As in all other cases, the application of these procedures will need to consider the balance between further protection of the marine environment and the development of human society.

DUMPING OF WASTE AT SEA

9.28 The categories of waste which have in the past been dumped at sea include liquid industrial waste, solid industrial waste (largely fly ash from power stations), radioactive waste, waste munitions from the armed forces, sewage sludge, waste rock from collieries and dredged materials.

9.29 Major developments have taken place in recent years within the context of the Oslo Convention and the decisions taken in the Commission established by it. These developments have now been embodied in the new Convention for the Protection of the Marine Environment of the North East Atlantic, which will replace the Oslo Convention when it enters into force. The dumping of liquid and solid industrial waste and of waste munitions has ceased. The UK is committed to phasing out the dumping of sewage sludge at sea by the end of 1998. The dumping at sea of waste rock from collieries ("minestone") will cease by the end of 1997, unless no practicable land-based methods are available.

9.30 The remaining permitted dumping at sea will, therefore, be limited to dredgings from ports and harbours and fish wastes from fish-processing vessels. These activities will be regulated by the international agreements under the Oslo Convention and its eventual replacement. The amount of dredged materials dumped at sea has fluctuated in recent years, but is expected to continue at much the same general levels. No licences are now issued to dump heavily contaminated dredged spoil. Tighter controls over the load limits in dumping licences, coupled with changes in the nature of the sediment to be dredged (resulting from stricter controls over discharges of effluents into rivers and estuaries and better treatment of sewage), are leading to lower levels of deposit of potentially polluting substances in estuaries and coastal waters.

9.31 The disposal of high-level radioactive waste at sea is prohibited globally under the London Convention 1972 (formerly known as the London Dumping Convention). In the past, drummed low-level radioactive waste has been dumped at specific deep-water sites in the Atlantic. This practice was suspended in 1983. As part of the new North East Atlantic Convention, the UK has now agreed to a moratorium on any further dumping of any type of radioactive waste until, at least, 2008. A meeting of the London Convention in November 1993 agreed an indefinite ban on the sea disposal of all radioactive wastes. The UK and four other countries abstained. Countries have 100 days to notify the International Maritime Organisation of their acceptance of the ban. The UK is considering its response.

9.32 No significant questions of sustainability are expected to result over the next 20 years from the dumping of waste at sea.

OFFSHORE ACTIVITIES

9.33 The offshore oil and gas industry has been developed alongside growing public concern for the protection of the environment. Environmental considerations have, therefore, been taken into account in the grant of exploration and exploitation licences; operational controls include, in particular, controls over the discharge of oil-contaminated drill cuttings, the type of chemicals used on offshore installations and the discharge of "produced water".

9.34 Resources are finite, but the industry is no less sustainable than other exploitation of fossil fuel sources. As existing resources are exhausted, there will need to be continuing consideration of the environmental impacts of exploration for new resources; and, as production conditions change, the exploitation of existing developed resources must also be considered. An example of the latter is given by the discharge of "produced water" (the water, with an inevitable oil content, which is drawn from wells along with oil or gas). This increases in volume as wells approach the end of their usable life. The oil content of discharges of produced water is regulated (for the future, the upper limit is 40 parts per million). With increasing volumes discharged, and in the absence of some new initiative, there would be larger absolute discharges of oil. A new initiative might be, for example, the development of more efficient treatment units (and requirements for their use) or new controls on the rate of discharge (and hence on the rate of exploitation). Decisions must be made in the future to help deal with this issue.

Oil spills

9.35 Marine ecosystems and marine life may also be affected by oil spills from ships or offshore installations. These may be either recurrent operating discharges or the result of accidents, some of which may have substantial impact on the marine environment (depending on the type of oil discharged, weather conditions and so on). Many oil spills, however, are small, and the oil is dispersed and degraded naturally. Around 20–25% are spills of over 100 gallons (2.5 barrels). In 1991, around 60% of these involved offshore installations in the North Sea.

9.36 During the 1980s, there was a substantial increase in the number of reported offshore North Sea incidents, and a rising number of incidents in most coastal areas around the UK. Part of the explanation for these increases seems to be the more comprehensive reporting of incidents, encouraged

by improved surveillance techniques, which began in 1986. However, the number of incidents has fallen in the last three years, largely on account of the considerable reduction in offshore incidents in the North Sea.

9.37 Although suitable dispersants will help the process of biodegradation of spilt oil, they do not themselves remove oil from the marine system. However, they are still an important element of the National Contingency Plan for oil spills. Marked improvements have been made in reducing the toxicity of oil dispersants. The existing system for testing oil dispersants for efficacy and toxicity has been in place for some years; MAFF are currently reviewing the arrangements under which such chemicals are approved.

Aggregate dredging

9.38 Another form of exploitation of the resources of the sea-bed is the winning of aggregates. More attention is likely to be focused on this source with the exhaustion of acceptable sources on land. Regulation will continue to be required to ensure that the disturbance to the environment is taken into account in the same way as the extraction of aggregates on land.

Shipping

9.39 The most obvious impacts of shipping on the marine environment arise when there is a collision or shipwreck. Since the seas are open to ships of all nations, there are obvious difficulties in regulating ship traffic to avoid such accidents. Nevertheless, over the past 20 years, the

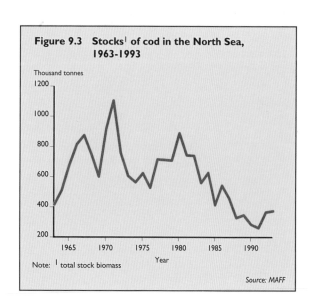

Figure 9.3 Stocks[1] of cod in the North Sea, 1963-1993

Note: [1] total stock biomass

Source: MAFF

international community has agreed a range of measures to improve the safety and operations of ships and to avoid collisions. This process continues. As well as accidents involving oil and other cargoes, oil and chemicals discharged from ships in the course of their normal operations are a major concern, since they pollute shores as well as affecting the sea. As a result of the Third North Sea Conference[3] in the Hague in 1990, the North Sea states have taken an initiative in the International Maritime Organisation which has led to a global tightening of the standards for such discharges. The North Sea states are further discussing how cooperative enforcement arrangements can be instituted to ensure that all ships operating in the North Sea observe the internationally agreed rules. Provided that ways can be found to ensure that ships do observe these rules, there seems no reason why, over the next 20 years, shipping should not continue to play its vital role in the world economy without affecting the sustainable use of the seas.

Fishing

9.40 The sustainable exploitation of the living natural resources of the sea is affected both by the human inputs to the sea (which is an important reason for regulating land-based inputs and dumping) and the scale and nature of the fishing itself. The side-effects of fishing on the conservation of the ecology of the sea (especially the sea-bed) also have to be considered. Many changes in fish stocks can be explained in terms of fishing intensity and natural factors; the state of stocks is not generally affected by the relatively low levels of inputs from anthropogenic sources which are found in UK waters. Populations of fish species have been heavily exploited in areas such as the North Sea for most of this century. The increasing power of fishing vessels and improved fishing technology are now posing serious problems for many fish stocks around the UK, particularly certain demersal species, notably cod (see Figure 9.3).

9.41 Given the international and intensive nature of fish stock exploitation, it is essential that regulations are agreed and enforced uniformly by all the countries involved. To this end, the EC Common Fisheries Policy is the most significant tool for the regulation of the scale and nature of the fishing

industry: it is therefore crucial that it does not allow fishing that is unsustainable.

INSHORE ACTIVITIES

9.42 The cumulative effects of human activity are most obvious close to the shores. Just as sensitive areas on land need protection against the combined effect of a wide range of activities, so similar measures are needed in inshore areas, where local ecologies are found which are at least as interesting and important as those on land. The expected growth of leisure activity over the next 20 years is likely to increase this pressure (see chapter 27). The leisure value of the waters is often dependent on maintaining and improving their environmental quality. The Government has recently published a review of the controls over development below the low-water mark[4]. This review puts forward a number of suggestions on how the controls might be improved, particularly by making more explicit the means whereby environmental factors are taken into account in making decisions. The Government has also published a discussion paper on the form and content of coastal management plans[5]. Both papers emphasise the significance of adopting a strategy for the sustainable use of inshore waters.

Bathing water quality

9.43 One aspect of this sustainable use should involve ensuring the quality of bathing waters with regard to discharges from the land: 80% of bathing waters in the UK complied with the EC Bathing Water Directive coliform standards in 1993, compared to 66% in 1988. Steps are being taken to bring the remaining bathing waters up to standard by an investment programme, including the installation of long sea outfalls and improvements to sewage treatment works and storm sewage overflows.

9.44 Current available evidence indicates that, even though some bathing waters breach EC limits, bathing water quality around the coasts of the UK does not present any significant health hazard. Research is under way to improve understanding of the relationships between the microbiological quality of coastal waters and the risk of health to bathers.

REFERENCES AND FURTHER READING

1   *Agreed Red List of Dangerous Substances confirmed by Lord Caithness.* DOE – Press release No. 194, 10 April 1989.

2   *Convention for the Protection of the Marine Environment of the North-East Atlantic,* Joint Oslo/Paris Conventions Secretariat, 1992.

3   *Third International Conference on Protection of the North Sea.* UK Guidance Note on the Ministerial Declaration. DOE, 1990.

4   *Development Below Low-water Mark: a review of regulation in England and Wales.* Department of the Environment/Welsh Office. 1993.

5   *Managing the Coast: a review of coastal management plans in England and Wales and the powers supporting them.* Department of the Environment/Welsh Office . 1993.

CHAPTER 10

SOIL

SYNOPSIS

10.1 The protection of soil is crucial for future sustainability, since it plays a vital role in food and timber production, in the maintenance of our biodiversity, as a reservoir for water and as a buffer and filter for pollutants. In recent decades, however, agricultural intensification, afforestation and increased pollution from industrial sources has resulted in some loss of soil function and structure in localised areas. Recent measures to reduce agricultural intensification and make farmers more aware of soil's importance should help to alleviate these problems. Measures to reduce emissions of sulphur dioxide (SO_2) and oxides of nitrogen (NO_x), coupled with the decreasing heavy industry sector in the UK, have reduced the rate of soil contamination, but in some areas the loss of soil function may be irreversible. Changes in the UK climate, if realised, will cause changes in the soil water balance and have implications for water resources.

10.2 The key sustainability issues are:
- to protect soil as a limited resource for the production of food and other products and as an ecosystem for vital organisms;
- to ensure that land management practices effectively utilise this resource and take account of the need to maintain soil functions by avoiding inappropriate use and development, by preventing erosion, contamination, burial and loss, and by preventing irreversible declines in organic matter and pH levels.

INTRODUCTION

10.3 Soil forms the surface layer of most of the earth's land area, varying in thickness from less than a centimetre to many metres. It has a complex and dynamic structure, consisting of living organisms, dead and decaying organic matter and mineral particles. It performs a wide range of functions which sustain either directly or indirectly the world's human population, plants and other animals.

10.4 Soil is essential for food and timber production, and also provides habitats for millions of plant and animal species. Other less visible roles include an ability to filter, transform and buffer potentially polluting substances which may enter the soil from rainfall or other sources. It also acts as an important reservoir for water and as a physical base for buildings, roads and other structures, and can provide protection for archaeological remains. Soils store about twice as much carbon as is in the atmosphere, and are an important link in the natural cycle that determines atmospheric carbon dioxide (CO_2) concentrations.

10.5 Soil is, therefore, essential to the maintenance of the environment, and loss of soil function is an important issue when considering sustainability. The 1972 *European Soil Charter*[1] recognised soil as a vital limited resource which is easily destroyed, and as a major support for human life and welfare. The *Charter* was strengthened in 1992 with the addition of a further recommendation on soil protection[2]. The Royal Commission on Environmental Pollution is currently examining the scientific and technical issues involved in soil protection, in order to help the future development of proper soil management.

10.6 The degradation of soils can be physical, chemical and biological. A number of potentially degrading processes are discussed in this chapter, including erosion, acidification, loss of structure, eutrophication, contamination with toxic substances, climatic change, and removal or burial. The chapter also describes the environmental impacts of land use and land management practices on soil functions, and the policy mechanisms that are in place to address these impacts.

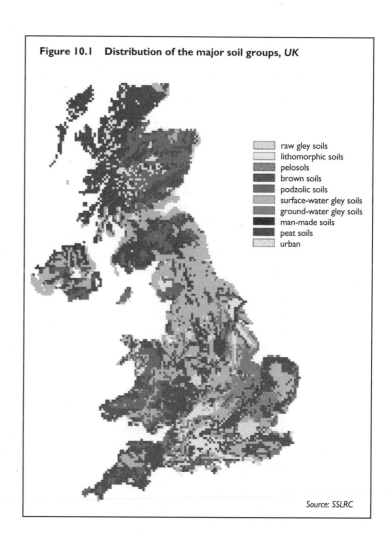

Figure 10.1   Distribution of the major soil groups, *UK*

- raw gley soils
- lithomorphic soils
- pelosols
- brown soils
- podzolic soils
- surface-water gley soils
- ground-water gley soils
- man-made soils
- peat soils
- urban

Source: SSLRC

Figure 10.2   Organic Matter, England and Wales.

■	< 1.5
▓	1.5 – 2.0
░	2.0 – 4.0
▒	> 4.0

Source: SSLRC

SOIL TYPES

10.7 The size and nature of soil particles and the way they fit together determine the characteristics of individual soils. Spaces between particles provide for the movement and storage of water, oxygen and other gases which are essential for healthy plant growth. They provide gaps through which plant roots can extend and organisms living in the soil can move. Soil patterns are complex and soils vary from place to place in their physical, chemical and biological properties. The main soil types[3] found in the UK and their broad distribution are shown in Figure 10.1. A wide variety of other soil types exist on a global scale.

ORGANIC MATTER LOSS

10.8 Organic matter is a vital component of soils. If the content declines, the soil becomes less stable, resulting in a loss of structure, a lower capacity to store nutrients and water, and an increased susceptibility to erosion. It also supports fewer organisms, including those that develop and maintain good soil structure.

10.9 The ploughing up of grassland, the loss of rotations in some agricultural systems and other arable farming practices

have reduced organic matter to low levels in some soils. The organic matter content of soils in England and Wales is shown in Figure 10.2. The optimum amounts of organic matter vary for different soil types and land use practices; it is not, therefore, possible to determine from this map areas where low organic matter content is causing serious land management problems at present. Under continued intensive arable agriculture, further decreases in organic matter are expected to continue into the next century in many areas. It is recognised that there has been an irreversible loss of organic matter where peat soils have been drained and used for intensive arable agriculture in the East Anglian Fens and in parts of Lancashire.

10.10 Recent measures to promote environmentally sensitive agricultural practices may also help maintain or increase the organic matter content of soils. The recent ban on straw burning is likely to result in more crop residues being ploughed back into soils. The Set Aside and Environmentally Sensitive Area schemes (see chapter 15) should lead indirectly to improvements in organic matter content in some areas, although they are designed to address other issues. The more widespread introduction of grass into arable rotations, which could include conversion to organic farming, can also help maintain or increase organic matter.

10.11 The forthcoming ban on dumping of sewage sludge at sea is likely to lead to increasing amounts being spread on the land, which will also enhance the organic matter content. However, the area of land likely to be affected by increased spreading of sewage sludge will be relatively limited (see 10.20) and the accumulation of organic matter will be limited by the need to control associated contaminants.

SOIL EROSION

10.12 In the international context, soil erosion in the UK is a relatively minor problem, but there is concern in some areas about the degree to which soil erosion has increased in the last 20 years as a result of changing agricultural practices. Water and wind erosion are the two main types of erosion which occur in the UK. Recent research suggests that sheet erosion, which occurs on steep slopes during very heavy rainfall, may be significant. Wind erosion is thought to be a potential problem on 5% of land, but preventive measures such as shelter belts and guard crops have been introduced to control it in many areas. Problems are, however, still to be found on some upland peat soils.

10.13 Within the UK, the main concern has been water erosion which occurs over a wide range of soils in many areas. Weather, slope and soil type all affect erosion rates.

Certain farming practices can accelerate erosion, including removal of hedgerows, increased field size, up and down slope cultivation, and late sowing of winter cereals which exposes the soil to adverse weather conditions in autumn and winter. If erosion continues at present rates, this will result in further deterioration of soil structure, a loss of nutrients and a reduction in the water holding capacity of soils, which will reduce soil fertility. In the uplands, overgrazing by livestock and the opening up of drainage channels up and down slopes contribute to soil erosion. The Government's agri-environmental schemes should help to control some of these problems by promoting better land management.

10.14 It is difficult to quantify how much soil is lost through erosion, as evidence of this can be masked by cultivation. Water erosion varies each year in relation to rainfall, and whether this falls when the soil is vulnerable. Present models[4] estimate, however, that over 20% of the arable lowlands of England and Wales are vulnerable to such erosion (Figure 10.3). There is also particular concern about some areas of the uplands, for example, the Peak District[5] and parts of Scotland, where erosion is thought to be sufficient to lower the land surface by 5–15 mm a year. The four main causes of this erosion are the fragile nature of the peat, burning of the vegetation, overstocking with sheep and increasing tourism.

10.15 Soil erosion has impacts beyond the areas in which it occurs. Movement of large volumes of sediment to roads and houses can lead to significant clean-up costs in some local authority areas. Soil erosion can also affect water quality by transferring pesticides, nutrients and sediment from fields to surface waters (see chapter 8) and silt into reservoirs, which gradually reduces their water storage capacity and shortens their useful life. Many erosion incidents have been triggered by soil compaction in the past, but these have been mainly localised events. Improved cultivation techniques have reduced the amount of compaction, but there still remains a problem of surface capping on arable soils low in organic matter.

10.16 Ways in which farmers can reduce soil erosion in lowland arable Britain have been set out in the Code of Good Agricultural Practice For The Protection of Soil[6], produced by the Ministry of Agriculture, Fisheries and Food (MAFF) (see chapter 15).

ACIDIFICATION

10.17 Acidification is a natural process in soils where there is an excess of rainfall over evaporation and water use by plants. The excess rainwater passes through the soil, removing

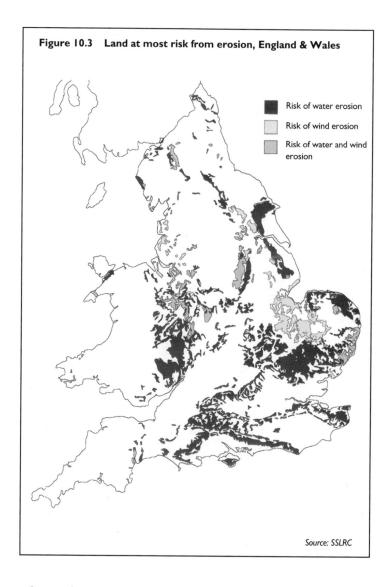

Figure 10.3   Land at most risk from erosion, England & Wales

Risk of water erosion

Risk of wind erosion

Risk of water and wind erosion

Source: SSLRC

calcium and magnesium and leaving behind a larger proportion of acidifying components. Emissions of acidifying gases, such as NO_x, SO_2 and ammonia, from industrial and agricultural sources are also a significant contributor to soil acidification. The acidifying effect is often neutralised by minerals in the soils but, where it is not, the soil gradually becomes more acid. Soils vary greatly in their ability to neutralise (buffer) acidity, depending on their texture and the amount of carbonates present. Sandy soils have a lower buffering capacity and are more prone to acidification than clay soils. Poorly buffered soils occur most frequently in North and West Britain (Figure 10.4).

10.18 Acidification can slow down organic matter breakdown in soil but it can also release metals bound within the soil, such as iron, aluminium and some heavy metals, which can adversely affect plant growth. These metals can leach into watercourses at levels which are toxic to

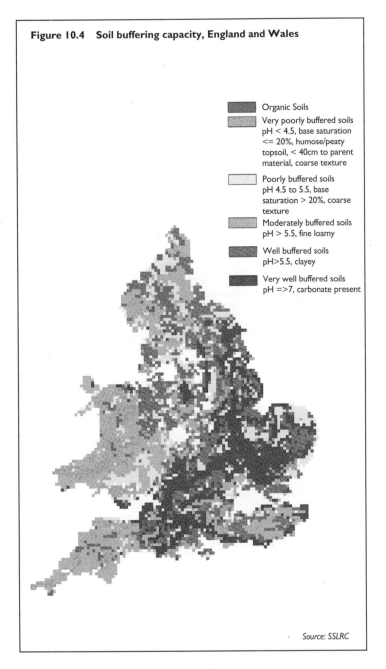

Figure 10.4   Soil buffering capacity, England and Wales

Organic Soils

Very poorly buffered soils pH < 4.5, base saturation <= 20%, humose/peaty topsoil, < 40cm to parent material, coarse texture

Poorly buffered soils pH 4.5 to 5.5, base saturation > 20%, coarse texture

Moderately buffered soils pH > 5.5, fine loamy

Well buffered soils pH>5.5, clayey

Very well buffered soils pH =>7, carbonate present

Source: SSLRC

freshwater organisms. The possible damage to soil and its ecosystems by acidification is assessed using the concept of critical loads, which are discussed more fully in chapter 7.

10.19 Afforestation, particularly with conifers, and the use of some fertilisers have the potential to increase soil acidification. Drainage of some wetland soils, such as alluvium and peats containing sulphides, can also lead to acidification. New land drainage schemes aimed at agricultural intensification are no longer permitted although, in some areas, water levels may still be declining because of existing schemes. In agricultural areas, the acidity of soil is reduced by liming. In some cases, however, it is important to maintain certain acid soil habitats to protect biodiversity.

CONTAMINATION

10.20 Soil can be regarded as contaminated when it contains substances which, when present in sufficient quantities or concentrations, are likely to cause harm, directly or indirectly, to human health or the environment. These substances include heavy metals, such as cadmium, zinc and mercury, and organic compounds such as polychlorinated biphenyls (PCBs) and dioxins. Contamination may result from deposition from air pollution, from point source contamination from industrial installations, such as factories and gas works, or from the spreading of sewage sludge and other wastes. The ban on dumping of sewage sludge at sea by 1998 is likely to result in sewage sludge being spread on 2% of agricultural land annually, compared to 0.3% in 1990–91. Natural processes may remove some contamination from soils only slowly, so that in many cases a legacy of soil contamination will remain long after the contamination originally occurred. The Government has recently published the results of an independent review of soil fertility and other aspects of sewage sludge use in agriculture[7].

10.21 Industrial and agricultural activities can significantly increase local concentrations of contaminants, such as cadmium, chromium, copper, mercury and zinc, which can impact on soil micro-organisms, plants, animals and humans. Figure 10.5 illustrates the wide variability of concentrations of zinc within different soils in the UK, both the underlying levels and those which result from human activities.

10.22 There are many possible contaminants, and knowledge of their effects within and on soil is far from complete. In some cases they may have long term effects which hamper the soil's ability to produce food and support biodiversity, but these have not yet been quantified. Government research is in hand to help improve understanding of the effects of contaminants on soil health, and to ensure that the environment and human health are adequately protected.

10.23 A range of methods has been developed for treating soil to reduce concentrations of contaminants to levels appropriate to the intended use or environmental setting of the site, or at least removing the soil to where it is likely to be less of a problem. The methods include washing, vitrification, removal to landfill sites and electrochemical treatment. Measures to deal with contamination are discussed in more detail in chapter 24. However, remediation can be very costly.

NITROGEN

10.24 Nitrogen is essential for plant growth. Soil plays an important role in the cycling of nitrogen and regulates its transfer to aquifers and surface waters and to the atmosphere. Nitrate in soil arises from the natural oxidation of organic matter and from fertilisers and manures. Any nitrate not used by plants or crops will also accumulate in the soil. However, when the soil is saturated with water, further rainfall can cause excess nitrate to leach into groundwaters. Most nitrate leaching occurs in the autumn when fields are either fallow, recently sown or awaiting sowing. Some 30% of England and Wales have soils with a potential for high nitrate leaching. However, the amount of leaching depends on the soil, the local climate and farming practice.

10.25 Since the 1950s, the amount of nitrogen fertiliser applied to agricultural soils has increased markedly, although this trend has reversed in recent years. The average amount of nitrogen fertiliser applied to arable and grassland crops in England and Wales increased from 19 kg per hectare in 1953 to 147 kg per hectare in 1987, but fell back to 125 kg per hectare in 1992. Research has shown, however, that fertiliser application alone is not responsible for nitrate leaching, and attention needs to be given to many aspects of land husbandry to bring it under control.

10.26 The Government's policies on nitrate leaching are discussed further in chapters 8 and 15.

PHOSPHORUS

10.27 Phosphorus is also essential for plant growth. However, on average, only about 3% of the total phosphorus in soil is available for plant uptake. The availability is often less than optimum for plant growth in intensive agricultural and forestry systems, and additional quantities are usually added in the form of fertilisers and manures. Where run-off or erosion occur, excess applications can contribute to the eutrophication of adjacent surface waters, although this is not generally regarded as a widespread problem. Studies on the River Severn have indicated that the levels of phosphates doubled between 1974 and 1991. About 20% of phosphates found in water come from agricultural activities, and about 75% from domestic sewage.

10.28 MAFF has set up a research programme to investigate all major avenues by which phosphates are likely to enter water from the land. A parallel research project, the Land-Ocean Interaction Study, funded by the Natural Environment Research Council (NERC), is reviewing movement of nutrients, including phosphates and pollutants, from the land to the North Sea.

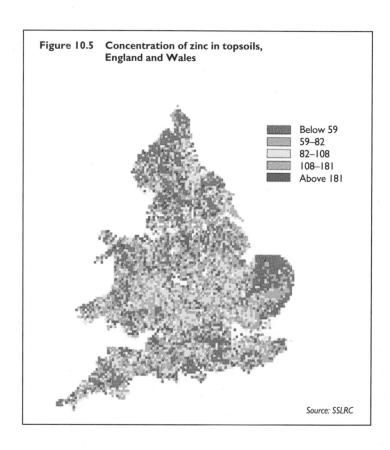

Figure 10.5 Concentration of zinc in topsoils, England and Wales

Below 59
59–82
82–108
108–181
Above 181

Source: SSLRC

SUBSIDENCE

10.29 Most clay soils in Britain are prone to swell when wet and shrink when dry. This tendency can be exacerbated by the presence of certain types of vegetation, particularly trees, which remove water from soil at greater depths. This leads to a reduction in soil volume and the consequent shrinkage causes differential movement in the foundations of buildings and damage to the structure. In recent years, there has been a large increase in claims made to insurance companies for damage to buildings as a result of subsidence after the dry years of 1976 and 1989. Claims totalled £5 million in 1975, but rose steadily to reach almost £100 million in 1988. Thereafter, claims rose sharply to £250 million in 1989, and to around £500 million in 1990 and 1991. These sharp rises in claims prompted insurance companies to make large increases in premiums for domestic buildings insurance; this has contributed to the halving of subsidence claims to £260 million in 1992.

10.30 A possible knock-on effect of these increased insurance claims and payouts for subsidence is that insurance companies could impose more stringent requirements for the construction of buildings on greenfield sites in high-risk areas, as a pre-condition of providing buildings insurance cover. This could lead to higher construction costs, but these costs should be mostly offset by reduced prices for land in high-risk areas.

THE IMPLICATIONS OF CLIMATE CHANGE

10.31 A changing climate (see chapter 6) is likely to have an effect on soil quality[8]. Increases in temperature will cause changes in soil water balance which may lead to an increased need for irrigation, with implications for water resources. Changes to the soil water regime may also cause shifts in the distribution of natural and semi-natural ecosystems. Different cropping patterns may emerge as the climate becomes warmer, whilst changing seasonal patterns may have a large impact on the types of crops grown. Climate change is also likely to affect soil structure, with drier conditions causing soil shrinkage and cracking. However, owing to the uncertainty about potential future climate change, it is not possible at present to quantify these effects.

10.32 Climate change may also have an impact on the amount of carbon in soil. It might cause further sequestration,

thus reducing the amount of atmospheric CO_2, or conversely it might cause greater organic matter turnover, releasing CO_2 to the atmosphere. The Government is sponsoring research at the Institute of Terrestrial Ecology into the impacts of climate change on carbon sequestration in UK soils.

SOIL BURIAL AND LOSS

10.33 Over the period 1981 to 2001, it is predicted that 105,000 hectares of land in England will pass into urban use (see chapter 11). This represents less than 1% of total land in England. The percentage is likely to be substantially less for the rest of the UK. The urbanisation of land can lead to the permanent loss of soil resources and functions, and may also affect soil functions on adjacent land. Land use planning policies aim to maximise the reuse of vacant and derelict land and to keep development on best quality agricultural land to a minimum.

REFERENCES AND FURTHER READING

1 *European Soil Charter.* Council of Europe. B(72)63, May 1972.

2 *Recommendation on Soil Protection.* Council of Europe. R(92)8, May 1992.

3 *Soil Classification in England and Wales (higher categories).* B. W. Avery. Soil Survey Technical Monograph No 14, 1980.

4 *Risk of Soil Erosion in England and Wales by Water under Winter Cereal Cropping.* R. C. P. Palmer. Soil Survey and Land Research Centre, 1993.

5 *Peak District Moorland Erosion Study. Phase 1 Report.* J. Philips, D. W. Yalden, J. H. Tallis. Peak District Joint Planning Board, 1981.

6 *Code of Good Agricultural Practice for the Protection of Soil.* Ministry of Agriculture, Fisheries and Food. MAFF Publications, 1993.

7 *Review of the Rules for Sewage Sludge Application to Agricultural Land: soil fertility aspects of potentially toxic elements.* Report of Independent Scientific Committee. MAFF Publications, 1993.

8 *The Potential Effects of Climate Change in the United Kingdom.* First report of the UK Climate Change Impacts Review Group. HMSO, 1991.

CHAPTER 11

LAND USE

SYNOPSIS

11.1 Despite being one of the most densely populated countries in the world, the UK remains a mainly rural land, with 77% used for agriculture, 10% covered by forest and the rest used mainly for urban purposes. There are, however, increasing pressures for development as the size and structure of the population changes and living standards increase. The urban area of England is projected to increase by 105,000 hectares (0.8% of the land area) between 1981 and 2001, with the main pressures occurring in regions to the South and East of the country. Government policies aim to minimise the impact of this development on rural land, through designating Green Belts, encouraging reuse of vacant and derelict land, and protecting landscapes and habitats of environmental value. On the coastline, problems still remain in some areas of degradation from development. The built heritage is an important source for understanding the UK's past and needs to be protected to prevent irreversible loss.

11.2 The key issues for sustainability are:
- to balance the competing demands for the finite quantity of land available and, in particular, to optimise the use for development of vacant urban land and to reclaim and develop derelict or contaminated land;
- to protect, as far as possible, the countryside for its landscape, wildlife, agricultural, recreational and natural resource value;
- to maximise access to facilities for individuals and to markets for business, while minimising the amount of travel required.

INTRODUCTION

11.3 Land is a finite resource of fundamental importance to the economy and the environment. There are competing demands for it: for agriculture, timber and minerals production; for housing, retail and industrial development and for roads; and for natural and semi-natural areas, which provide important habitats for wildlife, the national heritage of landscapes and open spaces for recreation.

11.4 The quality of land is also important. Some areas are affected by contamination from industrial activities. Agricultural intensification as well as land abandonment can also spoil the appearance of a landscape. The use of land is changing, with people moving to suburbs or to satellite towns and villages, and with the development of retail centres and office parks away from the centres of towns and cities. This has led to the run down of some inner cities and towns, and to people making longer journeys to work and for shopping, often by car, contributing to traffic congestion and pollution.

11.5 This chapter presents trends and projections in land use and conservation, and identifies gaps and inconsistencies in the data. Information on land use for mineral workings can be found in chapter 12.

CURRENT PATTERNS OF LAND USE AND RECENT TRENDS

11.6 Nationally, the proportions of land used for agriculture, forestry and urban uses change only slowly. In 1992, about 18.5 million hectares (77%) of land was used for agriculture, compared with 19 million hectares (79%) in 1972. Forestry has been increasing steadily over the last 20 years and covered about 2.4 million hectares (10%) of land in 1992 compared with 1.9 million hectares (8%) in 1972. Other land, the major part of which is in urban use, has barely altered in extent over the last 20 years, increasing by 0.1 million hectares to 3.4 million hectares (14% of the land area) in 1992. However, these figures may under-estimate the increase in urban land over this period. Results from the 1990 *Countryside Survey*[1], recently published by the Government, show an increase of built up land in Britain of about 13,000 hectares per year between 1984 and 1990. There are large margins of error associated with these estimates, since the Countryside Survey was not designed to measure the use of urban land, and they should therefore be treated with caution.

11.7 Department of the Environment (DOE) Land Use Change Statistics[2] for the second half of the 1980s show that, of land developed for urban uses in Britain, nearly 40% was previously in agricultural use, over 40% was previously developed for urban uses (including vacant land which had previously been developed), and a further 7% was also in built-up areas but had not been developed before.

GROWTH IN URBAN AREAS

11.8 Around three quarters of the population of the UK lives in urban areas (those with a population greater than 10,000). Most of the buildings in these areas, and in smaller towns and villages, are sound and represent national capital from which future generations will benefit. However, more buildings will be needed. A recent DOE study[3] concluded that 105,000 hectares of land in England would convert to urban uses between 1981 and 2001. At the end of that period, 11% of land would be in urban use, compared with 10.2% in 1981. The study is currently being updated. No projections have yet been made as far as 2012. Although half of new residential development in England takes place in urban areas, the pressures for new housing (see chapter 5), make it highly likely that there will be demands to use further rural land, in some areas, for urban growth up to 2012 and beyond.

11.9 Based on current trends, the increase in urban area for England as a whole is projected to be relatively small (0.8% of the total land area). This represents a rate of growth of urban areas of 8% between 1981 and 2001, or about 0.5% a year on average.

11.10 Large differences are expected in the predicted demand for urban growth for different English counties (Figure 11.1). These indicate where future pressures for urban development may come and reflect the varying rates of household growth expected for different counties (see chapter 5). If these demands were to be met, Somerset, Northamptonshire, Shropshire, Buckinghamshire and Cambridgeshire would have rates of urban growth at least double the national average (around 15% or more), representing an increase in the total area of land in these counties covered by urban development of between 0.8% and 2%. Areas such as London, Liverpool, Birmingham, Manchester and Newcastle, are forecast to have demand rates for urban growth of less than 5%. The lower rates for these areas reflect the existing high levels of urbanisation and the scope for reusing derelict and unused urban land.

11.11 However, these predictions of urban growth take no account of the role of planning policies and other factors in determining the extent, distribution and density of future development (see chapter 35). In many of the areas facing the greatest pressures for urban growth, strategic planning decisions should reflect environmental and other considerations when assessing the location and size of future developments; as a result, urban growth in these counties will not be as high as unconstrained demand would deliver.

THE DEMAND FOR HOUSING

11.12 The demand for more homes is being driven by an increasing population which is living longer, and by more people living on their own. The declining number of marriages and increased divorce rate have increased demand for household formation and reduced household size (see chapter 5). Improved living standards and higher aspirations have also contributed to smaller household size, as more people can afford to set up their own home rather than remain with their family or share with friends.

11.13 Between 1972 and 1992, on average some 250,000 dwellings were built each year in the UK. As a result, the stock of dwellings increased by 5 million to reach 24 million by the end of 1992. Over the same period, the number of households in the UK is estimated to have increased by

around 3.5 million to almost 23 million in 1992. The latest Regional Planning Guidance has provided for an estimated 3 million additional dwellings to be built across England over the next 20 years. This is similar to the projected growth in households of around 3 million across the UK over the same period.

CHANGING PATTERNS OF DEVELOPMENT AND TRANSPORT

11.14 Alongside a growth in the number of households, there have also been changes in attitudes to residential location, quality and space. The General Household Survey[4] shows that the average number of rooms per person increased from 1.8 in 1981 to 2.0 in 1991. The 1992 Household Attitudes Survey (HAS) of England[5] found that half of those who lived in flats would prefer to live in houses, which in general are more spacious, and that almost a quarter of households would prefer to have more rooms. Only 6% felt they had too many rooms, with more than half of these outright home owners at, or near, retirement age. The utilisation of housing space can be expected to decrease over the next 20–40 years as the elderly population increases.

11.15 There has also been a tendency to move out of town centres into suburbs and villages, with more commuting into town to work. In the last decade, there was a 6% increase in population in the remoter rural areas. This trend has been made possible by the growth in car ownership, which in turn has facilitated a significant increase in car use. The number of road vehicles registered in Britain[6] increased by 5 million to 24.5 million vehicles between 1981 and 1991. In some areas, the pressures from increasing car ownership are greater than in others. By county, car ownership in 1991 was highest in Wiltshire, Berkshire and Hertfordshire and lowest in Strathclyde, the Western Isles and Tyne and Wear (Figure 11.2). The growth in car ownership is expected to continue into the next century, when large increases in road traffic are expected (see chapter 26).

11.16 Increased car use has also led to changes in the pattern of retail and commercial development, to congestion in some urban areas and to parking problems. Retail stores are being developed away from town centres. This not only encourages the use of the car, but can lead to loss of vitality in town and city centres. Between 1982 and 1992, 4.1 million square metres of new floorspace was opened on out of town sites and 3.4 million square metres in town centres[7]. This compares with 1.0 million square metres of new out of town floorspace and 6.0 million square metres of new town centre floorspace opened between 1960 and 1981 (Figure 11.3). These data overestimate the extent of development in town centres, since they do not take account

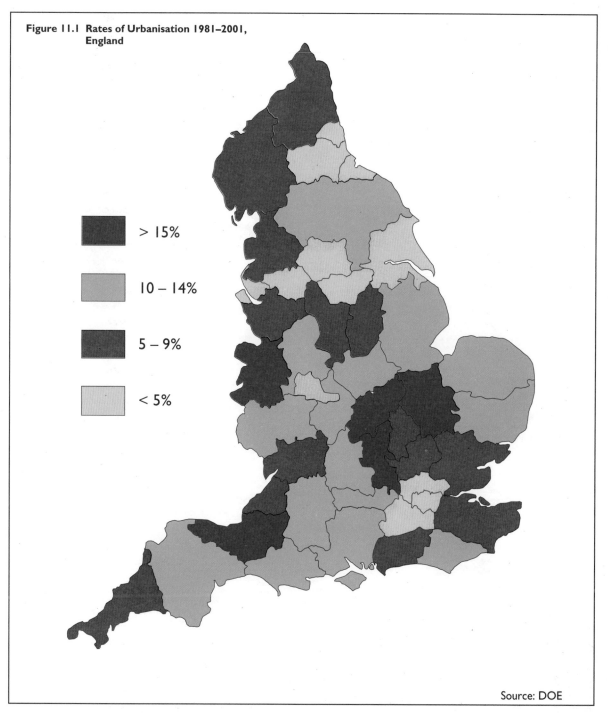

Figure 11.1 Rates of Urbanisation 1981–2001, England

> 15%

10 – 14%

5 – 9%

< 5%

Source: DOE

of the loss of floorspace owing to shops and other commercial outlets closing down in these areas. The extent of net development is, therefore, less than these figures suggest.

11.17 The changing relationships between residential, employment and retail uses are posing various social and environmental problems. More people use cars for more journeys and those journeys are lengthening. People travel further to work, for shopping, and especially for leisure, often by car, causing congestion, pollution and noise (Figure 11.4). They demand additional residential development away from town centres, often on previously open land. As people and businesses move away, some former town and city centres are becoming run down. Those without access to a car are being disadvantaged, and cannot share the same quality of life, for example, in the form of access to shops or leisure facilities.

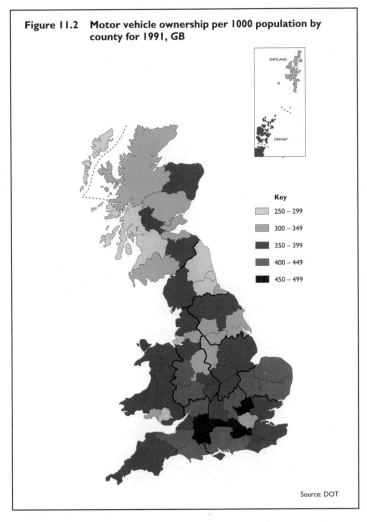

Figure 11.2   Motor vehicle ownership per 1000 population by county for 1991, *GB*

SHETLAND

ORKNEY

Key

	250 – 299
	300 – 349
	350 – 399
	400 – 449
	450 – 499

Source: DOT

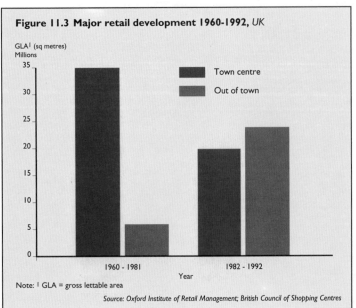

Figure 11.3 Major retail development 1960-1992, *UK*

GLA¹ (sq metres)
Millions

- Town centre
- Out of town

Year

Note: ¹ GLA = gross lettable area

Source: Oxford Institute of Retail Management; British Council of Shopping Centres

Some data on these demographic changes are available. What is less clear, however, is the impact of these changes on resources such as landscape quality and wildlife habitats. The Government will seek to quantify these aspects over the next few years through a number of research projects.

11.18 The need to travel to and from the workplace and during working hours is, however, beginning to be reduced as the increasing availability and affordability of information systems, including personal computers, fax machines, electronic mail, and video conferencing facilities, has allowed some employees to work at home; this has similarly enabled companies to conduct aspects of their business without employees having to leave their offices, while at the same time maintaining productivity and efficiency levels. A recent survey[8] found that 11% of employers were employing some people who worked from home, with around half of those employing workers who used information technology when working at home (teleworking). A further 8% of the employers surveyed said they were considering introducing teleworking in the future. Employers who had introduced teleworking were particularly concentrated in the South East of England, where commercial property costs and transport pressures are greatest. Teleworking was found to be most prevalent in the financial and business services sector and the public sector. Opportunities for teleworking are likely to increase as technological advances are maintained and the costs of information systems continue to fall.

11.19 Increasing car ownership and use has resulted in more land being used for road building. About 1.2–1.5% of the UK land area is covered by roads. Between 1985 and 1990, 9,000 km of new roads were built in Britain by the Department of Transport and local highway authorities, covering an estimated 14,000 hectares (0.06% of the land area). It is expected that the Government's road building programme (outlined in the White Paper *Roads for Prosperity*[9] and subsequently updated) would require up to 9,000 additional hectares of land in England. This will impact directly on landscapes and wildlife habitats and indirectly lead to more land being used for aggregate provision (see chapter 12).

VACANT AND DERELICT LAND

11.20 Vacant and derelict land is a potential resource to absorb some of the demand for further urban development. In England, in 1990, it was estimated[10] that there were 60,000 hectares of vacant urban land, about 5% of the total urban area. Of this, over 40% (25,000 hectares) had been previously developed. Regions with the highest proportions of vacant land, such as the North of England, are generally areas where the pressures to develop land are weakest.

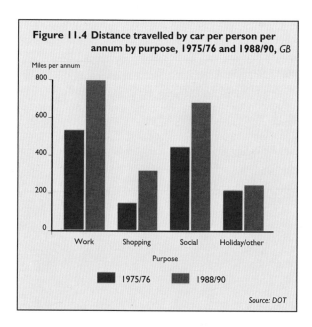

Figure 11.4 Distance travelled by car per person per annum by purpose, 1975/76 and 1988/90, *GB*

Miles per annum

Purpose: Work, Shopping, Social, Holiday/other

■ 1975/76 ■ 1988/90

Source: DOT

11.21 In 1988, there were an estimated 40,500 hectares of derelict land in urban and rural areas of England (0.3% of the land area) compared with 45,700 hectares in 1982[11]. About 14,000 hectares were reclaimed between 1982 and 1988 and, of this, around 12,600 hectares had been brought back into active use, with 63% for such uses as recreation, agriculture and forestry, and 27% for uses such as industrial and housing development. Around 31,600 hectares were considered by local authorities to justify reclamation in 1988. A new derelict land survey is under way which will identify the uses this land has been put to since then. English Partnerships, the new urban regeneration agency, and its equivalents in the rest of the UK, will have a key role to play in encouraging the development of derelict land (see chapter 24).

11.22 In Wales, in 1988, there were approximately 10,900 hectares of derelict land requiring reclamation and, of this, some 2,500 hectares were judged to require relatively low funding to enhance vegetation[12]. Much of the dereliction in Wales is being tackled progressively through the land reclamation programme of the Welsh Development Agency.

11.23 In Scotland, around 12,100 hectares of land were recorded as vacant or derelict in 1990[13]. Almost half of all derelict land and 60% of vacant land was concentrated in the Strathclyde region. The survey also recorded that 586 hectares of derelict land were brought back into use over the previous two years. A new survey is under way.

11.24 Some vacant and derelict land will also have been contaminated by its former use. Estimates vary greatly of the amount of such land in the UK but the range is likely to be in

the order of 100,000–200,000 hectares directly affected by former use. Other sites are affected by natural or migrated contamination. Some of these sites still retain their original use; others have been redeveloped. The DOE is carrying out research into the identification, assessment and treatment of contaminated land as part of its wider policy (see chapter 24).

11.25 Policies aimed at bringing into productive use vacant, derelict and contaminated land are being vigorously pursued, but are unlikely to fulfil all the future demand for new land for development, owing to the location and condition of much of this land.

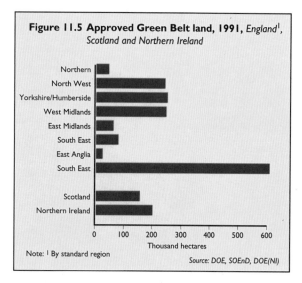

Figure 11.5 Approved Green Belt land, 1991, *England[1],* *Scotland and Northern Ireland*

Northern, North West, Yorkshire/Humberside, West Midlands, East Midlands, South East, East Anglia, South East, Scotland, Northern Ireland

0 100 200 300 400 500 600
Thousand hectares

Note: [1] By standard region

Source: DOE, SOEnD, DOE(NI)

GREEN BELTS

11.26 Green Belts are areas of designated land in which strict control over development restricts the sprawl of built-up areas, preserves the special character of historic towns and assists in urban regeneration (see chapter 24). They are important tools for the delivery of compact, energy efficient cities, rather than being of particular environmental value or quality in their own right. Green Belts in England cover 1.5 million hectares, almost 12% of the country and more than double the area designated in 1979. In Scotland, there are five Green Belts covering over 155,000 hectares (2% of the country), while in Northern Ireland, Green Belts cover 200,000 hectares, 17% of the land area (see Figure 11.5). There are no Green Belts in Wales.

PROTECTED AREAS

11.27 National Parks, Areas of Outstanding Natural Beauty (AONBs) in England, Wales and Northern Ireland, and National Scenic Areas in Scotland are the major areas which have been designated by legislation to protect their landscape

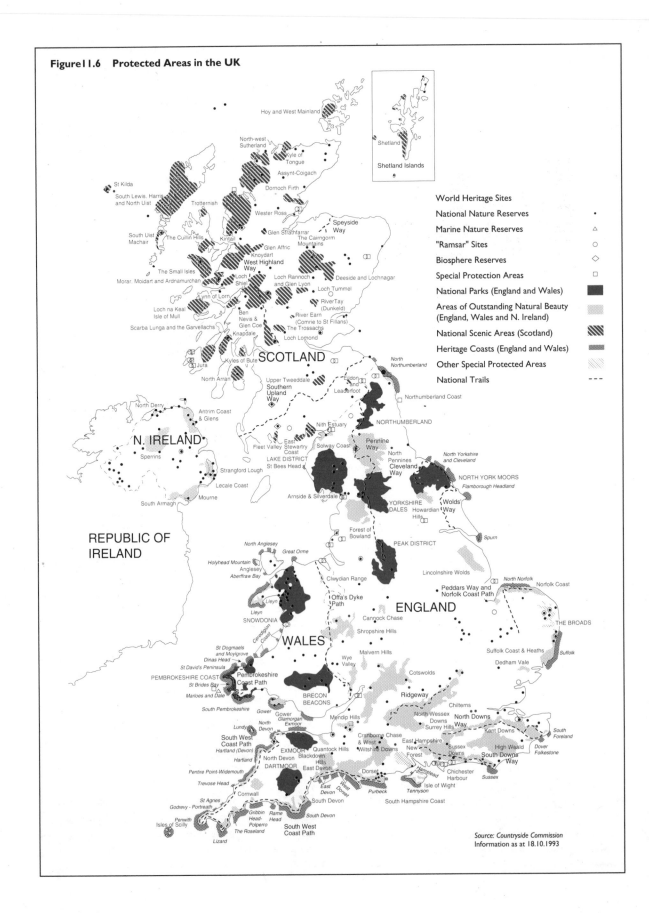

Figure 11.6   Protected Areas in the UK

Hoy and West Mainland

Shetland

Shetland Islands

North-west Sutherland

Kyle of Tongue

Assynt-Coigach

St Kilda

South Lewis, Harris and North Uist

Dornoch Firth

Trotternish

Wester Ross

Speyside Way

South Uist Machair

The Cuillin Hills

Glen Strathfarrar

The Cairngorm Mountains

Kintail

Knoydart

Glen Affric

The Small Isles

West Highland Way

Morar, Moidart and Ardnamurchan

Loch Shiel

Loch Rannoch and Glen Lyon

Deeside and Lochnagar

Lynn of Lorn

Loch Tummel

River Tay (Dunkeld)

Loch na Keal Isle of Mull

Ben Nevis & Glen Coe

River Earn (Comrie to St Fillans)

Scarba Lunga and the Garvellachs

Knapdale

The Trossachs

Loch Lomond

SCOTLAND

Jura

Kyles of Bute

North Arran

Upper Tweeddale

North Northumberland

Southern Upland Way

Eildon and Leaderfoot

North Derry

Antrim Coast & Glens

Northumberland Coast

N. IRELAND

Nith Estuary

NORTHUMBERLAND

Sperrins

East Stewartry Coast

Fleet Valley

Solway Coast

Pennine Way

North Pennines

North Yorkshire and Cleveland

Strangford Lough

LAKE DISTRICT

St Bees Head

Cleveland Way

NORTH YORK MOORS

Lecale Coast

Flamborough Headland

REPUBLIC OF IRELAND

Mourne

South Armagh

Arnside & Silverdale

YORKSHIRE DALES

Wolds Way

Howardian Hills

Forest of Bowland

Spurn

PEAK DISTRICT

North Anglesey

Great Orme

Lincolnshire Wolds

Holyhead Mountain Anglesey

Aberffraw Bay

Clwydian Range

North Norfolk

Norfolk Coast

Lleyn

Peddars Way and Norfolk Coast Path

Lleyn

Offa's Dyke Path

ENGLAND

SNOWDONIA

Ceredigion Coast

Cannock Chase

THE BROADS

Shropshire Hills

WALES

Malvern Hills

Wye Valley

Suffolk Coast & Heaths

Suffolk

St Dogmaels and Moylgrove

Cotswolds

Dinas Head

Dedham Vale

St David's Peninsula

PEMBROKESHIRE COAST

Pembrokeshire Coast Path

St Brides Bay

BRECON BEACONS

Ridgeway

Chilterns

Marloes and Dale

South Pembrokeshire

Gower

Gower Glamorgan

Mendip Hills

North Wessex Downs

North Downs

North Downs Way

Lundy

North Devon

Exmoor

Cranborne Chase & West Wiltshire Downs

Surrey Hills

Kent Downs

South Foreland

South West Coast Path

EXMOOR

Quantock Hills

East Hampshire

New Forest

High Weald

South Downs Way

Dover Folkestone

Hartland (Devon)

North Devon

Blackdown Hills

East Devon

Sussex Downs

Chichester Harbour

Sussex

Pentire Point-Widemouth

DARTMOOR

Dorset

Hampstead

Isle of Wight

Trevose Head

East Dorset

West Dorset

Purbeck

Tennyson

St Agnes

Cornwall

South Devon

South Hampshire Coast

Godrevy - Portreath

South Devon

Penwith

Gribbin Head-Polperro

Rame Head

Isles of Scilly

The Roseland

South West Coast Path

Lizard

World Heritage Sites

National Nature Reserves ·

Marine Nature Reserves △

"Ramsar" Sites ○

Biosphere Reserves ◇

Special Protection Areas □

National Parks (England and Wales) ■

Areas of Outstanding Natural Beauty (England, Wales and N. Ireland)

National Scenic Areas (Scotland)

Heritage Coasts (England and Wales)

Other Special Protected Areas

National Trails - - -

Source: Countryside Commission
Information as at 18.10.1993

84

importance. Together with other protected areas such as Special Protection Areas (SPAs), they account for nearly 20% of the total land area of the UK. Figure 11.6 shows the main protected areas in the UK.

11.28 There are also a number of areas which are protected because of their value as wildlife habitat, especially for endangered species. The most important of these are sites protected in order to meet international obligations, such as SPAs for Birds, Wetlands of International Importance under the Ramsar Convention and, soon, Special Areas of Conservation (SACs) under the EC Habitats Directive. National Nature Reserves (NNRs), Sites of Special Scientific Interest (SSSIs) – Areas of Special Scientific Interest (ASSIs) in Northern Ireland – have been established under UK legislation and these networks underpin the international designations. Table 11.1 shows the numbers and total area covered for each statutorily protected area in 1992. Sites are selected on the basis of scientific evidence of the importance of the habitat for the species to be protected and the numbers and the richness of the assemblage of flora and fauna to be found there. That evidence can be reviewed over time to assess whether the environmental resource is being sustained.

Table 11.1	Statutory protected areas, November 1993, UK	
Status [1]	Number	Area (sq km)
National Nature Reserves [4]	304	1,895
Local Nature Reserves [1,4]	371	206
Sites of Special Scientific Interest (SSSIs) [2]	5,999	19,370
Area of Special Scientific Interest [3]	46	481
Special Protection Areas	74	2,450
Biosphere Reserves	13	443
"Ramsar" Wetland Sites	68	2,519
Environmentally Sensitive Areas [5]	33	27,207

Note: [1] Some areas may be included in more than one category. For example, in Great Britain NNRs, SPAs, Biosphere and Ramsar Sites are all SSSIs (see also Figure 8.1)
[2] Great Britain only
[3] Northern Ireland only
[4] As at March 1993
[5] As at December 1993

Source: DOE(NI), MAFF, EN, Countryside Council for Wales, SNH

11.29 Clearly there is a special responsibility to protect sites of international importance within the terms required by the relevant EC Directives or international conventions. The Government has also developed clear policies for the protection of sites designated under national legislation. In all cases, however, there can be situations where a balance must be struck between the importance of the site for nature conservation and the need to cater for other legitimate

needs, such as human safety or health, or economic or social factors. The Government has taken care to ensure that the decision-making processes for such cases give full weight to nature conservation objectives.

11.30 Within the various types of designated area, those of international importance could be deemed closest to being inviolable natural capital. Those of national importance must be protected, but may need to be traded against equally important economic objectives, in which case it may be necessary to look at the scope for designating compensatory resources.

RURAL LANDSCAPE

11.31 The landscape of the UK countryside forms an important part of its national heritage, and it is important to measure how it is changing in response to the various pressures identified in this Strategy. The 1990 Countryside Survey provided information on the stock and distribution of land cover and landscape features in Britain. Data from field surveys carried out in 1984 provided a baseline for measuring change between 1984 and 1990.

11.32 The survey found that tilled and managed grassland, which is primarily used for agriculture, made up half the land area of Britain in 1990. Between 1984 and 1990, the area of this land fell by 380,000 hectares (3%) with about half this loss resulting from a doubling of fallow land, which increased by about 180,000 hectares. Semi-natural vegetation such as heath, moor and bracken, which is often used for rough grazing, accounted for 27% of land cover in 1990, with the overall cover little changed since 1984. Changes in the stock and distribution of vegetation species are discussed in chapter 13.

11.33 Landscape features, such as hedgerows and other boundaries, are important for land management, and often provide important wildlife habitats. There was a net loss of about 23% of hedgerows between 1984 and 1990, with most of this loss due to a change in the form of hedges, for example, from a managed hedge to a line of trees. About 20,000 km of walls were also lost over this period, 10% of the total. Boundary fences showed a net increase of 75,000 km over this period and were the most widespread boundary type, occurring in over 70% of the boundaries in Britain.

AGRICULTURE

11.34 Although the area of land used for agriculture has fallen marginally over the last 40 years, 77% of the land (18.5 million hectares) is still used for agriculture. Hence, most of the UK countryside and landscape is not "natural", but has been created and is maintained by agricultural activities. In

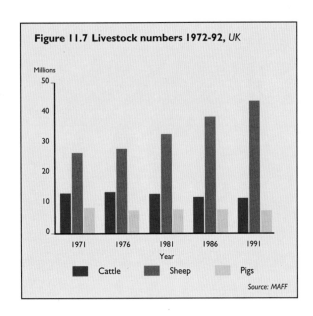

Figure 11.7 Livestock numbers 1972-92, *UK*

Millions

Year

Cattle   Sheep   Pigs

Source: MAFF

larger numbers of dairy and beef cattle and sheep than would be the case if they had to sell their produce at prices determined by an open and competitive market. The 1992 reforms of CAP, which will reduce support prices and limit eligibility for livestock subsidies, should help reverse this trend (see chapter 15).

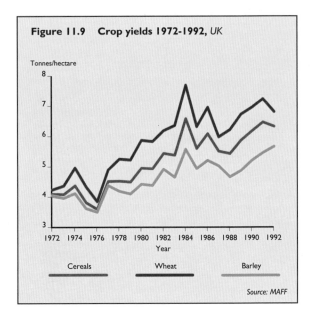

Figure 11.9   Crop yields 1972-1992, *UK*

Tonnes/hectare

Year

Cereals   Wheat   Barley

Source: MAFF

most areas some form of land management is essential to maintain the character of the landscape and the environment.

11.35 Around 73% of agricultural land is used for dairy farming, grazing by livestock or for growing grass. Changes in livestock numbers from 1971 to 1991 are shown in Figure 11.7. The large increase in sheep over this period (68%) has led to overgrazing of heather in some upland areas, which is assumed to have had adverse consequences for wildlife species that depend on this habitat (see chapter 13). Levels of support under the EC's Common Agricultural Policy (CAP) (see chapter 15) have encouraged UK farmers to maintain

11.36 The remainder of agricultural land, some 27%, is used for growing crops, mainly cereals. Changes in the area used for growing different crops over the last 20 years are shown in Figure 11.8. Since 1981, there has been an increase of over 40% in the area used for growing arable crops other than cereals, with the major change being the fourfold increase in the area used for growing oilseed rape. This accounted for 9% of the total crop area in 1992.

11.37 The trend towards more intensive arable farming practices is reflected in the higher yields for cereal crops (Figure 11.9). These have been accentuated by the high levels of support for food production under the EC's CAP (see chapter 15), which has encouraged farmers to take former grazing land into arable production.

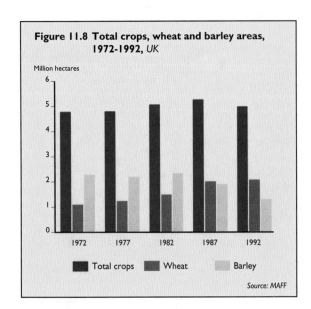

Figure 11.8 Total crops, wheat and barley areas, 1972-1992, *UK*

Million hectares

Total crops   Wheat   Barley

Source: MAFF

11.38 Higher yields have resulted, in part, from increased use by farmers of fertilisers to replace soil nutrients where crops are repeatedly harvested, and of pesticides, including herbicides, to control weeds and pests. The volume of these products used in agriculture increased steadily throughout the 1970s and part of the 1980s, but has fallen in recent years. This is largely due to economic and technical factors, but to some extent it also reflects changing consumer preferences.

11.39 Farmers have also improved efficiency by increasing farm and field sizes, thus giving economies of scale through use of larger machinery, and reductions in manpower. In some cases, fields have been enlarged by removing hedgerows with resultant loss of some habitats for wildlife (see chapter 13).

FORESTRY

11.40 The UK was once heavily forested, with about 80% tree cover according to some estimates. Over the centuries much of it was felled for agriculture, for settlements and for roads, so that by the beginning of this century forest cover stood at 5%.

11.41 In the past 70 years, during which the UK has had a policy of forestry expansion, more than 1 million hectares of land have been restored to forest and woodland. Tree cover now stands at 2.4 million hectares (10%) of the land area. About 250,000 hectares (13%) of this area is ancient semi-natural woodland. The tree cover is not evenly distributed; Northern Ireland, for example, has only 5% forest cover. With the exception of the Republic of Ireland (5%) and the Netherlands (9%), the UK now has the lowest tree cover of any European country, and significantly less than the 25% average for the EC.

11.42 Forest cover is continuing to expand steadily with more than 500,000 hectares established since the early 1970s. In restoring forest cover, non-indigenous coniferous species have generally been favoured over broadleaved trees because they are generally more productive and adaptable to UK soils and climate. However, there is now greater emphasis on broadleaved species, new plantings of which have increased more than tenfold in the last 20 years. Substantial scope remains for the UK to increase its woodland and forest area.

11.43 In 1993, UK forests supplied some 7 million cubic metres of wood, equivalent to 13% of UK wood consumption. They have the capacity for a sustained yield of about 14 million cubic metres per year, and this will increase as new forests mature, peaking at around 20 million cubic metres between 2020 and 2030.

11.44 The UK monitors tree condition under the joint EC-UNECE monitoring programme (see Figure 11.10). For all species, there were sharp increases in the number of trees with more than 10% foliage loss in 1992 compared with 1990. Much of this decline in condition can be attributed to the drought conditions caused by recent hot, relatively dry summers. There is some evidence that air pollution is affecting the condition of some species, but further monitoring will be required before a proper analysis can be made of the long-term effects on tree cover and its associated ecosystems.

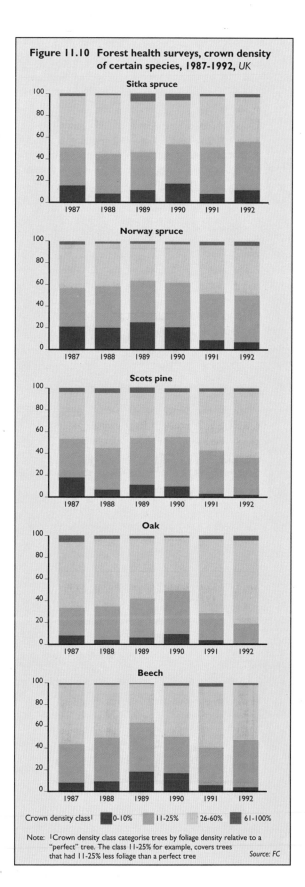

Figure 11.10 Forest health surveys, crown density of certain species, 1987-1992, *UK*

Crown density class[1]   ■ 0-10%   ■ 11-25%   ■ 26-60%   ■ 61-100%

Note: [1]Crown density class categorise trees by foliage density relative to a "perfect" tree. The class 11-25% for example, covers trees that had 11-25% less foliage than a perfect tree

Source: FC

COASTAL AREAS

11.45 The protection of coastal and estuarine areas from over development is vital if the UK coast is to maintain both its economic viability and unique biodiversity.

11.46 Different economic and social activities require coastal locations, and certain natural and historic landscapes and habitats are specific to coastal areas. Around 30% of the coast of England and Wales is developed, although the proportions are much smaller in Scotland and Northern Ireland. Special policies apply to those areas designated for their landscape or wildlife interest, which include parts of the coastal zone (see paragraphs 11.27–30). More specifically, 45 Heritage Coasts have been defined in England and Wales to protect and manage effectively the finest stretches of undeveloped coastline. They account for 1,500 km or 33% of the coast. In Scotland, over 7,500 km of the mainland and island coastline are defined as Preferred Coastal Conservation Zones to protect them from development (Figure 11.5).

11.47 The coastline is shaped by powerful natural forces. Coastal erosion rates vary greatly around the UK, with rapid erosion found along parts of the coast of South and East England, where relatively soft geological formations are found. Surveys of the saltmarshes along the North Kent and Essex coasts were carried out in 1973 and 1988 to assess the degree of loss of this habitat to factors other than development. These found that, over 15 years, between 10–40% of saltmarsh area had been lost in each surveyed estuary owing to coastal erosion and land claim.

11.48 Further pressures on the coastline may come from flooding caused by rising sea levels. Over the past century, the mean sea level is estimated to have risen by 10–15 cm; the rate of rise is thought likely to increase over the next 50 years or so, owing to the anticipated effects of global warming (see Chapter 6). Areas at particular risk from erosion and flooding include some major conurbations, together with high grade agricultural land, road and rail links and power stations in coastal areas. The Government has recently published a strategy[15] that encourages the operating authorities engaged in flood and coastal defence measures to carry out their responsibilities in ways which are as technically and economically effective, and as environmentally sustainable, as possible. The strategy reflects the Government's intention that natural river and coastal processes should only be disturbed by the construction of defence works when important natural or man-made assets are at risk, and that in considering future defence schemes and in operating existing systems, the potential impact on wildlife habitats should be a key consideration.

11.49 Planning policy towards the coast was recently updated and guidance[16] emphasises the need for development in coastal areas to be sustainable. The undeveloped coast will seldom be the most appropriate location for new development. A recent review of development below low-water mark[17] establishes criteria for systems of control, and draws attention to their need to contribute to a strategy of sustainable development. Parallel advice on the role of coastal management plans[18] states that the Government's aim is to promote the sustainable use of the coast, to reflect its human uses as well as its nature conservation value.

BUILT HERITAGE

11.50 The built heritage comprises remains of past human settlements, religion, industry and land use. It includes ancient monuments, archaeological sites, historical buildings and gardens, industrial remains and other landscape features of historic interest. For the prehistoric and many other historic periods, such remains form the only source of evidence for understanding the UK's past. It is, therefore, important that historically and aesthetically important monuments, buildings, sites and landscapes are maintained and protected for future generations. Failure to do so would result in irreversible loss of the nation's heritage.

11.51 Built heritage features survive throughout the countryside, in underwater, marine and coastal environments, and in urban locations. They are affected by a wide range of environmental factors and development processes, including air, ground and water pollution; coastal erosion; agriculture, forestry and peat extraction; development for housing, industry and transport; mining activities; and derelict land reclamation. The scale and rate of these pressures pose major problems for the built heritage and mitigation strategies, as well as procedures for monitoring and active management, are required to ensure its long term conservation.

11.52 There are currently around 560,000 listed buildings in the UK, compared with 310,000 (excluding Scotland) in 1981. In 1990–91, consent was given to demolish or partially demolish over 1,100 listed buildings in England and Wales. Consent was also given to alter or extend about 21,500 listed buildings. In Scotland, in 1992–93, some 2,000 listed building consents were handled. The level of government expenditure for the conservation of the built heritage in Britain was £142 million in 1992–93. Further protection is afforded to the built heritage through scheduling, the planning system and in forestry and agricultural regulations.

11.53 A survey[19] carried out in 1990–91 found that most listed buildings in England are in reasonable condition, but that 36,700 listed buildings (8%) are at risk from neglect, with a further 72,850 being vulnerable.

11.54 The pressures facing the built heritage mirror those affecting the natural environment, and can be addressed through the policies set out in this Strategy. It is therefore important that the impact of environmental pressures and development proposals on the built heritage are considered as these policies are formulated, to ensure that a holistic view is taken of the whole environment.

REFERENCES AND FURTHER READING

1 *Countryside Survey 1990 Main Report.* Countryside Series 1990, Volume 2, Department of the Environment, 1993.

2 *Land Use Change in England.* Statistical Bulletins 86(1), 87(7), 88(5), 89(5), 90(5), 92(3), 92(4), 93(1), Department of the Environment, annual.

3 *Rates of Urbanisation in England 1981–2001.* Department of the Environment. HMSO, 1990.

4 *1991 General Household Survey.* Office of Population Censuses and Surveys. HMSO, 1992.

5 *1992 Household Attitudes Survey of England.* Department of the Environment. HMSO, 1990.

6 *Transport Statistics, Great Britain 1992.* Department of Transport. HMSO, 1993.

7 *The Effect of Out of Town Retail Development: A Literature Review for the Department of the Environment.* BDP Planning & Oxford Institute of Retail Management. HMSO, 1992.

8 *Teleworking in Britain. A report to the Employment Department.* U. Huws, Analytica. Employment Department, 1993.

9 *Roads for Prosperity.* Cm 693. Department of Transport. HMSO, 1989. ISBN 0–10–1069324.

10 *The National Survey of Vacant Land in Urban Areas of England 1990.* Department of the Environment. HMSO, 1992.

11 *Survey of Derelict Land in England 1988.* Department of the Environment. HMSO, 1991.

12 *Survey of Derelict Land in Wales 1988.* Welsh Development Agency, 1993.

13 *Scottish Vacant and Derelict Land Survey 1990.* Scottish Office Environment Department, 1992.

14 *Forest Monitoring Programme 1992 Results.* Forestry Commission, HMSO, 1992.

15 *Strategy for Flood and Coastal Defence in England and Wales.* MAFF/Welsh Office. HMSO, 1993.

16 *Planning Policy Guidance: Coastal Planning – PPG20.* DOE/Welsh Office, HMSO, 1992.

17 *Development Below Low-Water Mark: a Review of Regulation in England and Wales.* Department of the Environment/Welsh Office, 1993.

18 *Managing the Coast: a Review of Coastal Management Plans in England and Wales and the Powers Supporting Them.* Department of the Environment/Welsh Office, 1993.

19 *Buildings at Risk: a Sample Survey 1991.* English Heritage, 1992.

CHAPTER 12

MINERALS INCLUDING FOSSIL FUELS

SYNOPSIS

12.1 Very large quantities of mineral resources exist, sufficient, in many cases, to last far into the foreseeable future. Nevertheless, it is becoming increasingly difficult to find sites that can be worked without damaging the environment to an extent that people find unacceptable. Thus, while it may be unlikely that there will be a problem of physical exhaustion of resources, in terms of what can be extracted from environmentally acceptable locations, the supply of minerals should not be viewed as infinite.

12.2 The key issues for sustainability are:
- the use and management of mineral resources and the environmental constraints placed on the availability of resources in the longer term, having regard to the implications of present and future demand, and the contribution which minerals make to economic growth;
- the environmental impact of minerals provision and the overall quality of the environment achievable after restoration.

INTRODUCTION

12.3 A wide range of minerals is worked in the UK. Principally, they include:

Minerals used in construction, such as:
- sand and gravel, and crushed limestone, igneous rock, and sandstone used as aggregates;
- chalk, limestone, clay/shale used in cement manufacture;
- common clay/shale for use in brick/tile manufacture;
- slate for roofing;

Energy minerals:
- coal, oil and gas;

Other industrial minerals, such as:
- barytes, mainly used in drilling muds;
- chalk/limestone for industrial processes;
- fluorspar, mainly used in the chemical industry and as a flux in some processes;
- specialist clays (such as china clays, ball clays and fireclays) for the ceramics industry;
- gypsum, for plaster/plasterboard but also for the cement industry;
- peats, for horticulture;
- potash, mainly used for fertilisers;
- salt (rock salt, used for snow and ice clearance on roads, and white salt, used in the food and chemical industries);
- silica sand, used for glass, foundry castings, and ceramics (and for silicate bricks).

In quantity terms, the main minerals extracted in the UK are aggregates (sand and gravel, and crushed rock), and energy minerals.

12.4 Minerals extraction can have environmental impacts in areas of attractive countryside and on communities (for example, noise, dust, visual impact, traffic). Whilst sites can be restored to a high standard, it may take some time for the soil on restored areas to develop or for vegetation to be established. Mineral workings can often be concentrated in a locality for many years. However, modern best practice is to avoid or mitigate adverse long term effects, so that many impacts of extraction are usually temporary. Chapter 18 describes current controls on minerals workings designed to promote sustainable management of minerals extraction.

12.5 It is difficult to be precise about which minerals in the ground may be regarded as an economic resource in the long term since this will depend on demand and, in particular, on the extent to which new and different materials will be developed as substitutes. Nevertheless, it will become increasingly important to have reliable information about the nature, quantity and location of mineral reserves as workable resources in environmentally acceptable areas become scarcer.

NON ENERGY MINERALS

Aggregates for construction

12.6 The majority (90%) of aggregates supplied is from primary materials: 32% sand and gravel from land-based sources, 7% sand and gravel from marine dredging and 51% crushed rock. In addition, a number of secondary materials are used as aggregates, including wastes (such as china clay sand, slate waste, colliery spoil, pulverised fuel ash, and blastfurnace slag) and recycled materials, such as demolition arisings. However, economic, geographical and technical reasons currently constrain secondary use to about 10% of total aggregate requirements.

12.7 Of the 106,900 hectares of land recorded as having permissions for surface mineral workings in England and Wales in 1988 almost half were permissions to work minerals used for primary aggregates (28% sand and gravel and almost 20% other aggregates including limestone/dolomite, sandstone and igneous rock). In the period 1982–1988 in England and Wales, 10,750 hectares of land were restored following extraction of aggregate minerals. Most of this was areas worked for sand and gravel (9,680 hectares or 90%), where the most common after-use was for agriculture (over 50%), but about 36% was for amenity uses, and about 7% each for forestry and other uses.

12.8 The principal uses of aggregates are roads construction and maintenance, and new housing and housing maintenance

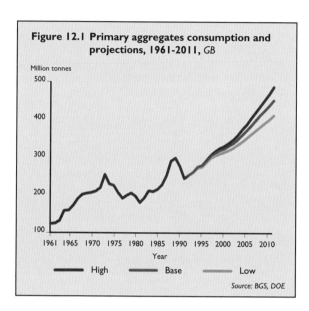

Figure 12.1 Primary aggregates consumption and projections, 1961-2011, *GB*

Million tonnes

High — Base — Low

Source: BGS, DOE

(approximately 30% each). Past trends in the consumption of primary aggregates in Britain are given in Figure 12.1. There has been a substantial increase in consumption of primary aggregates over the last 30 years (reflected chiefly in increased use of crushed rock).

12.9 Projections of demand for primary aggregates to 2011 are also shown in Figure 12.1. These projections anticipate a growing need for primary aggregates over the next 20 years in Britain (in the range 6,600–7,200 million tonnes (mt)). A total demand of 7,300 to 7,900 mt including 700 mt of secondary materials (representing approximately 10% of total aggregates consumption) is anticipated. Annual demand by 2011 could be between 410–490 mt; this is an increase of between 40% and 60% on 1989 consumption levels.

12.10 The aggregates demand projections are derived from an economic model which projects construction activity. The relationship between construction investment and primary aggregate consumption is then modelled to estimate primary aggregates demand. The projections provide an informed guide to future demand only and are not targets for production. There are likely to be significant fluctuations around the trend, roughly in line with economic growth (see Annex IV for more details).

12.11 Consented reserves for England and Wales (that is, onshore reserves with full planning permission for extraction), as estimated at mid-1993, are in excess of 5,900 mt for crushed rock and more than 940 mt for sand and gravel; corresponding figures for Scotland are 821 mt and 132 mt. Further reserves will need to be released to meet the projected demand (see paragraph 12.9) and to provide for the period after 2011.

Other non-energy minerals

12.12 Figure 12.2 shows past trends in the production of the main non-energy non-aggregate minerals: china clay, common clay and shale, chalk, gypsum and silica sand. Planning permissions for working of these minerals amounted to 20% of land recorded as having permissions for mineral workings in England in 1988. Production of clay and shale has reduced by almost 60% over the last 20 years partly because changes in building design have meant more use of concrete and less of bricks, and there has been some reduction in new house construction in the last few years. The production of chalk has also declined by 40% because of factors such as the increased use of limestone in cement manufacture. There has been little change in the production of china clay and gypsum. Production of silica sand has declined by around 25% over the last 20 years.

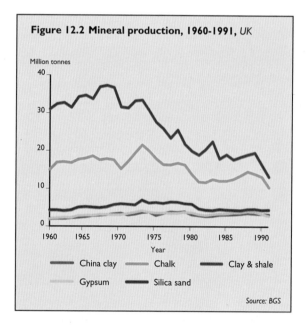

Figure 12.2 Mineral production, 1960-1991, *UK*

Million tonnes

China clay — Chalk — Clay & shale

Gypsum — Silica sand

Source: BGS

12.13 Projections are not generally available except for silica sand and the combined raw materials required for cement manufacture (limestone, chalk, clay and gypsum). The silica sand projections indicate only a very slight rise in demand to 2011 compared to recent levels. Requirements for silica sand in the future will depend on a number of factors including the extent to which glass and foundry sand is recycled.

12.14 Demand for minerals to produce cement is projected to rise considerably from under 25 mt in 1989 to 35–45 mt a year by 2011, reflecting forecast growth in construction. The introduction of flue-gas desulphurisation (FGD) in coal-burning power stations will increase the demand for limestone used in the FGD process. There is also likely to be an impact on the demand for natural gypsum since gypsum is

Table 12.1 Oil and natural gas reserves, 1981-1992, *UK*	1981	1982	1983	1984	1985	1986	1987	1988	1988	1990	1991	1992
Oil (million tonnes)												
Remaining reserves (1 Jan)	1436	1271	1468	1378	1302	1235	1328	1285	1190	1200	1195	1230
Change in estimation[1]	-75	300	25	50	60	220	80	20	102	87	125	230
Extraction in year	90	103	115	126	127	127	123	115	92	92	91	95
Remaining reserves[2] (31 Dec)	1271	1468	1378	1302	1235	1328	1285	1190	1200	1195	1230	1365
Natural Gas (billion cubic metres)												
Remaining reserves (1 Jan)	1101	1007	941	1149	1325	1242	1325	1298	1195	1185	1200	1235
Change in estimation[1]	-58	-30	244	212	-43	125	17	-61	32	61	87	166
Extraction in year	36	36	36	36	40	42	44	42	42	46	52	51
Remaining reserves[2] (31 Dec)	1007	941	1149	1325	1242	1325	1298	1195	1185	1200	1235	1350

Note: 1 Changes in estimates are due to new finds and re-assessment of existing reserves
2 Figures are proven plus probable reserves

Source: DTI

produced as a by-product of the FGD process. The extent to which this will be the case is not yet known. (See Annex IV for more details on projections for silica sand and minerals to produce cement).

12.15 In 1991, peat production in England was 1.204 million cubic metres, more than 99% of which was for horticultural uses. In Scotland, production was 357 thousand cubic metres, of which 68% was for horticultural uses. Annual total use of peat in UK horticulture is estimated to be approximately 2.3 million cubic metres, of which about 40% is imported.

COAL, OIL AND GAS

12.16 Figure 12.3 shows the trends in the production of coal, oil and gas in terms of tonnes of oil or oil equivalents. Demand for coal, oil and gas will depend on the demand for energy generally and the extent to which other energy sources such as nuclear power and renewables are utilised. While forecasting the level of overall demand in these areas is difficult, it will depend on fuel prices and the evolution of the economy, and the effectiveness of energy efficiency measures. Chapter 36 considers issues surrounding energy efficiency.

Opencast coal

12.17 Opencast coal production rose from 14 mt to 19 mt in the 5 year period up to 1991, but is now falling. Total reserves with planning permission for opencast working were 87 mt at the end of 1992, mainly contained in large British Coal sites. It is an important source of low cost energy, which was recognised in the Government's Interim Planning Guidance on coal issued earlier this year (see chapter 18).

12.18 Opencast coal extraction, in common with the extraction of many other minerals, can be noisy, dusty, visually intrusive, and can give rise to heavy traffic movements. It can be disruptive of landscapes, but it can also create opportunities for major improvements, including the clearance of derelict land. About a quarter of the land used for opencast coal mining was previously derelict. Restoration to "hard" after-uses can, moreover, reduce pressure for development on other land.

12.19 In the period 1974–1982, approximately 6,200 hectares of land worked for opencast coal in England were restored. For the period 1982–1988, the figure was

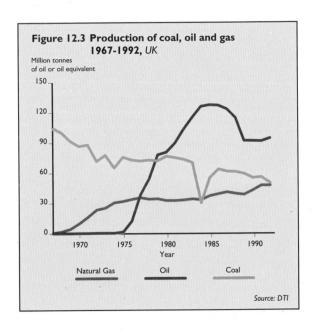

Figure 12.3 Production of coal, oil and gas 1967-1992, *UK*

Million tonnes of oil or oil equivalent

Natural Gas   Oil   Coal

Source: DTI

approximately 4,100 hectares (broken down as 82% to agriculture, 1% to forestry, 13% to amenity uses, and 4% for other uses).

12.20 For Wales, in the period 1974–1982, more than 1,700 hectares of land worked for opencast coal were restored. For the period 1982–1988, the figure was approximately 1,200 hectares (broken down as 87% to agriculture, 9% to forestry, and 4% to amenity uses).

Deep mine production

12.21 In the five years ending March 1992, UK production from deep mines fell from 82.4 mt to 71 mt, and the number of collieries from 94 to 50. British Coal stocks at the end of 1991–92 totalled 10.8 mt, and consumer stocks stood at 42.2 mt.

12.22 The particular planning problems associated with deep mining are subsidence, disposal of wet and solid waste, visual intrusion, traffic and the lengthy duration of mining operations.

12.23 In the period 1974–1982, approximately 4,000 hectares of land worked for deep coal in England was restored. For the period 1982–1988, the figure was approximately 2,600 hectares (broken down as 54% to agriculture, 7% to forestry, 30% to amenity uses, and 9% for other uses).

12.24 For Wales, in the period 1974–1982, approximately 920 hectares of land worked for deep coal was restored. For the period 1982–1988, the figure were approximately 580 hectares (broken down as 34% to agriculture, 2% to forestry, 56% to amenity uses, and 8% for other uses).

Oil and gas

12.25 Table 12.1 shows oil and natural gas reserves for 1981–1992. In the last five years, production of UK oil fell from 123 mt to 95 mt, while production of gas rose from 44 billion cubic metres (bcm) to 51 bcm. Remaining reserves, excluding reserves which are thought unlikely to be economically or technically producible, now stand at 1,365 mt for oil and 1,350 bcm for gas.

12.26 Production of oil and gas can give rise to problems of pollution from spillage, the discharge of oil-based muds used in drilling, the need to flare unusable gases, and the abandonment of disused installations and pipelines.

12.27 Since 1986, the UK has carried out surveillance flights over offshore installations using aircraft fitted with infrared and ultraviolet detectors and side-looking radar. The number of spills has decreased significantly over the last three years: 353 in 1990, 249 in 1991, and 183 in 1992 according to the Advisory Committee on Protection of the Sea[1].

12.28 From 1 January 1992, the level of oil permitted to be discharged with cuttings when drilling using oil based muds was lowered from 15% to 10%. From 1 January 1994, the level of oil on cuttings that may be discharged must be less than 1% for exploration and appraisal wells and for new developments drilled with oil-based mud. All other wells must achieve this target by 1997.

REFERENCES AND FURTHER READING

[1] *Oil pollution surveys, 1982 to 1992.* Available from the Advisory Committee on Protection of the Sea, 11 Dartmouth Street, London SW1H 9BN.

CHAPTER 13

WILDLIFE AND HABITATS

SYNOPSIS

13.1 The number and range of plant and animal species ("biodiversity") in the UK has been affected over the centuries by man's activities. In the last 50 years, there have been many losses as a result of urban and transport developments, growth of plantation forests, and intensification of agricultural production. The Government has a three-pronged approach to conservation: designation and protection of specific geographical areas; specific actions targeted towards individual species; and measures aimed at the wider countryside. The *Biodiversity Action Plan*[1] emphasises the need for partnership between individuals, conservation bodies and government to preserve UK wildlife.

13.2 The key issues for sustainability are:
- to conserve, as far as possible, the wide variety of species of flora and fauna found in the UK, particularly those whose population is of international significance;
- to ensure that the UK's objectives in landscape and wildlife conservation are given their full weight in policies for other sectors, particularly agriculture, industry, forestry, land use and transport planning, and coastal protection;
- to ensure that commercially exploited species are managed in a sustainable way.

INTRODUCTION

13.3 The UK's geographical position, as a collection of temperate offshore islands on the North East Atlantic edge of Europe, together with its diverse geology, geomorphology, soils, and the results of past human management, has resulted in a diversity of habitats, each with characteristic populations of plants and animals.

13.4 The changes in land use referred to in chapter 11, such as increased urbanisation, industrial development and transport, modern agricultural practices, mineral extraction, and the resultant pollution of air, water and soil, all affect significant areas of the countryside on which wildlife depends. During the 20th century, some species have become extinct, and many have suffered significant population decline.

PRINCIPLES AND OBJECTIVES

13.5 The *Biodiversity Action Plan* has redefined underlying principles and objectives (see Box 13.1).

UK statutes

13.6 The UK has a long tradition of legislation designed specifically to protect wildlife. Parliament passed the first Act to protect birds in the 1880s, and a comprehensive statutory framework has gradually been built up, not only to protect threatened or endangered species, but also to conserve important habitats for wildlife. The basis of nature conservation in the UK is the species protection provisions and the system of notification of special sites established by the Wildlife and Countryside Act 1981 and parallel legislation for Northern Ireland.

The Statutory Agencies

13.7 English Nature, Scottish Natural Heritage and the Countryside Council for Wales, together with the

---

BOX 13.1
OVERALL GOAL

To conserve and enhance biological diversity within the UK, and to contribute to the conservation of global biodiversity through all appropriate mechanisms.

UNDERLYING PRINCIPLES

1. Where biological resources are used, such use should be sustainable.
2. Wise use should be ensured for non-renewable resources.
3. The conservation of biodiversity requires the care and attention of individuals and communities, as well as Government processes.
4. Conservation of biodiversity should be an integral part of Government programmes, policy and action.
5. Conservation practice and policy should be founded upon a sound knowledge base.
6. The precautionary principle should guide decisions.

OBJECTIVES FOR CONSERVING BIODIVERSITY

1. To conserve and where practicable to enhance:
   a) the overall populations and natural ranges of native species and the quality and range of wildlife habitats and ecosystems;
   b) internationally important and threatened species, habitats and ecosystems;
   c) species, habitats and natural and semi-natural habitats that are characteristic of local areas.
2. To increase public awareness of, and involvement in, conserving biodiversity.
3. To contribute to the conservation of biodiversity on a European and global scale.

Countryside Commission and the Environment Service of the Department of Environment for Northern Ireland (DOE(NI)), are responsible for providing advice to the Government on policies affecting landscape and nature conservation in the UK; for notifying land of special interest for its wildlife, geological and natural features; for establishing and managing National Nature Reserves (NNR); for disseminating information about nature conservation and advising on the effects of ecological change; and for carrying out or commissioning research in support of these duties. Through the Joint Nature Conservation Committee, they discharge their special functions for landscape and nature conservation throughout the UK, and provide a collective view on international matters and those questions which affect the UK as a whole. Current annual expenditure of these bodies is of the order of £140 million.

The voluntary movement

13.8 The voluntary movement continues to play a conspicuous part, often owning and managing nature reserves and other areas of wildlife importance. Wildlife protection remains an objective of the National Trust, which has become the largest private landowner in Britain with an estate of over 600,000 acres. The Royal Society for the Protection of Birds (RSPB) was founded in 1889 and acquired its first reserve in 1931. It is now the largest voluntary wildlife-conservation body in Europe, with some 850,000 members, and a sizeable research department. Its 120 nature reserves cover 76,000 hectares. The Society for the Promotion of Nature Reserves evolved over the years, through the Royal Society for Nature Conservation (RSNC), into the RSNC Wildlife Trust Partnership, the major voluntary organisation in the UK concerned with all aspects of wildlife protection. At its core are 47 County Wildlife Trusts and 50 Urban Wildlife Groups. With a total membership of over 250,000, they own or manage over 2,000 nature reserves. There are many specialist bodies whose activities both add to knowledge of the natural environment, and preserve and enhance it in practical ways.

BIODIVERSITY

13.9 The Countryside Survey 1990[2] provides an important base line of information on biodiversity. The Government will undertake another major survey in the year 2000, and in the interim more research is in hand to follow up the Survey's findings, both to monitor trends and to understand their underlying causes.

Habitats

13.10 There is a close link between species and habitats. Changing a habitat will often affect the diversity of species contained within it. Through the centuries, the UK's landscape and wildlife habitats have been largely shaped by man's interventions. These include clearance of ancient forests for timber and in order to use the land for agriculture. This century has seen further loss of countryside to urban and transport developments, the growth of plantation forestry and increasing arable and livestock outputs from intensively managed farmland.

13.11 The main UK habitats include woodlands, heathlands, lower grasslands, coastal areas (cliffs, estuaries, saltmarshes, sand dunes and shingle shorelines), marine, freshwater habitats (lakes and ponds, rivers and streams, canals and grazing marsh ditches), peatlands, uplands and farmland. A fuller description of each of these habitat types is contained in Chapter 3 of the *Biodiversity Action Plan*.

13.12 The best and most recent estimates for the land cover of Britain, including the more common semi-natural habitats, are provided by the 1990 Countryside Survey. Semi-natural habitats cover about one-third of Britain. Although no clear trend towards a loss of semi-natural habitat was evident, the Survey was based upon a broad aggregation of habitats and a sample based approach; more local and detailed surveys reveal losses of the rarer and conservationally important habitats such as species-rich grasslands.

Species

13.13 Even in a well-studied country such as the UK, knowledge of the major groups of living organisms is uneven. Microbial organisms, such as bacteria and protozoa, are much less studied than larger plants and animals. The algae, fungi, ferns, bryophytes and lichens are, in turn, less well-known than flowering plants. For flowering plants, the location and even population size are known for the most threatened species. The abundance of more widespread plants is harder to assess, although the Countryside Survey gives information from fixed quadrats in sample 1 km squares. Invertebrates are generally less well known than vertebrates. For birds, and now increasingly for reptiles, amphibians and mammals, most species have national population estimates. Overall, birds are the best known in terms of their ecology, behaviour and changing numbers over time. Long term trends (over 10 years) in numbers at sample sites are known for a few flowering plants, for butterflies, larger moths, aphids, some mammals, as well as for breeding and wintering birds.

13.14 Many bird species typical of lowland farmland in the UK have become scarcer since the mid 1970s. The declines of the grey partridge, barn owl and lapwing are well documented. Many other, more common, farmland bird species have also severely declined over the last two decades. For example, recent monitoring by the British Trust for Ornithology suggested that 10 out of 12 seed-eating birds that are found on farmland showed signs of decline between 1977 and 1991, although for all other bird species there was a very slight increase over the same period. These include linnet (36% decline), reed bunting (–46%), skylark (–53%), corn bunting (–62%) and tree sparrow (–81%). These declines in farmland bird populations coincided with major changes in agricultural practices in lowland Britain. These include the switch from spring to autumn sowing of arable crops, which has also led to the loss of winter stubble; a move away from crop rotations and mixed farming; an increase in the inputs of inorganic fertilisers and pesticides; and the intensification of pasture management.

13.15 In global terms, the UK is not particularly rich in species; for example, it has only 210 of the 9,881 species of breeding birds in the world. Nevertheless, the UK has a rich and characteristic biological diversity for an island of its size, isolation and geographical position. Many aspects of the UK's biodiversity are linked with biodiversity elsewhere, notably in the case of migratory birds, sea mammals and fish. Box 13.3 and Box 13.4 show respectively species which are peculiar or

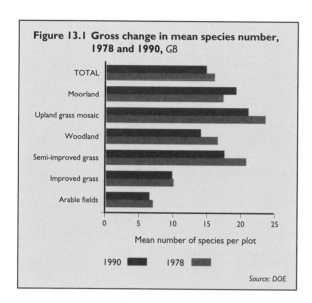

Figure 13.1 Gross change in mean species number, 1978 and 1990, *GB*

Mean number of species per plot

1990 ■ 1978 ■

Source: DOE

Figure 13.2 Change in mean species numbers within habitat types, 1978 and 1990, *GB*

Mean number of species per plot

1990 ■ 1978 ■

Source: DOE

unique to the UK ("endemic" species) and examples of species where the UK holds a significant proportion of the European or world population.

13.16 An analysis of changes in plant species diversity surveyed in 1978 and 1990 was included in the 1990 Countryside Survey. In 1978, over 1,000 vegetation plots (200m quadrats) were located at random within a sample of 256 1 km squares representative of Britain. The same plots were resurveyed in 1990. The plots have been grouped into six broad habitat types in Figures 13.1 and 13.2.

13.17 Figure 13.1 shows the gross change in mean species number for all plots surveyed in both 1978 and 1990, regardless of whether the plots remained in the same broad habitat type. In this analysis, there were significant losses of species diversity in semi-improved grassland (–13%), woodland (–14%) and upland grass mosaics (–11%). There was a gain in diversity in moorland habitats (+7%).

13.18 The second analysis in Figure 13.2 shows the change in species numbers for the plots that remained within the same habitat type in 1978 and 1990. In this analysis, there were significant losses of diversity in arable fields (–29%) and woodlands (–20%), and a gain in diversity in moorland habitats (+8%).

13.19 The results show a general reduction of plant species diversity between 1978 and 1990 in the most widely occurring vegetation of fields and woods. In contrast, the plant species diversity of moorland habitats has increased, although this may be associated with disturbance, and the spread of acid grassland in these inherently species-poor habitats.

13.20 Between 1984 and 1990, there was a net loss of 23% of hedges (about 130,000km) in Britain. This was the result

both of hedge removal and degradation, and it occurred despite the planting or regeneration of about 50,000 km of hedges. There was also a loss of quality. Between 1978 and 1990, on average, one plant species was lost from each 10 metres of hedge, an 8% loss of plant species diversity.

BOX 13.3
ENDEMIC SPECIES IN THE UK

GROUP	NUMBER OF ENDEMIC SPECIES
Lower plants	About 20 bryophyte species
Higher plants	About 43 species (excluding microspecies)
Invertebrates	About 9 species
Vertebrates	One species: Scottish Crossbill

BOX 13.4
EXAMPLES OF SPECIES WHERE THE UK HOLDS A SIGNIFICANT PROPORTION OF THE EUROPEAN OR WORLD POPULATION

SPECIES	PROPORTION OF POPULATION
Bluebell (endemic to Europe)	Unknown; Estimated over 30% of the European/World population
Snail Leiostyle anglica	Unknown: Estimated 70% of world range
Grey seal	About half world population
Gannet	About 60% of the world population nest in Britain
Pink-footed Goose	About 80% of the world population overwinter in Scotland and England

CONCERNS

13.21 The main factors affecting biodiversity in the UK are:

- loss and fragmentation of habitats such as chalk grassland, heather moorland, hay meadows and wetlands, and of linear features such as hedgerows, as a result of such factors as intensified farming practices, abstraction of water, and development and road construction;

- declining quality of habitats in terms of species diversity, resulting from neglect or abandonment and from the decline of traditional forms of management of land and woodland as they become increasingly uneconomic and difficult to sustain;

- point source or diffuse pollution arising from a variety of sources including effluent from sewerage treatment works and industrial processes, run-off from agricultural chemicals or farm waste, and acid deposition as a result of burning fossil fuels.

CURRENT PROGRAMMES

Species conservation

13.22 To conserve species effectively, the UK needs to take a variety of actions. Concentrating on the conservation of sites and habitats addresses the needs of many species concentrated within particular areas. Many plants and animals, however, have widely dispersed populations. They are not generally amenable to site-based conservation initiatives but, instead, require the retention of such features of the wider countryside as hedges, copses, ponds and flushes. Such features can be essential in preventing populations becoming isolated, vulnerable to extinction, and incapable of natural recolonisation. The conservation of species where individuals are small or difficult to identify, or where the population is not mobile and inhabits a very small area (for example, a lichen on a tree trunk), presents special problems.

13.23 Rare and vulnerable species require more specific action. Many of these are protected under existing legislation. The Wildlife and Countryside Act 1981 gives specific protection to all whales, porpoises, dolphins and bats, six other mammals, all species of reptiles and amphibians, five species of fish and 64 invertebrates, to 168 species of plants, and to all birds.

Species recovery and Species Action Plans

13.24 In 1990, the Nature Conservancy Council produced a report, *Recovery: a proposed programme for Britain's protected species*[3], explaining the action required to achieve a return to a more favourable status of all the UK species other than birds protected under the Wildlife and Countryside Act 1981. The report is an important source for selecting species needing help. In 1991, English Nature launched an innovative Species Recovery Programme to assist specific endangered native plants and animals. Species are selected because they can benefit from targeted help. Each is tackled through its own costed plan, and English Nature work in partnership with landowners and voluntary bodies. In 1993, 22 species are being given assistance under the programme, including the fen violet, the dormouse, the red squirrel and the large blue butterfly. Two projects, for the rough marsh-mallow and the starfruit, have already been completed. The RSPB has launched an initiative under which, in conjunction with the country agencies and other relevant organisations, it will prepare an action plan for each of the 117 species listed in the Red Data Book on birds. Box 13.5 gives an example of how voluntary conservation organisations, landowners and Government Departments can help with the plan, in this case for the stone curlew.

13.25 Many of the projects in the "recovery" programme are already producing encouraging results – such as the initiative to reintroduce the Large Blue Butterfly which became extinct in this country in 1979 (see Box 13.6). Thanks to the programme, this species has now been re-established on four sites. Recovery needs to be seen as the next stage in the successful conservation of endangered species. Perhaps the most notable recovery is in many birds of prey, for example sparrowhawks and peregrines, which have come back from being severely endangered.

Protected areas

13.26 Since 1949, there has been a framework of statutory measures to safeguard wildlife habitats and natural environmental features. Some of these, such as NNRs and Sites of Special Scientific Interest (SSSI), are established under UK legislation. Others represent the UK's response to international obligations.

Sites of Special Scientific Interest

13.27 Sites of Special Scientific Interest (SSSIs) are sites that are identified and protected because of their importance to

Table 13.1	Areas of special scientific interest, 1993, *UK*		
	Number	**Hectares**	**% of territory**
England	3,759	885,742	6.8
Scotland	1,364	845,609	10.7
Wales	876	205,714	9.9
Northern Ireland	46	48,083	3.4
Total	6,045	1,985,148	8.1

Source: EN, SNH, CCW, DOE(NI)

BOX 13.5

ACTION FOR THE STONE CURLEW: AN EXAMPLE OF THE ROLE OF GOVERNMENT DEPARTMENTS IN BIODIVERSITY ACTION.

The stone curlew provides an example of how national priorities for species should be translated into specific action within targeted areas, and of how Government itself, as a landowner and policy-maker, has a major role to play in sustaining and enhancing the country's biodiversity.

The Stone Curlew Action Plan aims to increase the breeding stone curlew population in England from around 160 pairs to 200 pairs by the year 2000 within their present distribution, while encouraging recolonisation of sites within the past breeding range, and increasing the proportion of the population breeding on semi-natural grassland habitats.

The stone curlew is a rare migrant breeder, mainly confined to the Breckland of East Anglia and the Wessex downlands. The species traditionally nested on short-cropped turf containing areas of bare ground. Their conversion to arable use as afforestation, together with a relaxation or cessation of grazing pressure on the remaining grasslands, has significantly reduced the extent of suitable habitats across the traditional range of the stone curlew. A high proportion of nests are now found within arable crops, especially sugar beet, where the nests and chicks are highly vulnerable.

The main objective of the Plan is to secure the long-term future of the stone curlew in its principal population cores by, firstly, enhancing the management of existing semi-natural grasslands, and secondly, re-creating habitats suitable for colonisation. This involves a wide range of actions promoting the sympathetic management of land for stone curlews. They include influencing agricultural policy, including ESA management prescriptions and designations, cereal extensification and set-aside, and encouraging positive management of SSSIs supporting breeding stone curlew through advice to landowners and management entering into agreements with English Nature.

As major landowners within Breckland and Wessex, the Ministry of Defence (MOD) and the Forestry Commission must play a major role in re-establishing appropriately managed areas for recolonisation by stone curlew. MOD training ranges on Thetford and Salisbury Plain already hold important stone curlew populations. The MOD is already involved in management experiments on its ranges, leaving bare soil areas for nesting and feeding. Achieving suitably high levels of grazing, by sheep or rabbits is another issue under consideration. In addition, forest restructuring plans in the Forestry Commission Thetford Forest are an opportunity for re-creating areas of grassy heath suitable for stone curlew.

The policies of the Ministry of Agriculture, Fisheries and Food are key to the future of the stone curlew on existing farmland. The Brecklands Environmentally Sensitive Area includes prescriptions aimed at re-establishing grass heaths. The Arable Set-Aside scheme will allow large areas of former cropland in both Breckland and Wessex to be left bare in the spring which could provide ideal nesting conditions. In the longer term, a carefully targeted Habitat Scheme may create new grass heath areas, helping to link existing, fragmented heaths.

Britain's natural heritage. These sites may be of interest because of flora, fauna, geological or physiographical features. The statutory conservation bodies have a duty to identify and notify landowners and occupiers, local planning authorities and the appropriate Secretary of State of all those sites which have a special scientific interest. Areas of Special Scientific Interest (ASSIs) are notified by the DOE(NI) and are protected by similar legislation to that for SSSIs in Britain (see Table 13.1).

National Nature Reserves

13.28 NNRs are areas of national and sometimes international importance, which are owned or leased by the appropriate statutory conservation body, or bodies approved by them, or are managed in accordance with Nature Reserve Agreements with landowners and occupiers. For most of these reserves, management plans have been prepared and implemented. NNRs serve a variety of purposes, notably the conservation of the special interest of sites, the provision of

BOX 13.6
RE-ESTABLISHMENT OF THE LARGE BLUE BUTTERFLY

The large blue butterfly is the rarest of the British blue butterflies.

In England it was formerly found in some 90 sites in the Midlands and South West and it finally became extinct in Devon in 1979.

The demise of the butterfly was caused particularly by the loss of its habitat. It needs very closely grazed grassland, often on steep sided chalk valleys containing patches of wild thyme on which the females lay their eggs.

The caterpillars feed on the thyme and, after three weeks, flick themselves on to the ground where they wait to be found by one species of red ant attracted by a secretion from the caterpillar. Within four hours the caterpillar mimics an ant grub by inflating the skin behind its head. Believing it to be an ant grub, the ant carries it back to its nest where the caterpillar feeds on the grubs (before and after hibernating in the nest) until it emerges from the ground as an adult the next June.

Scrub encroachment and lack of traditional grazing on original sites have eliminated the ants and the thyme crucial to the existence of the large blue.

Experiments to re-establish the butterfly have been ongoing since 1983. In 1991, a five year programme was initiated as a partnership between English Nature's Species Recovery Programme, the Institute of Terrestrial Ecology and the British Butterfly Conservation Society, with support from the National Trust, the County Wildlife Trusts and other landowners at the sites concerned.

Key objectives of the programme are to recreate the habitat on at least six sites and establish viable self sustaining populations of 400–5,000 on each. Traditional grazing levels are being re-established and the levels of thyme and red ants are being carefully managed and monitored to achieve a favourable balance in the overall species composition and vegetation structure. Five sites have already been restored.

Caterpillars from Sweden are being reared to the stage that they can be released on site to be transported by ants to their nests. The numbers of those reaching maturity and the quantity and distribution of their eggs are being carefully monitored. The butterflies have been successfully introduced to four of the sites. Early results of the breeding and egg laying on two of these are promising. An important feature of the project is the benefit to other species in the habitats concerned, many of which are themselves rare or uncommon.

Other butterfly species to have increased as a result of this project are the high brown and small pearl bordered fritillary.

sites for research and study, the provision of advice on, and the demonstration of, conservation management, the furtherance of education, and the provision of facilities for amenity use and access for the quiet enjoyment of nature. NNRs are also classified as SSSIs and attract similar protection.

13.29 At the end of March 1993, there were 45 NNRs in Northern Ireland with an area of 4,322 hectares. In Scotland, the equivalent figures were 70 (114,486 hectares), in Wales 49 (13,397 hectares) and in England 140 (57,335 hectares). The figures for Britain are included within those for SSSIs in Table 13.1.

13.30 Conservation legislation in the UK has developed alongside a comprehensive system of town and country planning legislation, and focuses on the wise management of the nation's land resources and the safeguarding of NNRs and SSSIs (see Chapter 35). The use of land for nature conservation is a material consideration for planning authorities when considering planning applications likely to affect a protected site. Planning authorities must consult the appropriate statutory conservation agency before granting permission for development within, or which may affect, such a site. Since the Environmental Protection Act 1990, planning authorities also have to consult about planning applications in any consultation area around an SSSI defined by the statutory conservation agency.

13.31 In addition, the amended SSSI system, introduced in the Wildlife and Countryside Act 1981, was designed to protect SSSIs from operations outside the scope of planning controls. Owners and occupiers of SSSIs are required to give the appropriate statutory conservation agency four months notice in writing if they intend to carry out, or cause or permit to be carried out, any potentially damaging operation (PDO), listed in the notification of the SSSI. The agency can seek to persuade owners or occupiers to modify or refrain from their proposals, or may offer to enter into a management agreement under which compensation may be paid if the owner or occupier agrees to retain the special interest of the site.

EC Birds Directive: Special Protection Areas

13.32 The Directive requires the designation of Special Protection Areas (SPAs) for breeding and migratory species of bird and measures to prevent damage or disturbance to SPAs. By November 1993, 74 SPAs had been designated in the UK, covering over 245,000 hectares. Some further 150 sites have been identified provisionally as meriting designation and there is an active programme in hand.

EC Habitats Directive – Natura 2000: Special Areas of Conservation

13.33 The Habitats and Species Directive sets out requirements for the creation of Special Areas of Conservation (SACs). These SACs, with SPAs classified under the Birds Directive, will form an EC series of sites to be known as Natura 2000. This coherent European ecological network is designed to maintain habitats and species of community interest at favourable conservation status: defined in terms of the natural range being stable or increasing and of the existence of structures and functions necessary for the long-term maintenance of that status.

13.34 The Annexes of the Directive list habitats and species of EC interest. They are listed because, within the EC, they are endangered, vulnerable, rare or endemic, have a small natural range, or are outstanding examples of characteristics typical of the community's biogeographical regions. Annexes I and II of the Directive list those habitats and species whose conservation requires the SAC designation, which will contribute to the Natura 2000 network. Of these, some 75 habitat types and 40 taxa of animals and plants occur within the UK. Some are classed as priority habitats and species for which stronger protection within SACs is required.

13.35 In the UK, the protection of SPAs and SACs will be based on the habitat conservation measures which derive from the notification of SSSIs. Additional measures necessary to ensure that the requirements of the Directive can be delivered will be enacted by Regulations under Section 2 of the European Communities Act 1972. This will ensure that damage or deterioration to Natura 2000 sites is only permitted, if there is no alternative, for reasons of overriding public interest.

13.36 The Directive requires member states to bring the necessary legislative and administrative provisions into force by June 1994. National lists of candidate SACs should be submitted to the European Commission by June 1995. The Commission must then agree the EC list with member states by June 1998. Designation of SACs to secure the Natura 2000 network must be in place by 2004. The UK intends to meet these deadlines.

Other designations and schemes

13.37 Since their inception, the Forestry Commission (FC) and the Department of Agriculture for Northern Ireland (DANI) have had, as one of their objectives, the use of their landholding for purposes other than forestry. As well as providing for recreation, the FC and DANI regard state-owned forests as an important ecological resource. Management aims to enhance the nature conservation value of these forests as a whole as well

as safeguarding special habitats. The FC and DANI have designated certain forests (17 in Britain and 9 in Northern Ireland) as National Forest Parks. In addition to SSSIs and ASSIs, special habitats include Forest Nature Reserves and other conservation areas identified in forest conservation plans which have been drawn up for all national forests. There is considerable scope for the enhancement of biodiversity as the new forests created this century are restructured and redesigned for their second and third rotations.

13.38 The Agriculture Departments, in consultation with other organisations, have been developing a package of programmes to encourage farming practices that protect and enhance wildlife habitats, valued landscapes and natural resources, as well as promoting new opportunities for public access to the countryside. A designation which is of great importance for wildlife habitats is that of Environmentally Sensitive Area (ESAs). ESAs are areas of high landscape and conservation value in which farmers and crofters may benefit from payments for managing their land in ways which conserve and enforce the landscape and wildlife habitats. Participants in the scheme enter 10 year management agreements, which are reviewed after five years. Each designated area has its own distinctive character and the payments offered relate to specific requirements supporting and promoting local diversity.

13.39 By December 1993, there were 16 ESAs in England, totalling 831,000 hectares, and six more were planned, covering 318,000 hectares. There were four in Wales, totalling 358,700 hectares, and two more were planned, covering 143,000 hectares. In Scotland, there were 10 ESAs, totalling about 1.4 million hectares. In Northern Ireland, there were three ESAs, totalling 131,000 hectares, and two more were planned, covering 116,700 hectares. The scheme's flexibility means that it can match incentives to specific local requirements and can therefore support and promote local diversity.

13.40 The Agriculture Departments plan to launch a number of other incentive schemes in 1994, including a Moorland Scheme to protect and improve heather and other shrubby moorland; a Habitat Scheme to re-create a range of specific habitats such as water fringes, upland scrub and saltmarshes, and new Nitrate Sensitive Areas. These initiatives have been developed in response to the EC Agri-Environment Regulation, an important element in the Common Agricultural Policy reform package agreed in 1992. The Agriculture Departments also operate the Farm Woodland Premium Scheme which encourages farmers to plant new woodlands, especially broadleaved, on land taken out of productive agriculture. These schemes offer considerable potential for enhancing biodiversity.

THE WAY FORWARD

13.41 Many policies and programmes are already in place to conserve UK wildlife and habitats. The Government recognises, however, that further work is needed to achieve the UK's conservation goals over the next 20 years.

13.42 Chapter 10 of the Biodiversity Action Plan sets out a list of actions, to which the Government and its agencies are committed, to conserve, and, where practicable, enhance wild species and wildlife habitats. To ensure that this work is focused to the best advantage, the Government proposes to establish a Biodiversity Action Plan Steering Group with representatives drawn from central and local government, agencies, institutions holding significant collections of materials, voluntary organisations and academic bodies. As its immediate remit, it will have responsibility for overseeing:

- the development of a range of specific costed targets for key species and habitats for the years 2000 and 2010, to be published in European Nature Conservation Year 1995;

- a working group, established in June 1993, designed to improve the accessibility and coordination of existing biological datasets, to provide common standards for future recording, and to examine the feasibility in due course of a single UK Biota Database;

- the preparation and implementation of a campaign to increase public awareness of, and involvement in, conserving UK biodiversity;

- the establishment of a review process for the delivery of commitments set out in Chapter 10 of the Biodiversity Action Plan.

13.43 The Group will be set the target of reporting on the specific elements of its remit, and particularly on targets for key species and habitats, during the European Nature Conservation Year 1995.

REFERENCES AND FURTHER READING

1   *Biodiversity: The UK Action Plan.* Cm 2428. HMSO, 1994. ISBN 0–10–124282–4.

2   *Countryside Survey 1990 Main Report.* Countryside series 1990 volume 2. Department of the Environment, 1993.

3   *Recovery: a proposed programme for British protected species.* Nature Conservation Council Publication, 1990.

SECTION 3
ECONOMIC DEVELOPMENT AND SUSTAINABILITY

CHAPTER 14

ECONOMIC ACTIVITY

14.1 One of the keys to sustainable development is to be found in the integration of economic development and environmental protection. This Section therefore turns to the main sectors of economic activity and the issues they raise for sustainability.

14.2 Sustainable development does not mean the preservation of the environment at all costs; nor does it mean that development must always have priority because of its importance for wealth and job creation. Much economic activity will have an impact on the environment, although this will not necessarily be harmful and in some cases is beneficial. An important concern is to establish precisely what environmental impacts arise from the development of the economy, and what problems they cause.

14.3 At present, future levels of harmful emissions, mineral extraction and so on, are forecast on the basis of assumptions about growing Gross Domestic Product (GDP). Since 1945, annual GDP growth has been around 2.3% and this might be expected to result in more pollution and resource depletion. Against this, the evidence is that, as economies advance, industrial and service activity is increasingly resource efficient: energy use is a striking case in point. There is no reason to assume that the potential for this kind of change is exhausted although, of course, its achievement requires continuing effort to be devoted to research and development, and to investment in new and more efficient processes.

14.4 Decision-makers throughout the UK, and in other countries, need to understand how these links between economic activity and environmental impacts will change. New technologies will often reduce environmental impacts, but will sometimes create new (and possibly less tractable) ones. As the structure of industry changes in response to changing demands, the scale and nature of polluting impacts will also change. Increasing the resource efficiency of industry will be good for the environment. Steady economic development should allow investment in new technologies, development of cleaner products, and further reductions in the resource intensity of production.

14.5 This is the positive side of the story. The other side must be a continuing concern to identify the impacts that are potentially harmful, whether through the demands for natural resources, or through the emissions of pollutants and waste. This Section identifies the main issues that arise in the different economic sectors.

14.6 Concerns about sustainability relate not only to a country's own environment but to the environmental impacts which its economic activity has beyond national boundaries. The UK, like other countries, thus needs to consider the impact of its international economic activity (trade and investment) globally and in individual overseas countries. Some academics have described this as a "footprint", which may have positive or negative impacts and cover both deliberate action and unintended side-effects. The following chapters explain some of these impacts sector by sector.

CHAPTER 15

AGRICULTURE

A Sustainable Framework

- To provide an adequate supply of good quality food and other products in an efficient manner.
- To minimise consumption of non-renewable and other resources, including by recycling.
- To safeguard the quality of soil, water and air.
- To preserve and, where feasible, enhance biodiversity and the appearance of the landscape, including the UK's archaeological heritage.

Trends

- The drive for increased food production during and following the Second World War had a major effect on the countryside.
- The level of support under the EC Common Agricultural Policy (CAP) has encouraged a further intensification of production, with consequent adverse effects on the environment.
- The 1992 CAP Reform represented an important change of emphasis but the full effects are still to be seen.

Current Responses

- There is a range of UK schemes in operation to encourage environmentally friendly farming and, in accordance with the 1992 CAP reform, further measures have been announced.
- In addition, advice, research and monitoring and, where appropriate, regulation play important roles.

The Way Forward

- For the future, the Government will encourage environmentally sensitive agriculture, and will work for further CAP reform to reduce levels of support and integrate fully environmental considerations.

THE ROLE OF UK AGRICULTURE

15.1 The UK enjoys a range of natural characteristics that combine to favour farming over most of its land area. A wide variety of agricultural systems has evolved over the centuries to match local environments. An advanced infrastructure to support the resulting production has also developed. The efficiency of UK agriculture has been increasing rapidly over a long period. This has led to greatly increased food production, although in recent years, it has manifested itself as reduced inputs rather than increased output: the 18% increase in efficiency since 1985 comprises a 3% increase in output and a 15% reduction in resources used.

15.2 The industry contributes nearly £7 billion to the UK Gross Domestic Product (GDP). Self-sufficiency in those foodstuffs which can be produced in the UK rose from 60% in 1970 to around 75% in the early 1980s, which level has been sustained. Since the 1950s, the area of land used by agriculture has fallen marginally, but the condition of over 18.5 million hectares (nearly 77% of the land area) remains dependent on the farmers who work it and whose predecessors have shaped it over the centuries. Over the same 40 year time scale, the industry's productivity has increased markedly – as evidenced by the two thirds reduction in the agricultural labour force. Over 0.5 million people remain directly employed in agriculture today, around 2% of the total work force, although this has much greater importance in some rural areas. Many other jobs in the supply trade and food manufacturing industries are dependent on agriculture. Moreover, agriculture's role in providing an attractive and varied countryside makes a significant contribution not only to quality of life, but also to rural economic activity, particularly tourism.

15.3 Thanks to the advanced development of its agriculture and general economic prosperity the UK is able to pay more attention to the way in which food supplies are produced and, in particular, to the impact of agriculture on the environment. These are important public concerns. But the production of food and the protection of the environment need not be conflicting activities. They are best seen as mutually dependent – a point that is particularly clear in the UK where, to a greater degree than in many countries, the countryside owes much of its appearance and diversity to generations of agricultural processes. Agriculture today remains the main influence over the appearance of the countryside.

AGRICULTURE AND SUSTAINABLE DEVELOPMENT

15.4 To meet the needs of sustainable development, agriculture needs to balance a number of aims:
- to provide an adequate supply of good quality food and other products in an efficient manner;
- to minimise consumption of non-renewable and other resources, including by recycling;
- to safeguard the quality of soil, water and air;
- to preserve and, where feasible, enhance biodiversity and the appearance of the landscape, including the UK's archaeological heritage.

15.5 The industry's interdependence with the environment is probably unique. Farmers rely on the fertility of their soils and an adequate water supply for their crops and livestock. The crops and livestock themselves form part of the natural nutrient cycle, drawing on soil resources and fertilisers and returning them through crop residues and animal manures to the land. Landowners, therefore, have a long term interest in the productive capacity of their land; farmers' own interests are best served by utilising natural resources wisely. Nevertheless, this tradition of stewardship is not always sufficient to ensure protection of the environment.

15.6 Changes in agricultural production have the potential to cause considerable environmental effects, particularly as agriculture occupies so much of the land area. The drive for increased food production during and since the Second World War has certainly had a substantial effect on the rural environment and the appearance of the countryside. Old grassland has been ploughed up, wetlands drained and traditional features, such as hedgerows, removed or neglected. These changes, combined with the substantial increase in the use of fertilisers and pesticides, have had a major impact on the wildlife of the countryside. The level of agricultural support under the EC Common Agricultural Policy (CAP), together with continuing technological improvements, has stimulated further intensification of production. Heather moorland continues to be overgrazed in places. Nitrates, farm wastes and pesticides cause problems of water pollution in some areas. Agriculture is also a source of greenhouse gases and ammonia. These developments are explained in more detail in Section 2.

15.7 The financial costs of agricultural support, meanwhile, have been high for taxpayers and consumers, and have resulted in a misallocation of national resources. Internationally, the CAP has imposed other costs. Producers outside the EC – including those in developing countries – have found the market for their goods distorted by the CAP's system of support subsidies and import levies (see Box 15.1 for a brief explanation of how the CAP support system works).

CURRENT POLICIES

15.8 Within the EC, the UK has consistently worked for lower CAP support prices. Lower support levels not only reduce economic and international trade distortions, but also help to reduce the environmental pressures from agriculture. The 1992 CAP reform package marked significant progress in reducing EC support prices – and hence consumer prices – and in decreasing the proportion of farmers' support which is linked to how much they produce. For cereals the assistance provided through price support is being sharply reduced and replaced by payments linked to the cropped area; and payments on other major crops have been converted from a quantity to an area basis. Farmers are only eligible for these payments if they set aside a proportion of their arable land. Moreover, payments are restricted to land which was already in arable use in 1991; there is thus no incentive for a farmer to create new arable land. The crops subject to these arrangements account for some 85% of the total arable area. Reductions in prices and increases in direct payments are also a feature of changes in support for the livestock sector. Although the payments remain linked to animal numbers, they are limited by quotas and, in some cases, are subject to progressively reducing limits on stocking density (see Box 15.2).

BOX 15.1
HOW THE CAP WORKS

The CAP supports EC agriculture in two ways: through commodity support measures and through measures to improve agricultural structures. Some 90% of EC expenditure on the CAP is directed towards commodity support.

Traditionally, the aim of assistance to agriculture under the CAP has been to safeguard the level of producers' returns by supporting market prices at predetermined levels. A number of devices are used for this purpose: surplus products are removed from the market by intervention buying and by export to non-EC countries with the assistance of export refunds; imports from outside the EC are subject to levies to ensure that they do not undercut the EC's support price.

Notable developments over the last 10-15 years have included: increasing use of **direct payment** to farmers instead of complete reliance on price support; **automatic adjustment of prices** in relation to the volume of production; or, in some cases, **limits per farmer on supported production**. These developments have all been taken further by the 1992 reform of the CAP (see 15.8 and Box 15.2).

There are a number of EC schemes to improve agricultural structures and to **encourage environmentally friendly farming**.

In 1992, expenditure on such support in the EC reached £22 billion under the guarantee section of the European Agricultural Guidance and Guarantee Funds (EAGGF).

15.9 The recent CAP reforms should do much to reduce environmental pressures. Many of the land use and landscape changes which have resulted from agricultural developments since the Second World War are the result of production incentives which are now being reduced. For example, although the usage of pesticides and fertilisers had increased significantly in previous decades, since the early 1980s the tonnages used have fallen. By 1992, the amount of nitrogen fertiliser used was 5% lower than a decade earlier[1]. Between 1980 and 1992, the amounts of pesticide (measured in terms of active ingredient) applied in England and Wales fell by more than 29%, although the area treated (counting subsequent treatment of the same area as additional area treated) rose by about 10%[2]. With the implementation of the CAP reforms the trends towards lower tonnages of pesticides and fertilisers are likely to continue.

15.10 The UK has also strongly advocated the integration of environmental considerations into the CAP and has played a leading role in getting the EC to include, in the CAP, measures to encourage environmentally friendly farming. In 1989, the EC agreed that the support arrangements for upland livestock

---

BOX 15.2
1992 CAP REFORM

The CAP reform agreement of May 1992 dealt with the major agricultural commodities, namely arable crops and the livestock sector. The agreement represented a significant shift in the direction of the EC's agricultural policy by switching support away from the end product and towards the producer. The significant cuts in support prices and reduced access to intervention should reduce over-production, encouraging farmers to look to the real market for their returns. Furthermore, by narrowing the gap between internal and world prices, international trade tensions should be eased. For the first time, environmental considerations were made an integral part of agricultural policy.

For individual commodities, key elements of the reform were:

Cereals
- support prices will be reduced by up to 35% over three years from 1993;
- farmers will receive compensatory direct payments, on an area basis, provided that they set aside 15% of the area for which they are claiming (small claims, less than about 15 hectares in the UK, are exempt from the set-aside requirement);

Oilseeds, "fodder" peas and beans
- these come under the scheme described above, with separate rates of direct payment;

Beef
- support prices will be cut by 15% over three years and new restrictions will be introduced on intervention;
- both the beef special premium and the suckler cow premium will be substantially increased, but claims to be limited by stocking rates;
- individual producer quotas introduced for the suckler cow premium, together with regional ceilings on numbers of claims for the beef special premium;

Sheep
- individual producer quotas to be introduced for the annual premium with producers receiving quota at the level of their 1991 claim;

Milk
- the intervention price for butter to be cut by 5% over two years (equivalent to a cut in the support price for milk of around 2 %);

Accompanying measures
- member states are required to introduce a programme of measures to assist environmentally friendly farming and afforestation.

farmers should be adjusted to allow overgrazing conditions to be applied; and, in 1991, it was agreed that member states should attach environmental management conditions to set-aside payments. In the 1992 reform package, the EC agreed that all member states should introduce programmes for encouraging environmentally friendly farming, and recognised the need for greater integration of environmental considerations into the CAP. More recently, the UK has made further progress in securing acceptance within the EC that CAP support payments can be subject to environmental conditions.

15.11 The Government has also worked at national level to encourage farmers' dual role as producers of food and guardians of the countryside. There is a range of schemes

BOX 15.3
MAIN UK ENVIRONMENTAL SCHEMES RELEVANT TO AGRICULTURE

There are, at present, five national schemes where the Government offers economic incentives to farmers to manage their land in a way which delivers environmental benefits. Three of these schemes are available in specifically defined parts of the country.

- The largest scheme operates in 33 **Environmentally Sensitive Areas** (ESAs), covering over 2.7 million hectares, where incentives are offered to farmers to farm in ways designed to protect or enhance the environmental quality of parts of the country noted for their natural beauty, rich habitats and historic interest.
- On designated **Sites of Special Scientific Interest** (SSSIs), the Government may provide payment for adopting particular management practices to protect a habitat or species. Such agreements currently cover approximately 98,500 hectares.
- In 10 areas in England where high nitrate levels have built up in groundwater, local farmers are asked to restrict their agricultural activities in return for payment under the pilot **Nitrate Sensitive Areas** (NSAs). These areas cover over 10,700 hectares.

The other two schemes are not restricted to specifically designated areas:

- The **Countryside Stewardship** scheme in England aims to protect and enhance valued landscapes and habitats and to improve opportunities for public enjoyment of the countryside. It now covers over 60,000 hectares. In Wales, the **Tir Cymen** scheme operates on similar lines, although there is an additional basic requirement that the whole farm should follow a code of good environmental practice.
- Under the **Farm Woodland Premium Scheme**, payments are offered to farmers who take land out of agricultural production and convert it to woodland, with the assistance of establishment grants under the **Woodland Grant Scheme**.

Alongside these land management schemes are separate grants paid on environmentally beneficial works. The largest is:
- The **Farm and Conservation Grant Scheme**, which provides grants for pollution control equipment and environmental improvements such as hedge planting.

In addition, a range of **new** voluntary schemes have recently been proposed in order to fulfil the requirements of the EC "Agri-Environment Regulation" which the UK successfully maintained should form part of the 1992 CAP reform package. These are:
- new **ESAs**, expanding the areas covered by the scheme to over 3.2 million hectares;
- new **opportunities for public access in ESAs**, to provide opportunities for public enjoyment of the UK's most beautiful countryside;
- new **NSAs**, to help protect groundwater catchments affected by high nitrate levels;
- a **Moorland Scheme**, to reduce overgrazing of heather and other shrubby moorland by sheep;
- a **Countryside Access Scheme**, to provide opportunities for public access to the most suitable set-aside land;
- a **Habitat Scheme,** to create and improve a range of valuable wildlife habitats in areas removed for the long term from agricultural production;
- an **Organic Aid Scheme**, to assist conventional farmers to convert to organic production. References and further reading

which provide financial assistance and incentives to encourage environmentally beneficial farming. Box 15.3 provides further details, including a list of the measures planned for the UK programmes under the EC scheme for encouraging environmentally friendly farming. These existing and planned new environmental schemes represent a substantial commitment to protecting and enhancing the wildlife habitats and landscape of the countryside. The schemes include measures to protect and improve the condition of heather in the uplands; to reduce the leaching of nitrates into water used for public supply; to safeguard and improve wildlife habitats including water fringes; to provide more access to the countryside; and to assist farmers to convert to organic production.

15.12 Livestock support payments, including Hill Livestock Compensatory Allowances, also play a key role in maintaining viable farming populations in the UK's less favoured areas and in conserving the upland countryside. The environmental schemes are complemented by the Government's efforts to ensure that the various flood defence agencies manage wetlands so as to safeguard their environmental value. Information and advice also make an important contribution. Farmers can obtain free advice about how to avoid pollution and assistance in drawing up farm waste management plans. Free *Codes of Good Agricultural Practice* on the protection of water, air and soil are available[3]. The Government helps to fund the Farming and Wildlife Advisory Group (FWAG), the Agricultural Development and Advisory Service (ADAS), the Scottish Agricultural College and the Game Conservancy which advise farmers on conservation.

15.13 Where necessary, regulations are used to provide essential environmental safeguards. The Government's policies for minimising pesticide use and ensuring that the pesticides which are used are not a hazard to human health or the environment are underpinned by statutory controls on both their approval and use. The storage of agricultural wastes and fuel oil is also subject to regulations aimed at avoiding pollution; and in 1992 planning regulations were introduced to allow local planning authorities to control aspects of agricultural development, such as siting of new farm buildings, which had been causing public concern.

THE FUTURE

15.14 The effects of the reforms and initiatives described in the preceding paragraphs have not yet all been seen. The 1992 CAP reforms will not be fully implemented until 1995 and their full effects may take even longer to work through. None of the new measures to encourage environmentally friendly farming, which are described in Box 15.3, has yet

been introduced pending the EC Commission's approval. However, within the period covered by this Strategy, the policies which are already in train should achieve substantial improvements. In particular, having regard to the key aims in 15.4, there should be further reductions in agriculture's contribution to the environmental pressures identified in Section 2 of this Strategy. As explained in 15.8, the main reason for this will be the reduction in levels of price support which will, in turn, reduce the incentives to intensive production and which, from the point of view of the UK environment, is the most important feature of the 1992 CAP reform. The Government will continue to work for further improvements in the CAP and, in particular, for:

● further reductions in support levels;
● a higher proportion of EC expenditure on direct payments to farmers to be applied to encouraging more environmentally sensitive farming;
● the application, wherever appropriate, of environmental conditions to support payments;
● the EC to give more attention to environmental considerations in deciding how to implement the various support mechanisms, such as set-aside.

15.15 In addition the Government will be pursuing a range of more specific policies and initiatives aimed at reducing the potentially polluting effects of agriculture. For pesticides, the UK and the EC have embarked on a review process which will ensure that pesticides used throughout the Community meet high standards of environmental protection. There will be a continuing programme of publicly funded research, aimed at identifying ways of further reducing pesticide use and encouraging integrated crop management systems with lower chemical inputs, together with a substantial research programme on all aspects of organic agriculture. Research into new plant varieties with resistance to pests and diseases will complement this work. The use as fertilisers of farm wastes, such as manures and slurry, is also subject to a range of initiatives aimed at minimising pollution risks and ensuring that these valuable by-products are used more efficiently in the future. A further advisory programme to help farmers with their waste management has been announced; and there is to be continued publicly funded research into farm waste problems, in particular to identify ways in which farmers themselves can minimise the pollution risks. Agriculture's contribution to excess nitrate levels in water is also to be tackled by the expanded programme of Nitrate Sensitive Areas which is mentioned in Box 15.3: new areas covering some 35,000 hectares are to be designated in 1994. In addition, the Government will be bringing forward proposals for more extensive Nitrate Vulnerable Zones which will include measures to reduce nitrate pollution from agricultural sources.

15.16 Section 2 of this Strategy also refers to problems, which are arising in some localities, of soil erosion and loss of quality due to intensive agricultural production. The *Code of Good Agricultural Practice for the Protection of Soil* will provide farmers with advice based on the latest research to help minimise such problems. The Code emphasises the importance of soil as a finite resource and recommends a range of cropping and cultivation practices aimed at protecting soil for the longer term. This advice will be reviewed from time to time to ensure that it takes account of advances in our knowledge of soils. The Royal Commission on Environmental Pollution's forthcoming study on soil will also influence future policies. The Government's general policy of protecting the best agricultural land from irreversible development also helps to safeguard this important resource for the long term.

15.17 Publicly funded research and monitoring will also make a crucial contribution to the Government's future agricultural policies and the development of environmentally sensitive agricultural practices. Specific monitoring and review arrangements will check the effectiveness of individual measures to tackle environmental problems. In addition, there will be more general monitoring arrangements including, for example, the Government funded Environmental Change Network, which is monitoring a range of key environmental indicators on a number of sites, five of which are at agricultural research centres.

15.18 This chapter also sets out some of the areas where publicly funded research is investigating ways of minimising agriculture's adverse environmental impacts. These are only a part of a wide-ranging research programme which underpins the Government's policies for achieving more sustainable agricultural practices. Environmental and economic research helps to inform the Government's various initiatives for encouraging environmentally friendly farming. A four year collaborative LINK programme on Technologies for Sustainable Farming Systems was set up in 1991 with the aim of developing new production systems which are profitable, environmentally friendly and meet consumer demands: it is expected to lead to new farming techniques, using novel methods of weed, pest and disease control, integrated crop management and reduced chemical inputs, while retaining farm profitability. There is a need for further research into ways to reduce ammonia and greenhouse gas emissions which are practicable and cost-effective, and do not have adverse effects on other aspects of the environment. Other areas of research include the development of new crops, including new renewable energy sources, and possible new non-food uses for established crops. As necessary, the Government's policies for

agriculture will be adjusted to take account of the results of these monitoring and research programmes.

15.19 The industry itself, and others, also have a part to play in encouraging the sustainable use of resources. Many of the courses provided by agricultural colleges already cover the principles of sustainability. The demand for such training may well increase. The Training and Enterprise Councils, the Scottish Enterprise Companies and the Agricultural Training Board, who conduct regular training needs surveys, should identify the demand for training in sustainable agriculture issues and ensure the necessary training provision. Organisations, such as FWAG, which are partly industry-funded also provide advice to farmers on conservation matters; and, on some issues, distribution and supply organisations can help by keeping farmers informed of current best practice. Organisations such as the Guild of Conservation Grade Producers and LEAF (Linking the Environment and Farming) and those involved in organic production are examining existing industry-based initiatives to try to establish environmentally beneficial production standards.

15.20 There is scope, too, for increased cooperation among farmers themselves in the interest of better resource conservation. This opportunity has been illustrated recently by the steps which farmers have taken in some low rainfall areas to invest jointly in reservoir facilities. Farmers are also collaborating with the National Rivers Authority and the Ministry of Agriculture, Fisheries and Food (MAFF) in some areas over the continuity of irrigation supplies during spells of drought. In some parts of the country, joint ventures of this kind may offer the most practical solution to the industry's needs.

15.21 For its part, the Government will encourage sustainable agricultural policies and practices by pursuing the following aims and objectives:
- to work for more liberal world trade in agricultural products in the interests of more rational use of resources, and to remove current international trade distortions;
- to work for further reform of the CAP and, in particular, to reduce the levels of support and the resulting pressures on the environment, and to integrate environmental considerations fully into the CAP;
- to encourage an internationally competitive and environmentally sensitive UK agriculture, which has regard to the commitments in the *Biodiversity Action Plan*[4];
- to protect the best and most versatile agricultural land from development;
- to minimise the environmental impacts of agricultural wastes, particularly on water quality and emissions to air;
- to minimise the use of pesticides through the rigorous approval and review of products, through guidance to

users and through research and development;

● to facilitate access by farmers to reliable and up-to-date information on good environmental practice based on sound science, and to encourage them to act on these findings.

REFERENCES AND FURTHER READING

1   *British Survey of Fertiliser Practice.* MAFF/Scottish Office/Fertiliser Manufacturers Association, 1993.

2   *Report of Pesticide Usage Survey Group.* MAFF, 1993.

3   *Code of Good Agricultural Practice on the Protection of Water.* Ministry of Agriculture, Food and Fisheries. MAFF Publications, 1991.

    Code of Good Agricultural Practice on the Protection of Air. Ministry of Agriculture, Food and Fisheries. MAFF Publications, 1992.

    Code of Good Agricultural Practice on the Protection of Soil. Ministry of Agriculture, Food and Fisheries. MAFF Publications, 1993.

4   *Biodiversity: The UK Action Plan.* Cm 2428. HMSO, 1994. ISBN 0–10–124282–4.

CHAPTER 16

FORESTRY

A Sustainable Framework

- To manage forests in a way that sustains their environmental qualities as well as their productive potential.
- To apply the principle of multipurpose forestry to the creation of new forests and woodlands.
- To assist developing countries to produce timber more sustainably.

Trends

- A history of decline in forest cover, halted by Government intervention, which has secured a steady expansion of forest cover since the beginning of this century.
- The proportion of broadleaved planting has increased following the introduction of additional incentives.
- Timber production from existing woodlands and forests will rise to around three times the current level over the next 30 years.

Problems and Opportunities

- Income from the sale of forest products may not be sufficient to sustain the environmental benefits of forests. In such cases, Government support in the form of incentives will be needed.
- The creation of new forests and woodlands is a commercially marginal activity in the UK.
- The Government will continue to press for changes in the EC set-aside rules to encourage planting on set-aside land.
- The markets for hardwood timber need to be developed.
- Recent surveys of forest condition in the UK give cause for concern about tree health.

- A continuing expansion of tree cover will help to offset the UK's carbon dioxide emissions.

Current Responses

- Measures aimed at the retention and sound management of existing forests and woodlands are already in place.
- The Government and its agencies sponsor research into techniques of forest management and disseminate best practice.
- The Government is a signatory to the Helsinki Guidelines for the sustainable management of European forests and the conservation of their biodiversity.
- The Forestry Commission has announced a biodiversity initiative for Britain's forests.

The Way Forward

- The Government is committed to improving the management and conservation of existing woodlands and encouraging the expansion of forest cover.
- The Government will continue to promote multipurpose forestry in accordance with the Rio Principles.
- Expansion will be promoted through initiatives such as the new National Forest and Community Forests as well as through more broadly targeted incentives.
- The use of indigenous hardwoods will be promoted through research into innovative uses in energy production and construction.
- The Government is working through the Convention on International Trade in Endangered Species (CITES) to control the trade in rare and endangered species.
- Through multilateral aid programmes, the Government is assisting less developed countries and economies in transition to conserve and manage their forest resources.

INTRODUCTION

16.1 Forestry is generally an environmentally benign activity. The key to sustainability lies in protecting and enhancing the existing resource, and enabling timber production to increase whilst, at the same time, protecting the environment and increasing the many other benefits forests provide.

16.2 The Government is committed to a policy of setting multiple objectives for forestry. This means that the UK's forests are valued not only for their commercial potential but also for recreation, nature conservation and landscape enhancement. Forestry also has a part to play as a significant carbon sink.

HISTORIC AND FUTURE TRENDS

16.3 Over many centuries there has been a gradual loss of forest cover. From a peak of possibly as much as 80% of land area 7,000 years ago, cover declined to 20% by 1000, and fell to its lowest level of 5% at the start of this century.

These losses led to an overdependence on imported timber, which was the catalyst for the initiation in 1919 of a forest expansion programme. This programme has resulted in the doubling of cover to just over 10% (2.4 million hectares) of land area today. UK timber production from existing forests is set to rise to around three times current levels in about 30 years time.

16.4 The rapid expansion through this century brought a number of problems. New woodlands were sometimes poorly designed and sited, adversely affecting the landscape. Often, insufficient account was taken of the biodiversity value of land converted to forest use; and in some areas airborne pollutants captured by new forests led to acidification of soil and groundwater to levels which were harmful to wildlife.

16.5 The UK has, however, learnt from experience. Multipurpose objectives are now enshrined in the grant-giving and regulatory regimes which ensure that the full breadth of factors, including landscape, biodiversity, water, archaeology and recreation, are fully taken into account before planting is allowed to proceed with Government assistance.

16.6 The Forestry Commission (FC) is the Government Department with lead responsibility for forestry in mainland Britain (a function held in Northern Ireland by the Department of Agriculture (DANI) Forest Service). The FC's regulatory and grant-giving functions are carried out by its Forestry Authority arm; its Forest Enterprise arm manages the state-owned forests. Other Departments, particularly the Agriculture and Environment Departments, also have significant roles to play.

16.7 The UK *Forestry Programme*[1], published in conjunction with this Strategy, gives a detailed account of the Government's forestry policies and programmes.

PROTECTION AND MANAGEMENT OF FORESTS

16.8 Surveys of forest condition have given cause for concern about the health of UK forests in recent years. Many factors are involved and, although natural phenomena such as weather, insect pests and diseases are probably the main influences, it seems likely that air pollution does play a part. Despite substantial Government research in this area, it has not proved possible to disentangle all the factors relating to forest health and so quantify the amount of damage caused to trees by air pollution. Research in this area continues while air pollution itself is being tackled at source.

16.9 The FC, DANI Forest Service and the conservation agencies offer special grants to encourage the regeneration of native woodlands. In addition, there are several special programmes designed to halt decline of these natural resources and to encourage regeneration by bringing woodland into sustainable management: for example, the FC's Native Pinewoods and Highland Birchwoods projects in Scotland; the Cumbrian Broadleaves Project; the Anglian Woodlands projects in England; and Coed Cymru in Wales.

16.10 Since the mid 1980s, the previous loss of native woodland through deliberate conversion to agriculture and other forest types has virtually ceased. Felling is regulated by means of felling licences, grant scheme plans of operations, tree preservation orders and statutory development control. The Government operates a general policy that felled areas will be replanted. In addition, areas of broadleaved trees which are felled must be replanted with broadleaves and there is a general presumption against the conversion of ancient and semi-natural woodlands to other forest types. Regulations provide for action through the courts against illegal felling and replanting orders may be enforced in addition to fines.

16.11 The process of notification of Sites of Special Scientific Interest (SSSIs), or Areas of Special Scientific Interest in Northern Ireland, by the nature conservation agencies includes the identification of woodlands which meet appropriate scientific criteria. Some of these are designated as National Nature Reserves (NNRs), and the international significance of some types of ancient woodland has been recognised by their inclusion in Annex 1 of the EC Habitats Directive which provides special protection. All NNRs and many SSSIs are managed according to plans agreed with the owner. These plans are regularly reviewed and updated, and consultation always takes place where these sites are managed by the FC or are affected by an application under the Woodland Grant Scheme.

Research and training

16.12 There are many ways in which the practice of sustainable forestry is supported through research and training. Forestry related research is coordinated in Britain by the Forestry Research Coordinating Committee, which assesses research priorities, ensures liaison between forestry research organisations, and coordinates specific programmes. Similar arrangements apply in Northern Ireland. In recent years, there has been a considerable shift in emphasis towards wildlife management, broadleaved silviculture, energy cropping, and protection of water quality. Research programmes are also under way to improve the non-market benefits of forestry, such as recreation and wildlife conservation.

16.13 Research results are published and widely disseminated. They are fed into FC guidelines against which applications for grant aid for new planting are judged. In this way research is fed back directly into improving practice on the ground. The FC and the DANI Forest Service are also involved in the education and training of new entrants into the forestry industry, thereby ensuring that the best practices form the core of early training experience.

International initiatives

16.14 In June 1993 at Helsinki, the Government signed resolutions setting out guidelines for the sustainable management of European forests and for the conservation of their biodiversity[2]. The Resolution for Sustainable Management described sustainable management as the stewardship and use of forests and forest lands in a way, and at a rate, that maintains their biodiversity, productivity, regeneration capacity, vitality and their potential to fulfil, now and in the future, relevant ecological, economic and social functions, at local, national and global levels, and that does not cause damage to other ecosystems. The Resolution included general guidelines thought to be particularly appropriate for forests in Europe and these are reflected in the UK's policies and programmes.

16.15 The Resolution for the Conservation of Biodiversity provides specifically for the enhancement of biodiversity as part of sustainable forest management. In 1993, the FC announced a complementary Biodiversity Initiative for forests in Britain. As part of this, a multidisciplinary biodiversity research programme will be promoted and a biodiversity policy for the management of all types of woodland developed. The aim is to identify methods for improving biodiversity and to develop biodiversity standards for managed forests.

AFFORESTATION

16.16 For many of the UK's woodlands, income from the sale of forest products is not sufficient to sustain the environmental benefits for which they are valued. Even where this is not the case, sustaining and enhancing environmental benefits will result in some income being foregone. The Government currently provides a degree of financial support to woodland and forest owners to achieve sustainable forest management.

16.17 The creation of new forests and woodlands requires an initial capital investment. Income from the sale of forest products does not start to accrue for many years and, depending on the nature of the new woodland, may produce only a small return. Forestry expansion is thus a commercially marginal activity in the UK and requires Government support.

16.18 The principal vehicle for grant aid to the private sector is the Woodland Grant Scheme and, allied to it, the Farm Woodland Premium Scheme. The Woodland Grant Scheme is structured according to the nature of the planting proposed and the likelihood of environmental benefits being achieved. For example, broadleaf planting benefits from a higher rate of grant to reflect its low commercial but high environmental value. Again, extra incentives are given for planting on improved agricultural land (which is less likely to be of conservation value) and for planting designed to provide recreational benefit for local communities.

16.19 All new forestry proposals must be accompanied by a comprehensive plan which will identify any areas of special status and other sensitive areas to be protected or specially managed. These plans are subject to consultation by the FC with other authorities and must show that the applicant is following detailed management and environmental guidelines which cover landscape design, nature conservation, archaeological sites, effects on water supply and catchment, and recreation. In certain circumstances, management grants are also available to encourage continuity in management after initial establishment and to assist with the costs of special recreation, conservation or landscape enhancement measures.

16.20 Alongside the 1992 reforms in the EC Common Agricultural Policy, a measure was introduced which required member states to encourage afforestation on agricultural land. This is implemented in the UK by the Woodland Grant Scheme and the Farm Woodland Premium Scheme. However, there are other ways in which EC rules could allow more scope for conversion of agricultural land to forestry, for example, by allowing such land to count towards the set-aside requirement for the arable aid regime. The Government is pressing for such a change to be made.

16.21 Government is also exploring other ways of promoting woodland planting by, for example, linking planting to suitable development proposals and recreational schemes. Local authorities are encouraged to promote these ideas through the development of indicative forestry strategies, and through the promotion of community forests around towns and cities.

NEW WOODLAND INITIATIVES

The Government is supporting several new initiatives to create extensive areas of new woodland near major urban areas.

In August 1993, the DOE approved business plans for three Community Forests in England – Thames Chase to the East of London, the Forest of Mercia in the Midlands, and the Great North Forest on Tyneside. These three forests are the pace setters for a programme of 12 community forests on the fringes of urban centres. Similar initiatives are in hand in Scotland, Wales and Northern Ireland.

These new forests will bring a variety of improvements to neglected urban fringe areas. The forest strategies aim for the mixed forests based on a mosaic of open space, wooded areas and farmland. This planting will provide landscape improvement, habitat creation, and new recreational opportunities. In future years the forests will also produce timber. They will generate a new renewable resource and contribute towards sustainable development by increasing tree cover.

The National Forest in the English Midlands is an ambitious project to create a new forest in the centre of England large enough to be of national importance. It will promote the economic regeneration of the area by reclaiming mineral workings, improving the landscape and providing recreational areas. It will cover 200 square miles and planting will be more extensive and rapid than in the Community Forests. Consultation on the *Forestry Programme* opened in October 1993.

MARKET FOR TIMBER

Domestic

16.22 An important part of financing the sustainable management of the UK's forests and woodlands is the sale of the timber they produce. The timber market is dominated by demand for conifer timber. The forecast threefold increase in production will require a corresponding increase in market penetration by the UK's wood processing industry. For hardwood timber there is a lack of bulk markets for thinning and much of the larger dimension timber is of poor quality. These problems have led to the neglect of many broadleaved woodlands. The most environmentally important native woodlands tend to be the least commercially viable since much of the timber they contain is of poor value and there are few markets for it.

16.23 The Government is encouraging discussion between groups representing owners and the processing industries, both at local and national levels. It supports research into the development of new markets, such as energy production and charcoal, and assists with the promotion of both new and traditional wood using trades. The diverse and small scale ownership of woodlands is an obstacle to successful exploitation of single bulk markets such as hardwood pulp or energy. The FC is holding a conference in 1994 on the Marketing of Small Dimension Hardwood. This will provide a focus for discussion of the marketing problems, publicise successes and opportunities and review strategy. In addition, the Department of the Environment (DOE) is sponsoring a competition to promote innovative uses of indigenous hardwoods, and is considering research into new construction methods using such materials.

16.24 Residues from harvesting and processing timber could be an important precursor in the development of electricity generation using trees grown specifically for this purpose, for example, willow and poplar grown as short rotation coppice. The Government has promoted species selection and cultivation techniques for such plantations as a means of cutting down consumption of fossil fuel and hence of net CO_2 emissions to the atmosphere. This energy plantation programme could have the added advantage of taking land out of agricultural production and, through suitable design, could also provide environmental benefits.

International

16.25 Despite increasing forest cover, the UK imports 87% of its timber requirements, 70% of which is for softwoods and 30% for hardwoods. Much of this comes from old growth forests that are not all sustainably managed.

16.26 Forestry expansion will go some way to reducing dependence on imports but lead times are long, and there is no doubt, even with the forecast trebling of domestic production, that the UK will continue to import the majority of its timber requirements for many years.

16.27 The UK Government is continuing to work through CITES and the International Tropical Timber Organisation (ITTO) to control trade in rare and endangered timber species and, through multilateral aid programmes, to assist less developed countries to conserve and manage their forest resource. The UK Government is also working for the effective implementation of the Earth Summit Forest Principles, the ITTO Year 2000 Target and the Tropical Forestry Action Programme.

CARBON DIOXIDE SINK

16.28 Forest expansion could have a significant role to play in tempering carbon emissions from other sectors, and so help to offset global warming. Growing trees remove CO_2 from the air and store the carbon in wood. The current forest resource of 2.4 million hectares offsets approximately 2% of the UK's industrial CO_2 emissions. Further planting should increase this benefit proportionately.

16.29 Felling and utilisation of wood products will eventually release some of the CO_2 locked up during growth but there will remain a net addition to the UK's store of carbon in the form of biomass and soil carbon. When wood is used for fuel, carbon is released almost immediately but, if the resource is continually replaced, this use is fully sustainable with no appreciable net effect on the carbon budget.

REFERENCES AND FURTHER READING

1 *Sustainable Forestry: The UK Programme.* Cm 2429. HMSO, 1994. ISBN 0–10–124292–1.

2 *The Second European Ministerial Conference on the Protection of Forests in Europe* – Helsinki, June 1993. ISBN 9–51–478283–6.

CHAPTER 17

FISHERIES

A Sustainable Framework

● To balance catches against the natural ability of fish stocks to regenerate.

Trends

● Fish stocks are now being exploited at, or beyond, their capacity.
● Technological developments mean that fish are becoming easier to catch.

Problems and Opportunities

● The main problem is over-fishing, with the danger of depleting the stocks to a level where the resource is threatened and unable to renew itself adequately.
● Both sea fishing and fish farming can give rise to environmental damage.

Current Responses

● Within the EC the main instrument for control is the Common Fisheries Policy (CFP).

The Way Forward

● Further development and tighter enforcement of the CFP.
● Further development of techniques and equipment which could reduce catches of immature fish and non-target species and minimise damage to the sea bed.
● Research will help to give more information on reasons for the decline in fish stocks, and also to develop methods for avoiding catching non-target species and for reducing environmental damage.

FISHERIES ACTIVITY AND ITS CONTRIBUTION TO THE ECONOMY

17.1 The UK fishing industry is based at many locations around the coastline. The areas fished range from North Norway and Greenland to the Azores, but the bulk of activity takes place in the North Sea, English Channel, western approaches, Celtic Sea, Irish Sea and the waters to the west of Scotland. In addition there are some 2,100 fish and shellfish farming sites on the coast and inland.

17.2 Fishing and fish farming are very important to the local economy in certain coastal areas, both directly and through the industries dependent on them, including food processing. The fishing industry employs some 24,200 fishermen and, indirectly, employs another 32,600 people in ancillary industries and fish processing. Fish farming is estimated to employ a further 5,000 people directly, and a similar number indirectly.

FOOD PRODUCTION

17.3 Fish stocks are a renewable resource and a valuable source of food. Unlike most other food sources, the majority of fish are harvested from the wild. In order to ensure the continuing sustainable harvest of fish, measures have to be taken to balance fishing effort with the natural ability of fish stocks to regenerate. In 1992, some 599,000 tonnes of fish (with a value of £395m) were landed into the UK by UK vessels (see Figure 17.1). In addition, 36,000 tonnes of salmon, 15,000 tonnes of trout and 5,000 tonnes of shellfish were cultivated, realising a first sale value of £150m. In 1992, the UK exported 421,525 tonnes (value £569m) and imported 731,600 tonnes (value £1,049m) of fish.

PRESENT SITUATION

17.4 Since 1983, fishing within the waters of EC member states has been managed through the EC Common Fisheries Policy (CFP). The CFP was the EC's first attempt to manage a resource which cannot be contained within national boundaries. CFP management options include the mechanisms of Total Allowable Catches (TACs), quotas and technical conservation measures. CFP management, marketing and control are outlined in Box 17.1. The EC conservation measures are intended to conserve and rebuild stocks, and

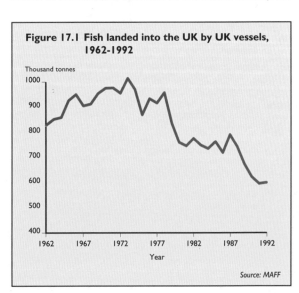

Figure 17.1 Fish landed into the UK by UK vessels, 1962-1992

Thousand tonnes

Year

Source: MAFF

BOX 17.1 COMMON FISHERIES POLICY MECHANISMS

Total allowable catches (TACs), quotas, fleet structure and technical conservation

Each year TACs are set for the major fish stocks on the basis of scientific advice or, in the absence of adequate scientific advice, on a precautionary basis. Traditionally, TACs are set on a single species basis for one year. But, following mid-term review of the CFP in 1992, the EC Council of Fisheries Ministers may now consider longer-term conservation objectives for the stocks where appropriate. TACs are divided into national quotas and member states' quotas reflecting their agreed share of the relevant stocks.

Third country fishing agreements with countries outside the EC help provide opportunities for EC fleets to augment fish supplies to the EC market which in most cases are insufficient to meet EC demand. The agreements of most importance to the UK are with Norway, Greenland and the Faroe Islands. There are also opportunities for EC vessels to fish on the High Seas.

To complement TACs and quotas, the CFP also includes:
- programmes to bring fleet structure into better balance with the stocks (Multi-annual Guidance Programmes), which originally focused on vessel capacity but now deal with fishing activity as well;
- a range of technical conservation measures including minimum landing sizes for fish, mesh sizes for tow nets, net configuration restrictions and attachments, limitations on power of certain vessels working up to 12 miles from the coast and closed areas.

Marketing

The EC's marketing regime makes provision for the formation and recognition of fish producers' organisations (FPOs), whose aims are to ensure that fishing is carried out along rational lines and that the conditions for the sale of their members' produce are improved. The legislation also provides various market support mechanisms which are designed to ensure stability on the market. The scheme most widely used in the UK is the degressive compensation scheme, whereby fish not meeting a minimum EC withdrawal price may be permanently withdrawn from the market for human consumption, and appropriate compensation paid to the FPO on a sliding (reducing) scale. Other schemes provide for the payment of aid by the EC for the storage of fish. The quantities withdrawn from the market are, however, minimal compared with the total put up for sale by the FPOs.

Enforcement and control of the CFP

No fishing regime can be effective unless there is a reliable control system in place. In recognition of this, the EC Council of Ministers has adopted a regulation (EC Reg. 2847/93) establishing a control system applicable to the CFP. For the first time, controls are extended to structures and marketing in a comprehensive enforcement policy. The agreement strengthens the European Commission's power to audit the enforcement procedures operated by individual member states, and generally tightens and extends existing control procedures to increase the effectiveness of enforcement throughout the EC. The new regulation allows EC Inspectors to make unannounced visits and to verify member states' planned programmes of enforcement. Annual reports will be published on member states' implementation of the Control Regulation. There will be tighter controls over third country vessels fishing in EC waters and all catches and landings will be more closely monitored. In addition, pilot projects are to be carried out before June 1995 to evaluate the costs and benefits of using satellite equipment in fisheries enforcement. This trial will include other systems such as automatic position recorders.

thus seek to ensure both sustainable harvesting of fish and the livelihoods of those dependent, directly or indirectly, on fishing. Nonetheless, stocks in EC waters are generally over-exploited and need extremely careful management if they are to provide the basis for a viable long term industry.

PROBLEMS AND ISSUES

17.5 The heavy exploitation of most stocks within the waters of EC member states is a cause for considerable concern. The key issue is how to achieve a better balance between the overall fishing effort and the level of harvesting which fish stocks can sustain. The existing CFP mechanisms have not hitherto been able to avoid increasingly powerful fishing technology exerting too much pressure on the stocks, particularly by killing too many immature fish. It is in the interests of the fishing industry's own viability that fishing effort is carried out at a sustainable level. To this end, the EC has adopted new technical measures to require the use of more selective gear, and new programmes for the progressive reduction in the capacity and activity of member states' fleets. In February 1992, the UKGovernment announced a package of measures aimed at reducing UK fishing effort, including new licensing rules, a £25 million decommissioning scheme and controls on vessels' days at sea. The new licensing rules are now in place and will, among other things, prevent further growth of the under-10-metre fleet; decommissioning grants have been offered for 140 vessels, representing some 2.5% of the fleet's tonnage; however, days at sea controls have been suspended pending a judgement by the European Court of Justice. There is a recognised world wide problem of over-exploitation of fisheries. The EC is already playing a major role in the UN Conference on Straddling Stocks and Highly Migratory Species set up to address this international problem.

17.6 The CFP also has regard to the needs and sustainability of the wider marine ecosystem, not just to commercial fish stocks. A specific environmental concern is that heavy towed gear, such as beam trawls and dredges, may have a long term harmful effect on the sea bed and the benthos (the flora and fauna at the bottom of the sea). The UK Fisheries Departments are funding research and development to examine this problem. There is also concern about the incidental capture of birds and marine mammals in fishing nets. In UK waters, incidents involving birds are comparatively rare and there is currently no evidence that the survival of any species is threatened. For mammals, CFP rules limit the length of drift nets and prohibit the practice of "setting" on groups or schools of marine mammals with purse-seine nets. The UK played a major role in bringing forward the Agreement on the Conservation of Small Cetaceans of the Baltic and North Seas (ASCOBANS) which it ratified in July 1993. In the spirit of that agreement, the UK is trying to establish the true level of accidental capture of marine mammals in UK fisheries and is funding research on increasing the acoustic detectability of nets to small cetaceans. These issues are addressed more fully in the *Biodiversity Action Plan*[1].

17.7 There is increasing interest in the environmental impact of fish farming. Much of this impact is on a local scale, but can be addressed through existing UK planning and environmental legislation. This includes concerns about siting and appearance of fish farms, water abstraction, effluent discharge, predator control and use of medicines. There are also wider issues, however, including the introduction of non-native species,

escapes of fish into the wild and risks of the spread of disease. Environmental assessment is required for marine salmon farming wherever it is likely to have significant environmental effects. Most shellfish farming activities are conducted on a small scale and have limited environmental effects. But there can be operations – for example, mussel dredging – which may have an ecological effect on particular shores. UK Fisheries Departments' research and development programmes are increasingly addressing questions related to the impact of fish farming on the environment.

FUTURE DEVELOPMENTS

17.8 It is essential that, in the waters of EC member states and elsewhere in the world, fishing effort is brought into better balance with what fish stocks and the wider marine ecosystem can bear. Otherwise, sea fishing will not be sustainable. The CFP has to be implemented successfully and made to work. The new EC control regulation[2] already provides a framework for more effective enforcement of the CFP by all member states.

17.9 All EC fishing fleets face the need for significant and permanent reductions in their fishing effort over the next few years. Provided the necessary measures are taken, the stocks can be restored to a properly renewable basis. In support of the wider marine ecosystem, the UK will continue to promote development of the CFP and of national fisheries policies in ways which take proper account of the impact of fishing, fishing methods and fishing gear.

17.10 The UK will honour the further commitments enshrined in the *Biodiversity Action Plan*. As the Plan notes, "...in many cases, the full environmental impact of fisheries policies and practices is not fully understood..."[3]. This points to the need to take account of the precautionary principle in deciding on the level and methods of fishing employed; it also identifies the need for more research into the processes that control the production and survival of fish, and into such issues as the interaction of towed gear and the sea bed and the means of making accurate and timely assessment of fish stock numbers. Within available resources, the Government will ensure that fisheries research continues to address these issues.

REFERENCES AND FURTHER READING

[1] *Biodiversity: The UK Action Plan.* Cm 2428. HMSO, 1994. ISBN 0-10-124282-4.

[2] *Council Regulation 93/2847/EEC establishing a control system applicable to the Common Fisheries Policy.* Official Journal of the European Communities L261, 20 October 1993.

[3] *Biodiversity Action Plan,* Chapter 6.

CHAPTER 18

MINERALS EXTRACTION

A Sustainable Framework

- To conserve minerals as far as possible, while ensuring an adequate supply to meet the needs of society for minerals.
- To minimise production of waste and to encourage efficient use of materials, including appropriate use of high quality materials, and recycling of wastes.
- To encourage sensitive working practices during minerals extraction, and to preserve or enhance the overall quality of the environment once extraction has ceased.
- To protect designated areas of critical landscape or nature quality from development, other than in exceptional circumstances where it has been demonstrated that development is in the public interest.

Trends

- Increasing demands for minerals, especially aggregates for construction.
- Higher environmental standards being required during minerals working and in restoration.

Problems and Opportunities

- The need to balance society's demands for minerals against the need to conserve resources for future generations, and to prevent unacceptable damage to the environment or to other finite resources.
- The existence of older planning permissions which do not include controls on how the site should be operated and how restoration should be managed, and which do not provide a level playing field between operators.

- The need to consider the potential contribution from alternative sources, in view of the increasing difficulty in finding environmentally acceptable sites.

Current Responses

- Government review of existing minerals planning guidance.
- Consultations on proposals for dealing with old mineral permissions to be announced in 1994.
- Ongoing research programme into minerals planning.
- Development by industry of Environmental Codes of Practice for mineral workings.

The Way Forward

- Government to ensure that society's needs for minerals are met while encouraging greater efficiency, effectiveness and economy in the supply and use of resources.
- Government, local authorities and industry to pursue opportunities for promotion of reuse and recycling of waste materials where they can substitute for primary minerals.
- Government, local authorities and industry to work towards improving standards of operation of mineral workings.
- Government, local authorities and industry to work towards ensuring high and consistent standards for restoration.
- Government to take forward the aims of sustainable development in research on a wide range of minerals issues.

INTRODUCTION

18.1 Chapter 12 described the range of minerals worked in the UK, both onshore and offshore, and highlighted that the main minerals extracted are aggregates for the construction industry (sand and gravel, and crushed rock) and energy minerals (coal, oil and gas).

18.2 Minerals make an essential contribution to national prosperity and quality of life. The total value of minerals production in the UK in 1991 was £17 billion. The extraction of minerals is economically vital because it provides essential inputs to many industrial processes. Direct employment in the minerals industry (including

British Coal opencast sites worked under contract, but excluding British Coal deep mines, and offshore oil and gas) is of the order of 43,500[1], but the industry also sustains a wide range of ancillary employment.

18.3 The UK exports some minerals, chiefly crude petroleum, natural gas, china clay and ball clay, coal and potash. The value of these exports was £4.9 billion in 1992. A wide range of minerals are imported, the most significant being crude petroleum, coal, natural gas, iron ore, titanium and zinc concentrates, magnesite and magnesia and potash, valued at £5.9 billion in 1992. For aggregates the trade is very small – less than 1% of total UK production and consumption over the period since 1985. In recent years, exports of aggregates to other European countries have increased to approximately 2% of UK production. For marine aggregates, this figure is higher; in 1990 and 1991 respectively, approximately 17% and 25% of marine aggregates dredged in England and Wales were exported. There is currently no marine dredging activity in Scottish waters.

POLICY DEVELOPMENT

Evaluation of costs and benefits

18.4 A sustainable approach to minerals requires that the costs and benefits of minerals extraction should be evaluated and internalised as far as practicable. The Department of the Environment (DOE) intends to commission research on this, to establish the feasibility of such an approach. The costs of minerals extraction could include an assessment of the landtake (which would otherwise be available for alternative purposes or undeveloped for future generations) and of the environmental impacts on localities and communities. These costs would need to be carefully balanced against the need for the minerals and their contribution to economic growth, and the benefits of reclaimed or restored land for other uses, ranging from agriculture through forestry and nature conservation to housing and industry. In addition, minerals extraction can provide opportunities for landscape enhancement, reclamation of derelict land, and creation of new habitats. Use of minerals will also increase human resource capital in terms of infrastructure, such as roads and buildings; the revenues generated by minerals working can also be put to other productive uses.

18.5 Planning for the supply of minerals – like most other forms of development – involves, therefore, the need to reconcile various social, environmental and economic costs and benefits. This suggests that a proper evaluation is necessary, not only of the resources themselves and the wealth their extraction creates, but also of natural and environmental resources such as soil, water, landscape, fauna and flora.

18.6 Questions arise about whether there are some critical environmental assets which should be permanently protected, and others which can be released on a "temporary" basis to allow extraction to proceed, provided that an acceptable new environment is created afterwards. These concerns relate to the landscapes with statutory designations (such as National Parks, Areas of Outstanding Natural Beauty (AONBs), National Scenic Areas, and Sites of Special Scientific Interest (SSSIs) – in particular, those designated as Special Areas of Conservation and Special Protection Areas), which account for nearly 20% of the total UK land area. They are also relevant to landscapes of locally designated value and areas highly regarded for their heritage and amenity value by local people. But it needs to be recognised that National Parks, AONBs, National Scenic Areas and locally designated areas occupy very large areas of land in Britain, and that certain minerals are predominantly found in these areas. Government minerals planning policy has proposed a strengthening of the policies with respect to these areas.

EC implications

18.7 The policy needs to be developed in the context of the EC's *Fifth Environmental Action Programme*[2], agreed in December 1992. This recognises that:

"...since the reservoir of raw materials is finite, the flow of substances through the various stages of processing, consumption and use should be so managed as to facilitate or encourage optimum reuse and recycling, thereby avoiding wastage and preventing depletion of the natural resource stock ... one individual's consumption or use of these resources must not be at the expense of another's ... neither should one generation's consumption be at the expense of those following."

18.8 This implies a positive policy to conserve raw materials; to ensure their efficient and effective use; to encourage recycling and use of secondary materials; and to consider whether high quality resources which are limited in supply require special husbanding.

MINERALS PLANNING

18.9 The Government wishes to see indigenous mineral resources developed within its broad objectives of promoting economic growth, assisting the creation and maintenance of employment and protecting the environment. For the economic well being of the country, it is essential that there is an adequate and steady supply of minerals to meet the needs of the community and that economic growth is not hindered. At the same time, the Government recognises that mineral extraction can have a significant environmental impact, and often takes place in areas of attractive countryside.

18.10 There is concern that it will become increasingly difficult to identify extraction sites which are environmentally acceptable. The marginal environmental cost of meeting

BOX 18.1

MINERAL PLANNING GUIDANCE NOTES

No	Title	88	89	90	91	92	93	94
1	General Considerations & the Development Plan System	■						●
2	Applications, Permissions and Conditions	■						
3	Opencast Coal Mining	■						●
4	The Review of Mineral Working Sites	■						
5	Mineral Planning and the General Development Order	■						
6	Guidelines for Aggregates Provision in England & Wales		■				▼	
7	The Reclamation of Mineral Workings		■					●
8	Planning & Compensation Act 1991: Interim Development Order Permissions (IDOs) – Statutory Provisions and Procedures.				■			
9	Planning & Compensation Act 1991: Interim Development Order Permissions (IDOs) – Conditions					■		
10	Provision of Raw Material For the Cement Industry				■			
11	Control of Noise at Surface Mineral Workings						■	

NEW MINERAL PLANNING GUIDANCE NOTES

No	Title	88	89	90	91	92	93	94
13	Treatment of Disused Mine Openings and Availibility of Information on Mined Ground					▼		
—	Peat Extraction							●
—	Provision of Silica Sand in England & Wales							●
—	Landslides and Planning							●
—	Stability in Quarrying							●
—	Oil & Gas							●

(MPG6 and MPG13 are to be published in final form in early 1994.)

■ Publication date.

▼ Consultation draft issued.

● Expect new consultation draft in year indicated.

increased demand for minerals is likely to rise over the longer term; the Government believes that ways of minimising future demand will need to be considered.

18.11 The issue is one of balance, that is, how to balance society's need for minerals and mineral-based products to contribute to economic growth (including improvement to the built environment and the development of goods and services) against the need to conserve resources and protect the environment.

18.12 The long term objective should be to seek ways of meeting society's needs while using less primary minerals, by employing alternative materials, technologies, and patterns of design. This may mean, for example, seeking to substitute waste and recycled materials for primary aggregates, exploring substitutes for peat, recycling silica sand and products derived from it, including glass, and pursuing energy efficient processes.

BOX 18.2
AGGREGATES PLANNING AND SUSTAINABLE DEVELOPMENT

The review of Minerals Planning Guidance Note 6, Guidelines for Aggregates Provision in England and Wales, and the preparation of guidelines on land for mineral workings in Scotland (draft National Planning Policy Guideline 4, Land for Mineral Working), have provided a timely opportunity for Government to examine the implications of sustainable development for aggregates planning.

As part of the review of MPG 6, projections of demand commissioned from consultants indicated that up to 6.4 billion tonnes of primary aggregates may be required in England and Wales over the next 20 years. These projections suggested that demand could be between 370-440 million tonnes per annum (mtpa) by 2011, compared with 212 mtpa in 1991. These projections are not production targets which must be met by the extraction of new materials, but indicated the potential demand brought about by a steady rate of economic growth. The projections provided a starting point for consideration of policy options and to inform the preparation of planning guidelines.

The draft MPG 6 set out Government's views on what sustainable development means for aggregates planning. The implications centre around two key themes:
a) making the best and most efficient use of all available resources, so that extraction of new resources is limited to what is necessary to meet the current generation's needs;
b) ensuring that the overall quality of the environment affected by aggregates extraction should be preserved or improved over time, so that future generations are not disadvantaged by the activities of the present one.

The draft guidelines sought views on how the supply requirements indicated by the demand projections could be met while pursuing the goals of sustainable development. They proposed that an increasing contribution to aggregate needs should be met from alternative sources, including secondary and waste materials and remote coastal superquarries, thereby reducing the pressure on traditional land-won resources. Views were sought on the level of provision that can come from land-won primary aggregates in England and Wales without an unacceptable level of damage to the environment; and on the contribution which should come from remote coastal superquarries outside England and Wales and secondary/waste materials.

The major public consultation exercise on MPG 6 has highlighted key differences in opinion between the main interested parties. The minerals industry maintained that demand should be met in full, and that this can be done in an environmentally acceptable manner by their continued efforts to improve operating performance. The industry regarded the draft proposals as not providing any environmental advantages over policies based on a continuation of the current approach. The local authorities and environmental groups, including the statutory advisory bodies, accepted the proposals as a positive move towards sustainable development, though not going far enough. They argued for the management of demand and the introduction of fiscal measures to influence the market share of alternative materials.

These matters are currently being considered. Final guidance is due early in 1994.

Current minerals planning approaches

18.13 Minerals planning control is a positive instrument in the UK to reconcile conflicting claims on land of mineral working, agriculture, building development or other surface uses and recreation and amenity. The DOE and Welsh Office series of Mineral Planning Guidance Notes (MPGs) (see Box 18.1) provide information and advice in England and Wales about planning policies, best practice and the legislation relating to minerals planning; they set a framework within which environmental considerations can be balanced against social and economic ones. The similar system of planning guidance in Scotland is described in chapter 35.

18.14 Built into the MPG/NPPG system is a commitment to regular monitoring and review, which will provide an opportunity to assess whether sustainable development aims are being achieved over time. Development of minerals planning policy is supported across the whole of Britain by research carried out in England, Wales and Scotland under the DOE's Geological and Minerals Planning Research Programme (see 18.24).

18.15 The issues surrounding sustainable development and the mineral planning process will be considered in the context of the revision during 1994 of MPG 1 (*General Considerations and the Development Plan System*) for England and Wales. NPPG 4, *Land for Mineral Working*, issued as a consultation draft in July 1992, is currently being finalised and will provide a sustainable development framework for all types of minerals extraction in Scotland.

18.16. For aggregates, the DOE and Welsh Office have recently completed a consultation exercise on revised planning guidelines for provision for aggregates in England and Wales (MPG 6: *Guidelines for Aggregates Provision in England and Wales*) which seek to identify how aggregates requirements should be met in a way which takes account of sustainable development principles (see Box 2). The Scottish Office's draft NPPG 4 also includes guidance on aggregates.

18.17 For energy minerals, the Government recognises that development of hydrocarbons will continue to make a valuable contribution to the national economy and to local economies. It is Government policy to ensure the maximum economic exploitation of oil and gas reserves over time, consistent with good oilfield practice and with the protection of the environment.

18.18 In March 1993, the Government announced, in a statement of Interim Planning Guidance, some changes to MPG 3[4], and set out the principles on which revised planning guidelines covering both opencast and deep mine operations

would be based. These included the principle that it is not the function of the planning system to seek to set national limits on, or targets for, any particular source or level of energy supply. Nevertheless, coal which can be produced economically is an important indigenous energy resource; it would be against the national interest to prevent its extraction where that can be done in an environmentally acceptable way and consistently with wider environmental objectives, including the principles of sustainable development.

18.19 Issues surrounding the need to provide and maintain supplies of peat for the country's horticultural and landscape industries, and the place of alternatives, are being discussed through a Working Group. This Group, which was set up in 1992 and is chaired by the DOE, represents interests across Britain. Key land use and land cover issues include consideration of future obligations to conserve a range of peatlands under the EC Habitats Directive. It is intended that a report from the Working Group, with any proposed national guidelines, would be the subject of future consultation. A Policy Statement[5], relating to the conservation and use of peatland in Northern Ireland, was issued in June 1993.

18.20 An MPG on the provision of silica sand in England and Wales will be the subject of consultation in 1994. This will provide guidance on how silica sand should be supplied consistent with sustainable development principles. It will consider the role to be played by recycling of silica sand and products derived from silica sand including glass.

Development plans, Regional Planning Guidance (England) and Strategic Planning Guidance (Wales)

18.21 Development plans provide an opportunity for local authorities to ensure that mineral supplies are obtained from areas where the environmental costs are acceptable. Under the Planning and Compensation Act 1991[6], Mineral Planning Authorities in England and Wales (MPAs) are required to prepare mineral local plans; there should be complete coverage of these by 1996. The forthcoming MPG 1 will advise MPAs on sustainable development in the context of development plans. In Scotland, there is no statutory requirement for planning authorities to prepare mineral local plans. However, draft NPPG 4 suggests that in areas of significant mineral resources, and where local plan coverage is well advanced, planning authorities should consider the need for mineral local plans.

18.22 Regional Planning Guidance in England, and NPPGs in Scotland will give guidance on policies to encourage sustainable development of regional resources. Again, monitoring and review will be an important part of these processes.

18.23 The Secretary of State for Wales invited the Assembly of Welsh Counties (AWC), in collaboration with other bodies, to assess the existing strategic planning framework of Wales. The AWC also submitted a report to the Secretary of State, which includes a chapter on minerals. In considering the report, the Secretary of State for Wales will take account of the sustainable development of resources.

The DOE's Geological and Minerals Planning Research Programme

18.24 Development of minerals planning policy is supported by research carried out under the DOE's Geological and Minerals Planning Research Programme, which has been investigating, for over 20 years, issues with a bearing on the sustainability of development. Over the last few years, the programme has been more closely focused on the key factors to be resolved in developing planning policies for sustainability, particularly alternatives to the utilisation of primary materials and ways of achieving the optimum use of those minerals which are extracted. This research also needs to address how practical encouragement can best be given to promoting the reuse and recycling of minerals, and how the appropriate use of high quality minerals, and avoidance of their use in less demanding applications, can be encouraged. The research will also contribute to the handing on to future generations of an enhanced technical methodology, and supporting knowledge base for minerals provision and its environmental management (see Box 18.3).

PRACTICAL IMPLICATIONS OF MINERALS PLANNING

18.25 The Government wishes to ensure that society's needs for minerals are met while encouraging greater efficiency, effectiveness and economy in the supply and use of resources. Sustainable development has the following practical implications for minerals planning and for the future development of the extractive industry:

- **During extraction:** operations should be managed to high standards. Sensitive working practices are required to reduce the environmental impacts of quarrying and to avoid wastage, so as to conserve minerals as far as possible. Recovery of reserves from a given working area should be maximised, consistent with environmental constraints, to avoid future sterilisation of unworked material.

- **In restoration:** land taken for minerals should be reclaimed at the earliest opportunity, and should be capable of an acceptable use after working has come to an end. Restoration and aftercare should preserve or enhance the long-term quality of land worked for minerals, so that there is no net loss of land for use by future generations and the community is provided with an asset of equal or added value. The long-term potential of best quality agricultural land worked for minerals should be preserved or enhanced.

- **In use of minerals:** steps should be taken to encourage appropriate use of high quality minerals, and to prevent them being used for less demanding applications. Over-specification and wastage of materials in use should be avoided and recycled/waste materials should be used where environmentally and economically advantageous.

- **Avoidance of sterilisation:** adequate protection should be provided in order to prevent mineral resources from being sterilised by other forms of development. Efforts should be made to extract minerals in advance of development.

18.26. Implementation of this sustainable approach requires contributions from different sectors:

- the **minerals industry**, in its approach to site management, restoration and future identification of areas for exploitation;

- those **industries which use minerals** for processes and end-products, particularly in their use of technology to increase efficiency of use and reduction of waste;

- **local planning authorities**, through their development plans, development control, and purchasing/specifying roles;

- **central Government**, in its advisory, regulatory and legislative roles, in its role as specifier for public works contracts, in the integration of policies in different areas, and in its research programmes;

- **conservation bodies**, particularly through joint initiatives with industry for site enhancement;

- **landowners**, through their responsibility for management, restoration, and aftercare of mineral workings and subsequent management of the land.

Minerals extraction

18.27 Modern planning permissions have conditions attached to them, governing how the mineral site is to be operated. These conditions may be used to control potential environmental disturbance. Many older permissions do not have such controls and, in the context of sustainable development, it is essential to bring permissions up to date. Following the Planning and Compensation Act 1991, Interim Development Order (pre-1948) permissions are being

BOX 18.3

GEOLOGICAL AND MINERALS PLANNING RESEARCH PROGRAMME

The aims of the Programme are:

i) to establish the availability of, and demand for, minerals by determining:
   - the nature and extent of mineral resources and the environmental limitations on exploiting these;
   - the likely demand which will need to be met from these resources in the short, medium and longer term;

ii) to ensure that those minerals which are won are used wisely by:
   - establishing the extent of high quality materials;
   - reviewing the standards and specifications for various uses of minerals in order to identify possibilities for substitution;
   - identifying options for increasing the efficiency of use of minerals;

iii) to increase awareness of alternatives to traditional sources of supply from environmentally sensitive areas by:
   - identifying mineral resources in less constrained areas;
   - examining the potential for increased recycling of mineral and construction wastes;

iv) to improve appreciation of the environmental, social and economic costs and the benefits of mineral working to enable these to be reflected in minerals planning policy;

v) to develop the basis for reducing the environmental effects of working, processing and distributing minerals by:
   - identifying, developing and disseminating good practices for control of development during extraction, restoration and aftercare of sites;
   - by monitoring the effectiveness of restoration of mineral workings.

updated. Further action is now being considered to update permissions granted in the 1950s, 1960s and 1970s. Consultation papers[7] were published in 1992 in England, Wales and Scotland, setting out alternative ways of moving forward; firm proposals for a further round of consultation will be published in 1994.

18.28 The Government is committed to ensuring that the minerals industry itself is responsible for carrying out its operations in an environmentally acceptable manner, as a "good neighbour". The industry has recently taken steps to encourage operators to work sites to a high standard of environmental performance. A number of trade associations have introduced Environmental Codes of Practice, as have a number of individual companies. This approach is welcomed by Government; all operators are urged to adopt this practice.

18.29 The DOE has sponsored a number of research projects aimed at encouraging higher operating standards throughout Britain. One of these, *The Minerals Industry Environmental Performance Study*[8], recommended that:

"a system of Environmental Management should be established as an integral part of each company's organisation;

this would include a corporate environmental statement, environmental site appraisals, regular monitoring of performance and periodic environmental audit/review."

18.30 A further study, *Environmental Management in the Minerals Industry*[9] provides practical advice on how to achieve the higher standards now expected. It establishes principles for environmental management of sites, and advice on how a more sustainable approach to site development might be achieved by operators. The report provides practical examples of how minerals operators can work to such objectives, for example, by carrying out crushing and screening of imported wastes to help provide restoration material on site. Use of recycled packaging for mineral products and monitoring of energy consumption are also suggested as ways of securing a more sustainable approach to operations. Another report, *Environmental Effects of Surface Mineral Workings*[10] provides guidance on the issues that need to be considered by local authorities and operators.

18.31 The DOE and Welsh Office have recently issued minerals planning guidance on the control of noise from surface mineral workings (MPG 11). This provides advice, in England and Wales, to the minerals industry and planning authorities on how the environmental performance of the industry can be improved, through the use of planning controls and the industry's own efforts to be a "good neighbour". Research is being commissioned on the control of blasting and dust associated with mineral working, on traffic at mineral workings, and on the effects of minerals extraction on hydrogeology, including water supplies. The research may lead to the issuing of further minerals planning guidance on these subjects in the future.

Site restoration and after-use

18.32 Government policy is to ensure that land worked for minerals is restored to a beneficial after-use at the earliest opportunity. The DOE has commissioned a number of research projects to establish what is technically feasible, to assess how far high quality restoration and aftercare of mineral workings is presently being achieved, and to provide guidance on how performance can be improved in future.

18.33 Research which has examined restoration to amenity and agricultural after-uses, as well as specific studies to examine the restoration of particular mineral types, is being used to update MPG 7 (*Reclamation of Mineral Workings*).

18.34 To ensure that a sustainable approach to site restoration is secured in future, the Government takes the view that, wherever possible, mineral operators should aim to secure positive enhancement of sites during and following extraction. For restoration and after-care of sites, "landscape fit" and the land use suitability and sustainability of completed sites should be important guiding principles, and the extent to which future generations inherit an asset of value.

Efficient use of materials

18.35 To conserve resources, it is important to achieve efficient use of minerals. A study by the Building Research Establishment (BRE)[11] found that there is currently little or no incentive to use lower grade and secondary materials in place of high quality ones. BRE reported cases of "overspecification", leading to unnecessary wastage of aggregate materials in construction. Such overspecification takes the form of both excessive margins of safety, and lack of appropriate specifications for some alternative materials.

18.36 The plentiful supply and relatively low price of certain minerals has, in some cases, meant that there may be wastage during processing and use. For example, BRE reported that up to 10% of building materials, including aggregate minerals, may be wasted on construction sites.

18.37 BRE recommended several steps which could be taken to promote overall efficiency of use of all available materials including wastes. These include increased publicity, the setting of targets or quotas for secondary materials, and risk-sharing in construction to encourage use of innovative design and materials, especially, and in the first instance, by the public sector. Chapter 25 considers the issues involved in a more sustainable approach to management of resources within the construction sector.

18.38 The movement in the EC is towards performance specifications so that, provided materials are fit for their intended purpose, they should not be precluded from use. This philosophy towards specifications is also being adopted by the Department of Transport (DOT). Further research is being carried out by BRE to look into the scope for accommodating waste and recycled materials into European construction specifications.

18.39 The DOE and Welsh Office are now considering what further efforts are needed to promote the most efficient and effective use of aggregates in construction, in the context of the review of MPG 6.

Waste and recycled materials

18.40 More action is required to substitute waste and recycled materials for primary ones wherever practicable (see chapters 23 and 25). In this context, the Government is considering how to encourage the use of secondary materials as aggregates, and the recycling of silica sand and products derived from it (such as glass). The aim should be to recycle as far as is environmentally and economically justified.

18.41 The DOE and Welsh Office policy on the use of waste and recycled materials as aggregates is set out in MPG 6 (May 1989). The draft revised MPG 6 (see Box 18.2) and the Scottish Office's draft NPPG 4 include policies to encourage the use of such materials, to reduce the demand for newly quarried materials and to reduce dereliction caused by tipping.

18.42 The draft MPG 6 states that it is in the national interest that aggregates, and products manufactured from aggregates, should be recycled wherever possible, as this reduces the demand for primary minerals. The draft guidelines also say that the Government is committed to increasing significantly the level of use of recycled materials from the present position. However, there are a number of obstacles which currently reduce the ability of these materials to replace primary aggregates.

18.43 The key problems are:

- **Transport costs:** for most secondary materials, the transport costs from source to principal markets mean that they are not price-competitive with locally-won primary aggregates.
- **Technical standards and specifications:** some lack of customer acceptance of secondary aggregates constrains their use, and further consideration of specifications for the use of recycled materials is needed.

18.44 The environmental problems associated with supplying primary aggregates are also often common to the reworking of waste tips and processing of secondary aggregates: for example, dust, noise, visual intrusion and transport impacts. The transport of secondary materials to relatively distant points of consumption creates its own additional environmental impacts, including the consumption of energy.

18.45 Work being undertaken by BRE should indicate what further efforts are needed to broaden specifications to give waste and recycled materials the best chance of being used. This is being carried out alongside a number of DOT research projects to broaden the technical scope for use of waste materials in roads construction.

18.46 The DOE has commissioned a study of the extent of recycling of demolition and construction wastes in the UK, and the constraints on this type of recycling, by both fixed-site and mobile plant. The research will make recommendations about a desirable level of recycling of such wastes for use as aggregates, and how it can be done in an environmentally acceptable manner. This study will be completed in early 1994. The research is running concurrently with a Priority Waste Streams initiative by the European Commission to increase recycling of such wastes, which aims to produce firm measures as the basis for a draft regulation, directive or

code of practice. Landfill prices can be expected to rise in the future as new licensing arrangements for waste disposal sites come into effect following the introduction of the Environmental Protection Act (EPA)1990[12]. The extent to which these will affect inert wastes from demolition and construction projects is not yet known, but one effect could be to encourage recycling, particularly if a landfill levy were to be introduced in the future.

18.47 More information is needed on the use of waste materials generally, on their substitution for primary materials, on regular monitoring of waste arisings and their use as substitutes for minerals. The use and management of waste is considered further in chapter 23.

Sterilisation of assets

18.48 Questions arise about the extent to which the workings of materials are restricted, either by protection of land from development on environmental grounds or by other development which by its location precludes mineral workings. It is for land use planning and minerals planning together to seek to resolve these potential conflicts.

CONCLUSIONS

18.49 Government will take steps to ensure that society's needs for minerals are met in a manner compatible with the aims of sustainable development. Efforts will be made to seek better patterns of supply and use of resources, including greater use of waste and recycled materials. Improved operating standards for mineral workings will be pursued, and the aim will be to ensure high and consistent standards in restoration. Further research on a wide range of minerals issues will be carried out to enable the aims of sustainable development to be taken forward.

REFERENCES AND FURTHER READING

[1] *United Kingdom's Minerals Yearbook 1992.* British Geological Survey, Keyworth, Nottinghamshire, 1993.

[2] *Towards Sustainability: A European Community Programme of Policy and Action in relation to the Environment and Sustainable Development* (the EC's Fifth Environmental Action Programme). Commission of the EC. Official publication of the EC, 1992. (Cm (92) 23/II/Final).

[3] *Guidelines for Aggregates Provision in England and Wales: Revision of MPG 6* (draft consultation document). DOE, 1993.

[4] *Interim Planning Guidance (Minerals Planning Guidance) Note.* DOE Press Release 212, March 1993.

[5] *Conserving Peatlands in Northern Ireland: a Statement of Policy.* DOE Northern Ireland, Environment Service, 1993.

[6] Planning and Compensation Act 1991. HMSO, 1991. ISBN 0–10–543491–4.

[7] *Review of the Provisions of the Town and Country Planning (Minerals) Act 1981: Old Mineral Permissions.* DOE consultation paper, 1992.

Review of the Provisions of the Town and Country Planning (Minerals) Act 1981: Old Mineral Permissions. Welsh Office consultation paper, 1992.

Review of the Provisions of the Town and Country Planning (Minerals) Act 1981: Post-1948 Mineral Permissions in Scotland. Scottish Office consultation paper, 1992.

[8] *The Minerals Industry Environmental Performance Study.* Groundwork Associates Ltd, Macclesfield, 1991.

[9] *Environmental Management in the Minerals Industry; the Greensite Report.* Groundwork Associates Ltd, Macclesfield, 1993.

[10] *Environmental Effects of Surface Mineral Workings; report for the Department of the Environment.* Roy Waller Associates Ltd. HMSO, 1992.

[11] *Efficient Use of Aggregates and Bulk Construction Materials.* BRE, Garston, Watford, 1993.

[12] Environmental Protection Act 1990. HMSO, 1990. ISBN 0–10–544390–5.

CHAPTER 19

ENERGY SUPPLY

A Sustainable Framework

- To ensure secure supplies of energy at competitive prices.
- To minimise adverse environmental impacts of energy use.

Trends

- Supplies of reasonably priced energy seem adequate for the foreseeable future.
- Improvements in energy efficiency, increased utilisation of renewable energy sources, and changes in the fuel mix are ameliorating the environmental impact of increased requirements for energy.

Problems and Opportunities

- Environmental problems include the threat of global warming, and also regional and local issues, such as sulphur dioxide (SO_2) and nitrogen oxides (NO_x) emissions.
- Nuclear power can deliver electricity without carbon dioxide (CO_2) emissions but raises issues of public concern, including handling of resulting wastes.

- Opportunities also presented by renewables to reduce CO_2 and other emissions.

Current Responses

- Energy efficiency campaigns are being stepped up and the supply utilities involved through the Energy Saving Trust.
- Value Added Tax (VAT) is being imposed on domestic fuel supplies.
- Renewable energy is being further encouraged.
- Nuclear electricity generation has increased and is expected to rise further when Sizewell B comes on line.

The Way Forward

- Energy efficiency, involving all sections of the economy, needs to be developed further so that consumers can enjoy improved energy services without increased fuel use.
- Longer term prospects for the development of renewable energy sources and combined heat and power could be significant.
- The prospects for nuclear power will shortly be reviewed.

INTRODUCTION

19.1 For the first half of the 20th century, the UK economy was almost wholly coal based. Now, the UK has four main sources of primary energy: coal, oil, gas and nuclear. UK production of fuels has increased and considerably diversified over the past 30 years and is currently just over 210 million tonnes of oil equivalent (MTOE). Just under half of that total is petroleum, whilst coal and natural gas each represents a little under a quarter. Overall inland consumption of fuels for energy use in the UK is currently 208 MTOE. This is a similar level to that in 1973 before the sudden increase in oil prices that occurred in that year. Since 1973 UK Gross Domestic Product (GDP) has increased by 33%; significant increases in energy use have been avoided through increased energy efficiency and through structural change in the economy.

19.2 Outside the transport sector, natural gas is now the dominant fuel, amounting to 65% of domestic fuel use, 42% in the commercial and public sector and 32% in industry. In 1973 petroleum was the major fuel used by commerce and the public sector (51%) and by industry (44%). The switch

to natural gas can be attributed to the surge in supply that took place in the early 1970s offering relatively cheap and clean fuel to consumers. The switch has also been accompanied by a decline in the share of coal in final consumption, particularly in the domestic sector. The use of electricity has become more important in both industry and in the commercial and public sectors. This reflects the changing structure of industry, increased use of electricity based technologies and increased demand for lighting, power and air-conditioning. The growth of transport fuel demand means that petroleum still represents 42.5% of final fuel use (see Figure 19.1) .

19.3 As part of its preparation for developing a UK strategy on climate change, the Government published *Energy Paper 59*[1]. This shows possible levels of energy demand associated with different assumptions about two of the major factors which will influence future UK energy demand: economic growth and fossil fuel prices. Assumptions about other factors can also be very important and, because of the very wide range of uncertainties, no attempt can be made to identify the single most likely outcome; a substantial margin of error should be attached to the estimates of energy demand projected. The scenarios show that final energy demand may grow by between 0.6–1.9% a year in the period 1990–2020. In primary energy terms, the projected range of energy demand is 212–257 MTOE for the year 2005 and 241–361 MTOE for the year 2020.

19.4 The UK has abundant supplies of all the fossil fuels, long experience of nuclear power and the potential to extend use of renewable sources of energy. Furthermore, the world has vast supplies of fossil fuels and uranium, and global exploration is still adding to proven reserves of fossil fuels as fast as they are being consumed. These factors suggest that, despite the likely increases in demand for energy internationally, particularly outside the Organisation for Economic Co-operation and Development (OECD) area, energy markets are well equipped to meet it. A recent report by the World Energy Council noted[2] that world energy demand could in one of the scenarios double in the next 30 years, and this might eventually lead to higher prices for certain fuels. However, UK and world experience of the last 20 years suggests that such price rises would be likely to lead to further improvements in energy efficiency, shifts in the global fuel mix and the introduction of new technologies; and thus they should contribute to global environmental goals.

GOVERNMENT POLICIES

19.5 The aim of the Government's energy policy is to ensure secure and diverse and sustainable supplies of energy in forms that people and businesses want, and at competitive prices. It is the Government's view that this aim will best be achieved by means of competitive energy markets working within a framework of law and regulation to protect health, safety and the environment. The Government also recognises that predicting the future for energy is notoriously difficult. Accordingly, the Government does not produce central plans, setting out how much of the different kinds of energy should be produced or consumed and by whom. However, the Government will continue to monitor the operation of the energy market to ensure that the aim of its energy policy is achieved. Diversity and security of supply, the pricing of energy and the impact of energy on the environment have been and will remain priority areas. The Government's aim is to ensure that future generations can enjoy a quality of energy services comparable to that currently enjoyed.

19.6 Although the availability of sufficient energy to meet UK demand is unlikely to present a problem over the period of this Strategy, environmental issues related to energy production and use will include global warming (see chapter 6), regional air quality issues (see chapter 7), issues relating to mining and extraction of fuels (see chapter 12), and transport-

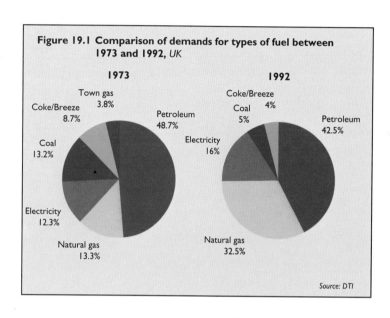

Figure 19.1 Comparison of demands for types of fuel between 1973 and 1992, *UK*

Source: DTI

related impacts (see chapter 26). There are two ways in which sustainability can be encouraged in the energy market:
- by encouraging consumers to meet their needs with less energy input, through improved energy efficiency;
- by supplying energy in ways which have less environmental impact.

This chapter discusses the questions which arise for the supply industries in consequence.

MEASURES TO REDUCE ENERGY CONSUMPTION BY 2000 AND BEYOND

Energy efficiency

19.7 Improvements in energy efficiency have real potential for minimising the environmental impact of energy use. The Government's Energy Efficiency Office (EEO) estimates that there is great scope for improvement without adverse economic impact and, indeed, in some cases with possible economic benefit. The prospects for improved energy efficiency, and action in hand to realize them, are described in chapter 36. They depend on influencing the decisions of many millions of individual consumers.

19.8 The energy supply industries also need to be fully involved in promoting energy efficiency. Energy markets should operate on "level playing fields" which do not undermine efforts to improve energy efficiency. Consumers are not interested in the amount of energy supplied to them as such, only in the services it provides, such as comfortable living and working temperatures, lighting levels, mechanical operations and transport. The development of competitive markets in energy supply has already given some encouragement to these industries to improve their services to consumers rather than to increase the quantity of energy they supply. The setting up of the Energy Saving Trust (see chapter 36) and recent changes in the price control formulae for gas and electricity supply are welcome steps in this direction. There is likely to be scope for further development in services, which could result in market opportunities for the supply industries.

19.9 Growth in energy demand for transport use has been underpinned by the availability of energy supplies and is itself a major contributor to overall increases in energy demand. Continuation of such growth is, therefore, a significant factor in considerations of a sustainable pattern of energy use.

Energy prices

19.10 As indicated above, in the short term at least, increased world fuel prices are unlikely to produce the degree of reduced demand needed to meet environmental objectives. Use of the price mechanism would, therefore, need Government action, for example, through taxation, to increase the price to the consumer. The UK Government has already taken action to increase the price of energy in the domestic sector through the phased introduction of Value Added Tax (VAT), and has incorporated its estimate of the effect of this increase in its *Climate Change Programme*[3] for returning carbon dioxide (CO_2) emissions to 1990 levels by 2000. The European Commission has proposed an EC-wide carbon/energy tax. Such a tax is not necessary in the UK to meet its current commitments on CO_2 emissions. The position for the longer term (post 2000), in relation to further market-based instruments, including fiscal measures, will be kept under review.

MEASURES TO REDUCE THE ENVIRONMENTAL IMPACT OF ENERGY SUPPLY

Fuel switching

19.11 Currently, coal fired plant dominates the UK electricity generation market. It can be expected to continue to make a significant contribution to electricity supply for the period of this Strategy. However, during the last few years, the use of gas for electricity generation has increased. This increased use has environmental benefits. The use of gas rather than coal can result in a halving of CO_2 emissions per unit of electricity sent out, together with substantial reductions in nitrogen oxide (NO_x) emissions and virtual elimination of sulphur dioxide (SO_2) and smoke emissions.

Part of this gain arises from the greater purity and higher heat content of the fuel, and part from the practicability of using gas at higher efficiency, in combined cycle gas turbine (CCGT) systems.

Technical developments

19.12 Technical developments are also beneficial in mitigating the environmental implications of energy supply. For example, sulphur can be removed from oil before combustion, or from flue gases after oil and coal combustion, but at a cost in both energy and financial terms as well as with some environmental impact. The usual form of removal is Flue Gas Desulphurisation (FGD). The most well established FGD processes use limestone, which needs to be quarried, often in areas of particular natural beauty. FGD also reduces power generation efficiency, thus increasing CO_2 emissions. Clean coal technologies can also provide more effective means of reducing sulphur emissions from coal burning, but they are unlikely to be in large scale use before the year 2000 and are likely to have much higher capital costs than the alternative of gas, although the overall economics will depend on the future price of gas.

Combined Heat and Power (CHP)

19.13 Use of the waste heat from power generation can increase the overall efficiency of fuel use still further, up to 80–90%. CHP is already being promoted as a priority area through the EEO's Best Practice Programme, and through an Energy Saving Trust Scheme (see chapter 36). Progress is such that the Government has recently been able to increase its target for installed capacity in 2000 from 4,000MW to 5,000MW, (compared to a 1990 figure of about 2,000MW). This increase corresponds to a reduction in CO_2 emissions of about 1 million tonnes of carbon (MtC) which is being incorporated in the *Climate Change Programme*.

19.14 The potential is there for further substantial increases in the years after 2000. However, progress so far has been largely in the industrial and commercial sector, and the potential after 2000 will depend to a considerable extent on the scope for using CHP in the domestic sector, that is to provide community heating for residential consumers on an attractive and commercial basis. This could require, for example, the installation of insulated pipes for delivering hot water to large numbers of separate domestic premises and the cooperation of most residents in the areas where it is introduced. As with energy efficiency, much will depend on the attitudes of many millions of individual consumers. The low emissions of gas fired power stations makes their siting near residential areas more acceptable than that of power stations using other fuels, and this could facilitate progress with such CHP schemes.

NON-FOSSIL ENERGY SOURCES

Renewables

19.15 During 1992, renewable energy provided about 2% of UK electricity supply, which had the effect of reducing annual CO_2 emissions by about 1 MtC. As stated in the *Climate Change Programme*, the Government is now working towards a UK figure of 1,500MW declared net capacity (DNC) of new electricity generating capacity from renewable sources by 2000. This would enable the most promising of the renewable electricity generating technologies to develop, and could increase the renewables contribution to about 5% of current UK electricity supply, reducing annual CO_2 emissions by possibly a further 2MtC. By 2025, renewables may be supplying between 5% and 20% of current UK electricity supply, with further significant contributions from the heat-producing new and renewable energy technologies (for example, the combustion of wood, straw and various wastes to generate heat). The future impact of these sources on UK energy supply will be dependent upon their economic viability, environmental acceptability and the success of the Government's programme.

Nuclear

19.16 Nuclear power provides a source of energy free from the pollutants that contribute to acid rain and global warming. It currently provides around 22% of the UK's electricity. This is expected to increase when the Sizewell B power station comes on stream in 1994; but, unless other stations are constructed, the figure may start to decline around 2000 as the magnox stations reach the end of their operational lives. In 1992, the UK's emissions of CO_2 would have been between 6 MtC and 15 MtC higher if the electricity generated from nuclear power had been generated from gas or coal plant. The UK's nuclear industry has made good progress in reducing the cost of electricity from existing nuclear stations. The Government is committed to maintaining the nuclear option for the future, provided that it can prove economic and maintains high standards of safety and environmental protection. The Government is considering options for the scope and format of a review of the future prospects for nuclear power in the UK.

19.17 It is important to ensure that the nuclear power industry operates to high standards of safety and environmental protection. Accordingly, nuclear power stations and other nuclear plants are subject to stringent regulation in their respective fields by the Nuclear Installations Inspectorate, Her Majesty's Inspectorate of Pollution (in England and Wales – in Scotland, Her Majesty's Industrial Pollution Inspectorate) and the Ministry of Agriculture, Fisheries and Food. This framework of regulation covers all aspects of nuclear power from design, construction, operation and maintenance of facilities, through to decommissioning and disposal of wastes. The safe transport of nuclear materials is regulated by the Department of Transport.

19.18 Nuclear power generation gives rise to radioactive waste both in the course of normal operations and in the decommissioning of nuclear power stations and fuel cycle plant. The nuclear industry is responsible for dealing with future waste arisings, as well as those which already exist, and this includes planning for decommissioning and securing the funds to pay for it. Both operational and decommissioning wastes are taken account of in the Government's radioactive waste management strategy. The Government's policy is to ensure that radioactive waste is managed safely and that the present generation, which receives the benefit of nuclear power, meets its responsibilities to future generations. Details of the policy are kept under active review and the Government receives advice from an independent committee of experts, the Radioactive Waste Management Advisory Committee.

19.19 Waste is categorised into low, intermediate and high levels (LLW, ILW, and HLW respectively). The Department of the Environment (DOE) and UK Nirex jointly fund the compilation of a radioactive waste inventory which assesses current stocks of wastes and arising up to 2030, and is updated regularly.

19.20 UK Nirex was formed by the nuclear industry in 1982, and incorporated in 1985. It is developing a deep disposal facility for the ILW and long lived LLW, and is currently investigating a site adjacent to British Nuclear Fuels' Sellafield works. Building on the results of its ongoing surface drilling programme, Nirex intends to apply early in 1994 for permission to construct a Rock Characterisation Facility (RCF), which will enable it to examine internally the strata in which it proposes to construct the facility. If the rock proves satisfactory, Nirex will apply in 1999 for planning permission to construct the facility itself, with the aim of completing construction some 10 years later. The Government is committed to holding a full public inquiry into the planning application for the repository itself, which will also need to be licensed by the appropriate regulatory bodies.

19.21 About 90% of annual arisings are LLW. Most of this is disposed of at BNFL's Drigg disposal facility, although some will be stored pending the availability of a Nirex disposal facility. Improved procedures, including categorisation and handling, have reduced LLW volumes by a factor of four over the last 10 years. ILW is currently stored, mainly at the sites of production, until it can be disposed of by Nirex. HLW from reprocessing spent fuel is stored at Sellafield and at Dounreay in Scotland. Such waste is being converted from liquid to a vitrified form at Sellafield. It will be stored for at least 50 years to cool.

19.22 Some liquid and gaseous LLW is discharged directly to the environment. These discharges are regulated to ensure that their radiological impact is as low as reasonably achievable, taking economic and social factors into account, and that radiation doses to the public remain well within internationally accepted limits. Levels of these discharges have been progressively reduced. For example, as a result of improved working practices and continuing investment, the level of radiologically significant discharges to the Irish Sea from Sellafield is now about 1% of peak levels of the 1970s. The new effluent treatment plant, EARP, which is awaiting authorisation, would provide a means to reduce further the discharges of the most radiologically significant nuclides, and the operation of the Thermal Oxide Reprocessing Plant (THORP) will still leave these discharges at a tiny fraction of the earlier levels.

19.23 Only 0.1% of the UK population's exposure to radiation comes from radioactive waste. 87% comes from natural sources, while almost all of the exposure from artificial sources is due to x-rays and isotopes used in medical diagnosis and treatment. Nevertheless, the Government's aim remains that of keeping the risks from radioactive waste as low as is reasonably achievable, taking economic and social factors into account.

REFERENCES AND FURTHER READING

[1] *Energy Paper 59 – Energy Related Carbon Emissions in Possible Future Scenarios for the UK.* Department of Trade and Industry. HMSO, 1992. ISBN 0-11-414157-6.

[2] *Energy For Tomorrow's World.* 1993. World Energy Council, 34 St James Street, London SW1A 1HD. ISBN 0-312-10659-9 (USA).

[3] *Climate Change: The UK Programme.* Cm 2427. HMSO, 1994. ISBN 0–10–124272-7.

CHAPTER 20

MANUFACTURING AND SERVICES

A Sustainable Framework

- To continue to work within a stable, transparent, effectively enforced regulatory system.
- To make appropriate use of economic instruments.
- To handle resource depletion, emissions and waste responsibly.
- To encourage voluntary action by industry to move towards best practice and good environmental management.
- To enable capital markets to take account of corporate environmental performance.
- To support and inform environmentally aware consumers, taking positive steps to support products less damaging to the environment.

Trends

- Leading businesses are already voluntarily adopting environmental policies and targets, and implementing management systems to achieve them.
- Some companies are producing corporate environmental reports.
- The link between environmental performance and competitiveness means that the financial community is increasingly taking account of environmental concerns in investment decisions.
- A growing number of firms are evaluating the environmental performance of their suppliers.

Problems and Opportunities

- Smaller businesses tend to lack information and resources, and, therefore, find it harder to adopt a proactive role.
- Financial institutions lack the comprehensive information on environmental performance needed to integrate it as a factor in project appraisal and investment decisions.
- "Bottom line" benefits from taking environmental action such as energy efficiency and waste minimisation.
- Expanding demand for environmental goods and services.

Current Responses

- Government action:
  - implementation of extensive environmental legislation;
  - promotion of voluntary schemes, such as Eco-Management and Audit and Eco-labelling;
  - raising awareness, particularly among small businesses;
  - continuing dialogue between Government and industry on environmental issues.
- Action by the manufacturing and services sector:
  - companies signing up to principles in the International Chamber of Commerce's (ICC) Business Charter for Sustainable Development;
  - progress towards best practice in environmental management, including use of BS 7750;
  - responding to the demands for more information on the impact of operations and particular products on the environment.

The Way Forward

- Government will work to establish the conditions for business to operate sustainably, looking where possible to rely on economic instruments rather than regulation to deliver environmental objectives.
- Industry should voluntarily adopt best practice in environmental management.
- The manufacturing and services sector should integrate environmental considerations into all aspects of policy and management, and report fully on performance.
- Research and development into problem-solving cleaner technologies is required.
- Managers, the workforce and consumers need education and training on environmental issues.
- Small businesses need particular help and advice in making best use of environmental messages.

INTRODUCTION

20.1 Continuing economic development is essential to maintain and improve the quality of human life; but it must be sustainable. Manufacturing industry in the UK today accounts for approximately 20% of employment, 82% of visible exports and 21% of Gross Domestic Product (GDP). The UK imports about 37% of its consumption of manufactured goods. Service industries, including banking, tourism, leisure, retailing and distribution have been taking a growing share of activity.

20.2 The manufacturing industry has direct impacts on the environment through raw material depletion, waste generation, emissions to air and water, and energy consumption both in the production process and through the movement of raw goods and finished materials. Service industries produce less direct pollution, but also have a major environmental impact through energy consumption and waste production. Some sectors, such as the tourism industry, can have intense local effects (see chapter 27), while others, such as the distributive trades, can have a major influence on transport demand and local land use. The consultancy sector can spread innovatory ideas and best practice. A productive manufacturing and services sector can make a major contribution towards sustainable development, generating economic growth, as well as developing technologies and services which can offer solutions to environmental problems.

20.3 Sustainable development involves identifying ways in which industries can flourish, while reducing impacts to levels the environment can sustain. By finding the right mix of regulation, economic instruments, voluntary action by industry and consumer-led developments, the UK will be able to strike a balance between economic development and environmental impact. The manufacturing and services sector has already taken steps on the path to sustainability, but there is still much more to be achieved. The responsibility for direct action lies with industry, but the financial sector, consumers and non-governmental organisations (NGOs) must all play a part.

INDUSTRY TODAY

20.4 Industry's environmental awareness and performance has improved dramatically over the past few decades. This is largely due to the need to comply with the growing body of environmental legislation, but also reflects a major change in attitudes among the leading companies, who have recognised that industry has a responsibility to take positive action to protect and conserve the environment. The rate of progress varies greatly between companies, reflecting the wide diversity of UK business.

20.5 The UK already has a substantial body of environmental protection legislation, some national and some agreed in the EC. This is outlined in other chapters. Legislation continues to play a key role in securing minimum standards, and this has been given extra impetus by the introduction of integrated pollution control (IPC), with its emphasis on securing the best practicable environmental option. However, the range and prescriptive nature of some regulation can cause difficulties for industry, hampering competitiveness and innovation, and offering limited flexibility for business to introduce change cost-effectively. The Government recognises that the regulatory route does

not necessarily promote the best environmental option, and is already committed to a policy of deregulation and rationalisation of legislation, without compromising the determination to achieve high standards. It is also committed to using economic instruments, where appropriate, and these measures usually allow industry greater flexibility. These issues are dealt with more fully in chapter 33.

20.6 Leaders in the field have already adopted environmental policies and targets and introduced management systems to deliver them. They have discovered that environmental reviews often identify potential for cost savings or product development and have started to consider the whole life-cycle of their products and processes. They are seeing benefit in reporting on their performance to shareholders and the wider public. A few reports have been externally verified, but in general the information in corporate reports is extremely variable both in quality and quantity. Some companies are already looking beyond their own operations to the performance of their suppliers, pushing awareness of environmental issues through the supply chain. Other companies, often the smaller ones, have yet to adopt a proactive approach. They may be limited by a lack of information and resources. This is why the Government is currently trying to encourage more smaller businesses to become involved in local green business clubs and environmental schemes where they can share information and expertise. The Government also supports initiatives, such as 'Business Links', to provide advice and guidance to companies on legislative requirements.

20.7 The environment is one of a number of issues which impacts on investment decisions. Protecting the environment is about managing operations well to minimise waste; this can be costly, but often results in substantial savings. The implications and weighting of environmental considerations in those decisions are changing as the impacts the environment can have on competitiveness and profitability become clearer. Environmental issues are of increasing importance in the evaluation of corporate performance; and the capital markets are having to take a more sophisticated view of the economics of long term investment in environmental protection measures.

20.8 Domestic consumers increasingly take environmental issues into account in their purchasing decisions – their most notable impact so far being their refusal to buy aerosols containing chlorofluorocarbons (CFCs). Proactive companies are responding by promoting cleaner products and technologies, entering new markets and publicising their own environmental programmes. "Green consumerism" is discussed in more detail in chapter 32.

TRENDS

20.9 Innovation has been a consistent feature of UK industrial history, and there is no reason to expect it to falter over the next two decades. Solutions will be found to some of the environmental problems the UK faces today, but it is not possible to predict to which problems or how they will be solved. Nor is it possible to rely on technological progress alone to tackle all problems. There are, however, some trends which it is useful to examine to consider how businesses may develop in the next 20 years.

20.10 Legislation will remain the main means of maintaining minimum standards for the foreseeable future, but it must be based on sound science and cost-benefit analysis, set long term targets, and be effectively enforced. Targets should increasingly be the subject of public discussion and consultation with industry. Provision of information to the public is already a key plank of Government policy and this information should be more readily and conveniently available, so that there is a basis of agreed facts underpinning the policy debate.

20.11 The financial sector should become better able to evaluate the financial implications of environmental risk and liability and should consider the potential impact of poor environmental performance on commercial performance when making investment decisions. The City may begin to consider environmental performance in rating companies.

20.12 Environmental considerations will be an important influence on purchasing behaviour over the next two decades; environmental criteria will become standard features of purchasing specifications, both in the public and private sectors. Consumers will have much more information at their disposal to inform their decision-making, as the eco-labelling and energy labelling schemes become more widespread in the UK and other countries. Product standards will have to be revised to take account of environmental considerations.

20.13 Environmental awareness among companies in 2012 will be much higher and more widespread than at present. Knowledge among employees, both of environmental issues and the impact they can have on the environment in the workplace, should have increased due to the expected growth in environmental education and improved industrial training in environmental issues. Training in environmental issues should also form an important part of any corporate training policy.

20.14 The anticipated improvements in the legislative and scientific base will help industry plan its long term investments. Increased internalisation of environmental costs and continued pressure from consumers and investors should strengthen business commitment to protecting the environment, with many companies likely to adopt principles such as those in the ICC's *Business Charter for Sustainable Development*[1]. Companies will increasingly integrate environmental considerations into business decisions and coordinate management of quality and health and safety with their management of the environment; BS 7750 (the new environmental management standard developed by the British Standards Institute), the EC's Eco-Management and Audit scheme and the chemical industry's Responsible Care scheme should also be useful tools in encouraging more companies to integrate the environment into their management systems. Industry will increasingly set targets for direct impacts on the environment (such as emissions, resource use and waste), and perhaps also for indirect impacts, such as product development, distribution networks, company transport and production processes – as they already do in areas such as product reliability and customer satisfaction.

20.15 Companies will, therefore, continue to find that openness about their environmental impacts reassures investors, employees, potential recruits and the local community. As environmental performance becomes a competitive issue, companies will find that they can reap commercial advantage from disclosure; this will be reflected in increased reporting on environmental performance as an integral part of the company report and accounts. It is likely that there will be well-developed environmental auditing techniques, which can be applied to environmental management systems and corporate environmental information as well as to financial results. There should also be professional qualifications and standards, and increasing integration of the required environmental expertise into the auditing profession.

20.16 These developing markets for environmental goods and services will also encourage more companies to consider the environment. New processes will increase industrial efficiency, minimise waste and use of resources and help prevent pollution, so making the products and the technology itself attractive to purchasers. Product and process design should take account of environmental impacts; durability, upgradeability and recyclability will be key criteria.

THE WAY FORWARD

20.17 Meeting the challenge of sustainable development will demand positive action from Government, industry, the financial sector, consumers and NGOs. Effective dialogue and cooperation are essential if all interests are to work towards this common goal.

Government action

20.18 The Government, working within the EC as necessary, will create the conditions within which the manufacturing and service sector can pursue sustainable development successfully. By determining the right mix of policies and implementing them effectively and equitably, the Government can create a stable and transparent legislative framework, established around long term environmental quality objectives. New legislation must only be introduced after thorough consultation with firms of all sizes, and to a realistic timetable, which takes account of industrial investment cycles. The Government must also ensure that legislation is based on sound science, and that it does not impose costs on industry that are disproportionate to the environmental benefit to be achieved. Cost benefit analysis will be an important tool for justifying government action, and further work is needed to improve the evaluation of environmental benefits.

20.19 The Government will increasingly favour economic instruments over regulation as a more effective way of changing behaviour, especially where knowledge and technology are changing rapidly. By putting a price on environmental impacts, economic instruments affect directly all aspects of a company's operations and can force the environment into mainstream business decision-making.

20.20 The Government will also continue to promote to industry, and to small companies in particular, the benefits of positive environmental management and of best practice in the use of environmental technology and techniques. The key message is that good environmental management is allied with good management generally and makes good business sense. The challenge is to move beyond the initial barriers of low awareness, to demonstrate the benefits and options available, and to convince industry of the value of environmental investment. In this way, industry will be helped to respond effectively to the very significant challenges and opportunities posed by environmental pressures. The Government will pay special attention to the information requirements of small businesses, since these have particular difficulties in finding the time and resources for environmental improvement, but are an important source of innovation.

20.21 Industry's cooperation and expertise is crucial in a move towards sustainable development. The Government will encourage innovation, not only by large companies but also by small firms, utilising their innovative abilities. Ongoing dialogue, such as through the Advisory Committee on Business and the Environment, is vital if the Government is to understand the constraints under which companies are operating, and if industry is to keep in close touch with Government thinking. By developing the existing consultation network, the Government will be able to involve small businesses more fully, so that their specific concerns can be taken into account at an early stage of policy development. The Government must also take into account wider interests by ensuring that there is an ongoing, balanced debate between industry and different interest groups to achieve and maintain a consensus on strategic policy, while ensuring that different perspectives are respected and taken into account.

Action by industry

20.22 The technological and productive capacity of industry gives it a pivotal role in achieving sustainable development. Some industrial sectors are in themselves solutions to environmental problems. The waste and water industries, for example, have an important role in clean up and pollution minimisation. The environmental technology industry has a function in developing and marketing equipment that enables industry to operate in a manner that is less damaging to the environment. The wealth created by industry is a key driver of environmental improvement.

20.23 Industry must continue to take a proactive stance on environmental issues, striving for best practice. Take up of voluntary schemes, such as Eco-labelling, Eco-Management and Audit and BS 7750, will be an indicator of the standards industry is prepared to set itself.

20.24 Industry should continue to integrate environmental considerations into all aspects of policy and management. In particular, industry must commit time and resources to environmental remediation, research and development, and the application of new, cleaner technologies. It should also set itself challenging targets for environmental improvement. By taking an appropriate life-cycle approach when considering the impacts of industrial operations, companies will be able to make informed decisions about the environmental impact of their activities. As part of this process, companies should consider their overseas operations as part of a total company approach to environmental standards.

20.25 More widespread reporting on environmental performance will enable investors to evaluate environmental risk, let Government know what improvements industry is prepared to make voluntarily, and improve public awareness about the performance of different companies. Such reports should set targets for action and monitor progress against those targets.

20.26 Companies in the forefront of developing positive environmental management will be able to lead by example, disseminating information on their experience and expertise widely through the business community. Business-led initiatives, such as the Confederation of British Industry's (CBI) Environment Business Forum and the growing network of local green clubs, will play an important role in promulgating information on the environment throughout the sector and in helping companies, particularly smaller companies, to take positive steps to improve their environmental performance.

Action by the financial sector

20.27 The growing evidence of the implications of environmental performance on profitability, and the increasing costs of poor environmental performance, should encourage investors to seek consistent and reliable information from companies on their environmental impacts, targets and progress towards them. Systems of environmental accounting and reporting will need to be improved in order to provide the necessary basis for good decisions.

Action by consumers

20.28 Both Government and industry need to promote greater awareness among consumers about the environmental consequences of their everyday actions; schemes providing official, reliable, information, such as eco-labelling and energy labelling will be valuable. Consumers have a responsibility to act on this information and make responsible choices about the products which they buy; their purchasing power is a key factor in forcing companies to improve their environmental performance. Consumers may sometimes, but not always, need to trade off price against environmental improvement. An important task is to identify the level of price increase which consumers will accept to cover the cost of environmental improvements.

REFERENCES AND FURTHER READING

[1]   *The Business Charter for Sustainable Development: Principles for Environmental Management.* International Chamber of Commerce, 1991, publication 210/356 A.

CHAPTER 21

BIOTECHNOLOGY

A Sustainable Framework

- To encourage the use of genetic resources whilst ensuring that this does not lead to long term, or severe adverse effects on the environment.

Trends

- The main biotechnological developments are being made in the areas of health care, bioremediation and agricultural applications.

Problems and Opportunities

- Biotechnology can contribute substantially to sustainability by encouraging economic use of genetic resources, which can lead to new and valuable products, and by helping to improve the environment.
- It is important to ensure that the technology is applied in a beneficial manner, and that any risks to humans and the environment are minimised.

Current Responses

- Legislation has been introduced in the UK to provide for protection of humans and the environment from all activities involving genetically modified organisms.
- Establishment of a new Research Council with responsibility for biotechnology.
- Ongoing research to identify risks associated with particular organisms.

The Way Forward

- Continued review of regulatory controls to ensure that they are commensurate with the degree of risk.
- Government will issue new guidance on risk assessment:
  − continued research to utilise the potential of biotechnology and to identify hazards and risks associated with genetic modification;
  − promotion of an international agreement on risk assessment and risk management of modern biotechnology with a view to an eventual convention.

INTRODUCTION

Applications

21.1 Biotechnology involves the use of biological systems, including living organisms, to create products for health care, industry, agriculture and the environment, and for service purposes, such as diagnostic kits and clean-up processes. Biotechnology has been used in traditional applications, such as baking and brewing, for centuries. However, the advent and development of new molecular techniques over the past 20 years have opened up a vast range of new possibilities. Certain of these "modern" techniques, often referred to as genetic modification, can allow parts of the genetic material of one organism to be incorporated into the genetic material of another, possibly non-related, organism. The resulting genetically modified organism (GMO) has one or more new characteristics and could not be produced using traditional methods, such as selective breeding. The technology offers opportunities for greater novelty and the possibility of crossing different species quickly.

21.2 The UK was one of the first countries to use modern biotechnology, initially by using GMOs in containment (within physical, chemical and biological barriers to limit contact with the environment) to produce chemicals and pharmaceuticals. Since 1986, biotechnology has been used in controlled releases to the environment, such as the planting out in trial of crop plants with specific modified characteristics for research purposes. Modern biotechnology has already produced developments in health care which had previously been considered to be unattainable, and this trend is likely to continue. Biotechnology also has enormous potential in other fields, such as environmental clean-up and veterinary medicine, and in the analysis of genetic determinants, which may allow for improving the quality of, and yield from, crop plants and livestock.

Research

21.3 As experience with modern biotechnology grows, countries are devoting more resources to the application of these techniques for specific needs. Biotechnological techniques are used in fundamental research, such as in the international human genome project, part of which is being conducted in the UK. Projects such as these have allowed significant progress to be made in the identification of genes responsible for certain inherited diseases. Gene therapy is already being carried out in the UK. Significant developments in disease treatment and prevention by vaccines are also under way. The Government will continue to support UK research in potential medical, scientific, environmental and agricultural applications of biotechnology, and is also participating in the EC Framework Programme.

21.4 In its White Paper *Realising Our Potential: A Strategy for Science, Engineering and Technology*[1], the Government announced the creation, on 1 April 1994, of a new Research Council, the Biotechnology and Biological Sciences Research Council, which will take over the majority of work in biotechnology currently carried out through the Agricultural and Food, and Science and Engineering Research Councils. In supporting a full range of basic, strategic and applied research in biological systems, the new Council will place special emphasis on enhancing the competitiveness and safety of the UK's biology-based industries.

PROBLEMS AND OPPORTUNITIES

Contribution of biotechnology to sustainable development

21.5 Traditional biotechnology, using non-genetically modified organisms, can continue to contribute to sustainability, particularly in less technologically difficult processes. For example, biotechnology has a prominent role in environmental remediation (clean-up processes), such as treatment of contaminated soil. It provides the basis for treatment which requires less intense use of resources and energy than many other types of treatment, whilst providing solutions to pollution and waste management problems which are at least equally beneficial to the environment. Energy derived from the fermentation of alcohol may also aid sustainability by reducing the demand for fossil fuels.

21.6 Modern biotechnology using GMOs has a prominent role to play in economic development and sustainability: not only does it have the potential to provide new and valuable products, but it can also help to improve the environment. The Government is encouraging the development of such "green" products. Biotechnology could provide cleaner processes, enabling industrial and agricultural activities to be carried out in ways which are more environmentally friendly than their non-biological counterparts. Examples are the use of biological agents in the chemical industry, in the treatment of wastes and in environmental monitoring. Furthermore, it is likely that biotechnology products will bring about a reduction in reliance on some chemical products in the future. For example, genetically improved crop varieties could lessen dependence on pesticides and fertilisers.

Problems and constraints

21.7 To achieve sustainability, it is important both to strive for appropriate application of biotechnology, and to minimise the risks of damage to the environment. In traditional biotechnology, any risks are usually known because there

has been a long experience of use. GMOs have now been used in containment for more than 20 years and, from this experience, categories of low hazard organisms have been identified. There is less experience with releases of GMOs to the environment, for which there are two main sources of risk:

- the possibility of transfer of inserted genetic material from the modified organism into other, related organisms;
- the survival and spread of the modified organism itself, which expresses new characteristics.

21.8 These hazards might affect the capacity of the GMO to exert adverse effects on other organisms or ecosystems. The risks depend on the frequency with which hazards might be realised, and the consequences for the environment. The risk can therefore be evaluated in terms of the impact on sustainability and, if necessary, appropriate management practices can be developed and applied.

21.9 The use of GMOs in the environment has so far been restricted mainly to experimental releases of modified crop plants, and no adverse effects on human health or the environment have been reported. This may, in part, reflect the intrinsically low risk associated with a particular organism or the way it is released. It also reflects the cautious approach to the new technology taken in the UK and in most other countries, which has been to examine proposals on a case-by-case basis, and to use earlier results to assess more extended operations in a flexible step by step approach.

CURRENT RESPONSES AND FUTURE ACTION

Regulatory approach

21.10 Controls over biotechnology are needed to allow rapid development, whilst at the same time giving the public and consumers the assurance of regulatory scrutiny. The UK adopted a precautionary approach to modern biotechnology because the lack of experience meant that it was not possible to predict the risks to humans and the environment. In 1978, shortly after modern biotechnological techniques came to be used fairly widely, the UK introduced human health and safety legislation covering all activities involving genetic modification. The Environmental Protection Act 1990[2] and *The Genetically Modified Organisms (Deliberate Release) Regulations 1992*[3] provide for the environmental safety of releases of GMOs to the environment and the marketing of GMO products. Regulatory control of contained uses of GMOs is provided by *The Genetically Modified Organisms (Contained Use) Regulations 1992*[4]. Together, this legislation implements two EC directives.

21.11 The Government has two independent expert committees to advise on the human and environmental safety of contained uses, and releases and marketing of GMOs: the Advisory Committee on Genetic Modification and the Advisory Committee on Releases to the Environment respectively.

21.12 The Government is keen to ensure that the degree of regulatory control applied to biotechnology is commensurate with the level of risk, with no unnecessary burdens being placed on the biotechnology industry and its considerable economic potential. As experience grows, and certain organisms and operations are shown to be of low risk and, therefore, to be compatible with sustainable development, regulatory control will be relaxed. This will necessitate continuous review and adjustment of controls to reduce unnecessary burdens on industry and to strike the right balance with environmental and safety issues.

21.13 As risk assessment is central to the development and control of biotechnology, the Government is focusing on methods of assessment and publishing guidance for users. In addition, the Department of the Environment and other Departments, including the Ministry of Agriculture, Fisheries and Food, have extensive research programmes targeted on identifying and assessing risks associated with particular organisms. The approach to risk assessment and risk management will be continually refined as more experience and data accumulate.

International action

21.14 The Government's aim is to promote a climate that will allow maximum trade in biotechnology products and impose minimum burdens on those investing in and developing the technology whilst, nonetheless, giving due attention to the protection of the environment and to human safety and well being. An international approach to biotechnology safety is needed quickly, because it is likely that there will soon be significant volumes of traded goods containing GMOs. Growth in biotechnology will probably be very rapid over the next few years, and it has been estimated that the world market might approach $80–100 billion by 2000. Without international collaboration on the safety testing of such products, non-tariff barriers to trade could arise. International agreements should also encourage the development of biotechnology products for a wide variety of environments.

21.15 The EC has adopted a policy based on collaboration between member states, and the establishment of a single market. This regional, harmonised approach to development in the context of safety is likely to take on increasing importance as more products of modern biotechnology flow from research investments. In the wider international forum, the UK and the Netherlands collaborated closely and participated actively in the preparations for the discussions on biotechnology safety at the Earth Summit in Rio. The Government is now pressing for the implementation of Agenda 21[5] to achieve international agreement on biotechnology safety. The Government welcomed the African Regional Conference, the first regional meeting on biotechnology safety, which was hosted by the Netherlands and Zimbabwe and held in October 1993 in Harare. It would like the existing national and international regulations and guidance, such as that produced by the Organisation for Economic Co-operation and Development, the UNCED Research Paper No 55[6] following the Earth Summit, and the results of the Harare and similar regional meetings, to provide the framework for an international instrument on safety in biotechnology.

REFERENCES AND FURTHER READING

[1]   *Realising Our Potential: A Strategy for Science, Engineering and Technology.* Cm 2250, HMSO, 1993.

[2]   Environmental Protection Act 1990. HMSO, 1990. ISBN 0–10–544390–5.

[3]   *The Genetically Modified Organisms (Deliberate Release) Regulations 1992.* SI 1992 No 3280, HMSO.

[4]   *The Genetically Modified Organisms (Contained Use) Regulations 1992.* SI 1992 No 3217, HMSO.

[5]   *Agenda 21* – an action plan for the next century, endorsed at UNCED, 1992.

[6]   *Environmentally Sound Managemnt of Biotechnology: Safety in Biotechnology. Assessment and Management of Risk,* UNCED Secretariat, Research Paper No 55, 1992.

CHAPTER 22

CHEMICALS

A Sustainable Framework

- To test and assess the risks of new and existing chemicals.
- To reduce point source and diffuse emissions.
- To develop less hazardous alternatives to the chemicals currently in use.
- To develop low waste technologies.
- To increase the use of recycling.

Trends

- The development of more specific, less toxic and more degradable chemicals.
- Improved test methods, including the use of fewer animals.
- Better understanding and greater use of risk assessment.

Problems and Opportunities

- Persistent chemicals, with long term damaging effects on human health or the environment, have become widely distributed.
- There is considerable uncertainty about the effects of long term, low-level exposure.
- Ecotoxicity testing is still in the early stages of development.
- The need to control environmentally damaging chemicals, and economic, social and regulatory pressures on the use of such chemicals, will force the development of new and improved technology.
- Chemicals will be assessed for their overall impact on the environment, and comparisons made with substitute materials or processes.

Current Responses

- Environmental legislation and pollution control regulate the use of chemicals.
- Statutory approvals procedure for biologically active compounds.
- Systematic assessment of new and existing chemicals.
- International Guidelines for the Exchange of Information on Chemicals in International Trade.

The Way Forward

- Adherence to the Agenda 21 programme for the management of toxic chemicals.
- International cooperation on the extension of information exchange on chemical risks.
- Voluntary agreements between Government and industry on use and recycling of chemicals.
- Industry Responsible Care programmes.
- Regulations to control the use of chemicals when necessary.
- Greater use of economic instruments to influence the use of chemicals.

INTRODUCTION

22.1 Modern society is dependent on the use of a wide range of chemical substances. Industry depends on the use of chemical substances as raw materials, solvents, lubricants, fuels, dyes, adhesives, intermediates, biocides and so on. The production of many consumer products, such as paints, plastics, detergents and disinfectants, which are important to quality of life depends on the availability of chemicals. Some of these chemicals are naturally occurring and are extracted from minerals or plants, but there is a growing number of synthetic chemicals produced by the chemicals industry. The number of chemicals produced has increased rapidly over the last 20 years; for example, the inventory of chemicals placed on the EC market contains over 100,000 substances. Some of these chemicals can cause serious threats to human health, to the natural environment and, ultimately, to the sustainability of the balance between human activity and the environment. The greatest threats are likely to arise from persistent chemicals which become widely distributed and have long term damaging effects on human health or the environment, or from excessive release of chemicals which cause irreversible changes in natural processes.

22.2 Many chemicals are released to the environment directly, or in products or as wastes. People may be exposed directly to chemicals during their manufacture, distribution, use or disposal, or indirectly to chemicals released to the environment. Whatever the source of a chemical, the potential harmful effects on people and on the natural environment will depend on the extent of exposure to the chemical and on its toxic and other properties. In some cases, the immediate exposure from a point source will be the most important; in other cases, cumulative exposure from all sources will be more important. It is clearly important to know whether exposure to chemicals can be harmful to human health or to the environment, and to take action to reduce the risks where necessary. Since exposure may occur at any stage, the full life cycle of a substance must be considered when estimating the potential for human and environmental exposure. In general, the control of risks arising directly from work activity is covered by employment legislation; the protection of people from risks arising indirectly, and the protection of the environment is covered by environmental legislation.

22.3 Direct releases of chemicals to the environment during manufacture or industrial use are usually controlled by the pollution control legislation, referred to in Section 2 of this Strategy. Emissions from the most polluting processes are subject to the integrated pollution control (IPC) regime described in chapter 4. Indirect or diffuse releases of chemicals to the environment, or release as a result of the use of chemicals in products, may need other types of control, such as restrictions on the use of certain chemicals. A discussion paper on reducing emissions of hazardous chemicals to the environment will be published early in 1994.

22.4 The overall objective of these controls is to manage the use of chemicals in a sustainable manner and to minimise or eliminate risks to human health or the environment, now or in the future. Certain special classes of chemical, such as agricultural pesticides, ozone-depleting substances and greenhouse gases, are covered elsewhere in the Strategy; but the general principles of risk assessment apply equally to these chemicals. Chemical wastes are covered in chapter 23.

RISKS TO HUMAN HEALTH AND THE ENVIRONMENT

Toxicity

22.5 Any chemical released in large quantities in the wrong place can cause problems, but toxic chemicals can cause problems even when released in small quantities. The toxicity of chemicals is usually measured by tests using laboratory animals, but it is important that all the available data are considered so that as detailed as possible a toxicological profile of the substance is built up.

22.6 In order to evaluate potential risks to environmental organisms, tests may be carried out on fish or other aquatic species, birds, plants, algae or micro-organisms. Ecotoxicity testing is a relatively new science and new test methods, for instance, to assess effects on terrestrial species such as earthworms and arthropods, are still under development.

22.7 The primary objective of most controls on the use of chemicals is the protection of plants, animals and human health, but it is also important to ensure that basic ecological

processes involving other organisms in the environment are protected. Experience has shown that there is great uncertainty about the effects of chemicals on the ecological and environmental processes on which human life ultimately depends. Long term sustainable development depends on maintaining the functioning and health of the organisms responsible for these processes.

22.8 Many of the toxic chemicals released to the environment are degraded by physical, chemical or biological processes into simpler compounds, and eventually converted to compounds such as water, carbon dioxide or inorganic salts. The micro-organisms in sewage treatment works and soil are extremely adaptable in converting many domestic, agricultural and industrial wastes into harmless degradation products. However, there are some substances which resist degradation and can accumulate in the environment or in particular species of animal. Elements such as lead, cadmium and mercury are non-degradable, and some organic compounds such as polychlorinated biphenyls (PCBs) and certain organochlorine pesticides are very resistant to degradation.

22.9 This group of persistent chemicals needs to be controlled with great care, particularly those which are toxic or which bioaccumulate, because of the long term damage they can cause and the uncertainties inherent in predicting the effects of long term, low-level exposure to chemicals (see Box 22.1). There is concern that continuous exposure to very low levels of certain chemicals in the environment could have complex long term effects on human and animal health, and also on other ecological processes that are not yet fully understood.

Risk assessment

22.10 The risk assessment procedure used for chemicals released to the environment is to compare the estimated exposure (dose) with the dose known to cause harmful effects. Information on ecotoxicity is used to estimate the lowest level of exposure likely to cause harmful effects to the most sensitive species. This is compared with estimates or measurements of exposure in the environmental medium of most concern (water, sediment, air or land). If there is no known threshold level below which harmful effects are not observed to occur, it is necessary to reduce exposure to the minimum level possible.

22.11 Because of the uncertainty about the effects of long term, low-level exposure to persistent or bioaccumulative chemicals, a precautionary approach must be adopted for these substances. When substantial quantities of a persistent substance are released to the environment, life cycle analysis is required to predict the pathways of the substance through the environment to decide how it will finally be degraded or immobilised, or whether it will continue to circulate in the environment.

22.12 If the risk assessment of a chemical reveals a significant threat to man or the environment, action must be taken to reduce the risk and a risk/benefit analysis will be required. This involves comparing the estimated risks to human health and the environment with the economic and other consequences of restricting use of the substance, taking into account the availability of chemical or non-chemical alternatives. This will help to identify the most cost-effective, and least burdensome, means of introducing the necessary control measures. Final decisions on the use of chemicals must be based on a full assessment of all the factors involved, including risks to workers, consumers, the public and the environment, as well as the benefits of using the chemicals concerned. A joint Government/Industry Working Group has produced guidance on risk assessment for chemicals[1] and work is currently under way on a methodology for risk benefit analysis.

REDUCING THE RISK OF CHEMICALS

Regulation

22.13 Pesticides, pharmaceuticals and veterinary medicines, which are potentially harmful because they are designed to be biologically active, are subject to statutory approval procedures in the UK and in most other developed countries. These procedures are expensive and require extensive testing to be carried out; it is not practicable or necessary to apply them to chemicals generally. However, there is an increasing emphasis on an anticipatory approach to chemical safety based on toxicity testing and risk assessment.

22.14 There are general obligations under the Control of Pollution Act 1974[2], the Environmental Protection Act 1990[3] (EPA) and the Water Resources Act 1991[4] to prevent the pollution of air, water and land by hazardous substances. Emissions of prescribed substances from the most potentially polluting processes require authorisation by the regulatory authorities under Part I of the EPA in accordance with the principles of IPC. *The Control of Substances Hazardous to Health Regulations 1988*[5] made under the Health and Safety at Work Act 1974[6] require employers to make an assessment of potential risks to employees and others before using a hazardous substance, and to take appropriate control measures. Accidental releases of

chemicals are controlled by *The Control of Industrial Major Accident Hazards Regulations 1984*[7] which, in certain cases, require companies to draw up detailed safety plans to demonstrate that they are operating their plants safely.

22.15 Industrial and consumer chemicals are now being systematically assessed for potential risks to man and the environment. EC legislation on the classification, packaging and labelling of dangerous substances requires that chemicals marketed in the EC must be classified and labelled according to their hazardous properties. The classifications include physical hazards such as explosivity and flammability, and health hazards such as toxicity and irritancy. An additional classification "Dangerous to the Environment", based on aquatic toxicity, has recently been introduced. New substances placed on the EC market for the first time above specified tonnage thresholds are subject to mandatory testing and notification requirements under EC Directive 92/32/EEC[8].

22.16 Similar procedures are now being introduced for chemicals already on the market in the EC (Council Regulation No 793/93[9]), which will require that basic information is provided on all chemicals produced in, or imported into, the EC in quantities over 10 tonnes per year. This information will be used to draw up priority lists for risk assessment and, when necessary, control measures will be proposed. The EC existing chemicals programme is being fully coordinated with a similar Organisation for Economic Co-operation and Development (OECD) programme which draws on information and expertise from all OECD countries, including the USA and Japan.

22.17 Chapter 19 of Agenda 21[10] aims to extend information exchange on chemical risks to developing countries, and to develop the necessary expertise to enable these countries to make informed decisions about production and use of chemicals, taking account of their own economic and environmental conditions. In 1987, the UN Environment Programme (UNEP) Governing Council adopted *Guidelines for the Exchange of Information on Chemicals in International Trade*[11], and the Food and Agriculture Organisation *Code of Conduct on the Distribution and Use of Pesticides*[12] contains similar requirements. Both documents have since been amended to include the principle of prior informed consent, which requires that importing countries must be informed of the risks of, and give their consent to, the import of certain specified hazardous chemicals. These procedures are now mandatory for EC member states (EC Regulation No 2455/92[13]).

Economic instruments and voluntary action

22.18 Regulation may be needed when other measures are not adequate to control chemicals which pose a serious threat to human health or the environment. But regulation may not always be necessary to achieve significant reduction in the use of chemicals. In some cases, voluntary agreements with industry to reduce or phase-out certain uses, or to increase recycling, may be sufficient to achieve the required reduction in use. Industry Responsible Care programmes, eco-labelling schemes or chemical release inventories may also help to achieve the same objective. The second year report on the Environment White Paper[14] sets out a presumption in favour of economic instruments rather than regulation to deliver environmental goals. Economic measures have been successfully used, for example, to encourage the use of unleaded petrol. There may be further scope for using such measures to reduce emissions of hazardous substances to the environment, for instance, by increasing economic incentives for recycling.

FUTURE ACTION

22.19 The main questions for the future are whether there is sufficient scientific understanding of the behaviour of chemicals in the environment to predict their likely effects, and whether current procedures for testing and assessing chemicals are good enough to detect future risks, including unexpected or unforeseen risks.

22.20 Some of the most environmentally hazardous substances, such as PCBs, heavy metals, persistent pesticides and ozone-depleting chemicals, have now been identified, and action has been taken to control or ban their use.

Residues of these chemicals will remain in the environment long after production and use has ceased. In some cases, remedial action can be taken to deal with particularly badly polluted areas but, in other cases, there will remain a legacy of past pollution until natural processes degrade or immobilise the most persistent historic pollutants.

22.21 It is always possible that new or unforeseen chemical risks will be discovered, possibly caused by chemicals which have been in use for a long time. The best protection against these risks is continuing study and monitoring of environmental processes, with systematic procedures for testing and evaluating the potential effects of persistent chemicals released to the environment.

22.22 Improved test methods for chemicals are under continual development as understanding of the underlying biological mechanisms of toxicity improves. Animal welfare considerations are another important driving force in efforts to reduce the number of laboratory animals needed, to refine testing techniques and to develop replacement methods which do not use animals. At present there is no alternative to using animals to test for some biological effects of chemicals, but continuing progress is being made in developing methods which use fewer, or no, animals.

22.23 Increasing understanding of the biological activity of chemicals at the molecular level is helping chemical manufacturers to design new chemicals which are more specific in their activity, more degradable and less toxic to people or animals. The development of structure-activity relationships, which relate the chemical or biological properties of a chemical to its structure, and increasingly

---

BOX 22.1
EXAMPLES OF CONTROLS ON PERSISTENT CHEMICALS

Chemical	Control action	Effect
Lead	Reduction of emissions and use in petrol, paint, plastics, batteries since 1974.	Average blood lead levels in children are decreasing by 5% per year.
Tributyltin	Use in antifouling on small boats prohibited since 1987.	Concentrations in affected areas have decreased by 90% and the diversity of marine species has recovered.
Pentachlorophenol	Phased introduction of controls on use and tighter emission limits since 1993 and 1989 respectively.	Reduction in water and soil pollution expected.

sophisticated models of the transport and distribution of chemicals in the environment, will help to improve understanding of the behaviour of chemicals.

22.24 There is less understanding of the long term effects of chemicals on basic ecological processes. But continuing research will improve understanding of the threat which chemicals may pose to other organisms, such as plants and fungi, and of underlying ecosystem processes. The techniques of biomonitoring which focus on particular indicators of environmental health at the molecular, cellular, organism or species level may be useful in detecting subtle long term effects which are not detected by laboratory testing.

22.25 This new knowledge, and the extensive testing and assessment programmes under way internationally, will help to ensure that risks from chemicals are better managed by screening and controlling them where appropriate. New chemicals under development or existing chemicals which pass these assessment procedures will pose fewer risks to man or the environment, but they may be more expensive than the older more hazardous chemicals they replace.

22.26 There will be other pressures in the future to reduce emissions to the environment of all chemicals, especially the most hazardous. Tightening of emission standards and IPC methods will reduce point source emissions. The introduction of low-waste technologies by industry, and increased recycling of some materials, will help to reduce emissions, as will the increasing cost of disposing of hazardous wastes. In some cases, chemicals may be replaced by less hazardous alternatives, such as water-based rather than solvent-based paints, or by non-chemical alternatives, such as biological agents or genetically modified organisms. At the same time, the development of new materials and new products is likely to lead to new uses for existing chemicals and the development of new chemicals to meet new requirements.

22.27 It appears likely, therefore, that a wide range of chemicals will be needed in the future, but that they will be more specific in their action, less toxic and more degradable than the older chemicals they replace. The knowledge is now available to understand many of the problems caused by chemicals in the past and to avoid them in the future. Progress has been made in managing chemical manufacture, use and disposal. Knowledge of the potential harmful effects of chemicals is now much more extensive with the likely impacts of individual chemicals more predictable. Continuing vigilance will be needed to detect unexpected or long term adverse effects on man or the environment, but there is no fundamental incompatibility between the managed use of appropriate chemicals and sustainability.

22.28 Developing countries may continue to manufacture and use some of the older, more hazardous, chemicals for longer, principally for economic reasons, and these chemicals may, therefore, continue to cause problems for some time to come. Increasing standards of living and growing populations in developing countries are also likely to lead to increasing numbers and quantities of chemicals used globally.

22.29 The knowledge and expertise gained by industrialised countries must be passed on to developing countries, to avoid repeating past mistakes and to ensure that chemicals are used sustainably. The UK Government supports a wide range of training activities on the safe use of chemicals through its bilateral aid programmes and contributions to international programmes, including the International Programme on Chemical Safety, which was identified at Rio as the nucleus for international cooperation on the environmentally sound management of chemicals. Chapter 19 of Agenda 21 provides a new framework for international activities on chemicals and the UK will continue to play an active role in these programmes in the future.

REFERENCES AND FURTHER READING

1   *Risk Assessment of Existing Substances – guidance produced by a UK Government/Industry Working Group.* DOE, 1993.

2   Control of Pollution Act 1974. HMSO, 1974. ISBN 0-10-544074-4.

3   Environmental Protection Act 1990. HMSO, 1990. ISBN 0-10-544390-5.

4   Water Resources Act 1991. HMSO, 1991. ISBN 0-10-545791-4.

5   *The Control of Substances Hazardous to Health Regulations.* SI 1988 No 1657, HMSO.

6   *Health and Safety at Work Act, 1974.* Reprinted in 1991, HMSO. ISBN 0-10-5437743.

7   *The Control of Industrial Major Accident Hazards Regulations.* SI 1984 No 1902, HMSO.

8   *EC Directive 92/93/ECC (Amending for the Seventh Time Directive 67/548/ECC).* Official Journal of the European Communities L154, Volume 35, 30 April 1992. HMSO.

9   *Council Regulation No 793/93 on the Evaluation and Control of the Risks of Existing Substances.* Official Journal of the European Communities L84, Volume 36, 5 April 1993. HMSO.

10   *Agenda 21 – action plan for the next century,* endorsed at UNCED, 1992.

11   *London Guidelines for the Exchange of Information on Chemicals in International Trade,* UNEP, 1989.

12   *International Code of Conduct on the Distribution and Use of Pesticides, 1990.* Food and Agriculture Organsiation of the UN, 1990.

13   *EC Regulation No 2455/92.* Official Journal of the European Communites L251, Volume 35, 29 August 1993. HMSO.

14   *This Common Inheritance. The Second Year Report.* Cm 2068, HMSO, 1992. ISBN 0-10-120682-8.

CHAPTER 23

WASTE

A Sustainable Framework

- To minimise the amount of waste produced.
- To make best use of the waste that is produced.
- To minimise pollution from waste.
- A hierarchy of waste management options can be defined:
  - Reduction
  - Reuse
  - Recovery
    i) materials recycling
    ii) composting
    iii) energy recovery
  - Disposal.

Trends

- Increasing amounts of waste.
- Higher standards of environmental protection required by EC and domestic waste management legislation.
- Growing public awareness and concern over some aspects of waste management, particularly recycling of household waste, siting of waste facilities and the disposal of hazardous waste.
- Increasing cost of waste disposal, creating pressure to minimise and recycle waste.

Problems and Opportunities

- Most waste disposal in the UK is to landfill. There is considerable scope for waste reduction, for greater reuse of existing materials, and for materials recycling and energy recovery.
- Stricter control over emissions to air and water will alter the nature, and increase the quantity, of waste needing to be disposed of to land.
- The prices of the different waste management options do not accurately reflect their full environmental impacts.
- Cleaner technology needs to be further developed and information about it disseminated.
- Adequate markets for reuseable/recycled products and energy recovered from waste need to be developed.

- New recovery/disposal routes need to be developed for some wastes such as sewage sludge.

Current Responses

- A framework of UK and EC regulation encourages minimisation of waste and controls the management of waste in order to protect the environment.
- Government funds research, pilot projects, advice, and information to industry, local authorities and community groups on waste reduction, reuse, recycling, and energy recovery.
- Government has set targets on waste recycling and is encouraging industry to set its own targets.
- Non Fossil Fuel Obligation provides financial support for energy from waste plants.
- Government is considering a range of economic instruments to address distortions in the waste market − especially to help ensure that waste management options bear their full environmental costs and, in turn, that the polluter pays.

The Way Forward

- Action needed by all. Government will be influenced by the extent to which businesses and consumers recognise the need to adopt sustainable practices towards waste.
- Government will continue to fund research, advice and pilot projects and provide an appropriate framework of regulation and market instruments to encourage sustainable waste management practices.
- Businesses can make a particularly significant contribution by taking greater responsibility for the waste they produce, agreeing and achieving recycling targets, and investing in processes to reduce or reuse wastes.
- The waste industry will need to invest in increased reclamation/reprocessing capacity and facilities for energy recovery from incineration/landfill.
- Individuals will need to take more care to minimise the amount of household rubbish they dispose of, accept less packaging and the increased use of reusable or recyclable products.

INTRODUCTION

23.1 In the UK and other developed countries, increased wealth has generally led to increased waste. In the Organisation for Economic Co-operation and Development (OECD) region, it is estimated that per capita arisings of municipal wastes have increased by 26% between the mid-1970s and late 1980s.

23.2 Increased industrial production, increased consumer spending and population growth, have all had their part to play. A society that is generally well off seeks to have the newest and best of everything and is less inclined to retain old or worn items, or to repair or reuse them. Without any immediately apparent shortages of goods or materials, there is no perceived need or pressure to recover, reuse or recycle items or materials. For an industrial society, the rapid replacement of goods can have economic benefits in creating a demand for production which, in turn, creates jobs and wealth in the short term. In the longer term, this is not sustainable because of the use and ultimate exhaustion of a finite supply of conventional forms of energy and raw materials.

23.3 It is evident, therefore, that any strategy for sustainable development must include two key objectives:
- to minimise the amount of waste that society produces;
- to make best use of the waste that is produced, and to minimise resulting pollution.

WASTE TODAY

Waste arisings

23.4 The UK generates about 400 million tonnes (mt) of solid waste each year. The main sources can be seen in Table 23.1.

23.5 Around 40% of this waste (the first five categories in the table) is defined as "controlled waste" under the Environmental Protection Act (EPA) 1990[1]. About 2.5 mt is hazardous or toxic, and is defined as "special waste" to which additional, more stringent, controls apply.

Table 23.1 Estimated total annual waste arisings in the UK, by sector		
Sector	Annual arisings (million tonnes)	% of total arising
Construction & demolition industry	30	7
Other industry	70	17
Householders	20	5
Commercial premises	15	4
Sewage sludge	36	9
Mining & quarrying	110	27
Agriculture	80	20
Dredged Spoils	43	11
	Source: DOE, MAFF, QI, WSA	

Waste management options

23.6 There are a number of options for dealing with this waste. Table 23.2 shows their use. Industrial, household and commercial wastes are mainly landfilled, although for some elements recycling and incineration are also important. In particular, incineration is the favoured disposal route for clinical waste; and certain wastes (such as some scrap metals and waste paper) can also become valuable raw materials and, therefore, provide the basis for extensive reclamation industries. Some other wastes are also put to beneficial use and, where this is the case, they may fall outside the legal definition of waste.

Table 23.2 Estimated disposal routes for the main elements of controlled waste in the UK				
	Approximate percentage of each source[1]			
Sector	Landfill	Incineration	Recycled/ Re-used	Other
Industrial	70	*	25	5
Demolition & Construction	45	0	55	0
Household	85	10	5	0
Commercial	70	5	25	0
All controlled[2]	70	**	25	0

Note: 1 To the nearest %5.
* equals less than 1%; ** equals more than 2.5%, but less than 5%

Sources: DOE, WSL

23.7 Power station ash and steel and blast furnace slags, are used as aggregates (approximately 10 mt in 1990). About 50–55% of construction and demolition waste is believed to be recycled as a substitute for primary aggregates. Most of this is roughly crushed and used in low grade end-uses, but approximately 1 mt is processed and graded aggregate. The rest is thought to be sent to landfill sites where it may be used for haul roads and inert fill.

23.8 Most waste material from primary aggregate quarries is either used on site or backfilled into related quarries to facilitate site reclamation to a beneficial after-use (about 10% of annual production). Of the remaining non-aggregate quarrying and mining waste, it is estimated that less than 10% is used as an alternative to primary aggregates. The remainder is largely stockpiled on site.

23.9 Most agricultural waste is returned to the land in the form of fertiliser or soil conditioner. Chapter 15 has further information on the management of agricultural waste.

International movements of waste

23.10 The UK's policy on transfrontier waste movements takes account of its international trade and environmental obligations. These include the General Agreement on Tariffs and Trade (GATT) and the UN Environmental Programme Basel Convention on the Control of Transboundary Movements of Hazardous Waste and their Disposal[2]. The UK, together with other EC member states, is working towards ratification of the Convention on 6 February 1994.

23.11 The UK is self-sufficient in the final disposal of its own waste, and it is Government policy not to export waste to other countries for final disposal. The UK also aims to reduce as far as possible the import of waste for final disposal, particularly from developed countries. Requests from exporting countries which lack and could not reasonably be expected to acquire appropriate facilities, will be considered on their merits. In 1992–93, the UK imported some 45,000 tonnes of hazardous wastes (1.5% of the UK total volume of such waste) for final disposal.

23.12 Waste destined for recovery operations offers a valuable alternative to the use of raw materials, and transfrontier shipments of waste for recovery – predominantly involving other OECD countries – are commercially important. The UK wishes to see such trade shipments continue, provided that the waste is dealt with in an environmentally sound manner at all stages.

23.13 Future action regarding these issues is being considered as the Government prepares for implementation of the EC Waste Shipments Regulation[3] and becoming a Party to the Basel Convention.

CURRENT POLICY RESPONSE

The hierarchy

23.14 The Government's waste policy is based on a hierarchy of waste management options:
- *Reduction* – by using technology which requires less material in products and produces less waste in manufacture, and by producing longer-lasting products with lower pollution potential.
- *Reuse* – for example, returnable bottles and reusable transit packaging.
- *Recovery* – finding beneficial uses for waste including:
  - materials recycling to produce a useable product;
  - composting – creating products such as soil conditioners and growing media for plants;
  - energy recovery – producing energy either by burning waste or by using landfill gas.

- *Disposal* – by incineration or landfill without energy recovery.

23.15 This hierarchy both embodies sound waste management practice and mirrors the requirements of sustainable development. It is salutary, therefore, to consider the extent to which current waste management practice in the UK operates towards the bottom of this hierarchy. For instance:
- 85% of controlled waste goes to landfill, mostly without energy recovery;
- only about 5% of household waste is recycled and energy recovered from a further 4%, when about half of it could be recycled;
- 30% of household waste is compostable, but only a small fraction is composted;
- 30% of sewage sludge is dumped at sea (although this will cease by the end of 1998);
- About 25 million tyres are scrapped annually, presenting in some cases a significant fire risk and environmental hazard – more of these could be reprocessed for other uses, or used for energy recovery.

23.16 Aiming for sustainable development requires that more UK waste management practices move from the bottom to the top of the hierarchy. This, however, needs to be achieved in a measured way, governed by the principle of using the best practicable environmental option (BPEO). Landfill, although at the bottom of the hierarchy, is not inconsistent with sustainability if properly managed and controlled, for example, where it provides land restoration of old mineral workings. Some hazardous wastes are best landfilled with other biodegradable wastes at co-disposal sites so that natural processes can render them less harmful over time. Other wastes will be best landfilled because the environmental cost of making any productive use of the material outweighs the benefits. Similarly, it may be best to burn some types of waste to generate energy, rather than using up energy and other resources trying to sort and decontaminate waste for recycling. It will certainly not make sense to collect more material for recycling than the market is capable of absorbing. Waste reduction should aim to achieve equality between the marginal social costs of the collection and disposal of waste and the marginal benefits associated with its production. The best practicable environmental option needs to be considered case by case, informed by careful environmental evaluation of the various options, their wider economic costs, and developments in technology and markets.

23.17 A sustainable approach to waste, moreover, needs to be based on an integrated multi-media approach – whereby the best practicable environmental option seeks the optimum balance between discharges to water, air, and land. In some cases, this may increase the quantity of waste needing to be disposed of on land. For example, flue gas desulphurisation plants installed at several power stations reduce pollution to air by removing sulphur dioxide, but this results in the production of gypsum. While some of this can be used for the manufacture of products such as plasterboard, the market is limited and any surplus will require disposal. Similarly, restrictions on discharges of sewage to sea increase the need for landspreading of sewage sludge.

Regulation and economic instruments

23.18 The Government's aim is to create an economic and legislative framework which encourages the optimum balance between the different waste management options. This means ensuring as far as practicable that each option bears its full cost, including the cost of any environmental damage which it causes; and that those full costs are borne by the polluter.

23.19 As part of its commitment to introducing economic instruments in support of its policies wherever appropriate, the Government has carried out over the last three years studies examining their use in the area of solid waste. This has included research on deposit/refund schemes, the case for recycling credits, the use of economic instruments to promote waste recovery and recycling, the feasibility and possible effects of introducing a landfill levy, and the external costs/benefits of landfill and incineration. The Government recently published the Pearce report[4] which evaluated the environmental impacts of landfill and incineration. It concluded that incineration with energy recovery produced a net environmental benefit – primarily because of the displacement of pollution from other forms of energy generation. The Government, in consultation with all interested parties, is considering the report's findings, together with the earlier work on a landfill levy, before deciding its policy.

23.20 The Government's research has identified two main failures in the operation of the solid waste market. Firstly, there is often no direct incentive through the pricing system to reduce or recycle waste. Secondly, it appears likely that the prices of the different waste management options do not accurately reflect their environmental impacts.

23.21 One way of addressing the first issue of ensuring that the polluter pays has been the introduction of a scheme of recycling credits. These are paid by local authorities to recyclers whose activities save them collection and disposal

costs. Another way has been recent arrangements for the introduction of a producer responsibility scheme, notably for packaging waste (see 23.37). The costs of achieving the designated recovery levels will be borne by producers and consumers. The Government has no plans to charge householders for the collection and disposal of their waste, however, since this would raise many practical difficulties.

WASTE REDUCTION

23.22 Waste minimisation is at the top of the Government's hierarchy of waste management options. It can reduce the potential pollution from industrial and waste disposal activities and bring significant savings in raw materials, energy, production and waste disposal costs.

23.23 Waste reduction in industry does not necessarily mean investing heavily in cleaner technology: a waste audit may be able to identify simple adaptations to processes which would both reduce waste and produce substantial savings. However, effective waste minimisation is not just a question of reducing unwanted outputs from the manufacturing process. It also involves the manufacture of products that are likely to result in less waste when they are used, for instance, by using less packaging, by using re-usable or recyclable materials, or by producing longer lasting products. Manufacturing processes should also avoid producing hazardous wastes, or reduce the toxicity of such wastes, especially where goods are designed for a short life.

23.24 The Government uses a variety of means to encourage industry to minimise waste. The EPA 1990 creates a framework which imposes stringent standards for disposal and pollution control. In particular, the system of Integrated Pollution Control (IPC) established under the Act is predicated upon the use of the best available techniques not entailing excessive cost (BATNEEC) to prevent the release of potentially polluting substances. This approach requires the operators of prescribed processes to consider all aspects of their activity with a view to minimising the potential to pollute. This approach will clearly favour the use of cleaner technology and will tend over time to discourage waste production. Similarly, if, in the future, the costs of disposal to landfill rise (for example through a landfill levy), this would have the effect of encouraging industry to think more carefully about its generation of waste.

23.25 A number of companies of different sizes and from different industries have modified processes to avoid or minimise waste production. Some firms are recycling wastes back into the manufacturing process, or are using potential wastes as raw materials in other production processes.

23.26 The Government has supported such developments through demonstration projects and by providing advice and information on cleaner technology through seminars and workshops and literature documenting best practice. It has also encouraged the formation of waste minimisation clubs where information can be exchanged. It is funding projects in the Aire and Calder region and in the Mersey Basin, which aim to demonstrate the benefits of a systematic approach to waste minimisation. It is also committed to establishing a Cleaner Technology Centre.

REUSE

23.27 There are many examples of reusable packaging in the UK – from doorstep milk delivery where bottles are routinely collected, cleansed and reused through to reusable transit packaging. Reuse can, therefore, be a commercially attractive and environmentally sound way of avoiding waste, and has particular potential for further development in the case of transit packaging. However, it may not necessarily be the best approach in every case once account is taken of the additional raw material and energy demands which can accompany production, recovery, cleaning and transportation of reusable containers.

RECOVERY

Materials recycling

23.28 This involves collecting materials from waste and processing them to produce marketable products. Recycling of glass and aluminium, for instance, can yield considerable

energy savings compared to virgin production. In some material sectors, there is already a high level of recycling. For instance, the scrap metal and waste paper industries are well-established, and manufacturing companies tend to recycle a high proportion of the waste which comes from their own processes. Figure 23.1 shows the percentage of different materials that are typically found in household (dustbin) waste in the UK. The hatched areas on the bars indicate what fraction of that material is recyclable. About 52% of household waste could be recycled; currently only around 5% is collected for recycling.

23.29 However, it is counter-productive to recycle if doing so has a greater impact upon the environment than disposing of the waste and manufacturing again from raw materials. A sensible decision on whether to recycle will take account of many factors, including the availability of alternative raw materials, the energy consumption in collection and processing, and the effect of releases to land, water and air. For rural areas, the sustainability equation will be different to that for urban areas because of the dispersed population pattern. More localised recycling initiatives may have to be found. It is clearly important for recycling capacity and the demand for recycled material to increase broadly in line with expanded recycling collections. There are no advantages in increasing the amount of material collected for recycling if the capacity to process that material, or the markets for recycled products, are not similarly expanded. To collect a waste material separately for recycling if there is then no market for it simply wastes additional energy with no environmental gain.

23.30 In its 1990 White Paper on the Environment[5], the Government set a target of recycling half of all household waste that can be recycled by the year 2000; this broadly equates to a target of 25% of all household waste. In parallel, the EPA 1990 introduced measures designed to create a more favourable climate for recycling, including a scheme of recycling credits (see 23.21) and a requirement on all waste collection authorities to produce recycling plans. In 1991, the Government issued guidance (*Waste Management Paper 28* on recycling[6]) to assist local authorities in producing their recycling plans, most of which have now been approved.

23.31 The Government is also providing financial assistance to recycling initiatives which will help to meet the year 2000 target. In 1991, it introduced a programme of supplementary credit approvals (SCAs) in England to enable local authorities to invest in recycling projects. This has made available capital investment of £42 million for recycling schemes between April 1991 and March 1994. This has supported, amongst others, pilot schemes for the kerbside collection of

Figure 23.1 Typical composition of household (dustbin) waste and its potential for recycling

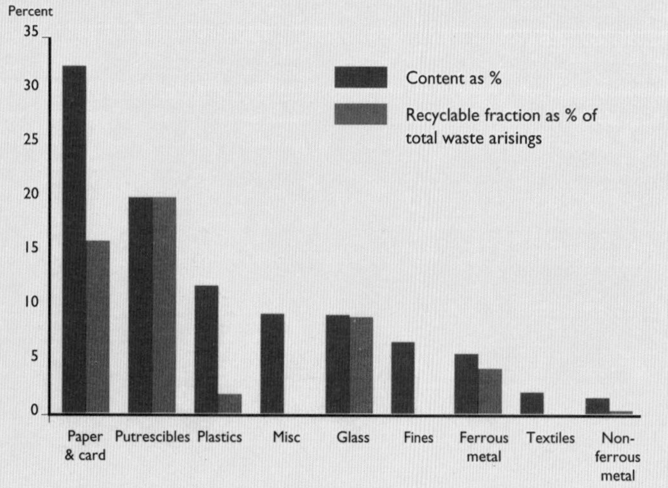

Source: WSL

recyclable household waste in Leeds and in Devon. Government financial support to Scottish local authorities in 1992–93 also took into consideration their priorities for expenditure on recycling.

23.32 Government grants have also been given to voluntary organisations and the private sector. For example, through its Environmental Action Fund (EAF), the Government funds national and regional bodies who act as enablers for local projects; it also funds specific schemes – such as, in 1993–94, the voluntary group Waste Watch which promotes waste reduction and recycling.

23.33 Since 1990, the Department of Trade and Industry (DTI) has committed £4 million to recycling projects under three environmental technology grant schemes:

- ETIS, the Environmental Technology Innovation Scheme (jointly with the Department of the Environment (DOE));
- DEMOS, DTI's Environmental Management Options Scheme, which promotes the spread of best environmental practice and technology among potential users;
- Euroenviron, part of the EUREKA initiative, which facilitates international collaboration on innovative environmental projects.

23.34 The provision of information about recycling is an important aspect of the Government's activity. Pilot recycling collection schemes, for example for the kerbside collection of recyclable household waste, are to be monitored and the results disseminated. As well as research programmes, it funds recycling information phonelines for companies and for members of the public, together with consultancy services to local authorities on composting and to community recycling groups. It also provides funding for educational materials, such as the Open University's book *Watch Your Waste*[7], which gives practical advice on recycling for individuals and community groups.

The 'producer responsibility principle'

23.35 Businesses, and the consumers who buy their products, can make a significant contribution by taking greater responsibility, physical and financial, for what happens to the waste they generate. The Government announced in July 1993 that it would discuss with a range of industries – including the packaging, newspaper, tyre, battery, vehicle and electronic equipment industries – ways in which they could increase recycling and recovery rates for their products when they become waste, and what would be appropriate targets.

23.36 Levels of recycling achieved in recent years by some

of the key industrial sectors and, where known, the targets they have set themselves are indicated in Table 23.3. The use of waste and recycled materials as aggregates is discussed in chapter 18.

Table 23.3	Recycling levels achieved by some key industrial sectors		
Material	**1990**	**1992**	**Target**
Glass	20.0%	26.0%	50% by 2000
Plastics	2.0%	5.0%	–
Steel cans	9.3%	11.9%	–
Aluminium cans	5.5%	16.0%	50% by 1997/98
Waste paper used in Newsprint	26.8%	28.1%	40% by 2000
Paper and board	31.0%	32.0%	–

Source: BGMC, BS, SCRIB, ACRA, BP&BIF, PPIC

23.37 The prospect of an EC Packaging and Packaging Waste Directive has given an added urgency to the discussions on packaging waste. Industries involved in the packaging chain were asked by the Government to prepare a plan by Christmas 1993 for introducing producer responsibility for packaging to include:

- the need for an effective organisation, spanning all the relevant business sectors, which can both prepare and implement the plan;
- commitment by industry that it will meet the costs necessary to fund new collection and processing capacity and the creation of a mechanism for raising the necessary finances;
- a staged plan building up progressively to overall recovery levels of between 50–75% by 2000, but recognising the scope to expand collection and processing capacity within the next year;
- a willingness by industry to increase demand for recycled material where it meets appropriate standards;
- immediate action to safeguard recycling infrastructure for plastics and paper and board threatened by subsidised German imports.

23.38 Newspaper publishers have agreed to a target of using newsprint with at least 40% recycled content by the year 2000. For its part, the Government has offered a £20 million grant for a newsprint mill in Kent which would produce newsprint made from 100% recycled paper, consuming over 350,000 tonnes of waste newspapers and magazines from households and other post-consumer sources each year.

Composting

23.39 In some cases, recycling can take the form of composting, since significant elements of some waste streams can be composted to make a usable product. The Government has funded research into the composting of mixed municipal waste over many years. Two of the main challenges are in finding outlets for the compost, and devising appropriate standards for waste-based composts. The Department of the Environment (DOE) also funds schemes providing advice to local authorities and community groups, including the pioneering composting project Wyecycle (linked to related work by Wye College, University of London).

23.40 The results of research[8] suggest that it may be better to separate so-called "green" waste (mainly parks and garden waste) from the municipal waste stream and compost it, thereby reducing problems of contamination from heavy metals or materials such as broken glass or plastics. In the past two years, several local authorities and other organisations have started schemes for collecting green waste for composting. Others have been promoting home composting, sometimes by offering householders free or subsidised composting bins.

23.41 There is also increasing interest in the scope for composting sewage sludge, with the 1998 deadline for ending disposal to sea. A DEMOS project is investigating the feasibility of co-composting municipal solid waste and sewage sludge.

Landspreading of sewage sludge

23.42 Some 50% of the UK's sewage sludge is spread on agricultural land as a soil conditioner and fertiliser. The nature of sewage sludge, the possible environmental hazards of using it in this way, and the various controls used to prevent these, are dealt with in chapters 8 and 10. The phasing out of sludge dumping at sea and the implementation of the Urban Waste Water Treatment Directive[9], will increase the volume of sewage sludge for which land-based waste management solutions need to be found – either landspreading, incineration or landfill.

23.43 The results of current research into the use of sewage sludge as a peat replacement, and for other horticultural purposes such as fertiliser on coppicing, may increase the demand for land spreading; there could also be scope for using sewage sludge (mixed with gravel) as an artificial topsoil for landscaping.

23.44 However, in the longer term, the scope for spreading will be limited by the area of suitable land available in proximity to sewage treatment works, and the need to prevent pollution of water and soil by heavy metals. Other options for the recovery or disposal of sewage sludge will, therefore, be important; incineration with energy recovery looks the most promising.

Energy recovery from waste

23.45 It is possible to recover energy from some wastes, either by burning them in an energy to waste plant or by burning methane produced from the decomposition of wastes (such as in some sewage treatment plants or landfill sites). Energy recovery can provide heat to adjacent buildings and/or power to the National Grid. The Government's intention is to work towards 1500 megawatts (MW) of new renewable electricity generating capacity by the year 2000. Waste to energy is sufficiently economically attractive for it to have the potential to make a substantial contribution to meeting this aim.

23.46 The Pearce report (see 23.19) discusses incineration with energy recovery. The Government is also currently considering the recommendations of a report by the Royal Commission on Environmental Pollution[10] into the merits of incineration with energy recovery, over landfill. This concluded that there was benefit in continuing to encourage incineration to provide energy.

23.47 All new incineration plants are likely to be able to utilise heat from the incineration process in some way to generate energy. Although the start-up costs and the potential risks from air pollution can be greater, they are able to achieve a higher overall energy recovery than landfill sites with methane-generated energy. Nevertheless, the recovery of energy from landfill gas will have an increasingly important role to play in making waste disposal more sustainable. Methane gas is produced from the anaerobic digestion of putrescible wastes such as household waste. Uncontrolled, it can be dangerous because the gas is explosive, and it is also a major greenhouse gas. Its utilisation therefore has the double benefit of reducing the level of emissions to the atmosphere, and providing a means of energy recovery. The gas can normally be exploited from two to three years after the deposition of the waste for a period of 10–15 years.

23.48 A range of Government action encourages the development of new waste to energy plant. The Electricity Act 1989[11] places an obligation on regional electricity companies in England and Wales to contract with suppliers of electricity from non-fossil fuel sources for a prescribed amount of electricity (the Non Fossil Fuel Obligation (NFFO)). The purpose of this is to create an initial market so that in the not too distant future the most promising renewables can compete without financial support. This will require steady convergence under successive orders between the price paid under the NFFO and the market price. It is recognised that an increase in the cost of waste disposal is one way in which this price convergence could be accomplished. Under the first two NFFO Orders, seven schemes with aggregate capacity of around 1.5 million tonnes of waste per year are likely to be in operation by 1995.

23.49 One such scheme will improve the management of waste tyres. A whole-tyres-to-energy plant at Wolverhampton (an NFFO 1 contract) will have the capacity to generate 25 MW of electricity and to absorb about 20% of UK annual scrap tyre arisings; 95,000 tonnes of tyres will be burned annually. Other proposed energy-related disposal routes for tyres include their use for firing cement kilns, and pyrolysis processes which can reclaim gas and oil for use as fuel. Neither option is in operation at present in the UK.

23.50 The availability of NFFO allocations is also encouraging landfill operators to make the necessary investment in energy recovery plant and equipment. 42 projects, which will generate 72 MW electricity from landfill gas, are operating already under the first two NFFO Orders. Landfill gas exploitation is on the verge of commercial viability, particularly at larger sites. The Third NFFO Order (see 23.52) proposes further support for landfill gas projects.

23.51 Sewage gas is another renewable technology which is considered close to commercial viability, The first two NFFO Orders should lead to the eventual exploitation of 33 MW of the 60 MW which the Government estimates to be accessible for electricity generation from sewage gas.

23.52 By the start of 1997, EC Directives concerning emissions from waste incinerator plant will take effect, resulting in the closure of much of the UK's waste incinerator capacity. In response to this, the Government announced, in 1993, a Third NFFO Order, a Scottish Renewables Obligation and a NFFO Order for Northern Ireland. The Scottish Renewables Obligation will generate 30–40 MW of new capacity.

23.53 Because of the phasing out of sludge dumping at sea and the implementation of the Urban Waste Water Treatment Directive, a number of water companies are considering the increased use of incineration with energy recovery for some sewage sludge.

DISPOSAL

Incineration

23.54 The incineration of waste without energy recovery is unlikely to be used for ordinary household and commercial waste after 1995, except where there are already existing facilities which can be economically upgraded to meet new EC emissions standards. All new mass burn incinerators for such waste will include energy recovery facilities. Specialised incinerators will, however, continue to be needed for the disposal of certain types of hazardous waste which cannot go to landfill. If environmentally acceptable facilities for burning clinical waste with municipal waste can be developed, less clinical waste would require specialised incineration. All incineration at sea ceased in 1990.

Landfill

23.55 Landfill remains the predominant route for waste disposal in the UK. Modern UK practice is to encourage biological processes within the mass of landfilled waste which degrade, neutralise, and stabilise the harmful components of the waste. Over a period of time, typically several decades, the waste ceases to present any significant threat to the environment. Landfill is in principle, therefore, an environmentally sustainable process.

23.56 Landfill offers particular advantages where it infills voids left from mineral workings[12], enabling them to be put to another use. A 1988 survey of mineral workings showed that some 9,500 hectares in England had permissions or requirements for restoration, including filling with wastes. A similar survey was carried out in Wales. While the equivalent volume is not known, the supply of void space and of other unproductive land is unlikely to be a significant constraint on landfill for the foreseeable future.

23.57 It is, however, essential that landfill is properly engineered and controlled so as to reduce the impact on amenity, and eliminate any dangers from leachate and landfill gas. In clay strata, geological conditions may enable wastes to be landfilled safely in voids with relatively little engineering. Such strata provide for slow migration of leachates, with little risk that pollutants will find their way from the landfill site to a water source to affect water quality. Where geological conditions are less favourable, or for more polluting wastes, more expensive and careful installation of suitable artificial linings may be needed. Even with such precautions, the risk of groundwater contamination may preclude the landfilling of all but truly inert wastes in the vicinity of major aquifers. In all cases, monitoring of adjacent water courses will be required; as will the monitoring and recovery of methane gas where necessary. Measures to guard against nuisance (smells, dust, litter, vermin) are required in all cases.

23.58 Environmental controls are provided by a requirement for operators to obtain licences from waste regulation authorities. Some 4,000 licences for landfill sites are currently in force in the UK. Tougher requirements will be introduced in the near future under Part II of the Environmental Protection Act 1990, requiring operators to prove their technical competence and financial viability, and to provide continued after-care of sites after closure.

23.59 About 300 landfill sites in the UK are licensed for a waste disposal route called co-disposal. Co-disposal is a calculated and monitored treatment of industrial and commercial liquid and solid wastes by interaction with biodegradable wastes in a controlled landfill site. It makes use of well understood natural processes in order to render less harmful over time the potentially hazardous elements of certain industrial wastes. Co-disposal is an important waste disposal method in the UK, and for some types of waste it is the best practicable environmental option. Some 70% of total annual arisings of difficult industrial wastes, for instance reduction slags from blast furnaces, are dealt with in this way. This practice would have to be discontinued if the draft EC Landfill Directive currently before the Council of Ministers, the need for which the Government questions on subsidiarity grounds, were to be agreed in its present form. It would instead be necessary to develop alternative mono-disposal bunker facilities, or to treat the waste prior to landfill, or to incinerate it. The UK has reservations about mono-disposal bunker facilities because they would require maintenance and monitoring in perpetuity.

23.60 The Landfill Directive would have an important bearing on the future use of landfill. This method of disposal will, however, remain the best environmental waste management option in a wide range of circumstances where the overall environmental costs of recycling, reuse or incineration would be greater. It will remain the only disposal route for ash from incinerators, and will continue to be the best practicable environmental option for a range of wastes that are difficult to burn or to recycle.

Sea disposal
23.61 Most forms of sea disposal are being phased out under the terms of the Oslo and Paris Conventions[13]. This is discussed more fully in chapter 9. Most of the waste which

is currently disposed of at sea – particularly sewage sludge – will therefore in future have to be disposed of to land, with implications for the main land-based methods of recovery and disposal.

THE FUTURE
23.62 The future of waste management in the UK depends on the pace of economic growth and developments in EC and other international legislation, and on the extent to which countries implement the Agenda 21 programme proposals. Above all, however, it depends on the extent to which individual householders and businesses recognise the need to adopt practices towards waste that will be sustainable. That, in turn, will influence the extent to which governments act to accelerate the transition towards more sustainable practices.

23.63 These uncertainties will tend to affect the pace of change more than its general direction – which will be towards waste reduction, reuse, recycling, and recovery, and away from simple disposal. The changes will be gradual rather than sudden, because changes in behaviour will take time to feed through and may need to be accompanied by major capital investment with long lead times.

23.64 For some time yet, waste disposal through landfill will continue to account for the majority of UK wastes. Better engineered sites and increased regulation will, however, reduce environmental risks. As a consequence, landfill will become more expensive, especially if a levy is introduced to reflect environmental impacts that remain even after regulation.

23.65 The waste industry will need to provide increased capacity for reclamation and reprocessing, and there should be a significant increase in new incinerators with energy recovery. Incineration without energy recovery will become insignificant. There will also be greatly increased energy recovery from existing landfill sites, and it will become the norm on new sites.

23.66 Technological advances will make recycling cheaper, and should be accompanied by developments in the size and range of markets for recycled products. Manufacturers are likely to invest in processes and introduce environmental management techniques, that reduce, reuse or recycle wastes, seeing greater economic advantage in doing so. Farmers will continue to use wastes and by-products to condition their land, but with greater understanding of the potential consequences for soil and water courses, and hence with reduced environmental risks.

23.67 It is hoped that the general public will give more thought to the disposal of their household rubbish, with an increased acceptance of sorting for recycling. They are likely to find that products have less packaging, and they may increasingly be required to return or reuse such packaging as remains.

REFERENCES AND FURTHER READING

1 Environmental Protection Act 1990. HMSO, 1990. ISBN 0–10–544390–5.

2 *United Nations Environmental Programme Basel Convention on the Control of Transboundary Movements of Hazardous Waste and their Disposal, 1989.*

3 *Council Regulation 93/259/EEC on the Supervision and Control of Shipments of Waste within, into and out of the EC.* Official Journal of the European Communities L30, 1 February 1993.

4 *Externalities from Landfill and Incineration.* CSERGE (Centre for Social and Economic Research of the Global Environment) with Warren Spring Laboratory. HMSO, 1993. ISBN 0–11–752825–1.

5 *This Common Inheritance. Britain's Environmental Strategy.* Cm 1200. HMSO, 1990. ISBN 0–10–112002–8.

6 *Waste Management Paper No 28: Recycling,* DOE. HMSO, 1991.

7 *Watch your Waste.* Open University/DOE. Open University, 1993.

8 *Municipal Waste Composting.* No: CWM/074/93 in the Controlled Waste Management Report Series, Warren Spring Laboratory. HMSO, 1993.

9 *Council Directive 91/271/EEC on Urban Waste Water Treatment.* Official Journal of the European Communities L135, 30 May 1991.

10 *Royal Commission on Environmental Pollution Seventeenth Report: Incineration of Waste.* Cm 2181. HMSO, 1993.

11 Electricity Act 1989. HMSO, 1989. ISBN 0–10–542989–9.

12 *Survey of Land for Mineral Workings in England.* DOE. HMSO, 1988. *Survey of Land for Mineral Workings in Wales.* Welsh Office, 1988.

13 *Convention for the Protection of the Marine Environment of the North-East Atlantic.* Joint Oslo/Paris Conventions Secretariat.

CHAPTER 24

DEVELOPMENT IN TOWN AND COUNTRY

A Sustainable Framework

- To provide for the nation's needs for food production, minerals extraction, new homes and other buildings, while respecting environmental objectives.
- To use the already developed areas in the most efficient way, while making them more attractive places in which to live and work.
- To conserve the natural resources of wildlife and landscape (safeguarding those identified as being of special interest or of national and international importance).
- To shape new development patterns in a way that minimises the use of energy consumed in travel between dispersed development.

Trends

- Increasing overall population, increasing numbers of smaller households, and the desire for more space in homes (10% more rooms per person in 1991 than in 1981) are the key factors behind the need for new housing development.
- Other structural changes in industry and commerce, and in lifestyles, are demanding different patterns of land use and different types of building.
- The resulting urbanisation is leading to a loss of open land; however, half the development takes place on previously developed, or vacant, urban land.
- During the 1950s–1970s, there was a substantial flow of population from big cities to new towns and other towns in the regions; more recently, the flow has been from towns into villages and the countryside.

Problems and Opportunities

- The demand for housing cannot be met entirely in the already developed areas, but new housing should be located in places where the resulting transport demands can be met in an energy efficient way.

- Similar problems and opportunities exist in relation to new shopping and employment buildings, and facilities such as schools, hospitals, and those related to leisure.
- Vacant, derelict, and contaminated land needs to be reclaimed and reused, but the market is not achieving this unaided.

Current Responses

- A positive land use planning system incorporating environmental constraints, backed by other controls over development.
- Reviews of planning guidance, which influence the way controls over land use are exercised.
- The work of Government agencies and the establishment of English Partnerships.
- Government research into the relationship between development and the environment, especially transport energy use.
- Contaminated land review.

The Way Forward

- The Government will encourage:
  – attractive and convenient urban areas, in which people will want to live and work;
  – new development in locations which minimise energy consumption over the lifetime of that development;
  – initiatives that lead to the regeneration of urban land and buildings, and to the restoration of derelict and contaminated land for development or open space;
  – development to sustain the rural economy, which is compatible with the protection of the countryside for its landscape, wildlife, agricultural, recreational and natural resource value;
  – through promoting research, and by other means, a better understanding of sustainable development by all those who have an interest in the development process.

INTRODUCTION

24.1 Chapter 11 presents information about the patterns of development and land use in the UK. Other chapters in Section 3 consider what sustainable development means for various sectors of the economy. This chapter considers issues arising from the likely demands for development over the next 20 years, and the choices in how and where that development takes place. The following chapter considers the construction industry itself – the buildings and structures, the materials used, and the wastes produced.

24.2 Land is a finite resource. Changes in its use, and new buildings, must respect environmental priorities. Development provides for people's needs, whether for food production or minerals extraction, for homes or workplaces, for transport or recreation. It is mainly initiated by the private sector to meet market demands. But it must respect the interests of the community as a whole in making the best use of the land resource. Government, at national and local level, seeks, therefore, to influence the way in which development takes place, and the way in which land is used. It can do this in different ways. The protection of the most sensitive areas demands the use of regulatory instruments, in particular the land use planning system. To encourage development in priority locations where the private sector alone will not invest, the Government works through agencies such as the Rural Development Commission, the new English Partnerships, and their equivalents throughout the UK. Fiscal measures and economic instruments influence the location of development, and how it takes place.

24.3 In providing for development, there are choices to be made about:
- how much development can be accommodated by reusing or using more intensively the existing stock of buildings and urban infrastructure; this influences the scale of new construction and the mineral resources to be exploited (see chapters 18 and 25);
- the pace of development in particular regions, which derives from changes in society and the economy;
- the balance between development in towns and in the countryside;
- how urban structures can be planned to be more ecologically coherent, in particular by seeking to influence the pattern of development to minimise the need for travel;
- the extent to which abandoned or under-used urban land can be economically recycled for development, thus avoiding the need to take green field sites for development.

24.4 Central and local government will keep the benefits of alternative approaches under review, so that plan preparation and decisions can properly accord with sustainable development principles, and so that other initiatives can be tailored to influence the market to deliver development that is compatible with that approach.

SCALE OF DEVELOPMENT

24.5 The scale of development clearly influences the land resources available to future generations. Each year in England currently sees approval for about:
- 150,000–200,000 new housing units;
- 2.0–2.5 million square metres of office floor-space;
- 11.5–12.5 million square metres of industrial and warehousing floor-space;
- 2.0–2.5 million square metres of retail floor-space.

Not all approvals are necessarily followed by development.

Housing

24.6 One major contributor to the scale of development expected over the next 20 years is a projected 14% increase in the number of households overall (see chapters 5 and 11).

24.7 Government housing policy aims for a decent home to be within reach of every household. Most people would prefer to own their own homes, and the Government has been keen to extend opportunities for home ownership to as many households as possible. Making sure that the markets for construction of new homes for sale, and for buying and selling homes, work efficiently is an important part of that.

24.8 Some households, however, will either need or choose to rent their home. Expanding the availability and choice of rented housing is, therefore, also an important objective. The Government works towards it by:
- encouraging the growth of private rented housing, thereby bringing empty properties back into use;
- promoting efficient management of the existing social housing stock;
- providing Government funding for housing associations to build new homes or convert existing buildings;
- targeting financial support on individual households so that they can rent privately.

To achieve Government housing policy objectives is clearly a key component of sustainable development.

24.9 Some demands for additional housing will be met through conversions of existing buildings, such as large houses or former commercial property. Much should, as now, be met through new housing on sites in urban areas. Indeed, an important element of government housing policy of relevance to sustainable development is the regeneration of run down areas, which often involves bringing derelict land back into productive use. However, some new housing will be needed on the edges of towns and villages, or in new self-contained settlements on green field sites. National and local government will need to decide, through regional and strategic planning decisions, whether demands can be met where they arise, or whether environmental constraints will require provision to be made in different locations.

Industry and commerce

24.10 Structural changes continue to affect the make-up of the economy, and the location of commercial and industrial businesses. The decline of traditional heavy industry in the industrial heartlands has brought with it a need to regenerate land and to create new jobs in other areas of the economy, such as the commercial sector and service industries, over the next 20 years. This process is expected to continue in response to world markets.

24.11 Future trends in demand for industrial and commercial development, and consequently for transport of all kinds, can only be predicted in the broadest terms. The Government expects a continuing trend towards service industries and away from manufacturing (at least in terms of numbers of employees and value added). This implies that more goods will be manufactured by more investment in capital, energy, and communication-intensive production. Changing communications technologies may reduce the need for routine journeys to work, making the actual location of businesses less critical and enabling economies in the use of office space. Developers will also seek to respond to new infrastructure investment and changing relationships, for instance, closer links to mainland Europe.

24.12 All these changes in society and in industrial patterns will give rise to other development demands, for schools, shops, hospitals, transport (see chapter 26) and ancillary services.

LOCATION OF DEVELOPMENT

The countryside

24.13 In the countryside, as elsewhere, there are competing demands for land. In rural areas, these demands have to be reconciled with the need to protect open countryside, for its importance as part of the landscape heritage and as natural habitat. Sustainable development objectives demand an approach which integrates rural development and conservation; development will continue to be needed, but of a scale and nature that protects the qualities of the countryside. Sustainable development also demands that considerable weight is given to protecting the best agricultural land as a national resource for the future.

24.14 Over most of the countryside, long term trends of rural depopulation and increasing unemployment have reversed. In many areas, the rural economy is now relatively buoyant, and the population is also growing — most rapidly in the countryside of the South East and South West. But there has been a loss of younger population, and a change in the nature of employment, with declining opportunities in agriculture and traditional employment, such as quarrying. These structural changes

will continue. The Government, therefore, encourages new forms of economic activity to sustain viable rural communities, especially in those areas hardest hit by the decline in traditional rural industries.

24.15 The guiding principle on development in the wider countryside is to look for benefits to the rural economy which also help to maintain or enhance the environment. The countryside can accommodate many forms of development without detriment, provided location and design are handled with sensitivity. Appropriate development in rural areas can help support local shops, schools and other facilities, and otherwise sustain the local economy and self-contained rural communities in which there is less need to travel, and less isolation for the elderly and economically vulnerable.

24.16 Many small towns and villages can accept new housing development that is sensitively related to the existing settlement. Even in villages where housing would normally be ruled out by environmental considerations, small sites may be released to meet local needs for affordable housing which can help to ensure the continued social health of small communities. However, expansion of villages and towns should not lead to further ribbon development or dispersed settlements; equally, any infilling of villages must have regard to the existing structure and character of the village.

24.17 New buildings away from existing towns and villages must be strictly controlled, in order to protect the qualities of the open countryside. Special restraints apply in statutorily designated areas such as the National Parks, Areas of Outstanding Natural Beauty and in Scotland, the National Scenic Areas. Such restraints also apply to areas which are important for nature conservation reasons, such as Special Protection Areas under the EC Wild Birds Directive, Ramsar Sites, National Nature Reserves and Sites of Special Scientific Interest (SSSIs). Where development is permitted in a designated area, it may be appropriate to consider how to compensate for the loss of environmental assets. For example, the loss of part of an SSSI might justify notifying a new area of similar quality nearby or, where practicable, the creation of a replacement wildlife resource.

24.18 Green Belts have been established in the countryside and open land around many major built-up areas. Their main purpose is to contain urban sprawl, so encouraging compact development in the urban areas and the reuse of urban sites. Their essential characteristic is their permanence. Inside Green Belts, development is normally restricted to agriculture, forestry, open air leisure and sport, and other uses appropriate to a rural area. Other development will not normally be allowed unless it involves the reuse of a redundant building. Green Belts and other controls over development in the open countryside help to focus development in urban areas, where sustainable development objectives are more likely to be met.

24.19 Major developments in the countryside, such as regional shopping centres and business parks, are almost entirely car-dependent and encourage people to travel long distances; they are, therefore, unlikely to form part of a sustainable approach. There may be scope for new settlements in some areas, especially where the provision of housing would otherwise significantly damage the character of existing places. However, research has shown that proposals for new settlements are unlikely to be sustainable unless they are of sufficient scale to support a wide range of local services and employment opportunities, and well-served by public transport. They would need to provide at least 10,000 dwellings, and the economics of development suggest that they will therefore be more likely to be created through building on existing smaller towns than starting from scratch.

Towns and cities

24.20 Urban growth should be encouraged in the most sustainable settlement form. The density of towns is important. More compact urban development uses less land. It also enables lower energy consumption through efficient generation technologies such as district heating and through the reduced need to travel, for example, from homes to schools, to shops, and to work. Larger towns can more readily develop the critical mass that enables them to offer a variety of facilities locally, thus reducing the need to travel to other towns for work, shopping or leisure. The scope for reducing travel, especially by car, is dependent on the size, density of development and range of services on offer at centres well served by public transport as well as local centres within walking distance.

24.21 Sustainable development within urban areas is closely bound up with the quality of urban life. The quality of urban areas should encourage people to want to live and work there, and to enjoy the culture and entertainment that only cities can sustain. This will help to counteract the current trend for people to move from urban to rural areas and help reduce development pressure on the countryside.

24.22 Building within existing urban areas might improve sustainability by increasing density, but there may be a limit to the benefits to be gained. Careful design will be needed to avoid loss of open space and environmental quality within urban areas. Research currently under way is looking at whether there is a clear limit to which built-up areas can be developed without resulting in loss of urban quality.

24.23 Urban quality depends on the creation and protection of green space in cities, for amenity and recreation. Decisions on alternative uses of open space should take into account the needs of future generations, for once developed it is gone forever. Everyone should have easy access to public open space, and deficiencies will need to be made good as opportunities arise. Maintaining green space, both public and private, and planting trees in urban streets will raise the environmental quality of urban areas.

24.24 Quality of life is also materially affected by factors such as the location of homes and work places, the availability locally of a wide range of goods and services, and the availability and use of energy efficient modes. Local facilities need to be accessible by a choice of means of transport, with more emphasis on short trips being undertaken on foot or by bicycle.

24.25 Developments which attract a lot of employees or customers, such as offices and shops, need to be located in town centres or other places which are well-served by public transport. In this way, they are accessible by a choice of means of transport. This improves the range of facilities available to those without cars. It enables people to choose more energy efficient means of transport, such as cycles and buses. And it enables a single journey to serve more than one purpose, thus increasing the business that can be achieved for each vehicle mile travelled.

24.26 Town and city centres must incorporate the best principles of urban design. They need to contain a variety of uses. These can reinforce each other, making town centres more attractive to local residents, shoppers, those involved in business, and visitors. Town centres are good locations, not only for offices and shops, but for restaurants and cafes, entertainment centres, theatres and cinemas, museums, hotels and conference centres, universities and colleges, and tourist attractions.

24.27 The public spaces in town centres need to be well-designed for people on foot, and kept clean to meet the needs of the businesses that operate there. They need to provide for disabled people, the elderly, and those with young children. Works of art and street furniture can provide a sense of identity and civic pride. Crime prevention and safety will also be key objectives, to be taken into account in planning for central areas that are full of life during the day and the evening. Investment in facilities for cyclists, and traffic calming measures, will also help improve the quality of urban life by reducing the effects of vehicles in towns.

24.28 Older industry in larger cities is tending to close and relocate, while new businesses focus on smaller towns or on the edges of urban areas where sites served by motorways and upgraded trunk roads have attracted developers. Such development can often be reached only by private car. This type of development is likely to be more wasteful in long term energy use than development within urban areas, and it undermines initiatives designed to put the heart back into cities. Government policy is now, therefore, to:

- encourage new industrial and commercial development, shops and offices, hospitals, and further education centres in locations which minimise the length and number of trips, especially by motor vehicle, and which can be served by more energy efficient modes of transport (particularly important in decisions about the location of office, light industrial and campus style developments – such as science and business parks – likely to have large numbers of employees);
- reserve space close to good inter-urban transport infrastructure – whether rail, water or road – for development that needs this (in particular warehousing, which uses large areas of floor-space and requires few journeys by employees, but many large goods movements).

Decisions on development will not be sufficient to achieve either the transport emissions or urban design objectives outlined above. A complementary approach is required. More details of action in the transport field can be found in chapter 26.

24.29 Sustainable development in run-down city areas entails making a concerted attack on the range of problems which affect such areas, and achieving a turnaround which prevents them from deteriorating to their former state. The principles of coordination and partnership are central to the Government's City Challenge initiative in England, and equivalent initiatives in Wales, Scotland and Northern Ireland. This approach harnesses the energies and resources of local authorities, the private sector, Government Departments and local communities themselves to target particular areas within cities. Concentrated efforts are made to provide jobs, improve housing, transport, health and education, control crime, reclaim derelict land and carry out environmental improvements. These integrated measures aim to provide the basis for long term revival in the chosen areas and decrease pressure for green field development.

24.30 The same considerations apply in disadvantaged housing estates on the periphery of major cities and towns which have been a particular focus of attention in recent Scottish urban regeneration activity. Physical and environmental improvements, for example, have featured strongly, alongside economic and social regeneration, in the programme of the four Scottish Office led Partnership Initiatives.

Reuse of vacant and derelict land and buildings

24.31 Vacant and derelict land in urban areas needs to be reused. The buildings occupied by industries created in the last century have become increasingly inappropriate, particularly in terms of size and location. Their lack of adaptability and inability to accept the demands and requirements of technological innovation mean that they may not be well placed to meet the requirements of the modern workplace. Some unoccupied office buildings also offer limited prospects for business use. In such cases, conversion to housing use, either through adaptation of existing buildings or through redevelopment, may be sensible.

24.32 In 1993, the Government set up the new body, English Partnerships, to promote the reclamation and development of vacant and derelict land and buildings throughout England, particularly in urban areas. It will offer grants, and promote the provision of industrial and commercial space (mainly in the areas most affected by industrial restructuring). Working in partnership with the private sector, local authorities and other bodies with a role in regeneration, its aim will be to make land available for housing, employment, green space or any other use that will help the regeneration process. Making better use of derelict land will also reduce pressure on green field sites.

24.33 In Wales, the Welsh Development Agency continues to make significant progress in terms of land reclamation and urban development, especially in areas affected by the run-down of traditional industries such as coal and steel. As well as having an economic impact on the towns and cities which so often relied upon these industries for an economic base, the decline has also left a very significant environmental legacy. The Agency's Urban Development Programme is designed to stimulate economic growth and operates on the basis of partnership with local authorities and, where possible, the private sector.

24.34 In the core of the most damaged urban areas in England and Wales, urban development corporations are working single-mindedly to diversify the economic base, to increase employment and access to jobs, and to revive areas as places to live by providing homes and leisure and community facilities. They also improve and protect the environment by dealing with contamination, greening derelict or unused space, and improving public access. The job of the corporations is a time-limited one.

24.35 Urban regeneration is a costly and time-consuming process. It requires sustained effort over many years to tackle the legacy of vacant land in our towns and cities. New areas of land become vacant and derelict all the time. Urban policy, therefore, needs to find lasting solutions, and to ensure that development is not achieved at the cost of new dereliction elsewhere.

Contaminated land

24.36 The quality of land is intimately bound up with its past and present uses. Whilst most land in the UK is not damaged, there is, nonetheless, a legacy of contaminated and degraded land which, whether in urban or rural areas, presents special problems. In a few cases, land which is damaged, physically or chemically, can be so hazardous as to be unusable without treatment.

24.37 The objective for the future is to prevent or to minimise further contamination through pollution control and market mechanisms. But land which is already contaminated should be dealt with where there is the risk of threatening health, safety or the environment; where practicable, it should be kept or brought back into beneficial use, so helping to minimise avoidable pressures on green field sites.

24.38 Dealing with the legacy of contaminated land is a considerable economic burden, and raises important issues of priorities for national resources. The Government's approach is that threats should be dealt with on the basis of a realistic set of priorities related to risk. Land should be treated where it is necessary or worthwhile to cure or to control the problem. The goal is to bring land to a standard where it is suitable for its actual or intended use; this may mean that it is better to use resources to treat five sites and carry out 80% treatment, than to restore one site fully. The objectives of sustainable development

do not mean that contaminated land must necessarily be brought to a standard where it is fit for any purpose.

24.39 There can be problems in applying the polluter pays principle to contaminated land. With historic pollution, the polluter may no longer exist or may be unable to meet the costs; ownership of the site may have changed; and contamination may sometimes remain on a site for many years with no harmful effects until activities or other changes many years later lead to problems.

24.40 There are difficult questions to address here, with no easy answers. The Government has, therefore, set up a review of the powers and duties of public authorities related to the identification, assessment and appropriate treatment of contaminated land and liabilities. The recommendations of that review will inform any decisions on the future approach to contaminated land.

Urban trees

24.41 Trees can contribute to a more pleasant urban environment. They may also reduce the deposition of airborne pollutants, particularly when planted alongside roads, act as windbreaks, or shield buildings from sun and wind. The Government is, therefore, encouraging the planting, management, and protection of trees important to amenity.

24.42 Tree planting is encouraged through a range of urban grants, a significant proportion of which go towards environmental enhancement programmes involving tree planting and management. Significant tree planting takes place in association with new roads. Other grants are made to voluntary organisations. An extensive programme of research into tree issues has led to wide knowledge of practical and cost-effective solutions.

24.43 Since the 1940s, the Tree Preservation Order system has helped to ensure the retention of some of the UK's most valued trees which come under threat of removal or inappropriate management. The Government has been consulting on proposals for streamlining and updating the system.

24.44 The Government and the Countryside Commission have published two complementary research reports on the stock and condition of trees in towns, entitled *Trees in Towns*[1] and *Action for London's Trees*[2]. These highlight the likely changes that will occur in the urban tree stock over the next 20 to 50 years as the legacy of large broadleaved species comes to the end of its natural life. The Government is consulting local authorities in England and voluntary groups through a series of seminars on how to respond to the research findings and is encouraging local authorities to develop long term strategies for the management and care of trees in their ownership. These strategies should plan for the eventual replacement of old trees; enable authorities to take advantage of new opportunities for tree planting provided by other urban improvement measures such as traffic calming; and integrate awareness of the contribution which trees can make to the quality of life in urban areas into the full range of local authorities' activities.

REFERENCES AND FURTHER READING

1   *Trees in Towns*, DOE. HMSO, 1993. ISBN 0-11-752845-5.
2   *Action for London's Trees,* Task Force Trees (Countryside Commission). ISBN 0-86-170403-7. Available from the Countryside Commission, John Dower House, Crescent Place, Cheltenham.

CHAPTER 25

CONSTRUCTION OF THE BUILT ENVIRONMENT

A Sustainable Framework

- To refurbish, adapt and reuse existing buildings.
- To design and construct new buildings which can be adapted to different uses, thereby extending their lifetime.
- To use recycled components and materials, or those from sustainable sources.
- To minimise the energy needed to operate a building.
- To reuse or recycle wastes produced during construction and demolition.

Trends

- There has been a continuing improvement in the energy efficiency of buildings, driven by Building Regulations requirements, recognition of the environmental and financial benefits of reduced energy use, and improvements in technology and techniques.
- Technology is also improving the ability of designers and constructors to use sustainable and recycled components, and to reuse and recycle construction wastes.

Problems And Opportunities

- Practices such as energy efficiency, recycling, and use of sustainable materials and products need to become inherent parts of the design and construction process and, in some cases, to displace traditional construction techniques and practices.
- The process has already begun, promulgated through a number of channels such as design leadership, education and training, regulation, research and development, and dissemination of information.

Current Responses

- Research and development activities are continuing into energy efficiency techniques, technology and best practice, and the results are being disseminated. Research is also being undertaken into recycling opportunities.
- The BREEAM environmental assessment methodology is continuing to make progress, with new applications under development.
- Training and career development programmes for building professionals are increasingly taking on board the principles and practice of environmental sustainability in the construction process, although further progress in this area is desirable.

The Way Forward

- Improved standards of thermal performance of buildings are planned under the Building Regulations.
- Further initiatives are needed between Government and the industry to bring forward ways of increasing recycling and minimising waste in the construction process.

INTRODUCTION

25.1 Construction and the related supply industries are of major importance to the UK economy, producing about 12% of Gross Domestic Product (GDP) and around 50% of gross fixed capital formation. The sector's size and diversity give it a widespread influence on sustainability issues. It is a major user of resources and materials, both in the construction process and in the use and maintenance of buildings.

25.2 Most buildings and land use patterns have a long life. Much of today's urban structure will endure well into the next century. Equally, decisions taken today on the design of those buildings will affect the people living there for a long time. The return from investments made in the interests of the environment today will be enjoyed for many years.

25.3 The design and location of development can influence the energy used within buildings and the amenity value of the locality. Features such as the adaptability of new buildings to different uses, and the ease with which the site can be returned to its original green field condition at some time in the future, are further important sustainable development considerations at this detailed level.

25.4 Other important factors include the external layout of new buildings, and their overall orientation to ensure that they are sited to make maximum use of natural heat and light. It is not yet possible to quantify with confidence the contribution to total lifetime energy use of buildings from materials, construction, location, services in use, transport, demolition and so on. However, current indications are that the energy used to provide appropriate internal conditions during the building's occupied life makes the dominant contribution.

25.5 As well as constructing new buildings, existing buildings can be adapted and converted for new purposes. Each generation inherits buildings and civil engineering structures from previous decades; where appropriate, these can be maintained and improved, and passed on to future generations for productive use. This, in itself, is a contribution towards sustainability, and can be encouraged through informed development and investment as a cost-effective option which at the same time preserves good quality older properties which dignify both towns and countryside. Much has been achieved in the last 20 years, due to active local authority planning policies, with advice towards the repair of the finest historic buildings from heritage bodies, and financial and other assistance from central Government.

25.6 In recent years, consumers have become increasingly aware of the environmental effects of their use of products. Despite this, they often do not appreciate the environmental impact of buildings and the potential for reducing environmental damage by improving the design of buildings. For example, activities which take place inside, and during construction of, buildings are responsible for about half the UK's emissions of carbon dioxide (CO_2), the gas that plays a dominant role in the greenhouse effect. Much is being done to encourage reduced energy use in buildings by the application of cost-effective current technology, through fiscal and financial measures, through the development of Building Regulations, and through the provision of information and advice. However, considerable potential remains, particularly in existing buildings, for the incorporation of further cost-effective energy efficiency measures. There is also considerable potential for improving on the efficiency of use of water in buildings and for the reuse or recycling of water used in industrial and commercial properties.

RESEARCH

25.7 The Department of the Environment (DOE) funds a continuing research programme, in collaboration with the construction industry, many aspects of which are relevant to sustainable development issues. In particular, the Energy-Related Environmental Issues (EnREI) Programme aims to reduce CO_2 emissions associated with energy use in non-domestic buildings, to support the commitments on climate change made by the UK Government at the Earth Summit in Rio.

25.8 The framework of the programme includes minimisation and efficiency of air-conditioning; control strategies for heating, ventilation and air-conditioning; efficiency and control of lighting; minimisation of embodied energy in building materials; application of new technologies; and effective integration of design, including use of thermal mass. The results of the research programme will be incorporated into the Best Practice programme of the DOE's Energy Efficiency Office (EEO), as appropriate.

ENVIRONMENTAL ASSESSMENT OF BUILDINGS

25.9 There is, as yet, no blueprint for the truly sustainable building. Many issues and factors are relevant. The Building Research Establishment Environmental Assessment Method (BREEAM), developed by the Government's Building Research Establishment (BRE) with private sector sponsors, provides a vehicle for the environmental assessment of buildings. BREEAM schemes now exist for the assessment of new and existing office designs, for new industrial buildings, for new home designs and for new superstores and supermarkets. Approximately 25% of all new office developments are currently applying to be assessed under the scheme.

25.10 In the case of new buildings, assessing a range of building characteristics at the design stage allows improvements to be incorporated before the design is fixed. The BREEAM scheme, therefore, changes the characteristics of new buildings, and is likely to become an important source of guidance to the building industry on how to make new buildings more compatible with the principles of sustainable development. For existing buildings, the assessment is in two parts, relating to the building fabric and services, and to operation and management.

25.11 On energy consumption, BREEAM provides an assessment of the expected release of CO_2 resulting from energy use in the building being assessed. This assessment is calculated from energy consumption predictions, taking account of the variation in CO_2 emissions from the combustion of different fuels. This approach enables designers and specifiers to include minimisation of CO_2 emissions as an explicit criterion and gives an indication of how performance can be improved.

25.12 A wide range of independent, authoritative guidance on how to improve the energy efficiency of buildings is available from the EEO's Best Practice programme. This guidance, which is produced in the form of publications, seminars and workshops, is disseminated on the EEO's behalf by the Building Research Energy Conservation Support Unit (BRECSU) at the BRE. The EEO cooperates closely with building professional institutions (such as the

Royal Institute of British Architects, the Chartered Institute of Building Services Engineers, and the Royal Institution of Chartered Surveyors) and the major interests in the building industry responsible for design, construction and management of buildings. As part of this cooperation, BRECSU has established, with the Royal Town Planning Institute, an informal group known as the Urban Energy Management Network.

25.13 In the BREEAM versions for new offices, houses and industrial buildings, the ecological value of the site is assessed and credit given for including design features which lead to positive enhancement of the site and its amenity value. A checklist of ways of minimising ecological damage gives further encouragement to designers to contribute to sustainable development.

USE OF SUSTAINABLE SOURCES FOR MATERIALS

25.14 It is important, when designing buildings, to avoid over-specification of materials and wastage in use. The resources used in the UK construction industry are dominated by primary aggregates (sand and gravel, and crushed rock). The extraction of these minerals can have environmental impacts on local areas and communities (such as noise, dust, visual impact and traffic problems). The need to conserve resources and to seek efficient and effective use of aggregates in construction is a sustainability issue for management of mineral resources (see chapters 12 and 18).

25.15 The use of timber in construction has important advantages: it is natural and renewable, absorbs CO_2, and has important attributes in terms of its strength, insulation properties, ease of use and low energy consumption in production. Thus, provided they are produced from regulated and well-managed forests designated for sustainable timber production, wood and wood products can play an important role in a strategy for sustainable development. Careful specification of timber from sustainable resources is an area where designers can make a significant contribution to using an environmentally acceptable material without deforestation. Studies by the International Tropical Timber Organisation in 1990 indicated that, at present, less than 0.2% of tropical forests are being managed sustainably for commercial production.

25.16 The UK Eco-Labelling scheme (based on the EC Regulation 880/92) was launched in 1993. It is voluntary, and criteria are set for each product category on the basis of a "cradle to grave" analysis of environmental performance.

Only those products which meet these criteria will be awarded a label. The scheme is designed mainly for consumer goods, although extension to construction products is being considered; paints and tiles have already been subject to pilot studies and work has started on insulating materials.

WASTE FROM CONSTRUCTION AND RECYCLING OPPORTUNITIES

25.17 The built environment, in particular, is associated with waste production in a number of ways, including the considerable proportion of landfilled wastes derived from demolition and construction activities. However, good site practice and management of resources can reduce wastage in construction and, where feasible, end-of-life buildings could be recycled.

25.18 There exist significant recycling opportunities in the engineering and civil building sector from:
- bringing into beneficial use derelict or contaminated land (subject to the planning process);
- reusing materials or components arising from demolition work;
- refurbishing buildings or structures;
- beneficial use of waste from the construction process;
- incorporating waste from other industries into construction materials or products.

25.19 Recycling of demolition materials, by sorting and using bulk materials as fill, is now possible in civil and building construction. Tests carried out in the UK and elsewhere have demonstrated that recycled building materials can be reused in road construction with no appreciable loss of performance. There are already practical schemes in Holland and Germany for full sorting, reprocessing and reuse of demolition waste. Research is under way in the UK to identify ways in which the Government can further encourage the recycling of demolition and construction wastes.

25.20 A major constraint to greater recycling (particularly of bulk materials) is the transport cost compared with the value of the materials. It is estimated that the demolition industry recycles about 11 million tonnes of the construction industry's waste, from structures that have reached the end of their life, but there is potential to recycle much more of the material currently going to landfill.

25.21 Certain building materials are manufactured from waste in preference to virgin materials. One example is the use of wood particles in chipboards, blockboard and fibreboards, which can be used as substitutes for timber; another is the use of pulverised fuel ash for concrete blocks. Blast furnace slag can also be incorporated into concrete. Technical standards and specifications need to be drawn up to allow for a greater degree of recycled material, where there is no significant effect on performance of the construction.

25.22 There are well developed markets for recycled ferrous and non-ferrous metals from construction waste. In addition, the reuse of bricks, roof tiles and slates is widespread. Doors, fireplaces and other interior items are also being recovered. Further details of reuse and recycling of all categories of waste are set out in chapter 23.

CHAPTER 26

TRANSPORT

A Sustainable Framework

- To strike the right balance between the ability of transport to serve economic development and the ability to protect the environment and sustain future quality of life.
- To provide for the economic and social needs for access with less need for travel.
- To take measures which reduce the environmental impact of transport and influence the rate of traffic growth.
- To ensure that users pay the full social and environmental cost of their transport decisions, so improving the overall efficiency of those decisions for the economy as a whole and bringing environmental benefits.

Trends

- Very strong growth in the use of private car and air travel; decline in other means of travel. Projection of a doubling of road traffic by 2025.
- Growth closely linked historically to the rate of economic growth, as people choose to spend disposable income on travel, and as more goods are moved.

Problems and Opportunities

- Traffic growth means more emissions, and more demand for road construction.
- Improvements in the efficiency and emission standards of vehicles will not be enough in themselves to meet environmental objectives.
- Effective transport is important for the economy; measures must take that role fully into account.
- Individual decisions lie behind the forecasts for growth – individuals can make a difference by changing their travel habits.
- Individual decisions are shaped by the framework set by Government; this could help to deliver environmental objectives.
- There is great potential for bringing home the full

costs of transport decisions, leading to increased efficiency for the economy as a whole.

Current Responses

- Government is pursuing steps:
  - to increase fuel duty by, on average, at least 5% a year to reflect wider costs and help to meet the UK carbon dioxide target;
  - to enable local authorities to manage transport demand in their areas, and to use land use planning policies to reduce the need for travel and to encourage less polluting means of travel;
  - to develop improved vehicle standards in the EC;
  - to improve the assessment of the environmental impact of transport programmes.
- Local authorities are taking steps to:
  - develop appropriate demand management programmes for their areas;
  - incorporate principles for reducing the need for travel into their land use plans.

The Way Forward

- Further measures will be necessary by Government to:
  - influence the rate of traffic growth and provide a framework for individual choice which enables environmental objectives to be met;
  - improve understanding of the costs and benefits associated with transport, to ensure that transport decisions reflect the full costs they impose, and to ensure that measures affecting the transport sector are the most efficient ones for the economy as a whole;
  - improve the environmental performance of vehicles;
  - increase understanding of environmental impacts and pollutant emissions from transport, such as those present in very small amounts in urban areas or those emitted at high altitude by aircraft;
  - explore the role for new technologies such as telecommunications.

TRENDS

26.1 An effective transport system is a necessary part of modern life. Commerce and industry depend on it, and changing patterns of transport have shaped today's social and recreational lifestyles. But the impact of ever rising levels of transport on the environment is one of the most significant challenges for sustainable development. At the heart of this challenge lie the continuing forecasts for long term growth in demand for transport, together with the wide variety and level of associated environmental impacts.

Transport growth 1952-1992, *GB*

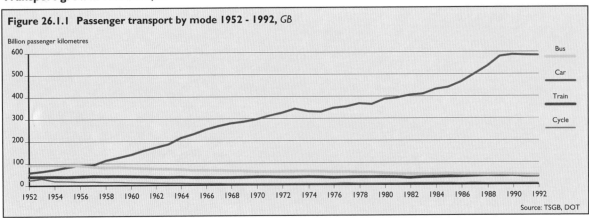

Figure 26.1.1 Passenger transport by mode 1952 - 1992, *GB*

Billion passenger kilometres

Bus
Car
Train
Cycle

Source: TSGB, DOT

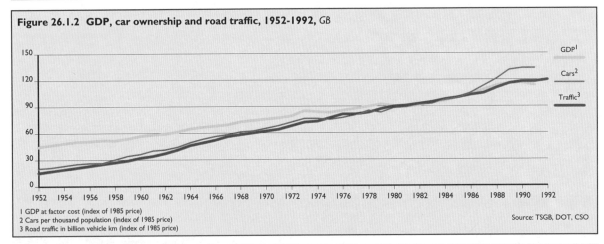

Figure 26.1.2 GDP, car ownership and road traffic, 1952-1992, *GB*

GDP[1]
Cars[2]
Traffic[3]

1 GDP at factor cost (index of 1985 price)
2 Cars per thousand population (index of 1985 price)
3 Road traffic in billion vehicle km (index of 1985 price)

Source: TSGB, DOT, CSO

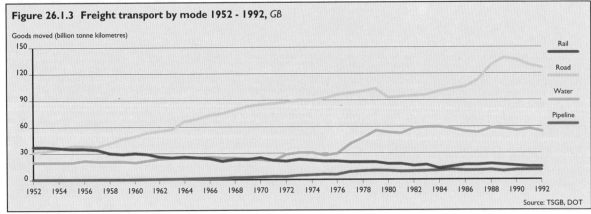

Figure 26.1.3 Freight transport by mode 1952 - 1992, *GB*

Goods moved (billion tonne kilometres)

Rail
Road
Water
Pipeline

Source: TSGB, DOT

26.2 Passenger travel has increased from 219 billion passenger kilometres in 1952 to 681 billion kilometres today (Figure 26.1.1). This growth has closely followed the growth in car ownership (Figure 26.1.2) which in turn has been closely connected to economic growth and, hence, people's ability to afford to run a vehicle. People with access to a car make more and longer journeys than those without access to one; they are also making progressively more use of their cars. The present forecast for traffic growth to 2025 – the National Road Traffic Forecast (NRTF) – is based on relationships found to exist under current policies at present and in the recent past. The key relationships are income growth and growth in car ownership and use, and economic growth and freight transport growth, together

Table 26.1   International comparisons, passenger and freight transport

	Passenger Transport						Freight Transport							
	Car		Bus		Rail		Road		Rail		Water		Pipelines	
	1981	1991	1981	1991	1981	1991	1981	1991	1981	1991	1981	1991	1981	1991
UK	388.0	586.0	49.4	44.0	34.0	38.0	90.9	127.2	17.5	15.4	51.8	54.1	8.7	11.1
Belgium	62.7	75.0	9.1	10.0	7.1	6.5	18.8	32.0	7.6	5.4	5.4	5.2	1.7	1.1
Denmark	37.4	53.3	7.4	9.3	4.5	4.9	7.1	10.0	1.6	1.9	1.8	2.5		2.3
Germany	448.0	681.0	93.1	68.0	64.8	57.0	119.9	173.8	116.8	133.1	53.8	57.7	17.4	14.0
France	466.3	599.0	38.5	43.0	55.7	62.1	93.3	112.0	64.4	53.7	11.1	8.4	28.8	22.5
Greece			5.8	5.3	1.5	2.0		12.4	0.7	0.6				
Eire					1.0	1.3	4.5	5.5	0.7	0.6				
Italy	335.8	494.0	85.4	85.0	40.1	45.5	129.1	168.0	17.1	2.0	28.4	35.1	10.4	10.0
Luxembourg					0.3	0.3	0.3	0.2	0.6	0.7	0.3	0.3		
Netherlands	110.5	133.9	11.4	13.5	9.2	12.0	17.8	23.3	3.3	3.0	31.8	35.7	4.7	5.4
Portugal	42.5	67.0	8.6	10.5	5.9	5.7		16.2	1.0	1.8				
Spain	131.8	145.4	28.3	38.6	15.5	15.0	114.6	150.0	11.0	10.5	28.6	30.0	3.1	4.8
Sweden	67.0	93.0	7.9	10.0	7.1	6.1	21.0	29.4	15.3	19.4	9.4	8.5		
USA	3,275.7	4,273.8	43.6	66.4	17.7	22.0	790.0	1,182.6	1,485.7	1,509.6	1,495.7	1,450.0	907.2	843.6
Japan	347.6	570.0	89.5	110.0	316.2	387.5	181.3	274.4	34.1	27.2	211.8	244.6		

Note: Freight: billion tonne kilometres   Passengers: billion passenger kilometres
Gaps are due to unavailable data

Source: DOT

with effects of fuel prices. The Department of Transport (DOT) is currently reviewing the methodology underlying these forecasts.

26.3 Bus use has declined progressively since 1952 and is now just 6% of distance travelled. Bus deregulation has not reversed the long-term trend. Rail use is roughly at the levels of the 1950s but has also fallen to 6% of total distance. Walking and cycling are now a small percentage of total distance travelled, and cycle use has fallen markedly since its peak after the Second World War. The picture is rather different if, instead of distance, it is based on the number of journeys by different means. 32% of trips are walk or cycle trips. Many of the recorded trips are very short, with about half of all journeys under 2 miles. 30% of these shorter journeys are made by car. The great majority of journeys are local journeys on local urban roads. Just 2% of journeys are over 50 miles, although these make up 29% of all mileage travelled.

26.4 There is substantial variation in the use of different means of transport across Europe. The UK has one of the highest mileages per car and one of the lowest levels of rail freight or public transport use. Countries such as the Netherlands and Denmark also have substantially higher use of cycles. But the basic trend towards more travel by car is seen, to some extent, throughout. Only the Netherlands experienced a growth in the share of travel by rail during the 1980s (see Table 26.1).

26.5 In the freight sector, there has been strong growth in road haulage, closely related to changes in the types of goods carried, improved roads and vehicles, deregulation

of road haulage, increased vehicle weights, and changing distribution methods (see Figure 26.1.3). Growth in recent years has been particularly strong in the very heaviest vehicles, introduced in 1983. These offer maximum loads (and hence flexibility of use) for operators. The light goods fleet has also grown strongly, with diversification of small service industries. Rail freight has declined in the face of road competition, and with changes in its traditional markets such as coal and aggregates. Now most long distance freight goes by road. Coastal shipping has maintained a steady volume of freight (much of it petroleum).

26.6 Air mileage remains a small share of total travel within the UK but growth trends for travel further afield and for

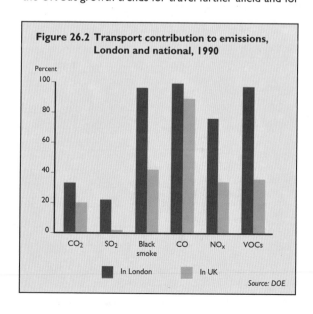

Figure 26.2 Transport contribution to emissions, London and national, 1990

Source: DOE

171

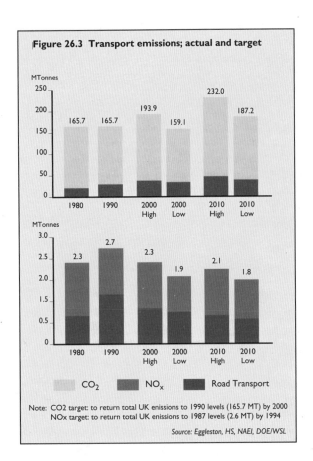

Figure 26.3 Transport emissions; actual and target

MTonnes

Year	value
1980	165.7
1990	165.7
2000 High	193.9
2000 Low	159.1
2010 High	232.0
2010 Low	187.2

MTonnes

Year	value
1980	2.3
1990	2.7
2000 High	2.3
2000 Low	1.9
2010 High	2.1
2010 Low	1.8

CO₂   NOₓ   Road Transport

Note: CO2 target: to return total UK enisssions to 1990 levels (165.7 MT) by 2000
NOx target: to return total UK enisssions to 1987 levels (2.6 MT) by 1994

Source: Eggleston, HS, NAEI, DOE/WSL

transport of freight are high. Between 1982 and 1992 the total number of passengers to or from UK airports doubled. Air movements in the South East of England are expected to grow to at least 75 million by 2000, compared to 69 million in 1992.

ENVIRONMENTAL IMPACTS

26.7 Transport has a wide range of adverse environmental impacts. Transport emissions (Figure 26.2) pose major challenges for the response to the threat of climate change, for air quality, and for reducing the levels of noise to which local populations are exposed. The provision of infrastructure to support growing demand in turn poses challenges for the protection of landscapes, of protected nature areas and of urban and rural quality of life. Wastes from transport, such as oil and tyres, are some of the most intractable forms of waste. Improved transport can also bring pressures for development which, if not resisted, can lead to the loss of green field sites and exacerbate reliance on the private car.

TRANSPORT IMPACTS AND NATIONAL TARGETS

26.8 The transport sector will have to make a contribution to meeting a number of international and domestic environmental targets. The exact contribution which the transport sector makes to environmental goals will need to take into account the costs and benefits of measures to reduce transport emissions relative to those in other sectors. Figure 26.2 shows transport's share of emissions to air in 1990 in London and in the UK as a whole. Figure 26.3 projects transport emissions against international standards for carbon dioxide (CO₂) and nitrogen dixoide (NO₂).

Climate change

26.9 Transport is responsible for some 24% of CO₂ emissions and the proportion is growing. These need to be reduced by some 2.5MtC by the end of the century against present trends if the UK is to achieve its target of returning total emissions to 1990 levels in 2000 (see chapter 6). There is a strong prospect of further international commitments after 2000, if current scientific predictions are confirmed.

Air quality

26.10 There are international standards and targets for a range of air pollutants, including oxides of nitrogen (NOₓ), carbon monoxide, smoke, and tropospheric ozone. Transport is the major single contributor to these pollutants, especially in urban areas most prone to incidents of high air pollution. In the short term, continuing growth in road transport threatens the prospect of meeting the UNECE target reductions for NO₂. Growth in the diesel fleet presents particular problems, due to its higher NOₓ emissions compared with petrol. Around 40% of transport NOₓ emissions come from road based diesels; shipping contributes a further 10%. Although new emission standards will begin to reduce most pollutant emissions per car over the next 10 years, by 2012, overall emissions will begin to rise again if no further action is taken, as growth in traffic overtakes these gains. The Government is also exploring the need for new standards for certain volatile organic compounds, such as benzene, which have been identified as carcinogens. Again, road transport is the principal source of these emissions. Emissions from air transport also raise concerns because of the high altitude at which they take place and the possible implications for stratospheric chemistry. Chapter 7 gives a fuller account of air quality.

Noise

26.11 In the regular monitoring undertaken for the Government by the Building Research Establishment, transport noise was identified as a major source of annoyance for over 10% of the population. Improving standards for noise levels of vehicles and aircraft have allowed transport noise to remain fairly constant, despite growth in traffic, but the area of land subject to noise, especially road noise, has increased over the period of surveys.

Waste

26.12 Some 25–30 million used tyres are disposed of each year in the UK, of which the majority are put to landfill. 25% are currently recycled. Water run-off from roads can put oils and other harmful wastes into groundwater, although to date these impacts are little understood. The problems of waste disposal are covered in chapter 23.

Aggregates

26.13 At present, 32% of aggregates are supplied to the road construction and maintenance industry. Even if current plans to increase use of recycled aggregates are successful, some 2 billion tonnes of primary aggregate will be required to 2011. Chapters 12 and 18 give further information on aggregates.

Wildlife and countryside

26.14 Transport infrastructure continues to place demand on land. Roads currently use 1.2–1.5% of the land area of the UK. Between 1985 and 1990, 14,000 hectares of land in Britain was used for road construction (mainly unclassified roads). Land take from rural uses of land (9,600 hectares) is second only to housing (23,300 hectares). The present road programme for England would increase the total area of land under roads by just under 5%, although the area of trunk roads and motorways would grow by 45%. Just under one fifth of the programme involves new roads through green field sites; about half is for motorway widening and the remainder is for rural bypasses.

26.15 Some road construction proposals threaten protected nature sites and other sensitive areas such as Areas of Outstanding Natural Beauty and Green Belts. The extent of impact on these areas depends on final decisions about the routes and designs of roads. A preferred route has been announced for 266 schemes in the road programme in England – 55% of all programme schemes. These affect 50 Sites of Special Scientific Interest (of 3730 sites in England).

26.16 Transport infrastructure brings pressures for other development. These impacts are complex and difficult to predict but developers are clearly attracted to sites with good national road links, such as the junctions of the motorway network. This can mean use of green field sites and the attraction of activity away from existing urban centres, which would benefit from that investment. Improved long distance rail services have also increased the length of commuting journeys and spread the housing pressures of urban centres across the rural surroundings. Such pressures put strains on the ability of the planning system to contain them.

ELEMENTS OF A SUSTAINABLE TRANSPORT POLICY

26.17 It is not the Government's job to tell people where and how to travel. But if people continue to exercise their choices as they are at present and there are no other significant changes, the resulting traffic growth would have unacceptable consequences for both the environment and the economy of certain parts of the country, and could be very difficult to reconcile with overall sustainable development goals. The Government will need to provide a framework in which people can exercise their transport choice in ways which are compatible with environmental goals.

26.18 A transport policy that is compatible with sustainable development objectives is one which strikes the right balance between serving economic development and protecting the environment and future ability to sustain quality of life. Serving economic development is an important objective of transport policy. But there are alternative ways in which that objective can be achieved. One aim of the Government's framework must be to enable people to enjoy the desired end of access to goods, services and other people (the reason for travel) while substantially reducing the amount of movement needed to achieve that aim.

26.19 A key principle in all sectors of the economy is to get the price right for the goods and services consumed. This means reflecting environmental and other costs in the price people pay for the benefits of transport. To the extent that current transport decisions do not do so already, new measures which lead to increases in user costs to reflect the full costs – including environmental costs – of transport will lead to more efficient decisions for the economy as a whole. They are likely to play an important part in setting the framework in which environmental objectives can be met.

TRANSPORT AND THE WIDER ECONOMY

26.20 Sustainable development is about getting economic and environmental trends working in harmony. Transport growth is the product of economic growth: higher disposable income means greater demand for travel and for goods which need to be transported. Forecasts of future traffic are based on a gradual weakening of this relationship, as more people have as many cars as they want and travel as much as they wish ('saturation'). Only significant social change (for example, in attitudes to use or ownership of the car which might reduce the propensity to travel at higher incomes) or structural change (such as changes in trends in the location of development or employment) are likely further to affect this relationship. In the absence of such changes, the only steps which would reduce the underlying rate of traffic growth would be measures which increased the cost of travel by road, either by raising prices or by otherwise making car travel relatively less attractive.

26.21 There are good grounds for increasing the price people pay for road use in so far as current prices do not reflect wider social and environmental costs (see 26.19). But any such measures will need to take account of distributional effects or impacts on competitiveness. Overall motoring taxes in the UK are close to the EC average, and lorry taxes are above average. Transport is a cost borne by the entire economy and some sectors are particularly dependent upon it. Transport industries are also an important economic sector in their own right. Any measures to increase prices will have to weigh the benefits, some of which may only be felt in the future, against the potential costs now.

EXTERNAL EFFECTS AND TRANSPORT EFFICIENCY

26.22 Decisions which people make when choosing whether and how to travel should reflect the true costs of those decisions. At present, prices paid by road users do not relate to the use made of particular roads, and most of the costs – such as the cost of the car, insurance, and vehicle excise duty – are sunk costs for the user which do not influence the choice of individual journeys. Journey choices are relatively little influenced at present by the

one marginal cost, fuel price, which is just a quarter of motoring costs and which has, in any case, fallen to historic lows in recent years (although the measures set out in 26.24 should begin to reverse this trend). Nor is it apparent that the prices paid fully reflect wider costs imposed on the environment and society, nor properly distribute the costs road users impose on each other through congestion. People's transport decisions can only be economically efficient if the prices paid reflect the full marginal external cost of road use. It is important that those costs which are currently averaged out or imposed on others should be more closely reflected in transport decisions.

26.23 The economic appraisal of the value of national road schemes is based on quantified benefits for users, largely derived from values of time saved and from any accident reductions. Environmental costs and benefits cannot be given monetary values at present but are covered by a separate environmental assessment.

PRESENT MEASURES

26.24 As part of the UK's commitment to the International Framework Convention on Climate Change, the Government is publishing its national programme to reduce UK emissions of CO_2, the principal greenhouse gas, to 1990 levels by 2000. This programme includes measures which will reduce transport emissions by 2.5MtC (or 5%) compared with the forecast levels. The principal measure is a commitment to year on year real increases in fuel duties of 5% which will, all other things being equal, put real fuel prices slightly above their 1980 historic high point.

26.25 To reduce the need for travel and encourage less polluting transport choices, the Government will shortly issue advice to local planning authorities on ways in which they can plan settlements so as to give people greater transport choice and more facilities close at hand, and to reduce the pressure for out-of-centre sites which can generate additional travel by road. This could bring significant benefits in the longer term by influencing the underlying trends, and will complement other proposed measures. A draft of the advice (*Planning Policy Guidance Note 13*[1]) was issued for consultation in England and Wales in April 1993. The Scottish Office is considering the need for similar guidance.

26.26 Since the end of 1992, all new cars sold or used in the UK have had to meet tough new EC standards for emissions to air. These reduce emissions of NO_x, hydrocarbons and carbon monoxide per vehicle by around 80% compared with existing levels (through the fitting of catalytic convertors). Tighter fuel and evaporative emission standards will also help.

26.27 The Government is asking local authorities to reduce traffic growth through their transport programmes. From 1993, local authorities in England have been invited to come forward with transport packages for funding which seek to improve public transport and manage the use of the car. This approach should become standard in future years, although packages will need to reflect resources available. The Scottish Office has also taken steps to explore multi-modal options in looking at the problems of the Edinburgh area. Local authorities have been given greater freedoms to enforce parking controls and introduce low speed limits. Traffic calming or management for environmental reasons, and facilities for public transport priority and for walking and cycling are receiving higher priority for Government funding.

26.28 A number of the UK's major roads are suffering from congestion at peak times. The Government's road programme is designed to address this. Failure to provide additional road space in the absence of measures to reduce or manage demand could result in increasing congestion and diversion on to less suitable routes. Less congested traffic moving at moderate speed gives lower emissions than the same volume of traffic travelling the same distance in congested conditions.

26.29 During 1993, the Government produced revised environmental guidance for its road schemes as part of the *Design Manual for Roads and Bridges*[2]. This guidance gives updated and expanded advice on environmental assessment of schemes to reflect current good practice. In Scotland, new practical guidance on road and environmental design – *Fitting Roads* – is in preparation. The Government has also recently published the *Good Roads Guide*[3] (the first comprehensive practical guide to environmental road design) and the *Wildflower Handbook*[4] (on methods of establishing wildflowers on roadside verges).

FUTURE DEVELOPMENTS IN TRANSPORT AND THE ENVIRONMENT

26.30 The DOT is currently reviewing the road programme to establish priorities ahead of the creation of a Highways Agency which will take responsibility for the executive task of improving and maintaining the national road network.

26.31 The DOT is also exploring the scope for environmental appraisal of transport programmes as a whole

with the Department of the Environment (DOE) as part of its commitments following the Standing Advisory Committee on Trunk Road Assessment (SACTRA) 1992 report *Assessing the Environmental Impact of Road Schemes*[5]. This should improve methods of taking account of the environmental impacts of transport proposals.

26.32 Improving road quality may be expected to increase demand, but it has proved extremely difficult to identify and measure this effect. SACTRA has been asked to provide the Government with advice on the extent to which new or improved roads might generate traffic. Its report is expected early in 1994.

26.33 If it were no longer acceptable to build some roads, prices and physical management measures would be the best way to ration the limited resource. Such steps are being developed in urban areas where the scope for new construction is physically limited. Variable speed limits and improved signing are being introduced to maximise the capacity of existing trunk roads and motorways. The Government is also exploring measures to ensure that its roads serve the strategic purposes for which they are designed. A programme to combine bypasses with traffic management in the towns bypassed is one such measure.

26.34 Following consulation[6], in November 1993, the Government announced its intention of introducing electronic tolling on the motorway network when the technology is available. Motorway charging will help to address congestion from rising demands for road capacity as the economy grows. It will improve the competitive position of rail and other forms of transport.

26.35 The Government is considering, with local authorities, the scope for road pricing in urban areas to help to manage congestion pressures. The extent to which such schemes will be acceptable or will deliver environmental benefits will depend on the application of funding and the levels of charges set. Research into the impacts of direct charging is continuing.

26.36 Better public transport will have an important role to play in a concerted programme of measures, including traffic management, to change existing trends – although improving public transport in itself is unlikely to create a major change in current trends, and investment in fast, long distance travel at the expense of local journeys might even increase the total amount of travel. The Government's reform of the railways should increase the competitiveness of rail and make the extent of subsidy more transparent. A more competitive railfreight industry could make a contribution to reducing freight volumes on the roads. Measures to extend the scope of support for the use of rail freight (beyond the proposals which followed the *1990 Environment White Paper*[7]) will help. These will offer a subsidy scheme for firms wishing to move their goods by rail, with funding up to the level of the charges made by Railtrack for the use of the lines. The Government is also looking at ways of improving public transport infrastructure through the use of private finance.

26.37 New computer and telecommunications technology has brought advances in the speed and ease of communication: developments such as video-conferencing, teleworking and shopping from home offer the potential to replace existing journeys. It is unclear at present what impacts such advances will have and whether more communication will stimulate more travel – as has sometimes been observed in the past – or supplant it. Businesses looking to reduce transport costs may well wish to explore these options. The Department of Trade and Industry has a research programme exploring the application of these technologies and the DOT is exploring the transport implications.

26.38 There is likely to be further action to tighten emissions standards. The United States is already developing standards which will require alternative power sources, including electric vehicles. Such steps may have a contribution to make to reducing emissions, but may also have a high cost and be unable to address the full range of the impacts imposed by transport.

26.39 Developing EC policy will play a part in the future debate. In 1992, the EC published its Green Paper on *Sustainable Mobility*[8], advocating traffic management for environmental improvement. The wider EC market and European transport networks will also be key elements in determining future transport priorities. These are covered in the EC White Paper, *The Future Development of the Common Transport Policy*[9].

26.40 *Agenda 21*[10] will also serve to shape the continuing debate. Among other things, this calls for a comprehensive approach to urban transport management and planning.

26.41 Continuing research to improve understanding of transport impacts will be important. The DOT recently issued a discussion document on its strategy for research, which recognises that the environmental impact of transport is a key issue. Research into demand management techniques and the application of new vehicle

and telecommunication technology could help to bring some of the benefits of mobility with less environmental impact. Other chapters of this Strategy set out the research being undertaken on environmental impacts by the DOE and others. For example, following the results of the recent *Countryside Survey*[11], the Government will be commissioning further research into the loss of hedgerows, which will look, among other things, at the impact of roads.

POTENTIAL BARRIERS TO FURTHER PROGRESS

26.42 Measures to deliver sustainable trends for transport will depend on public appreciation of the need for change and accurate knowledge of economic and other impacts. Costs of travel, particularly costs of road travel, may well have to rise to reflect environmental costs and to affect the levels of future demand for transport compared with those currently predicted. The impacts of such costs, and the way in which they could best be imposed (for example, by charges or through physical management of road use, such as partial traffic bans) will be a matter for debate. Individuals will need to reconcile their desire for a better environment for themselves and their children and for the protection of the natural world, with their desire to travel.

26.43 Some measures designed to reduce traffic impacts could have the effect of making many people better off – by improving the attractiveness of public transport and through improved environmental quality – but there will always be those made worse off, particularly those who may not be able to use their car or will have slower journeys. People will have to be certain that they will see the benefits of the additional cost in a better environment, for themselves and their children. They must appreciate why the framework is needed.

NEXT STEPS

26.44 To meet the needs of sustainable development, further measures will be necessary. Government as a whole should act to reduce environmental impacts and influence the rate of traffic growth. This will:

- require further study of the costs and benefits associated with transport;
- mean that transport decisions, including the provision of infrastructure, should reflect all the costs they impose;
- be based on improved knowledge of the relative costs of measures in the transport sector compared with other sectors.

26.45 The DOE and DOT, working together, must increase understanding of the interactions between transport and the environment, and develop policy as a result. Government needs to increase public involvement and understanding of the relationship between transport choices and the environment. This will require:

- improved information from central Government and local authorities;
- the provision of information on the interaction between prices, land use, transport and environmental impacts;
- clear guidance on how individuals can contribute to reducing transport impacts.

26.46 The Government also needs to increase understanding of pollutant emissions and other impacts from transport, how they arise and what costs they impose. This will need further research and monitoring by Government and other bodies.

26.47 Local government also has a significant role; local authorities must undertake measures to tackle transport issues and land use in their areas. They will need:

- to develop sustainable strategies for transport and planning;
- to manage the demand for transport in their areas and to develop clear environmental targets and criteria.

REFERENCES AND FURTHER READING

1 *Planning Policy Guidance note 13, Transport.* (consultation draft). DOE, April 1993.

2 *Department of Transport Design Manual for Roads and Bridges, Volume 11.* HMSO, 1993.

3 *The Good Roads Guide.* (Design Manual for Roads and Bridges, Volume 10, Sections 1 & 2). Department of Transport, 1993.

4 *The Wildflower Handbook.* (Design Manual for Roads and Bridges, Volume 10, Section 4, Part 1). Department of Transport, 1993.

5 *Assessing the Environmental Impact of Road Schemes.* DOT. HMSO, 1992. ISBN 0–11–55103–2.

6 *Paying for Better Motorways.* Cm 2200. HMSO, 1993. ISBN 0–10–122002–2.

7 *This Common Inheritance. Britain's Environmental Strategy.* Cm 1200. HMSO, 1990. ISBN 0–10–112002–8.

8 *The Impact of Transport on the Environment – A Community Strategy for Sustainable Mobility.* EC Green Paper, 1992. ISBN 9–27–741382–4.

9 *The Future Development of the Common Transport Policy; a global approach to the construction of a Community framework for sustainable development.* EC White Paper, 1993. ISBN 9–27–750663–6.

10 *Agenda 21 – action plan for the next century,* endorsed at UNCED, 1992.

11 *The Countryside Survey 1990 – main report.* Barr, C. J. et al. DOE, 1993.

CHAPTER 27

LEISURE

A Sustainable Framework

- To maintain the quality of the environment in which leisure takes place for future generations to enjoy.
- To contribute to the health, well-being and quality of life of those taking part in leisure activities without destroying the natural resources upon which leisure depends.
- To ensure that leisure activities are a major means of creating awareness of, and appreciation for, the environment.

Trends

- Leisure, which includes tourism, sport and active recreation, is now a major contributor to the national and many local economies.
- Much leisure activity is increasingly directly dependent on the natural environment.

Problems and Opportunities

- Effects of leisure can be directly on site (overcrowding, wear and tear, noise and disturbance) or indirect (traffic to and from attractions) or associated (demands for inappropriate development).
- Conflicts can occur between different forms of leisure pursuit or between those taking part and the local community.
- The leisure industries are a major source of employment and make a significant contribution to overseas earnings through income from foreign tourists.
- Leisure pursuits can provide a stimulus to local economies, including opportunities to conserve or restore natural resources.
- Leisure provides a special opportunity to educate the public about the impact of their behaviour on the environment and to influence that behaviour in a sustainable way.

Current Responses

- The Government has taken a number of steps to make the leisure industries sustainable, including the protection of the natural environment through appropriate planning policies, and promoting principles for sustainable tourism through the wide range of Government agencies involved in disseminating information, advice and good practice.
- The leisure industries have been particularly willing to adopt sustainable principles, largely because they recognise the direct relationship between the quality of the environment and their product.
- Sports and recreational bodies have also been keen to encourage their members to pursue their activities in a sustainable way.

The Way Forward

- Government will continue to pursue the principles already adopted and to ensure that the framework now in place is kept up-to-date.
- Local authorities can take forward the issues for leisure recognised in *Local Agenda 21*[1].
- The statutory agencies will have a key role in developing new initiatives, promoting good practice and participating in research strategies to establish more clearly the impact of leisure on the environment.
- The leisure industry will increasingly take a major role in promoting sustainable development amongst its members.
- Above all, the public needs to consider the impact of their leisure pursuits on the environment and to adopt sustainable forms of leisure behaviour.

INTRODUCTION

27.1 Many people in the UK today have the opportunity to spend a significant proportion of their lives on leisure activities, doing what they wish to, not what they must. One of the measures of quality of life is the way in which people's spare time is used.

27.2 Leisure takes many forms. This chapter concentrates on those aspects of tourism, sport and active recreation which have the greatest impact on the environment. It does not address the issues of home-based recreation nor look directly at the impact of leisure on the historic heritage or the cultural environment, although many of the issues discussed are also relevant to these matters. Leisure is linked to other types of economic activity such as transport, energy and urban and rural development; the principles of sustainable development in these sectors are just as relevant to leisure.

27.3 The character and effects of tourism, sport and recreation differ, but they have many common elements.

RECREATION IN THE COUNTRYSIDE

Walking remains the most popular form of active recreation; in the summer of 1992, over 50 million day visits were made for this purpose. To this, and other well-established pastimes such as riding, cycling and angling, have now been added new pursuits like orienteering, mountain biking and hang-gliding. The Government has specifically committed itself to bringing the 225,000 km network of public rights of way in England and Wales into "good order" by 2000. Public rights of way represent a unique legacy, providing unrivalled opportunities for people to enjoy the great variety of the UK's landscapes and the settlements within them. The Forestry Commission operates a "freedom to roam" policy, and is the largest single provider of countryside recreation with a wide range of forest-based recreation facilities and services. New opportunities for access to the countryside are being created. These include Government proposals for the provision of access over the most suitable set-aside land and, more generally, within Environmentally Sensitive Areas (ESAs) to complement the access prescriptions already included in the Countryside Commission and Countryside Council for Wales' 'Countryside Stewardship' and 'Tir Cymen' schemes. In Scotland, access to the countryside for recreation is being reviewed by Scottish Natural Heritage, who have undertaken a major consultation exercise. The Forestry Commission provides advice on the use of woodland for recreation through its *Forest Recreation Guidelines*[3] and access related grants through the Woodland Grants Scheme (WGS).

For many people, getting away from their everyday surroundings and experiencing somewhere or something different represents a welcome break from both home and work. Journeys may be short – much sport and recreation takes place locally – and there are many forms of enjoyment, from active, organised pursuits to a gentle stroll or simply admiring the scenery. The common thread is that all should be enjoyable experiences, contributing to the health and sense of well-being of those who take part. But, equally, damage to the natural environment should be avoided or minimized.

27.4 Leisure and the natural environment have a special relationship. Conservation of the environment is inherent to the pursuit of many leisure activities whether for the yachtsman, the climber, or simply the visitor drawn by the attractions of the scenery. This is also true for many of those who provide and earn their living from leisure.

THE ECONOMIC SIGNIFICANCE OF LEISURE

27.5 The last 30 years have seen an enormous expansion and diversification in leisure activity worldwide. The tourist industry in the UK currently has a turnover of some £25 billion, having doubled in value in the 1980s. The industry now contributes over 4% of national Gross Domestic Product (GDP), and provides work for one million people. The UK is the world's sixth largest holiday market and, in 1992, over 18 million overseas visitors spent £7.7 billion on UK holidays, whilst UK residents themselves spent some £7.8 billion on holidays in this country.

27.6 At a different scale, recreational day trips represent a further, massive source of expenditure in the economy. The UK Day Visits Survey[2] indicated that, in the summer of 1992, some 1.3 billion day visits were made for leisure purposes, and that 60% of the population made at least one leisure trip during any given two-week period. The commonest reason for day trips is to visit friends or relatives, but tourism, sport and recreation accounted for almost 500 million visits during that summer.

27.7 Similar growth to that in the tourism sector has occurred in sport and active recreation. For example, the Day Visits Survey estimated that over 250 million leisure trips in 1992 were for these purposes, and consumer spending on all sports related items in the UK amounted to nearly £10 billion in 1990, approximately 2% of national GDP. The sports industry provides jobs for nearly 500,000 people, employment having grown by some 22% between 1985 and 1990.

27.8 Leisure, therefore, has a considerable impact on the national economy, but also now dominates a number of local economies. Whereas, 30 years ago, leisure was recognised as a major provider of income and jobs only in some seaside towns, today tourism, sport and recreation are among the biggest employers and most significant sources of income for large areas of the countryside and coast, and for some cities. Leisure and sporting provision is now recognised as a major component in strategies for the economic regeneration of urban areas. There has been a movement towards larger and more sophisticated facilities with all-weather provision and a far greater application of technology. Some major developments link accommodation with a wide range of entertainment and sporting activities and aim to attract local, national and international visitors.

LEISURE AND THE ENVIRONMENT

Environmental impacts of leisure

27.9 The rapid growth and development in leisure in the UK has drawn attention to the way in which these activities impact upon the natural heritage. More and more people are seeking forms of leisure that provide the greatest possible contrast to an increasingly urbanised and technological everyday life. While, over the last decade, much greater use has been made of local sports and recreation facilities, "getting away from it all" remains a major theme of the leisure industries. The quality of the environment promotes many forms of outdoor recreation, especially those which make use of the countryside or coast as a resource.

27.10 The relationship between the participant and the environment is inevitably complex and lies at the heart of sustainability. That relationship may be local – the direct impact of activities on a site – or it may be associated or indirect. Spectators, or people travelling to and from the location, can pose greater problems as can the development and other pressures associated with leisure as a major industry.

27.11 The commonest environmental impacts of leisure, most of which apply whether the leisure activity takes place in town or country, are:

- **Overcrowding**: too many people at one spot at one time may lower the quality of the original attraction and harm the qualities of the location;
- **Traffic**: other than for very local recreation, leisure activity in the countryside now predominantly involves travel by road (70% of all day trips are made by car or van). Roads and parking are often inadequate and, in addition to the global implications of road transport, there may be disruption to local users, congestion, noise, pollution and visual intrusion;
- **Wear and tear**: pressure of numbers can have a detrimental effect on the fabric of the landscape, including trampling, erosion and vegetation loss, as can pollution;
- **Disturbance and noise**: although noisy leisure pursuits may be more associated with urban areas, the impact of noise can be far greater in the countryside, especially on wildlife;
- **Inappropriate development**: more visitors and

participants and new activities can produce demands for improved and enlarged facilities, whether this be for car parks or the development of the attraction itself. When out of scale, inappropriately located or insensitively designed, such developments can fundamentally change the character of an area.

The contribution of leisure to environmental protection

27.12 The relationship between leisure and the environment is neither simple nor one-sided. Information on the impacts of many forms of leisure pursuits is poor and needs improving; environmental impacts are sometimes assumed, rather then proven. Many damaged or threatened aspects of the environment have been restored or conserved through the resources which tourism, sport and recreation provide. For many sites, visitor income is crucial to their upkeep and, perhaps, even their long term survival. Sometimes, integration between conservation and the demand for leisure can be directly achieved, as, for example, in some of the Royal Society for the Protection of Birds' (RSPB) most popular reserves. Tourists can also provide a stimulus, and the resources, to restore derelict land. As a growth sector in the national and many local economies, tourism, sport and recreation can lead to greater prosperity and increased wealth, without which higher environmental standards cannot be attained.

27.13 The direct interest which leisure has in promoting other aspects of environmental protection is often as relevant to residents as to visitors. Two obvious examples are the quality of bathing waters and the promotion of a litter-free environment. Furthermore, when leisure provides a greater share of economic prosperity, environmental conditions which discourage visitors and set a poor tone for an area's attractions can have considerable implications.

27.14 Above all, the experiences which visitors gain can be a major factor in strengthening their appreciation of the environment, thereby building public support for measures which give environmental protection greater priority. That support may be passive, through membership of conservation organisations like the National Trusts or the World Wide Fund for Nature (WWF), or it may be active, through groups like the British Trust for Conservation Volunteers or the Scottish Conservation Projects Trust. People will be more inclined to support the protection of the countryside and natural heritage if they feel that they, too, share in the responsibility for its conservation and are able to enjoy the fruits of their effort, restraint, or money.

SUSTAINABLE LEISURE

27.15 In May 1991, a Task Force set up by the Secretary of State for Employment reported on the issues of tourism and the environment in England[4]. Many of its conclusions are applicable to the wider relationship between leisure and the environment, and it represented an important step towards integrating the principles of sustainable development into the leisure industry. The central conclusion of the Task Force's report was their belief:

"…that [the] concept of sustainability is the key to seeking a more productive and harmonious relationship between the three elements in our triangle – the visitor, the host community, and the place. In other words we are looking to achieve a situation which can be maintained without depleting the resource, cheating the visitor, or exploiting the local population."

Key principles

27.16 As a direct consequence of the Task Force's report, the Government adopted four objectives which it intends will shape the way in which it supports the tourist industry. These objectives, applicable across the whole span of tourism, sport and recreation, are:

- to look to support the development of leisure in ways which contribute to, rather than detract from, the quality of our environment;
- to promote environmental quality issues within the leisure industries as well as issues concerned with the quality of their services and products;
- to ensure that all leisure managers become increasingly aware of visitor management techniques and ways of protecting the environment whilst promoting their industry;
- to look particularly to encourage and disseminate those forms of tourism, sport and recreation which in themselves aim to safeguard the environment.

27.17 A similar commitment has been adopted with regard to sport. In December 1991, the Government's policy statement on Sport and *Active Recreation*[5] drew particular attention to the scope for management measures to reconcile leisure development with environmental concerns. Both the Government and the Sports Councils have emphasised the concept of "sustainable promotion" whereby people should be able to participate in recreation activities in the countryside whilst having regard to the long term need to maintain the natural resource. The (Great Britain) Sports Council's, *A Countryside for Sport*[6], and the Sports Council for Wales', *Changing Times, Changing Needs: A Strategy Review*[7],

both reflect this approach. A Countryside for Sport comments that:

"Sport for all in the countryside [should be] sustainable in the long term and achieved through strategic planning and management and, above all, based on the needs of the community."

Capacity

27.18 Environmentally, the concept of capacity is of crucial significance. Every site, facility or visitor destination has a threshold or capacity beyond which the numbers of visitors or participants begin to cause serious damage to the resource itself. Determining capacity is, therefore, the first step in sustainable management.

27.19 Determining capacity is not an exact science; the capacity to absorb use will vary significantly according to the parameters and priorities applied. Capacity may vary according to the weather or the frequency with which demands on any site occur. The same activity at the same level can produce very different impacts in different parts of the country depending on climate, geology or vegetation.

27.20 Ultimately, judgements have to be made about the degree of robustness of the local environment and the scale of pressures to which it is subjected. Those involved, who should include public authorities, the leisure industries and those directly participating, need to judge the level at which the character, ambience and environmental value of a site would be threatened, or the point at which the impact on the local community would become unacceptable. They also need to take account of health and safety aspects of visitor management. Identifying what irreversible damage might take place is especially significant for sustainability. Capacity may be capable of being increased by protective measures, and these techniques relate strongly to the more general issue of how demand can be managed.

The management of demand

27.21 Leisure activities lend themselves well to demand management at individual sites or facilities, but less easily over wider areas or when more general questions of influencing public attitudes and behaviour are raised. Techniques of site management have been well publicised, especially where sites are gated or self-contained; at the simplest level, facilities can be shut if there are too many visitors. But general strategies to restrict public access create the risk that such a denial may weaken people's interest in, and support for, preserving the environment. There is, however, scope for the wider application of sophisticated techniques for the management of visitors. Timed tickets, controlled routes leading the visitor away from sensitive areas and dispersal throughout sites, where possible, are now commonplace. Zoning in time and space can be appropriate on larger sites and has been recommended, for example, by the Government's recent consultation document on the form and content of coastal management plans as a way of coping with competing recreational demands in inshore waters[8]. Emphasis may also be placed on more robust environments. Forest-based recreation, for example, can reduce pressure on more fragile habitats.

27.22 Wider concepts of demand management, in terms of influencing the desire for leisure, are less well tested. Here, responsibility lies with public agencies rather than individual operators. Concepts are beginning to emerge, such as marketing places and areas taking account of the sensitivity of their environment, and providing alternative leisure opportunities with more limited environmental effects. However testing of ideas such as pricing or rationing is at an early stage, and it may be difficult to operate such concepts outside closed environments. One aspect of demand management which has been better tested is traffic management. Given the dominance of the car-borne visitor, this can be a key factor. Mechanisms to manage traffic or control parking at leisure attractions can, at least, mitigate the impact of visitors, although so far there is less evidence that similar measures can be applied to have a real impact over wider areas.

27.23 Demand management also has to recognise the requirement of local people for sports and recreation facilities. Although often on a smaller scale, local demands frequently represent a legitimate first call on scarce financial and natural resources.

Conserving the resource

27.24 The relationship between many forms of leisure and the environment in which they take place itself depends on positive measures to sustain that environment. Outdoor recreation, for example, often requires access to facilities or to natural resources. Loss of either may severely diminish choice and bring greater pressures upon those opportunities that remain. The Government promotes a range of policies designed to conserve and enhance the opportunities for leisure. These range from a general commitment to protect the countryside from inappropriate development, through specific initiatives to conserve special landscapes (such as National Parks in England and Wales, and National Scenic Areas in Scotland), to the Codes of Practice for water and sewerage undertakers on conservation, access and recreation, issued in England and Wales in 1989 and in Scotland in 1993. These policies to protect the natural environment go hand in hand with the promotion of sustainable tourism, sport and recreation, which will itself reduce pressures on the environment. Overall, however, the responsibility for conservation must be shared between public authorities, the leisure industry and those who participate.

Planning policy

27.25 The planning system provides a framework within which many key decisions are taken on the development of leisure activities which affect the use of land. Revised planning policy guidance notes (PPGs) on tourism, and on sport and recreation[10], have now been published in England and Wales; they give advice on how the planning system should reconcile the desire for development in these sectors with the need to protect the environment as a whole and to preserve the character of the areas which attract tourists. The PPGs are designed to secure speedy and satisfactory planning decisions on tourism and leisure developments. It is proposed to issue parallel guidance in Scotland through National Planning Policy Guidance (NPPG) and a Planning Advice Note (PAN).

27.26 The PPG on sport and recreation also gives emphasis to the important associated issue of ensuring sufficient protection for urban sports and recreation facilities. Not only does most sport and recreation take place in urban areas, but the protection and enhancement of such facilities provides an opportunity to reduce the impact on the natural environment of demands for leisure in the countryside. Further details on the planning system as a whole, are given in chapter 35.

27.27 Planning policies have an important role to play, not only in protecting opportunities for leisure and the environment in which it takes place, but also in providing new opportunities. The urban fringe, in particular, can provide leisure opportunities close to centres of population, which can be reached more easily with less travel, taking pressure off the countryside. The programme of 12 Community Forests, being jointly promoted by the Countryside Commission and Forestry Commission around major metropolitan areas in England, represents an example of the new opportunities that can be created.

Statutory agencies and the leisure industries

27.28 Sustainable leisure depends to a great extent on the leisure industries themselves. The Government has placed considerable emphasis on the Tourist Boards and other leisure agencies taking a lead.

27.29 In England, in December 1991, the English Tourist Board (ETB) with the Countryside Commission and Rural Development Commission launched *The Green Light: a guide to sustainable tourism*[11]. This publication provides advice and information to the tourism industry on a wide range of environmental issues, attitudes and trends, and has been followed up in September 1993 by a national demonstration project. This produced an environmental audit kit for small and medium-sized tourism businesses, emphasising how managerial improvements can reduce adverse impacts and

improve profitability. The Tourist Boards have also focused on the specific issues associated with tourism and recreation in sensitive areas, including the publication of *Tourism in National Parks – a Guide to Good Practice*[12]. Since 1988 the ETB has made a "green tourism" award as part of its England for Excellence scheme; this was renamed the Tourism and the Environment Award in 1991 to reflect the wider environmental issues associated with tourism.

27.30 The Wales Tourist Board (WTB) has published a draft consultative strategy, *Tourism 2000*[13], which places the aim of sustainable development at the forefront of its objectives. Policy principles dealing with the economic, environmental and community aspects of sustainability, and reflecting the particular circumstances and needs of Wales, provide a basic framework for the WTB's work. The document also sets out a series of action programmes to be implemented by the Board in conjunction with partner agencies within the public and private sectors. Welsh organisations have already had experience, for example, through the National Garden Festival at Ebbw Vale in 1992, of the way in which tourism and leisure can contribute, not only to environmental conservation, but to the regeneration and enhancement of an area.

27.31 In February 1992, the principles of sustainable tourism in Scotland were outlined in the Scottish Tourist Board's (STB), *Tourism and the Scottish Environment, A Sustainable Partnership*[14]. Following a detailed study into tourism's relationship with the environment, the Scottish Office set up in 1992 a Task Force, led by STB with representatives from key organisations in the public sector, to establish a national tourism management regime. The Task Force has published *Going Green*[15], giving practical examples of ways in which individual tourism businesses can help achieve the objective of an environmentally friendly tourism industry. Local interests have been encouraged to work together to establish pilot environmental tourism projects to test visitor management techniques and environmentally beneficial tourism developments in both urban and rural areas. National initiatives on coastal erosion, caravan parks and National Tourist Routes are also being implemented, whilst Scottish Natural Heritage are carrying out a review of arrangements for access to the countryside.

27.32 In December 1993, the Northern Ireland Tourist Board produced its own study of the relationship between tourism and the environment[16]. The strategy follows a detailed review of development policy, case studies and wide consultation. Nearly 80 action items have been identified, ranging from a sustainable tourism management initiative in the Mourne Areas of Outstanding Natural Beauty to marketing initiatives and good practice guidelines. Priority is also being given to introducing environmental impact tests for proposed tourist developments. Clear advice on sustainability is to be made available at all levels of decision-making and action.

27.33 Leisure operators have responded by beginning to show a direct concern for the environment upon which their operations may depend. Many tourism operators already recognise the importance of a quality product, and the Association of Independent Tour Operators is introducing an environmental policy as a part of its quality charter. Some individual companies make a selling point of their concern for the environment. The British Home and Holiday Parks Association's recent environmental code, produced in co-operation with the major touring caravan clubs, encourages the adoption of the highest standards by site operators.

27.34 Management measures are now also well developed to allow multi-use of recreational facilities which respect environmental quality. For example, British Waterways (BW) has become increasingly aware of the environmental problems associated with the multiple use

of canal towing paths. After wide consultation with interested groups, BW classified those paths which are suitable for cycling and added to its series of "waterway codes" a code of practice for cyclists. Agencies can also assist in the production of codes of practice designed to minimise environmental impacts of recreational activities. An example is English Nature's leaflet *Paintball Games in Woodlands – a guide to good environmental practice*[17].

27.35 The Sports Council has emphasised the scope for positive management in providing opportunities for sport and recreation in rural areas. Through the Regional Councils for Sport and Recreation, the Council sponsors bodies which bring together interests with the aim of achieving integrated strategic planning and management. It has been concerned to ensure that proper facilities are provided for people living in rural areas, including those in environmentally sensitive countryside. The Council has done much to promote responsible behaviour amongst those participating in sport and outdoor recreation. The Sports Council has also been concerned to ensure that sports and recreational facilities take account of the need for sustainable development. It has been working with the Building Research Establishment to make sports facilities more energy efficient,

---

BOX 27.3
LOCAL ACTION FOR SUSTAINABLE TOURISM

Between October 1991 and February 1992, eight very successful regional seminars were held in England to stimulate action at a local level. To reinforce this message, a series of pilot projects has been established to explore and further demonstrate techniques of visitor management, to monitor their effectiveness and to highlight the benefits of well-managed tourism. Similar pilots are being run in other parts of the UK.

These projects include:

The Peak Tourism Partnership, to tackle visitor pressures in villages and sites in an area which includes a National Park, and to look specifically at ways of raising funds from visitors to promote conservation measures;

The Purbeck Visitor Management Study, identifying ways of reducing pressure and looking at the consequences of extending a railway line;

The Lake District Traffic Management Initiative, in which ways to integrate a range of local schemes to reduce traffic congestion are being tested;

The Surrey Hills Tourism Initiative, looking at the potential for public transport and improving information for the visitor;

Stratford upon Avon, introducing a park and ride scheme, reducing coach congestion and setting up a visitor welcome training scheme.

The South Devon Green Tourism Initiative, encouraging good environmental practice within the tourism industry in south Devon; an Environmental Audit Manual, the first of its kind, has been published for the use of small operators.

All of these measures flow directly from, or are in line with, the recommendations of the English Task Force report and have had the assistance of the ETB or local Regional Tourist Board.

and aims to produce data sheets covering environmental and energy efficiency issues.

27.36 Environmental awareness is often high amongst those participating in outdoor recreation; many national governing bodies, such as the British Mountaineering Council and the British Water Ski Federation, now operate codes of practice which emphasise environmental issues. In May 1991, the Central Council for Physical Recreation (CCPR), the forum for such governing bodies in England, published its own policy statement, *Sport and Recreation in the Countryside*[18]. This emphasised that the natural fabric of the countryside was the fundamental attraction to visitors, who thereby had an interest in its protection; and that sport and recreation rarely required exclusive use of land and water and was therefore one of many diverse economic and social activities which the countryside could accommodate. It also encouraged its constituent bodies to develop codes of practice which promoted sustainable use of the environments, on which particular activities depend.

27.37 The responsible attitude expressed by the governing bodies of many sports also needs to be encouraged amongst the wider public. Bodies such as the Council for Environmental Education (CEE) are encouraging the growing interest in, and concern for, the environment. Emphasis is also being placed on providing better public information about leisure opportunities which are more sustainable. Public libraries, local authority funded information centres and Tourist Information Centres are increasingly able to alert regular visitors to the countryside to new opportunities which may be nearer their homes or which might occur in off-peak periods.

International dimension

27.38 Leisure is an international industry and, although recreation and tourism are not issues directly addressed in Agenda 21[19], recreational and tourist development are important components of sustainable land use. The UK Government has helped to bring the concepts of sustainable tourism to a wider international audience, particularly during the UK's Presidency of the EC in the second half of 1992. Tourism is one of the five main themes of the EC's Fifth Environmental Action Programme[20]. The Programme lays particular emphasis on developing environmentally friendly forms of tourism and encouraging the diversification of the tourist industry. Stress is laid on educating the tourist industry, and on increasing environmental awareness amongst both industry and local authorities. The UK is already implementing many projects along these lines.

27.39 As well as being a source for tourism, the UK itself generates considerable numbers of international tourists. Overseas visits for both business and pleasure by UK residents increased by over 75% in the 1980s. It would be irresponsible to pursue sustainable tourism at home, merely to export the problems to others. Environmental education of the visitor in the UK needs to accommodate the responsibilities of the tourist abroad. Some aspects of international tourism, including skiing and "ecotourism",for example in relation to wildlife watching, have already received attention in this context.

TRENDS

27.40 Trends in leisure can be difficult to predict, especially when so diverse a range of activities is covered and particularly when looking to the longer term. For tourism, the British Tourist Authority (BTA) forecasts continuing significant increases in the extent of, and expenditure on, tourism. The BTA expect incoming visits to rise by an annual increase rate of 5.2% between 1992 and 1997, with expenditure targeted to rise by 6.9% in this period. Domestic tourism activity is expected to increase by around 1.5% over this period. Day trips, too, are expected to continue to increase substantially by an anticipated 12–15% growth between 1990 and 1995.

27.41 If current trends continue, there could be more travel by car to leisure activities, with particular impact on rural areas. A growth in conservation-related activities is widely predicted, as are higher levels of participation in sport. Demographic changes may also affect the scale and pattern of leisure demands. An aging population might mean more modest demands involving less travel, although fitter, older people with larger disposable incomes may become a major niche in leisure markets. Changing work patterns may create a greater demand for short breaks, although technology could also increase home-based activities.

THE FUTURE

27.42 There is already a strong consensus that a sustainable approach is central to the future development and practice of leisure. All those involved with leisure and the leisure industries will need to ensure that this approach is translated from principles into practice.

27.43 For **Government,** this means pursuing the principles already adopted and ensuring that the framework now being put in place is kept up-to-date and relevant; that policies are developed which maintain a balance between economic development and the environment; and that appropriate priorities are identified for the direction of resources towards meeting those objectives.

27.44 Local authorities need to take forward the issues already identified for Local Agenda 21 in the context of leisure, incorporating, where appropriate, "green strategies" for tourism and recreation within their policies for the whole range of environmental issues with which leisure interacts.

27.45 A key role for the **statutory agencies** will be in developing new initiatives, spreading good practice and experimenting with novel management techniques which can be used to translate principles into sustainable action. The agencies have a vital role in providing knowledge, advice, skill training and other support to the leisure industries. They may also play a major part in research strategies to establish more clearly the impact of leisure activities on the environment.

27.46 The **leisure industries** themselves have now recognised the advantages of a sustainable approach and taken first steps to integrate these principles into the way they operate. This approach will benefit the industries' health and long term prospects. It will increasingly fall to the leisure industries to take the lead in promoting sustainable development in leisure.

27.47 Perhaps most importantly, the **public**, both as consumers and as participants, need to consider the impact of their leisure activities on the environment, whether it be through tourism, participation in organised sports or simply informal recreation. Only with public support will these objectives be achieved.

REFERENCES AND FURTHER READING

1   *Local Agenda 21 – Agenda 21: a guide for local authorities in the UK.* LGMB, 1992.

2   *UK Day Visits Survey, Countryside Recreation News, No 2.* Cardiff, June 1993.

3   *Forest Recreation Guidelines.* Forestry Commission. HMSO, 1992.

4   *Tourism and the Environment: Maintaining the Balance. Report of the Task Force.* Department of Employment, May 1991.

5   *Sport and Active Recreation: a Policy Statement.* Department of Education and Science, 1991.

6   *A Countryside for Sport.* The Sports Council. HMSO, 1992.

7   *Changing Times, Changing Needs: a Strategy Review.* Sports Council for Wales, 1991.

8   *Managing the Coast: a review of coastal Management plans in England and Wales, and the powers supporting them.* DOE/Welsh Office, October 1993.

9   *Planning Policy Guidance note 21: Tourism.* DOE/Welsh Office, November 1992.

10 *Planning Policy Guidance note 17: Sport and Recreation.* DOE/Welsh Office, September 1991.

11 *The Green Light – a Guide to Sustainable Tourism.* English Tourist Board, 1991.

12 *Tourism in National Parks – Guide to Good Practice.* English Tourist Board, 1991.

13 *Tourism 2000.* Welsh Tourist Board, 1992.

14 *Tourism and the Scottish Environment.* Scottish Tourist Board, 1991.

15 *Going Green, a report by the Task Force into Tourism and the Environment.* Scottish Tourist Board, 1992.

16 *Tourism in Northern Ireland – a Sustainable Approach.* Northern Ireland Tourist Board, December 1993. Available from the Northern Ireland Tourist Board.

17 *Paintball Games in Woodlands.* English Nature, 1993.

18 *Sport and Recreation in the Countryside.* Central Council for Physical Education, 1991.

19 *Agenda 21 – an action plan for the next century,* endorsed at UNCED, 1992.

20 *Towards Sustainability: a European Community programme of policy and action in relation to the environment and sustainable development (The EC Fifth Action Programme).* Commission of the EC. Official publication of the EC, 1992 (Cm (92) 23/11/Final).

SECTION 4
PUTTING SUSTAINABILITY INTO PRACTICE

CHAPTER 28

INTERNATIONAL CONTEXT

Current Responses

- The UK ratified the Climate Change Convention in 1993.
- The UK intends to ratify the Biodiversity Convention given satisfactory progress towards securing financial safeguards.
- The Government has discharged its commitment to publish this Strategy and the Climate Change Programme, the Biodiversity Action Plan and the Sustainable Forestry Programme.
- The UK successfully secured election to the UN Commission on Sustainable Development (CSD), which was established after Rio to monitor the implementation of Agenda 21, and contributed fully to the productive outcome of its first session in June 1993.
- The UK hosted a Global Technology Partnership Conference in March 1993.

The Way Forward

- The UK will continue to encourage multilateral organisations to adopt Agenda 21.
- Through its overseas aid programme the UK Government will continue to promote economic and social development in other countries, and the welfare of their people.
- The UK will continue to support developing countries to set priorities for their domestic resources.
- The UK has worked towards international agreement on the replenishment and restructuring of the Global Environment Facility (GEF).
- In the second half of 1994, the UK Government plans to host jointly with the Indian Government an international workshop to prepare for the 1994 session of the CSD, which will review the implementation of the Statement of Forest Principles.

INTRODUCTION

28.1 This Strategy is essentially national, and concentrates on achieving sustainability within the UK. However, the UK's pursuit of sustainable development will inevitably affect other countries, and vice versa. The UK can also make a positive contribution to help promote sustainability in other countries.

28.2 This chapter looks at the international institutional framework: environmental, economic and financial. It examines the UK's positive contribution to sustainable development in developing countries, Eastern Europe and the former Soviet Union (FSU), through private flows of finance and technology, and aid, both via official channels and through non-governmental organisations (NGOs).

INTERNATIONAL INSTITUTIONAL FRAMEWORK

28.3 The international framework inevitably shapes the UK's actions: the UK is only one country in a complex system in which individual states pursue their own national interests individually or collectively, and in which they seek to agree on common international objectives. The UK plays a prominent role in the international framework, through membership of the EC, the UN, the Commonwealth, the G7 group of major industrial nations, and many other multilateral organisations with more specific concerns. One of the UK's objectives is to ensure that environmental concerns are integrated into the agendas of these organisations as far as possible. Since the Earth Summit in Rio, the UK has been active in encouraging these international organisations to adopt *Agenda 21*[1] and to commit themselves to a continuing review of their progress in pursuing sustainable development.

28.4 Within the UN, the UK successfully secured election to the new Commission on Sustainable Development (CSD) which was established after Rio to monitor the implementation of Agenda 21; and it contributed fully to the productive outcome of the CSD's first meeting in June 1993. The UK's strategic objective at the CSD will be to maintain political interest in sustainable development, and to use it to apply effective pressure on the other members of the UN "family" to plan specifically for sustainable development and to report regularly on progress towards it. However, these arrangements will only be of maximum benefit if there is appropriate coordination between the international organisations' programmes and national plans and strategies.

ROLE OF SUSTAINABLE DEVELOPMENT STRATEGIES

28.5 The people and government of each country must take responsibility for pursuing sustainable development in their own activities. Each country must examine how to make best use of the resources available domestically. Countries should set priorities in the light of those resources and the recommendations set out in Agenda 21. Sustainable development is at least as much about changing old habits and ways of spending money as acquiring new ones, as Chapter 33 of Agenda 21 emphasised.

Indeed, reorientation of existing programmes can make by far the biggest contribution to implementing Agenda 21. Once a country's domestic priorities have been set out, it is possible to define the optimal role for external flows in helping promote sustainable development in the country concerned.

28.6 Each national government will wish to consider how best to determine coherent priorities for sustainable development. The UK Government has produced this Strategy, and will continue the series of White Papers on *This Common Inheritance*[2], which is the UK's process for establishing and recording its environmental priorities. The June 1993 session of the CSD considered what advice to offer countries on the design of national reports. The UK took an active part, and welcomed the encouragement and priority which the CSD gave to the production of such reports.

28.7 In many developing countries, these reports will be able to build on sectoral assessments and plans (for example, Tropical Forestry Action Plans and Biodiversity assessments) which the UK and others have already supported. Many developing countries have sought World Bank assistance for further National Environmental Action plans. The UK looks forward to the implementation of the programmes that will follow from these assessments. However, it is vital to ensure that both environmental action plans and sustainable development strategies are the result of widespread consultation within the country concerned, including discussion with and support from the major participants identified in chapters 23–32 of Agenda 21. Such plans cannot simply be imported from outside, if they are to be practical. The UK Government places much importance on these reports, and would therefore consider support for their production as a high priority for external assistance.

28.8 The UK is encouraging its Dependent Territories to pursue sustainable development strategies. Advice has been given to help them to determine their priorities for implementing the conclusions of the Earth Summit, and to identify the assistance they require in meeting the requirements of the conventions on climate change and biodiversity, and the Montreal Protocol[3].

THE EC ENVIRONMENTAL FRAMEWORK

28.9 Environmental policy in the UK is now inextricably bound up with EC policy. Within the Community, member states have responsibility to act when this is the most effective means of achieving Community and international environmental objectives. In the last 20 years, the EC has developed comprehensive measures across a broad range of environmental areas, in response to growing recognition of the value of common action to solve common problems. Much of the UK's environmental protection legislation is now developed in common with other EC member states; examples are water and air quality, waste management, wildlife and habitats protection, dangerous substances and environmental impact assessment (EIA). The EC also has a role in implementing agreements reached in wider international fora, such as the UN Economic Commission for Europe's work on air pollution, or global agreements on climate change and protecting the ozone layer.

28.10 In parallel with the Rio process, the EC developed its Fifth Environmental Action Programme, *Towards Sustainability*[4]. The UK played a leading role in developing and welcoming the Programme during its Presidency of the EC in 1992. The Programme was formally adopted by the Council of Ministers on 1 February 1993, and the Commission adopted new internal procedures to implement the Programme in June 1993. The Programme is linked closely to the principles and themes of Agenda 21 and addresses most of the areas covered by this Strategy. Its major theme – the importance of securing the integration of environmental considerations into all policy areas – lies at the heart of the pursuit of sustainable development. The Maastricht Treaty now in force states that, "environmental protection requirements must be integrated into the definition and implementation of other Community policies". The UK will do what it can to ensure that these principles are put into practice.

28.11 The Fifth Action Programme also highlights the importance of "shared responsibility", meaning that everyone – from international organisations through national governments to local authorities and individuals, as well as all economic sectors – has a role in delivering sustainable development. This ties in closely with Agenda 21 and this Strategy. An interim review of the implementation of the Fifth Action Programme will be conducted in 1994 with a full review in 1995. The UK will play a full part in these reviews. The national level action suggested in the Programme will be reflected in the Government's Third Year Report on *This Common Inheritance*, to be published early in 1994.

28.12 In some specific areas the EC has exclusive competence to participate in multilateral fora. The key example of this is the General Agreement on Tariffs and Trade (GATT), where the UK is involved in the development of the EC's Common Commercial Policy, through consultation with the Commission and with other member states. The Commission also speaks for the EC in some other commercial negotiations. The UK has worked to ensure that environmental questions and other aspects of sustainable development are taken into account at every stage in this process.

THE INTERNATIONAL ENVIRONMENTAL FRAMEWORK

28.13 The UK is active in a number of new organisations associated with the Earth Summit process, which have already been mentioned in earlier chapters. The UK ratified the Climate Change Convention at the end of 1993. The UK intends to ratify the Biodiversity Convention, given satisfactory progress towards securing safeguards regarding its concerns on the financial provisions of the Convention. The UK *Climate Change Programme*[5] and *Biodiversity Action Plan*[6] are being published in parallel with this Strategy. The UK is planning, through its share of the core fund of the Global Environment Facility (GEF), to finance its contributions to certain costs arising for developing countries to help to achieve global environmental benefits from both Conventions, and to help to prevent specific further global threats to the ozone layer and international waters. The GEF is available to assist countries in transition (Central and Eastern Europe and the FSU). The UK worked for international agreement on GEF restructuring and replenishment at the end of 1993. The Prime Minister has already pledged up to £100 million in new and additional resources for the replenishment of the GEF.

28.14 The Earth Summit agreed the Statement of Forest Principles for the management, conservation and sustainable development of the world's forests. The UK promotes the Principles internationally through the bilateral aid programme, participation in the Tropical Forestry Action Programme, membership of the International Tropical Timber Organisation, and support for international forestry institutions. The UK has strongly supported the agreement that the CSD should review the implementation of the Principles, which it will do in 1995. One of the primary aims of the Indo-British Forestry Initiative, which was agreed by the two governments in September 1993, is the plan to host jointly an international workshop in 1994 to prepare for the review. In June 1993, at the Ministerial conference on the Protection of Forests in Europe in Helsinki, the UK signed resolutions on sustainable management and conservation of biodiversity. The UK *Forestry Programme*[7] is being published in parallel with this Strategy.

28.15 The CSD is to consider reports from the various UN Agencies on progress in implementing the conclusions of the Earth Summit. The UK has encouraged this in the governing bodies of the UN Environment Programme (UNEP) and the UN Development Programme (UNDP).

28.16 At its Governing Council in May 1993, new priorities were agreed for UNEP based on Agenda 21. The Council also agreed that UNEP should cooperate closely with other UN agencies and the CSD. The UK fully supports the new Executive Director's aims to improve UNEP's efficiency and effectiveness. It is one of the largest contributors to UNEP, contributing £4.5 million in 1993–94.

28.17 In the case of UNDP, a capacity building programme in support of Agenda 21 was launched: 'Capacity 21'. This is designed to aid countries in the formulation and implementation of sustainable development strategies and national capacity-building programmes. The UK has emphasised that sustainable development principles should be applied across the board and integrated fully into all UNDP's activities.

28.18 The UK has stressed the importance of effective feedback from UNDP to the CSD. This feedback should reflect both UNDP's specific mandate with respect to sustainable development and its wider responsibility for UN coordination.

28.19 Earlier chapters demonstrate the extent of the UK's involvement in a wide range of international environmental and conservation bodies which predate the Earth Summit. The UK has:
- successfully pressed for a tightening of controls on CFC emissions through the Montreal Protocol on Substances which Deplete the Ozone Layer;
- enhanced protection for some of the world's most vulnerable species through the Convention on International Trade in Endangered Species (CITES)[8];
- fought hard to maintain the moratorium on commercial whaling through the International Whaling Commission;
- participated in the intergovernmental negotiations aimed at producing a convention on desertification.

ECONOMIC AND FINANCIAL FRAMEWORK

28.20 The Earth Summit also recognised the importance of a supportive external economic framework for sustainable development. This includes policies to promote free trade and economic growth.

28.21 Responsibility for sustainable development rests primarily with individual countries and their governments. But private investment flows, greater trade access to international markets, debt relief and overseas aid can all make an important contribution.

28.22 Most of these external flows contribute to economic growth and poverty reduction. Some of the worst degradation of the local environment is a by-product of poverty. Tackling poverty and promoting economic growth are therefore imperative for sustainable development. This is reflected in the objectives of the UK aid programme.

Trade

28.23 Trade is a key part of the UK's economic relationship with all parts of the world – the UK is particularly dependent for its own prosperity and development on both imports and exports. Trade and investment flows bind countries together. The main way the UK contributes to the economic development of developing countries is by buying their products. The impetus for trade lies with the private sector, but the Government's policy has consistently been to create the conditions in which trade can thrive. The UK has made a substantial contribution to the EC's negotiating position in the Uruguay Round of multilateral trade negotiations. A successful Round will lead to lower tariffs on goods and significant liberalisation of trade in services from which all countries will benefit. Developing countries will gain better access to developed country markets. A study[9] by the Organisation for Economic Co-operation and Development (OECD) sets out the eventual possible increases in developing countries' income – although the exact distribution of these benefits between countries is not yet clear.

28.24 The UK uses its membership of a number of commodity agreements and study groups to improve the functioning of commodity markets and to enhance transparency. It is a member of the Common Fund for Commodities, which develops commodity-based projects for developing countries. It participates actively in the UN Conference on Trade and Development (UNCTAD) discussions of commodity issues. The UK believes that producer countries gain more in the longer term from structural adjustment of their economies than continued reliance on one or two commodities, and supports developing countries' efforts to diversify and improve the efficiency of their export and import trade.

28.25 The importance of the interaction between trade and environment policies is now well established and is being examined in a number of international fora, principally the GATT and OECD, but also including UNCTAD, UNEP and the CSD. The UK plays a significant role in this work, for example, in considering the use of trade restrictions in environmental policies and international agreements, such as CITES and the Montreal Protocol. Governments are looking to develop and extend the important concepts, related to the proper pricing of environmental resources, which were reflected in the original development of the "polluter pays" principle in the early 1970s.

28.26 Trade liberalisation and economic growth change the impact of human activity on the environment. Views both within and between trade, environment and development communities on the relationship between trade and environment policies diverge considerably. This has engendered a lively debate. The UK believes that environmental and trade objectives can and should be mutually supportive: trade promotes growth and can help provide the economic and technical resources needed to protect the environment, while a sustainably managed environment provides the natural resources essential for this process of economic growth. The UK considers that environmental protection is best pursued domestically through national strategies for sustainable development and, internationally, through multilateral rather than bilateral action. Current work on trade and environment is likely to form the foundation for future negotiations on these policy interactions in the GATT and elsewhere (including in the negotiations of future environmental agreements). The Government is fully committed to playing an active role in this process, in consultation with EC partners and as part of a wider debate with all interested parties.

Foreign direct investment

28.27 Foreign direct investment (FDI) plays a significant part in the economic development of countries and can bring substantial environmental benefits. The policies of the UK Government have been effective in boosting FDI flows. The UK both provides and attracts substantial investment. The Government aims to encourage the widest possible adoption of liberal policies on foreign investment as a way of stimulating economic growth worldwide for the benefit of all. Work to encourage more liberal policies is continuing through organisations such as the EC, GATT, OECD, World Bank and UNCTAD, where the importance of FDI is fully recognised as a stimulus to domestic economic development. This, in turn, can have significant effects in generating the resources necessary to reduce environmental degradation.

28.28 Governments need to provide a liberal, transparent and non-discriminatory framework to promote investor confidence. Confidence is the key factor in encouraging foreign and domestic investment and, in particular, confidence that there will be economic and policy stability and transparency to enable investors to play a part in the development of the country. An increasing number of countries are recognising this and are taking measures to boost investment flows. This, in turn, is encouraging multinational companies to invest in new markets. With this comes greater exposure to and awareness of international environmental standards.

Technology cooperation

28.29 Technology cooperation, which includes technology transfer, is an important part of trade and FDI. Aid and development assistance is all about technology cooperation. Many of the technologies which improve environmental performance, protect the environment, or contribute to development are in the public domain, and therefore accessible. Several of the Department of Trade and Industry's inward technology transfer schemes have an environmental content. Thus the overseas Science and Technology Expert Mission Scheme, in which small teams of UK industrialists learn from the best practice overseas, has recently supported groups studying land and groundwater pollution in Czechoslovakia; wind energy in Greece; cryptosporidium in US water treatment; and sludge treatment in Japan. The Overseas Technical Information Service, which disseminates information gathered by British overseas embassies, found that the environment was the topic of most interest to governmental and industrial users of the service. Furthermore, the environment also features prominently in the bilateral science and technology agreements made with a number of East European countries.

28.30 Given the important contribution that technology can make to protecting the global environment, it is essential to encourage technology cooperation at both international and intra-national levels. 93% of technology flow takes place in the private sector, often as a result of FDI. A stable and liberal macro-economic framework, together with transparent non-discriminatory policies and the proper protection of international property rights, are fundamental to this flow. Governments play an important role in creating these conditions.

28.31 As the Prime Minister stated at the UK's Global Technology Partnership Conference in Birmingham in March 1993, commercial transactions are the most effective means of technology transfer because they have to pass the market test and each partner has a vested interest in their success. They take into account the economic circumstances, and the technical and managerial skills, needed to ensure that technologies can be absorbed, adapted, used and diffused by the recipient. They lead to

rewards that are essential for further investment and technological development. Any policy on technology cooperation must be based on these principles.

28.32 The UK therefore supports Trade Related Intellectual Property agreements (TRIPs) in the Uruguay Round, which will establish minimum standards for intellectual property rights and further encourage technology cooperation. The UK also encourages greater technology cooperation between businesses in developing and developed countries. The UK's Technology Partnership Initiative runs for three years, and will provide information to businesses in the developing countries on the technologies and management techniques widely adopted in the UK. These can lead to significant improvements in performance and profits, as well as reducing environmental impacts. In addition, the Initiative will strengthen the links between businesses in developing countries and businesses, scientific institutions and training centres in the UK.

Official aid

28.33 The UK's overseas aid programme is already very much in line with Agenda 21. The overall aim is to promote economic and social development in other countries, and the welfare of their people. The Overseas Development Administration (ODA) has seven specific objectives which reflect the principles agreed at the Earth Summit as part of Agenda 21, as shown below:

BOX 28.1

ODA Objective	Relevant Agenda 21 chapters
To promote economic reform	2
To enhance productive capacity	14 & 29–32
To promote good government	2
To undertake direct poverty reduction activities and programmes	3
To promote human development, including better education and health, and children by choice	5, 6 & 36
To promote the status of women	24
To help developing countries tackle national environmental problems	1 & 8

28.34 At the Earth Summit, the Prime Minister identified five key sectors of Agenda 21 on which the UK would concentrate activities and resources: forestry conservation (chapter 11), biodiversity (15), energy efficiency (9B), population planning (5) and sustainable agriculture (14). These were already important components of the UK's bilateral aid programme. In 1992-93, ODA had 179 projects under way whose principal objective was one of the Earth Summit priorities; these spent nearly £42 million, an increase of 21% over 1991–92. A further 162 projects included these priorities as a significant objective. Data for commitments since the Earth Summit will be included in future reports to the CSD.

28.35 The UK also attaches importance to encouraging and assisting developing countries to play their part in responding to threats to the global environment. For instance, India already contributes more than the UK to world emissions of greenhouse gases; and India and China, with other developing countries, are expected to contribute half the total by 2050, compared with a quarter in 1990. The world's species diversity of crops, plants and wildlife is overwhelmingly concentrated in the developing world, and thus can only be conserved by cooperative action with developing countries.

28.36 UK humanitarian assistance also has an important role. Given the damage to development prospects that can be done by natural and manmade disasters, it is often an essential prerequisite for any more sustainable process, as recent crises around the world have shown. Humanitarian assistance is intended to provide the necessary security for sustainable development, since without such security, sustainable development is not feasible. Equally, without sustainable development, there will not be security in the longer term.

28.37 At the Earth Summit, the EC agreed to commit 3 billion ecu for priority sectors of Agenda 21. The UK has played an active part in a series of expert groups to consider priority issues in the implementation of that pledge, including chairing the group on energy efficiency. The Development Council in May 1993 confirmed that a first tranche of 600 mecu will be committed in 1993, and agreed that member states would aim to commit 20% (120 mecu) on top of this in new and additional resources. This agreement will ensure that the EC's pledge is translated into effective action.

28.38 The UK is encouraging the International Financial Institutions (IFIs) to apply the principles of sustainable development, through membership of their Executive Boards. The UK was encouraged by the participation of the IFIs in the first meeting of the CSD. While it is ultimately for countries themselves to implement the reforms which lay

the foundation for sustainable development, the IFIs are well placed to provide financial support and technical advice.

28.39 The International Monetary Fund (IMF) has adapted to the changing needs and circumstances of its members by, for example, the introduction of concessional lending through the Enhanced Structural Adjustment Facility (ESAF), the Rights Approach to help countries with IFI arrears and, most recently, the Systemic Transformation Facility, which helps countries trying to make the transition from a command to a market-oriented economy. These are essential elements in creating sustainable development policies and structures.

28.40 The World Bank is paying increasing attention to the issue of sustainable development in its policy dialogue with borrowers; this was illustrated in the Bank's 1992 *World Development Report on Environment and Development*.[10] Particular features of Bank activities are the development of institutional capacity for environmental management; a greater emphasis on the social aspects of environmentally sustainable development; and the need to address global environmental problems through its participation in the GEF. The UK has played a leading role in supporting the Bank, for example, in the negotiations leading to the tenth Replenishment of the resources available to the International Development Association. Sustainable development will be one of the major objectives throughout the replenishment period. The UK will continue to support the Bank's efforts to raise standards of environmental appraisal and their integration into Bank lending.

28.41 The IFIs are increasingly encouraging governments to attach greater priority to social sectors within their budgets, in recognition of the importance of investments in human resources for successful and sustainable development. The IMF and World Bank help their members to assess the impact that policy reforms are likely to have on poor groups, through the integration of social safety nets into structural adjustment programmes.

Assistance for environmental problems in Central and Eastern Europe

28.42 In the countries of Central and Eastern Europe, tackling environmental problems and promoting sustainable development is closely bound up with economic and political reform. The UK is assisting this process both through multilateral channels (such as the EC's Phare programme, to which the UK is contributing some 17% of expenditure), and the bilateral Know How Fund. A dedicated tranche of the Know How Fund – the

Environmental Know How Fund (EKHF) – was established in 1992, to support the transfer of UK skills and expertise to help these countries build the management, institutional and policy infrastructure to bring about long term environmental improvement.

28.43 The EKHF is supporting a range of projects throughout the region which reflect Agenda 21 priorities. They include assistance with environmental legislation and planning; industrial pollution control, monitoring and inspection; environmental audit and impact assessment; sustainable tourism; nature conservation; and encouragement of NGOs.

28.44 The UK also plays a leading role in other international work on the environmental problems of Eastern Europe and the FSU. The Ministerial Conference "Environment for Europe", held in Lucerne in April 1993, endorsed an action programme setting out a strategy for environmental assistance to Central and Eastern Europe, based on the decisions taken at the Earth Summit. The action programme identifies policy reform, the strengthening of institutions, and investment as the main priorities to be addressed. The UK is active in the special Task Force and Project Preparation Committee which have been established to take work forward on these priorities. The UK is also an active member of the UNECE Working Group, which will coordinate the post-Lucerne process and preparations for the next Ministerial Conference (to be held in Sofia in 1995).

Official and commercial debt

28.45 While the worst of the 1980s "debt crisis" may have passed, some of the poorest countries are still bearing crippling burdens of debt and need some degree of external financial assistance to achieve economic viability and sustainable development. Many of these countries are in sub-Saharan Africa. In 1979, UNCTAD launched an initiative to encourage aid donors to adjust retrospectively the terms of old aid loans. So far the UK has applied to 29 countries retrospective terms adjustments, or equivalent measures, in respect of loans worth over £1,000 million in total. In 1990, at the Commonwealth Finance Ministers' meeting in Trinidad, the UK announced an initiative to reduce further the debt burden of the most indebted countries who were pursuing sound economic policies approved by the IMF and World Bank. These "Trinidad Terms" began to be implemented, in a modified form, by the Paris Club of government creditors in December 1991. Seventeen countries, including 13 in sub-Saharan Africa, have so far benefited. Over $4 billion of debt has been restructured, and nearly $2 billion will be forgiven

over the lifetime of these agreements. The UK expects more countries to benefit over the coming months. The current terms have the effect of halving the payments due to creditors over the period of an IMF agreement, and give a commitment to consider restructuring the whole stock of a country's eligible debt after a good track record of economic reform has been established. This would lead to significant additional relief in the medium term.

28.46 At the Tokyo summit, G7 Heads called for the Paris Club to look again at debt relief for the poorest, most indebted countries. For the first time, the possibility of earlier action on the stock of debt was included – a key objective of the original Trinidad terms proposal. The UK continues to press for full Trinidad terms, including up to 80% relief for the most desperate countries, on a case by case basis.

28.47 For some countries, particularly middle income countries, many of which are in Latin America, much outstanding debt is owed to commercial creditors such as banks. The UK has supported and provided its share of the finances needed to implement the Brady Plan, which helps debtor countries and banks reach voluntary agreements on commercial debt reduction. Around 90% of the bank debt of the major debtor nations is now covered by a commercial debt relief deal.

Non-governmental organisations

28.48 NGOs are another important source of external assistance. They receive funding from the UK Government and voluntary donations from the public. Cooperation between the UK Government and both UK and local NGOs overseas has strengthened over the years; the Government has a high regard for the development work of UK NGOs. Their rich and diverse experience is a valuable resource. In some instances, aid in areas of high priority for the UK aid programme can be better delivered through NGOs than government channels. NGOs are flexible and innovative in their approach, can react quickly to changes and have the capacity to work in the remotest of areas. Their projects cover almost all sectors of development, but areas in which NGOs work particularly well include primary health care, the needs of women, population, the provision of local infrastructure and the development and extension of rural technologies. NGOs are particularly effective in mounting poverty-alleviating projects at the village or urban slum level because of their willingness to study and understand the problems of the people and to deliver cost-effective services that satisfy the needs and assessed problems of the population.

28.49 UK NGOs seeking support from ODA are encouraged to focus upon issues of concern; at the same time, efforts are made to ensure that the independence of those NGOs is not compromised. Similarly, many UK-based NGOs have made it clear that they are willing to act as implementing agents for projects designed by ODA, provided these do not conflict with their own priorities and objectives.

28.50 NGOs are not only seen as effective conduits for aid, but also as valuable contributors to the development of the Government's aid policy, with regular dialogue taking place on both sectoral priorities within countries and on the possibilities for the integration of projects and programmes. For example, the establishment of BOND – the British Overseas NGOs for Development – in June 1993 has involved over 70 British NGOs in the setting up of a new network for sharing ideas and experiences with the ODA and between themselves. There are also regular meetings between ODA and the Aid and Environment Group of NGOs.

28.51 The development of local NGOs, through the provision of both professional and technical support, is high on the agenda of a number of UK-based NGOs and volunteer-sending agencies for whom financial support is given by ODA. The development of links with the local NGO community, the allocation of bilateral aid funds directly to local NGOs and a better understanding of their needs, provides ODA with the ideal opportunity to participate in their development. ODA has also found that the institutional strengthening and training of southern NGOs, which forms an ever-increasing component of projects, can and does increase pressure for good government and pluralism. The last few years have therefore seen an increased emphasis on the direct funding by ODA of local NGOs, particularly in countries such as Bangladesh, India, Pakistan, Kenya, South Africa, and Zimbabwe. Other countries will be benefiting from direct funding schemes in the near future.

REFERENCES AND FURTHER READING

1 *Agenda 21* – action plan for the next century, endorsed at UNCED, 1992.

2 *This Common Inheritance. Britain's Environmental Strategy.* Cm 1200. HMSO, 1990. ISBN 0-10-112002-8.
   This Common Inheritance. The First Year Report. Cm 1655. HMSO, 1991. ISBN 0-116552-8.
   This Common Inheritance. The Second Year Report. Cm 2068. HMSO, 1992. ISBN 0-10-120682-8.

3 *Montreal Protocol on Substances that Deplete the Ozone Layer.* UNEP, 1987.

4 *Towards Sustainability: a European Community programme of policy and action in relation to the environment and sustainable development.* Commission of the EC. Official publication of the EC, 1992. Cm (92) 23/Final/II.

5 *Climate Change: The UK Programme.* Cm 2427. HMSO, 1994. ISBN 0-10-124272-7.

6 *Biodiversity: The UK Action Plan.* Cm 2428. HMSO, 1994. ISBN 0-10-124282-4.

7 *Sustainable Forestry: The UK Programme.* Cm 2429. HMSO, 1994. ISBN 0-10-124292-1.

8 *Convention on International Trade in Endangered Species.* 1973.

9 *Assessing the Effects of the Uruguay Round.* OECD Secretariat, 1993.

10 *World Development Report on Environment and Development.* World Bank, 1992.

CHAPTER 29

CENTRAL GOVERNMENT

Current Responses

- Ministerial Committee on the Environment.
- "Green Ministers" in each Government Department.
- Publication of White Paper reports on environmental progress. Departmental Reports include further detail.
- Environmental appraisal of new policies.
- Network of "green contacts" across all Government Departments.
- "Green housekeeping" strategies in Government Departments.

The Way Forward

- To review effectiveness of measures for environmental appraisal of policies and programmes (1994).
- Government Departments to assess practicality of environmental management systems for green housekeeping.
- To publish further guidance on policy appraisal, including risk assessment.

INTRODUCTION

29.1 Other chapters deal with Government action to provide an effective framework for environmental protection, the statutory agencies involved and Government's links with the business, local government and voluntary sectors. This chapter focuses on the way in which central government integrates environmental concerns into its decision-making processes.

29.2 The Government has long been committed to the integration of environmental concerns into decision-making at all levels. It welcomes, therefore, the emphasis in chapter 8 of *Agenda 21*[1] on the need for an integrated approach. The need for integration also lies at the heart of the *EC's Fifth Environmental Action Programme*[2]. Not all government policies and programmes will have significant environmental effects; but all need to be examined on a consistent and systematic basis.

APPRAISAL OF CENTRAL GOVERNMENT POLICIES

29.3 When the Cabinet Committee structure was reorganised in May 1992, a Ministerial Committee on the Environment was established to provide a forum in which Cabinet Ministers from relevant Departments could collectively consider key environmental issues. This carried forward arrangements established in 1990. In addition, each Department nominates its own "Green Minister" whose job is to ensure that environmental considerations are integrated into the strategy and policies of that Department. Below this, a network of "green contacts" has links at official level across all Government Departments to develop best practice and to coordinate policy.

29.4 All Departments must ensure that papers for Cabinet and Ministerial Committees should, where appropriate, cover any significant costs or benefits to the environment. The effectiveness of these measures for the appraisal of new policies and programmes will be reviewed in 1994.

29.5 In September 1991, the Department of the Environment (DOE) followed up a commitment in *This Common Inheritance*[3] by publishing a guide to *Policy Appraisal and the Environment*[4]. This guide was designed to increase awareness within government of the need to examine systematically the effects on the environment of existing and proposed policies. It shows how these effects can be taken into account, both in environmental policies and in policies in other areas which have significant environmental impacts.

29.6 The *Second Year Report*[5] on This Common Inheritance contained a commitment to publish further guidance. This commitment is now being met in two new publications. Firstly, the DOE will publish a companion guide to *Policy Appraisal and the Environment* dealing with risk assessment[6]. Secondly, the DOE will publish a booklet[7] on *Environmental Appraisal in Government Departments* published by the DOE. This will give details of guidance on appraisal and evaluation currently in use in Government Departments and of case studies applying that guidance.

29.7 Assessing the costs and benefits of alternative courses of action is not an easy task. Guidance on economic appraisal has been available for many years in the Treasury "Green Book"[8], designed to help officials and managers in central government to appraise and evaluate expenditure proposals effectively. It describes the principles of project appraisal and evaluation and contains guidance on the treatment of non-marketed goods and services, including environmental impacts.

29.8 There are special problems in applying cost benefit analysis to environmental issues. Sometimes the consumption of resources or the by-products of pollution and waste may have delayed consequences; some effects may be irreversible, such as the depletion of natural resources in limited supply, the loss of species or the destruction of heritage sites; and some effects may be uncertain because not enough is known abut the scientific processes involved. Decisions about levels of protection should be based on the best possible economic and scientific analysis (see chapter 3).

BOX 29.1

EXAMPLES OF APPRAISAL GUIDANCE
1 DOE/Welsh Office, *"Environmental Assessment: A Guide to the Procedures"*. HMSO, 1989.

2 *Flood and Coastal Defence Project Appraisal Guidance Notes*. MAFF, 1993.

EXAMPLES OF CASE STUDIES
1 Report by London Economics on the potential role of market mechanisms in the control of acid rain. HMSO, 1992.

2 Report by Risk and Policy Analysts Ltd on the risk-benefit analysis of hazardous chemicals. RPA, 1992.

3 Report by the Centre for Social and Economic Research on the Global Environment (CSERGE) on the externalities of landfill and incineration. DOE, 1993.

29.9 Risk assessment is one of the great challenges in sustainable development policy; the best available science is required to identify the hazards and their potential consequences, and to weigh up the degree of uncertainty. Where appropriate (for example, where there is uncertainty combined with the possibility of the irreversible loss of valued resources), actions should be based on the precautionary principle if the balance of likely costs and benefits justifies it (see chapter 3). Even then the action taken and the costs incurred should be in proportion to the risk. Action justified on the basis of the precautionary principle can be thought of as an insurance premium that everyone pays to protect something of value.

29.10 To measure the precise extent to which people value environmental resources is an important task of environmental appraisal. The same is true of the valuation of environmental impacts. The booklet *Environmental Appraisal in Government Departments* includes examples of this kind of work. Yet, for environmental costs and benefits properly to be weighed against economic costs

and benefits, practitioners need to develop further their understanding of the issues involved. Significant progress on this front has been made in the last 20 years or so both in terms of theory and practice. It seems reasonable to suppose that the rate of progress in the next 20 years will be at least as rapid. There is already great potential for systematic appraisal of policies with environmental implications.

29.11 The key issue for sustainability is how proper consideration can be given to the interests of future generations and how these interests should be weighed in relation to present needs. The Government has developed a sophisticated approach to discounting techniques, which are themselves powerful tools for evaluating costs and benefits now and in the future. The use of these techniques when considering the impact of policy measures over very long periods, or when significant liabilities may be passed on to future generations, needs careful qualification – for example, in the case of decommissioning nuclear plant. But economic analysis alone will not resolve the ethical and practical issues at stake in determining the nature and value of bequests by individuals or society as a whole to future generations. Decisions about such benefits will also involve individuals' value judgements as well as careful consideration through political processes.

MONITORING THE IMPLEMENTATION OF GOVERNMENT POLICY

29.12 Since the publication of the first Environment White Paper in 1990, the Government has published two reports[5,9] reviewing progress and setting new targets. A third White Paper, covering policy development since October 1992, will be published early in 1994. Further information on each Department's environmental performance can be found in their Annual Reports.

29.13 The Government has also carried out a review of open government[10]. It is committed to a set of principles governing what information will be made available, including the facts and the analysis of the facts which the Government considers relevant and important in framing major policy proposals and decisions. This will take further the statutory rights of access the public already have to environmental information (see chapter 32).

GREEN HOUSEKEEPING

29.14 All Government Departments now have strategies in place for good environmental housekeeping, covering not only consumption of energy, water, paper and so on but recycling and pollution prevention (for example, minimising carbon dioxide and vehicle emissions and the use of ozone-depleting substances). By the end of 1994, all Departments will assess the practicality of developing an environmental management system for their green housekeeping activities which might, for example, follow BS 7750 (the environmental management standard developed by the British Standards Institute – see chapter 20), taking account of work already under way in Departments.

29.15 Departments and their executive agencies are also major purchasers of supplies. Treasury guidance has been provided to all Departments which recognises that specifications for goods and services should reflect the requirements of Departments' environmental strategies, seeking best value for money in the usual way.

REFERENCES AND FURTHER READING

[1] *Agenda 21 – action plan for the next century*, endorsed at UNCED, 1992.

[2] *Towards Sustainability: A European Community Programme of Policy and Action in relation to the Enviroment and Sustainable Development (The EC's Fifth Environmental Action Programme).* Commission of the EC. Official publication of the EC, 1992. Cm (92)23/final/Vol II.

[3] *This Common Inheritance. Britain's Environmental strategy.* Cm 1200. DOE. HMSO, 1990. ISBN 0-10-112002-8.

[4] *Policy Appraisal and the Environment: A Guide for Government Departments.* DOE. HMSO, 1990.

[5] *This Common Inheritance. The Second Year Report.* Cm 2068. HMSO, 1991. ISBN 0-10-120682-8.

[6] *Risk Assessment and Risk Management for Sustainable Development.* DOE, 1994.

[7] *Environmental Appraisal in Government Departments.* DOE,1994.

[8] *Economic Appraisal in Central Government: A Technical Guide for Government Departments.* HM Treasury. HMSO, 1991.

[9] *This Common Inheritance. The First Year Report.* Cm 1655. HMSO, 1991 ISBN 0-10-116552-8.

[10] *Open Government.* Cm 2290. HMSO, 1993. ISBN 0-10-122902-X.

CHAPTER 30

LOCAL GOVERNMENT

INTRODUCTION

30.1 Many local authorities have long been involved in developing local responses to environmental issues. Other chapters in this Strategy refer to local government's role in particular sectors. This chapter deals with the overall contribution that local government can make, its relationship with other key sectoral groups and its ability to enable these groups to consider local priorities together.

30.2 There are 541 principal local authorities in the UK. In England, most larger urban areas are covered by unitary authorities. In other parts of England and in Scotland and Wales, there are two tiers of principal authority. In Northern Ireland, many functions which in other parts of the UK would be undertaken by local authorities are exercised by central government departments or statutory agencies. There are also some 12,000 smaller authorities in parts of Britain serving more local communities. In each local authority, there is a council, consisting of directly elected members. Councils are responsible for the discharge of a wide range of functions. They are independent of central government but must act within the powers granted to them by Parliament.

30.3 The structure of local government in Britain is under review; proposals for single tier councils in Wales as well as Scotland have already been announced. Other measures (for example, covering finance, compulsory competitive tendering of certain contracts and the re-allocation of some functions) have provided a steady challenge to adapt and change. Local government recognises the importance of ensuring that environmental action meshes in with action on these other fronts.

30.4 Both central and local government acknowledge the importance of working in partnership to help identify priorities for action and the ways in which this can best be delivered. Local government's ability to innovate, to anticipate problems, to provide local leadership and processes for involving other groups, represents an important contribution towards the development of strategies for sustainability which reflect local needs and priorities.

LOCAL GOVERNMENT ACTION

30.5 There is already a substantial amount of activity under way in local government to carry forward much of the action required in *Agenda 21*[1]. One of local government's key strengths is that it is responsible for a wide range of functions which impact on the environment and has the ability to develop a strategic approach through its corporate processes, in consultation with other organisations. Much work is already ongoing which contributes to sustainable development through:

- contract specifications which minimise use of resources and maximise the use of the least environmentally damaging products, taking into account value for money;
- assessment of the state of the local environment and development of eco-management and audit processes (see 30.14–30.15) and local sustainability indicators;
- energy efficiency measures, for example, in local authority buildings, street lighting, transport fleets and local authority owned housing;
- integrating transport and land use planning strategies to reduce the need for travel and encourage less polluting means of travel (see chapters 26 and 35);
- transport strategies to include:
  - work to promote, improve and expand public transport to increase its use as an alternative to the private car;
  - traffic calming, bus lane and other bus priority measures, pedestrianisation, cycle lanes and other urban traffic management schemes, including investigation into parking restraint measures;
- local air quality strategies for integration with land use planning and transport strategies;
- waste minimisation and recycling initiatives and energy from waste schemes;
- work with local businesses on sustainable economic development strategies;

- local strategies for nature conservation, countryside, forestry and management and stewardship schemes reflecting national and international commitments;
- education and training schemes for local authorities' own staff, members and the community;
- measures to involve local communities in all of this work.

Local Agenda 21 Initiative

30.6 Local government is now developing its own policies and programme responses to many of the issues raised in Agenda 21 and the EC *Fifth Environmental Action Programme*[2] through its *Local Agenda 21 Initiative*[3]. The UK local authority associations have formed a coordinating group, including representatives of other key sectors, to provide a focus for action and to carry forward the Initiative. As part of this Initiative, local government has produced its own *Declaration on Sustainable Development*[4].

30.7 Chapter 28 of Agenda 21 encourages local authorities to adopt a Local Agenda 21 for their community by 1996. The UK local authority associations accept the challenge to their members to meet this target. In effect, local authorities are beginning to define their own sustainable development strategies at local level, focusing on initiatives that they themselves can influence through their statutory powers and responsibilities and coordinating initiatives across the community.

30.8 The approach to Local Agenda 21 will work in a variety of ways. Local authorities can coordinate local community interests to develop a local strategy. Many authorities have already taken specific initiatives such as adopting environmental charters, undertaking audits and reviewing purchasing policy in addition to delivering local services in an environmentally friendly way.

30.9 Local government is working to identify what sustainable development means at local level and how best to involve the business, voluntary and community sectors in that process. Local authorities will also share information about best practice – where it is taking place and the lessons to be learnt from it. Local government has already made significant progress on this front by developing and publishing its own account of environmental practice[5] together with many case studies.

30.10 The Local Agenda 21 Initiative aims to:
- interpret Agenda 21 for local authorities;
- define what sustainable development means at the local level;
- encourage and enable local authorities to prepare strategies for sustainable development;
- develop local environmental initiatives;
- develop information exchange on best practice;
- assist with education and training initiatives;
- assist with the creation of local partnerships, particularly with the business and voluntary sectors.

30.11 The Government welcomes and supports the Local Agenda 21 Initiative. It is supporting a series of round table meetings in 1993–94 to bring together local authority practitioners and specialists from other sectors to address key environmental issues of concern to local government, to produce best practice material and to set up an eco-management and audit scheme for local government (see 30.14–30.15). Both central and local government are working to develop sustainability indicators at national and local level respectively (see chapter 34).

Central and Local Government Environment Forum

30.12 Many local authorities have initiated local environmental fora, bringing together different sections of the community concerned about the environment.

30.13 To enhance cooperation and coordination between central and local government, a Central and Local Government Environment Forum was set up in 1991 to bring together Government Environment Ministers and the leaders of the local authority associations. The Forum has initiated valuable work on energy efficiency in local government, environmental publicity, environmental management and on a model local environment charter. It has published its own regular newsletter which has been widely welcomed in local government.

Eco-management and audit

30.14 There is an increasing recognition by local government that environmental considerations need to be built into the services it provides and the other functions it discharges as well as the management of its own buildings and vehicles. The joint central and local government work on the development of an eco-management and audit scheme for local government should be very valuable to local authorities in developing a more systematic approach to environmental issues throughout their activities.

30.15 The Government plans to introduce a voluntary local government scheme by 1995 based on an adaptation of the EC Eco-Management and Audit Regulation for Manufacturing Industry (see chapter 33). Guidance[6] has been published which provides a framework and a set of tools to develop

BOX 30.1
ENVIRONMENT CITY CASE STUDY: PETERBOROUGH

The most significant step forward in partnership environmental initiatives in Peterborough has been the establishment of the Peterborough Environment City Trust (PECT) in April 1993. PECT, a company limited by guarantee and a registered charity, provides a formal basis for the wide range of environmental partnership arrangements and working groups between public, private and voluntary sectors which have underpinned Peterborough's drive towards a more sustainable city. The Trust was established as a response to the designation of Peterborough as an 'Environment City' under the Royal Society for Nature Conservation's British Telecom Environment City Programme.

PECT was jointly set up and resourced by commerce and industry, Peterborough City Council and voluntary and professional groups in line with the national Environment City model. The Trust's board of management coordinates the work of seven specialist working groups (SWGs), each of which deals with a broad subject area. There are SWGs for energy, transport, the built environment, the natural environment, waste and recycling and so on. Membership of each SWG is widely drawn from all sections of the community and includes relevant officers from Peterborough City Council and Cambridgeshire County Council, specific voluntary and professional groups, commerce and industry and interested individuals. There are now over 140 organisations active within the Environment City partnership.

The Trust's board of management has set itself the task of producing and resourcing seven Peterborough Strategies for Sustainability. Each strategy will examine the effects and influences of all sectors of the community in a SWG subject area, and put forward a framework to build partnerships and undertake research and demonstration projects to further local understanding of sustainability. The range of projects in each strategy are specifically conceived to respond comprehensively to the range of issues and the "players" who influence that subject area. For example, the Strategy for People and Wildlife addresses not only habitat types and species but also the ways in which land owners and managers, the public authorities and nature conservation interests manage the natural environment. Implementation of each of the projects is designed to strike a balance between a sense of short term achievement and the production of properly researched and comprehensive databases over a period of two to three years. The databases will then be published as State of Environment reports for each subject area.

It is planned to complete and publish the seven strategies for sustainability and seven state of the environment reports by 1995–96. Peterborough then expects to have a firm basis to draw up a partnership Agenda 21 for the City and set real targets and limits, based on rigorous research, which command the support and commitment of all sections of the community.

environmental management systems. It offers local authorities not only the prospect of greater efficiency but the opportunity to provide the public with independently verified statements of progress in meeting environmental targets.

Overseas partnerships

30.16 In addition to the establishment of a national support framework for Local Agenda 21 initiatives, the UK Local Government International Bureau and the national associations are:

- assisting the International Union of Local Authorities (IULA) and the International Council for Local Environmental Initiatives (ICLEI) in laying foundations for a process of international and inter-municipal cooperation focused on Local Agenda 21;

- contributing to the coordination and implementation of ICLEI international programmes concerned with the reduction of carbon dioxide emissions and with the exchange of information and experience on local strategies for sustainable development;
- taking the lead in promoting local government capacity building initiatives within the context of North/South and East/West technical assistance partnership programmes.

30.17 In 1993, local authorities were given new powers to participate in overseas assistance programmes. Local government is giving priority to initiatives which both strengthen institutional capacity in the South and which promote North/South networks for exchange of experience and exchange of information about good practice.

30.18 In the two-year period 1993–95, there are also specific commitments to:

- provide local government training and work experience placements for personnel from local authorities in Africa, Asia, the Caribbean and Latin America;
- organise a series of sub-regional and national workshops on effective strategies for the management of local government, in association with the African Regional Secretariat of IULA;
- offer UK local government support for the establishment of an African Local Agenda 21 network (in association with IULA and ICLEI);
- promote a minimum of 10 new local government North/South partnerships as a basis for institutional strengthening and exchange of experience on local strategies for sustainable development;
- provide seconded staff, consultancy and advisory services to local government bodies in developing countries and in Central and Eastern Europe.

REFERENCES AND FURTHER READING

1 *Agenda 21 – action plan for the next century*, endorsed at UNCED, 1992.

2 *Towards Sustainability: A European Community Programme of Policy and Action in relation to the Environment and Sustainable Development (The EC's Fifth Environmental Action Programme)*, Commission of the EC. Official publication of the EC, 1992. Cm (92) 23/final/Vol II.

3 *Local Agenda 21 – Agenda 21: a guide for local authorities in the UK.* LGMB (on behalf of the Local Authority Associations and the Local Government International Bureau). Obtained free by writing to Anne Bubb, LGMB, Arndale House, The Arndale Centre, Luton, Bedfordshire LU1 2TS.

4 *Declaration on Sustainable Development* UK Local Authority Associations/LGMB, 1993.

5 *Environmental Practice in Local Government* (second edition). LGMB (on behalf of the Local Authority Associations), 1992. ISBN 0-7488-98549.

6 *A Guide to the Eco-Management and Audit Scheme for UK Local Government.* HMSO, 1993. ISBN 0-11-752719-X.

CHAPTER 31

VOLUNTARY ORGANISATIONS

Current Responses

- Voluntary sector action to influence policy development and tackle practical problems, locally, nationally and internationally.
- Involvement of voluntary sector in Local Agenda 21 initiative.
- Private sector, local and central government grants to voluntary organisations.

The Way Forward

- Government and environment groups to review ways to involve non-environmental groups in sustainable development.
- Follow-up action to Manchester Partnerships for Change Conference.

INTRODUCTION

31.1 The UK has a vigorous and independent voluntary sector with a key role in developing strategies for sustainable development at local and national level. There is no central register of all voluntary organisations. A recent estimate[1] suggested that there are between 230,000 and 300,000 groups in the UK on a relatively narrow definition of a voluntary group; 10 of the largest environment and conservation groups had a combined membership in 1991 of 4.3 million. There are also perhaps 150,000 – 200,000 autonomous local community groups, ranging from informal networks to more formalised groups and organisations. Many of these groups are concerned with environment and development issues.

POLICY DEVELOPMENT AND PRACTICAL OPPORTUNITIES

31.2 The voluntary sector provides a very wide range of opportunities for the public to contribute, at local and national level, towards environmental protection and sustainable development. Voluntary groups devise solutions to immediate and local problems, providing plenty of scope for practical action, such as work to protect the countryside, wildlife, to minimise waste and to green urban areas. They enable people to express their concerns about the environment and to become involved in debate about future priorities. They provide valuable mechanisms to help develop the concept of shared responsibility for the environment, which the *EC's Fifth Environmental Action Programme*[2] identifies as fundamental to continued progress on environmental issues.

31.3 Many groups are also active in seeking to influence policy development at national and international level. Voluntary groups, for example, are playing a key role in helping to develop and implement the Government's partnership approach in the carbon dioxide programme.

31.4 Voluntary bodies organise themselves for action in many different ways. Some develop expertise in particular policy areas, and groups form networks from time to time to focus on particular issues. Many local groups work with support provided by national umbrella organisations. Some groups develop connections with local schools, or provide specific opportunities for young people. Other organisations provide a brokering service for those who want to become involved in environmental work, including those from ethnic minorities. Other groups have been set up specifically to provide information about activities within a particular region. This is an important way of fostering cooperation and communication amongst existing groups. Education and training form a very important part of the sector's work.

31.5 To improve dialogue with the voluntary sector on practical and policy issues, the Government established, in 1991, a Voluntary Sector Environment Forum which includes individuals from major voluntary groups in England and which has been chaired by an environment Minister. There is no single body, however, which represents all groups and the Government recognises that in seeking views, it may need to consult many differing constituencies of interest within the voluntary sector.

Greater integration

31.6 Issues relating to sustainability cut across generally recognised separate areas of voluntary activity such as the environment, housing and low incomes. Action programmes will need to become increasingly integrated around the central theme of sustainability. This may well prove to be the key test of the voluntary sector's effectiveness over the next 20 years.

Involving other groups

31.7 The Government is keen to encourage the involvement of as many non-environmental groups as possible in debate and action on sustainable development issues, and has sponsored research on the barriers to such groups becoming more involved. Obstacles identified involve lack of access to simple, straightforward information about relevant issues, including grants; groups want as much notice as possible about new initiatives and practical ideas which are easy to implement and locally based. The Government has decided to review with representatives of the main environmental groups whether new initiatives are required to meet these needs.

31.8 The voluntary sector also recognises the importance of forging links with local government and industry. Voluntary bodies are closely involved in local government's Local Agenda 21 Initiative (see chapter 30). Many local groups look to business to provide sponsorship; business looks to the voluntary sector to provide opportunities for employees to become involved in the environment and to provide a bridge between the business sector and the wider community. Many groups engage central and local government and the private sector in debate on environmental priorities and targets for the future. Some groups take these links further and help form cross-sectoral partnerships for action on the environment.

Financial support

31.9 Many voluntary organisations receive substantial income from subscriptions, trading activities and donations. The private sector and local government also provide funding for specific activities. Groups sometimes, however, need central government assistance to tackle practical problems. Grants are, therefore, available to voluntary sector organisations; these are generally time-limited to allow new ideas to come forward.

31.10 In England, grant is provided through the Environmental Action Fund (EAF). The fund has two elements:
- funding for national/regional organisations to help with their strategic costs or regional projects;
- grants for organisations undertaking local projects.

In 1993–94, grants totalling just over £4 million are being paid to 90 organisations and many small local groups, carrying out a very wide range of work (see Figure 31.1).

31.11 In Scotland, support to the environmental voluntary sector is provided through the Special Grants (Environmental) Programme and through the funding of UK2000 Scotland. Some £334,000 is available in 1993–94 through the Grants Programme, and UK2000 Scotland will receive £420,000. In Wales, the main direct source of funding for the environmental voluntary sector is the Environment Wales initiative which combines the previous Special Grants (Environmental) Programme and UK2000 Cymru. The scheme is run by the Prince of Wales Committee on behalf of the Welsh Office. In 1993–94, £500,000 is available through the initiative. In

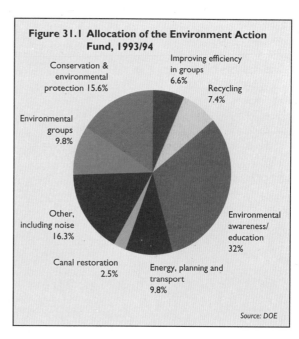

Figure 31.1 Allocation of the Environment Action Fund, 1993/94

Conservation & environmental protection 15.6%

Improving efficiency in groups 6.6%

Recycling 7.4%

Environmental groups 9.8%

Other, including noise 16.3%

Canal restoration 2.5%

Energy, planning and transport 9.8%

Environmental awareness/ education 32%

Source: DOE

Northern Ireland, support to the environmental voluntary sector is provided by the Environment Service of the Department of the Environment for Northern Ireland. The 1993–94 budget for such grant-aid is some £950,000. In addition, the Government's agencies for countryside and wildlife matters provide substantial funding for countryside and wildlife projects, as do some private sector sponsors.

31.12 It is important that Departments and agencies play complementary roles which reflect their respective responsibilities but with minimal overlap. Voluntary bodies of all kinds need clear and easily accessible information about grants available. The Government will continue to assess the ways of improving the voluntary sector's understanding about the purpose and availability of funding as well as encouraging the voluntary sector to seek support actively from elsewhere in the community. It also provides an opportunity for members of the voluntary sector to discuss possible priorities for the year ahead and to review grant allocations for the previous year. This helps to ensure that scarce resources are focused where they can do most good.

PARTNERSHIPS FOR CHANGE CONFERENCE, MANCHESTER 1993

31.13 The Government hosted an international conference for non-governmental organisations (NGOs) in Manchester in September 1993. This conference, Partnerships for Change, brought together over 300 representatives from all regions of the world, most of whom had practical experience of running sustainable development projects. An additional 70 representatives from the UK joined the conference for a special session looking at sustainable development projects in this country. The conference participants explored, through case studies and workshops, the conditions for success and the obstacles to partnership projects. The discussions held were very lively, stimulating and educative. The Government will draw on these discussions to produce a guide *Partnerships in Practice*[3], which will also include a record of the conference proceedings.

INTERNATIONAL INVOLVEMENT

31.14 The Government has strongly promoted the involvement of the environmental and developmental voluntary sector organisations at international level. In establishing the rules of procedure for the new UN Commission on Sustainable Development (CSD), the UK successfully pressed for NGOs to be given enhanced participation along the lines followed at Rio, going beyond the existing rules for observers in functional commissions of the UN's Economic and Social Committee. Where appropriate, NGOs can be included in UK delegations to international environment meetings on an ad hoc basis, as they were, for example, at the first substantive session of the CSD in June 1993.

31.15 The voluntary sector has also been closely involved in work in Central and Eastern Europe, either independently or managing projects funded through the Government's Environmental Know How Fund. Work has concentrated on training environmental groups and environmental education.

REFERENCES AND FURTHER READING

1 *Facts and Figures on the Voluntary Sector.* NCVO, 1993. ISBN 0-7199-1402-7.

2 *Towards Sustainabiltiy: A European Community Programme of Policy and Action in relation to the Environement and Sustainable Development (The EC's Fifth Environmental Action Programme).* Commission of the EC. Official publication of the EC, 1992. Cm (92) 23/Final/Vol II.

3 *Partnerships in Practice.* HMSO, 1994.

CHAPTER 32

INDIVIDUAL AWARENESS AND ACTION

Current Responses

- New rights of access to environmental information held by many public authorities.
- Publication (1992) of *The UK Environment*, a statistical report providing easily accessible environmental information.
- EC Eco-labelling scheme provides guide to products meeting stringent environmental criteria.
- Government-funded publicity schemes, for example, "Helping the Earth begins at Home".
- Environmental targets in National Curriculum in England and Wales across core subjects.

The Way Forward

- Review of Government's programmes encouraging individual commitment to environmentally friendly behaviour (1994).
- Three yearly revisions of eco-labelling criteria to ensure increasingly demanding standards.
- Government-sponsored public surveys to concentrate on identifying ways to translate public interest into action.
- Further guidance on schools' environmental management practices.

INTRODUCTION

32.1 Although the environment is not always the priority issue for people at any one time, it remains a long term concern. Interest ranges from very local environmental problems, such as litter and noise, to global issues, such as ozone depletion. This interest and concern must be channelled into positive action for sustainable development.

INDIVIDUAL AWARENESS

Current public attitudes

32.2 The Government monitors public attitudes to the environment. The Department of the Environment (DOE) has conducted three national surveys in England and Wales in the last eight years, and the Scottish Office carried out a similar survey in 1991. These have shown that most people are concerned about the environment in general, and would like more environmental information. Public concern extends across a wide range of local, national and international environmental issues, but people are mostly optimistic and believe much can be done about the problems.

32.3 In England and Wales, the majority of respondents thought the cost of dealing with environmental problems should be paid by the polluter, even if this meant that goods or services cost more. Only a small proportion thought the money should be raised by higher taxes (see Table 32.1). The Scottish Office Central Research Unit carries out similar surveys: in the most recent, over half of those interviewed thought that the public should pay higher taxes to protect the environment, and over 90% of people appreciated that it was up to them as individuals to protect the environment by changing their own behaviour.

32.4 The DOE conducted research among 8–15 year olds to establish interest levels in environmental issues. The findings reveal that children are very enthusiastic, particularly about local projects which can make a real difference to the area in which they live. They are enthusiastic about recycling, clean-up schemes, canal restoration and improving wildlife habitats. The research also showed that young people feel that they do not have a chance to say what they think about the environment, but are told by adults what is needed. In response, the Government has launched a new initiative (see Box 32.1 on the Green Brigade).

Access to environmental information

32.5 Not surprisingly, most people get their information on environmental matters from television, radio and newspapers; membership of environmental groups has risen over recent years and an increasing percentage of the population now receives information direct from that source. This interest leads to a healthy and vigorous debate on environmental issues. The answers to environmental questions are usually complex, and there is often dispute over the facts and science of a particular case. The Government wants to raise the level of public debate and improve the quality of environmental decisions by providing clear and up to date information (see Box 32.2 on air quality).

32.6 New rights of access to information on the environment held by many public authorities were introduced in 1992, subject to safeguards on commercial confidentiality and other matters. Under the *Open Government* White Paper[1], the Government is considering the case for an independent tribunal to hear disputes about requests for information. In the UK, much information is held on registers, for example, details about waste management licences. Copies of these and many other registers are held by local authorities and are available for the public to see. The DOE will produce in 1994 a booklet which brings together information about the different types of register and how to use them. In many cases people also have a chance to comment on proposals while they are under consideration, for example, applications for consents for industrial processes causing pollution are published in local press. In Scotland, research is currently under way to review the existing provision and accessibility of environmental information and to recommend ways in which it can best be made available to the public.

32.7 In 1992, a comprehensive statistical report, *The UK Environment*[2], was published. This provided, for the first time, environmental information for the lay reader, brought together in a single publication, and written and presented in an easily accessible form. The report complements other Government sources and covers most aspects of the UK environment, including details about health and the environment, public attitudes and expenditure. It provides an important contribution to international initiatives, particularly by the Organisation for Economic Co-operation and Development, to encourage countries to improve environmental reporting and thereby promote public awareness. Many children are now using this report in their schools.

Education for life

32.8 It is not only in schools that young people can learn about the environment. Voluntary groups – both those who have traditionally focused on environmental issues, such as the Royal Society for the Protection of Birds, the Royal Society for Nature Conservation and the World Wide Fund for Nature, and non-environmental groups, such as Scouts and Guides – provide many opportunities for young people to take practical action to improve their local environment (see chapter 31).

32.9 Youth groups are particularly active in this field and in many cases "peer education" – young people passing on their skills and knowledge to other young people – is used to great effect. Some surveys, however, show that 18–24 year olds are not very environmentally conscious. Research would be helpful to explore this.

BOX 32.1
INVOLVING CHILDREN IN ENVIRONMENTAL ACTION:
GREEN BRIGADE – YOUNG PEOPLE'S ENVIRONMENTAL INITIATIVE

In April 1993 a new initiative was announced to encourage children to take practical environmental action.

The "Speak Out" Competition
The first event in this initiative was the "Speak Out" competition – in June – in which young people were asked to devise a name for the environmental initiative and to suggest three topics to be discussed at a Young People's Environmental Summit.

The competition was open to children aged between 8 and 15 years old, and they each had to collect 20 empty cans for recycling. Everyone who entered got an activity sheet with ideas for summer action, and will be able to receive other "Green Brigade" Activity packs in the future.

The Summit
From the thousands of entries, it was 11 year-old Lydia Demetriou of Bury who suggested "The Green Brigade". She joined 59 other winners at the first ever Young People's Environmental Summit in Manchester on 18 September.

As well as discussing their environmental concerns, participants at the Summit were able to put their questions to the Secretary of State for the Environment. In workshop groups they looked at practical approaches to solving local environmental problems. The Summit selected nine projects to receive funding from the Green Brigade initiative, from a shortlist chosen to reflect the particular concerns expressed by entrants to the "Speak Out" competition. A total of £100,000 has been allocated to the projects which are located across the UK.

The Projects
The projects form the next stage of the Green Brigade Initiative. They are being coordinated by the Black Country Groundwork Trust. Young people will be involved in planning and implementing the projects. Their progress is being followed and reported, so that others can learn from the example they give and set up similar projects in their own local areas.

Public participation in decision-making

32.10 The Government is committed to consultation on environmental issues. There are already many opportunities for people to participate in environmental decisions. Examples include land use planning decisions, pollution consents, and recycling plans for local areas. People often choose to exercise these rights through local voluntary groups, especially where the subject is very complex.

32.11 Consultation usually reveals the conflicts between different people and interest groups in a particular area, rather than producing a consensus on a particular issue. Some people take the view that local groups and individuals should be involved in developing plans, rather than being consulted on fully worked up proposals. Of course, when people are closely involved "NIMBYism" (Not In My Backyard) may be a factor in the views they express. Some people feel that this is not necessarily a bad thing and, at least, is better than apathy. The likely areas for public concern in future include road building, out of town developments, pollution and habitat destruction.

EDUCATION

32.12 Education and training are crucial to the achievement of sustainable development. They can provide the population, including the workforce, with an understanding of how the environment relates to everyday issues and what action they can take personally to reduce their own impact on the environment at home, at work or in their leisure activities. The influence of education and training thus applies across the boundaries of the voluntary, public and the private sectors. In Scotland, the Secretary of State's Working Group on Environmental Education has made recommendations in their report *Learning for Life*[3] for strategies across the range of situations from home to workplace, the community, and in formal and informal education (see Box 32.3). Chapter 33 gives more information on training.

School education

32.13 Children need to understand the relationship between human activities and the environment, and the concept of sustainable development. They should be aware

---

BOX 32.2
AIR QUALITY – INFORMING AND INVOLVING THE CITIZEN

Measuring UK air quality is an essential part of the Government's approach to air pollution.

The Government introduced a system of daily air quality bulletins and forecasts in October 1990. These give air quality as "very good", "good", "poor" or "very poor" for sulphur dioxide, nitrogen dioxide, and ground level ozone in each of the main regions in the UK. These classifications take account of World Health Organisation and EC standards and other recent studies. Guidance is also available on implications for health.

All this material is available to the public on a free telephone service (0800 556677), and it is also carried nationwide on CEEFAX (page 404) and Teletext (page 187); these services are updated twice daily. The information is also sent to the press, television and radio. Some national and local newspapers take the bulletin daily, while others prefer only to print it when poor or very poor air quality is forecast.

In June 1993, an Air Quality card was launched in London's Evening Standard magazine. This card gives details on how to get information on air quality. To date over one million of these cards have been distributed and the impact on the number of calls received on the freephone has been monitored.

The Government will be extending the bulletins and forecasts to take in more pollutants as authoritative health advice becomes available on each and the monitoring network expands.

Such information should be particularly helpful to people who are sensitive to air pollution, for example, because of respiratory problems. They can take common sense precautions, such as avoiding outdoor exercise when pollution levels are high. However, in periods of poor air quality, everybody will want to play their part in improving air quality. In May 1992, the Government issued a booklet called *Summertime Smog*[4], with a range of suggestions for helping (such as minimising personal car use) during serious episodes of ground-level ozone. A follow-up booklet on winter air pollution was produced in November 1992[5].

of the opportunities that science, technology and other subjects can bring for environmental improvement, and not be daunted by negative images. Children should also be conscious of their responsibilities towards the environment and the contribution that they as individuals can make.

32.14 Schools have a vital role to play in both formal and informal environmental education. The National Curriculum is the focus for teaching and learning in compulsory education. Environmental education is, therefore, addressed through the individual subjects of the National Curriculum. The Government has specified for each subject the knowledge, skills and understanding which pupils of different abilities and ages are expected to achieve. Opportunities to study a range of environmental issues arise, in particular, through the study of geography, science and technology. Other subjects can also provide a context for pupils to examine environmental issues. Similar arrangements exist in Northern Ireland.

32.15 As part of the Government's drive to raise standards in compulsory education, the National Curriculum is currently under review. Although the broad structure is not expected to change, the need to reduce significantly the curricular load from 5–14, and to introduce additional flexibility for 14–16 year olds, may well mean that the balance between different elements of a subject may change, and that some will become optional rather than compulsory as now. Changes to the existing compulsory requirements for the National Curriculum subjects will need to be considered in detail, and new compulsory requirements will not be introduced into schools until the autumn of 1995.

32.16 In Scotland, the Scottish Office Education Department has published guidelines on all major components of the curriculum for 5–14 year olds; guidance on the curriculum for secondary schools is also issued by the Scottish Consultative Council on the Curriculum (SCCC). These include a number of attainment targets relating to the natural environment and man's impact upon it.

32.17 Teachers need support to help them give effective environmental education. Education authorities, the School Curriculum and Assessment Authority, SCCC, the Curriculum Council for Wales, Higher Education Institutions (HEIs) and others should assess what assistance teachers need. There is now a range of professional development opportunities in the field, including training courses to help update teachers' knowledge of recent developments.

32.18 Some local education authorities are scaling down their advisory staff and may be less able to offer support for environmental education. However, there is scope for exploring means of pooling expertise and sharing resources.

Teachers can also improve their lessons by using good quality teaching materials, of which there is a wealth available, but should make sure that the quality and coverage is appropriate to their pupils' needs. They should also satisfy themselves that controversial issues are dealt with in a balanced fashion and that there is no inappropriate emphasis on products offered by commercial sponsors. Teachers and school Governors will need advice, and there may be an opportunity for Government to play a part in setting standards against which environmental materials can be judged.

32.19 There are also a number of other bodies which support school education including the School Curriculum Industry Partnership (SCIP) and Business and the Community. Local Training and Enterprise Councils, and Local Enterprise Companies in Scotland, also have a role to play.

32.20 School grounds provide an important additional resource for teaching environmental issues, and for raising children's awareness. Pupils spend 25% of their time at school outside formal lessons. With the devolution of management decisions to school level, schools will have more flexibility and control over use of their school grounds, but they may need advice and support. The Government is keen to encourage the imaginative use of school grounds. The Department for Education's (DFE) Building Bulletin 71, *The Outdoor Classroom*[6], describes a range of options.

32.21 Schools, like other organisations, should adopt environmental management practices. The Government is developing further guidance to schools on this and on ways of involving the children themselves in eco-reviews and subsequent audits. In particular, the DFE aims to publish in 1994 a "Schools Environmental Audit Methodology" (SEAM) to assist teachers in evaluating the environmental impact of their school's building and grounds. The EC Eco-Management and Audit Scheme for local authorities also includes advice on assessment of schools' activities. The Government's Energy Efficiency Office has produced comprehensive advice on energy auditing of schools (see chapter 36).

32.22 Grants are provided by DOE under the Environmental Action Fund to support work on materials for teachers by the Council for Environmental Education, and the Scottish Office provided funding to the Scottish Environmental Education Council for the same purpose.

Further and higher education

32.23 In February 1993, the Toyne Committee (see chapter 33) established by DFE and the Welsh Office published a report[7] on environmental education in further and higher education (FHE). To ensure that employers' needs for environmental education are more clearly articulated, better communications must be developed, building on the networks that already exist. The Committee made a number of recommendations for the institutions and the professions to implement. It will be for institutions to monitor implementation of these recommendations, and academics themselves must keep up to date.

32.24 Research for the Toyne Committee's report shows that many school leavers are keen to pursue environmental careers, but have often taken inappropriate qualifications and are not aware of the opportunities available. Careers advice on education, training and employment in environmental careers may be available from local Careers Services and Education Authorities. The report recommends that ways of giving better careers guidance to potential students be explored. DOE has funded the Institution of Environmental Sciences to produce a careers handbook for students giving guidance on both career and course options.

BOX 32.3
EXAMPLE OF POLICY MAKING: THE SCOTTISH INITIATIVE.

The Scottish Office *Learning for Life* report in Scotland acknowledged the high degree of curriculum autonomy enjoyed by HEIs. It emphasised the need for universities and colleges to develop initiatives in environmental management policies and practices to complement environmentally sensitive teaching. Strong links already exist between research and teaching; and environmentally orientated research projects undertaken in the Scottish HEIs are likely to enhance environmental education generally.

Some institutions have been delivering environmental programmes for several years, and some interfaculty initiatives have been taken to help develop a shared sense of environmental responsibility. There is room for further development to ensure that these are relevant and effective.

32.25 Like schools, institutions should adopt positive environmental management practices and assess their wider impact on the environment, setting environmental objectives and targets, and introducing management systems to deliver them.

INDIVIDUAL ACTION

32.26 Sustainable development depends on changes in individual lifestyles: using the car less, saving energy, recycling, choosing environmentally friendly products and so on.

32.27 However, although many people claim to act in an environmentally friendly way (see Table 32.1), and say that they are prepared to pay a premium for less environmentally damaging products, they often do not do so in practice. As far as behaviour is concerned, the evidence shows that much more could be done. Many people still do not recycle their waste, for example, and more could be done to share transport and use public transport alternatives. Translating positive environmental attitudes into actual behaviour is therefore a key challenge for the future.

32.28 Experience shows, however, that changing people's behaviour is time consuming and resource intensive, even when there are immediate and tangible benefits to the individual, as in energy efficiency. Where people do not perceive any immediate personal benefit, the task is much more difficult.

32.29 The Government already funds a number of publicity schemes designed to encourage people to act, for example,

Table 32.1 Public concern about the environment and personal "green" actions, 1993, *England and Wales*		
Public concern	**Concerned**	**Not concerned**
Concern about the environment in general	85%	14%
Need for information	**More needed**	**No more needed**
Do the government provide enough environmental information?	84%	13%
Selected issues:	**Those worried**	**Those believing a lot could be done**
International issues		
Destruction of tropical forests	80%	78%
Global warming	71%	65%
National issues		
Chemicals put in rivers and seas	92%	91%
Disposal and import of toxic waste	87%	85%
Traffic congestion	75%	60%
Local issues		
Litter and rubbish	76%	79%
Quality of drinking water	70%	76%
Who should pay?		
Fairest way of finding money to solve environmental problems		
Polluter pays even if goods and services cost more		62%
Cut backs on other areas of public spending		19%
Higher taxes		14%
Personal actions		**Done on a regular basis**
Made sure that their noise did not disturb others		77%
Saved newspaper or other papers for recycling		48%
Took glass or bottles to bottle bank		44%
Cut down on the use of a car for short domestic journeys		26%
Deliberately used public transport instead of a car		8%

Note: See Techniocal Annex

Source: DOE

Table 32.2	Green consumerism and the need for product information, 1993, *England and Wales*	
Green consumers		**Done on a regular basis**
Avoided using pesticides in the garden		57%
Used unleaded petrol in their car		53%
Used recycled paper at home		45%
Bought phosphate free washing powder or liquid		17%
Used low-energy light bulbs in the home		16%
Bought organically produced food		12%
Need for product information	**More needed**	**No more needed**
Do manufacturers provide enough environmental information on their products?	88%	10%

Note: See Technical Annex   Source: DOE

the substantial campaigns to encourage people to save energy, including the "Helping the Earth begins at Home" campaign. In other cases, funding is channelled through a third party, such as Waste Watch or the Tidy Britain Group and its regional offices. Local authorities and voluntary groups also devote substantial resources to raising public awareness and encouraging local action.

32.30 In future, Government-sponsored public surveys will concentrate on identifying ways in which the enthusiasm and the interest of the individual can be translated into action. The Government, local authorities and voluntary groups all have a part to play in this.

32.31 There may be more that could be done to encourage individual commitment, to give incentives or to remove obstacles. The Government will look closely at its present programmes and at the work of others (such as local authorities) during 1994 and will consult on what might be done.

Green consumerism

32.32 One of the most powerful ways in which individuals can influence environmental matters is through the products they buy (see Table 32.2). Consumers can put substantial pressure on manufacturers to make environmentally less damaging products and on retailers to stock them: an example of this is the manufacturers' and the public's response in support of the need to phase out chlorofluorocarbons (CFCs) in aerosols and other products. Consumers need clear and comprehensive information, however, if they are to exert this power sensibly,

since balancing the environmental merits of different products or approaches is a complex issue.

32.33 In response to this demand, the Government pressed for an EC Eco-labelling scheme, which provides people with a reliable guide to greener products and will encourage manufacturers and retailers to make and stock these products. The label will only be awarded where a product has met stringent environmental criteria. These criteria will be based on an assessment of all the environmental impacts throughout the product's life cycle, "from the cradle to the grave". The first product criteria, for washing machines and dishwashers, have been published and those for a range of other products are being developed. As the scheme gathers momentum, it will be extended to an increasing range of consumer products, so that the distinctive flower logo will in time become a familiar symbol to shoppers. The criteria will be re-examined every three years to ensure that the standards are continually made more demanding.

32.34 The Government has already supported other consumer information initiatives, including a mandatory energy labelling system for domestic appliances in the EC, a voluntary energy labelling scheme for refrigerators and freezers, an energy labelling system for housing, and mandatory fuel consumption information about new cars. Manufacturers themselves chose to put energy labels on low energy lightbulbs.

32.35 However, the benefits of labelling products are limited. Research on the effect of energy labelling on electrical goods suggests that, apart from low energy bulbs, the labels themselves have only influenced a minority. The majority of consumers will only purchase the most energy efficient goods when there is no price premium; even then, the influence of the label is very weak compared to other factors. Similarly, the use of unleaded petrol (now 53% of petrol sales) only increased significantly when there was a price advantage.

32.36 However, the longer term influence may be the behaviour of manufacturers, who are reluctant to market products which will be labelled as having poor energy efficiency. Also, retailers who want to maintain their quality image will avoid stocking products with poor ratings on energy labels. The initial experience of the eco-labelling scheme is that the development of the criteria, through consultation with industry, consumer and environmental groups, can act as a spur to manufacturers to make and market less environmentally harmful products.

REFERENCES AND FURTHER READING

1   *Open Government*. Cm 2290. HMSO, 1993
2   *The UK Environment*. DOE. HMSO, 1992.
3   *Learning for Life*. Scottish Office, 1993. ISBN 0–74–800707–5.
4   *Summertime Smog*. DOE. May 1992.
5   *Wintertime Smog*. DOE. November 1992.

6   *Building Bulletin 71, The Outdoor Classroom*. Department for Education. HMSO, 1990. ISBN 0–11–270730–0.
7   *Environmental Responsibility: An Agenda for Further and Higher Education* (report of the Committee on Environmental Education in Further and Higher Education, Chairman Peter Toyne). Department for Education/Welsh Office. HMSO, 1993. ISBN 0–11–270820–X.

CHAPTER 33

SETTING THE FRAMEWORK FOR THE PRIVATE SECTOR

Current Responses

- Regulation has a key role in maintaining minimum standards. It is most effective where it considers impacts on the environment as a whole.
- The Government is committed to using economic instruments where appropriate.
- Many companies have voluntarily started to take action to improve their environmental performance further, responding to stakeholder pressures.
- Schemes, such as eco-labelling, BS 7750, Eco-Management and Audit and the Making a Corporate Commitment Campaign encourage companies to take positive action.
- Increasing the availability of information on environmental performance.
- Effective dialogue between Government and business on environmental issues.
- Provision of information and advice to small firms.
- Development of appropriate environmental training.
- Business-led initiatives to promote information exchange.

The Way Forward

- Deregulation and rationalisation of legislation. New legislation to be based on sound science and take account of relative costs and benefits of action.
- Development and introduction of economic instruments.
- Consideration of voluntary agreements between the Government and various industrial sectors.
- Companies to maintain a proactive stance on the environment, improving their performance in response to continued pressures from the financial sector, consumers, and shareholders.
- Continued increase in the availability of information on corporate environmental performance.
- Integration of environmental criteria into all purchasing and investment decisions.
- Review of way in which information is presented to small businesses.

INTRODUCTION

33.1 Government sets the framework of rules and incentives within which firms operate. Industry cannot simply be left unregulated if the necessary level of environmental protection is to be achieved and sustained, and if EC and other requirements and commitments are to be met. But nor should environmental regulation be excessive, or inappropriate, or used where other tools would be preferable. Regulation, economic instruments and voluntary action by firms all have their place. The balance will vary according to the differing conditions and expectations in various sectors.

33.2 The UK Government wants to shift the emphasis away from regulation and to use the incentives of economic instruments and market pressure where possible. Government and industry must remain flexible in their approach, ready to work together to achieve a common aim. Moreover, companies are increasingly moving beyond regulatory requirements, anticipating the future direction of legislation and of market forces. They realise that controlling the pace of change themselves can be more efficient and economic than reacting to events.

THE ROLE OF REGULATION

33.3 Regulation will continue to play a vital role in protecting the environment and in balancing the potentially conflicting demands of society for competitive industry, safe industrial activity and a clean and healthy environment. Where society determines that certain standards of environmental quality must be attained or preserved, regulation provides a means by which these can be ensured. It provides the foundation for a common approach to preventing, or minimising and rendering harmless, releases which can give rise to risks to the environment, taking account of the costs involved. And regulation provides a framework within which individual organisations can take the necessary steps to improve their environmental performance without the risk that their efforts will be rendered valueless or the company forced out of the market by the activities of competitor companies.

33.4 However, if regulation is not to lead to misallocation of resources, regulatory goals must balance the environmental benefits which will result from particular limits, for example, on releases and the cost of achieving these. Judgements on where this balance lies may be made at a macro level, such that on aggregate the benefits of attaining or preserving environmental quality goals are likely to justify the costs of achieving them, even if this will not necessarily be the case for individual regulated organisations. Or they can be made at the micro level, in relation to the individual process or plant authorised. Part I of the Environmental Protection Act 1990[1] incorporates the need for such judgements of balance through the concept of best available techniques not entailing excessive cost (BATNEEC).

33.5 It is now recognised that regulation is most effective where it considers the impacts on the environment as a whole. Within the UK, the system of Integrated Pollution Control (IPC) does this by requiring consideration of releases to air, land and water with authorizations based on the best practicable environmental option (BPEO). The challenge to the enforcing authorities is to find ways of applying the concepts of BATNEEC and BPEO to the wide range of individual processes requiring authorization so as to take account of the individual circumstances but on a consistent, transparent and auditable basis. The methodologies for doing this are expected to continue to develop as experience with the regime grows.

33.6 A key concern over regulatory approaches to environmental protection is that the cost of achieving a given level of protection may be unnecessarily high. This may arise either from the difficulty of identifying the appropriate balance of costs and benefits in each particular case or from the cost of applying regulatory systems. The Government is particularly concerned over possible impacts on small businesses where diversion of scarce human and financial resources could have a major impact on growth. One thrust of policy, therefore, is to seek ways in which burdens on regulated organisations can be reduced without weakening levels of environmental protection. One way of reducing such burdens is through increased professionalism and efficiency of regulatory organisations and a reduction in the number of regulators with whom individual organisations must deal. The proposed environmental agencies are part of the Government's response to this (see 33.8).

33.7 Another way of reducing the burden of achieving a given level of environmental protection may be to complement regulatory systems with voluntary agreements and economic instruments. One of the difficulties with regulatory approaches is that, as environmental goals become more stringent and all-embracing, the regulatory systems may become more complex and difficult to manage. Achieving sustainable development is, therefore, likely to depend upon finding increasingly effective ways of combining regulatory approaches with voluntary approaches and economic instruments.

33.8 The Government plans to establish new environmental agencies responsible for the regulation of air, water and waste. The Environment Agency in England and Wales will bring together Her Majesty's Inspectorate of Pollution (HMIP), the National Rivers Authority (NRA) and Waste Regulation Authorities. The Scottish Environment Protection Agency will bring together Her Majesty's Industrial Pollution Inspectorate (HMIPI), the Hazardous Waste Inspectorate, the river purification authorities, and the district and island councils in respect of their waste regulation function and some local air pollution controls. Both agencies represent a further step towards a more integrated approach.

THE ROLE OF ECONOMIC INSTRUMENTS

33.9 Economic instruments can work by encouraging efficiency, inducing innovation, providing flexibility, generating information about environmental damages and costs, and by providing additional public revenue. These instruments may take several forms: emissions charges, tradeable permits, product charges, deposit refund schemes, legal liability regimes and subsidies. Each of these instruments have their own particular advantage, and, like other policy instruments, they need to be assessed for environmental effectiveness, economic costs, effect on public revenues, dynamic incentives to innovation, effects on competition and competitiveness and fairness.

33.10 The rationale for the introduction of these instruments is that markets are the best way to find the most cost-effective methods of meeting environmental objectives. They ensure that resources are allocated efficiently by devolving decision-making away from the hands of regulators. If markets produce the most effective solutions, the result is that prices reflect the correct costs of environmental resources. Empirical studies suggest that using economic instruments in place of "command and control" regulation can often reduce significantly the cost of achieving environmental goals.

33.11 Different instruments can be used to achieve environmental objectives and all possible instruments should be considered. It will often be best to use a mix of policies; for example, a new economic instrument may well operate in conjunction with an underlying regulatory framework designed to prevent environmental degradation in the short term. It is important to consider how instruments fit together, to avoid perverse results. Where charges are the preferred instrument, they should ideally be set at a level which represents the costs of environmental damage, but when these costs are not clearly identifiable there are a number of alternative bases that can be used. Charges can, for example, be adjusted until a predetermined target is achieved, and this may be the most appropriate approach in some circumstances.

33.12 The Government has published a guide, *Making Markets Work for the Environment*[2], setting out this approach through the assessment, design and implementation of economic instruments. The Government is examining the possibility of :

- a levy on solid waste disposal;
- tradeable permit or charging systems for water pollution;
- tradeable permits or charges for water abstraction;
- a tradeable permit system for sulphur emissions.

ACTION BY FIRMS

33.13 Progress towards sustainable development will require continued profound change in the attitudes and aspirations that influence industrial activities. All firms will have to consider fully the impact their activities have on the environment, as some have already started to do, changing and improving the processes and technologies they use. One way forward is for businesses to take voluntary environmental action in response to public, consumer and stakeholder pressures; such action would be over and above, but complementary to, the requirements of Government regulation.

33.14 Self-regulation by business may be an effective course of action, complementing legislation. By entering into voluntary agreements or covenants with Government to reduce environmental impacts, individual sectors would have greater control over the implementation of agreed environmental targets. This would allow periodic review to take account of new information and changing circumstances. Some other countries have pioneered this approach but, before it could be adopted in the UK, further work would be needed on the scope of such agreements and how they could be negotiated, implemented and enforced.

Pressures for action

33.15 Many companies already recognise that measures which benefit the environment can also produce economic benefits. Alongside these internal incentives for action there are external pressures from groups such as consumers, local residents, employees, investors and insurers, as well as the Government, which will encourage companies to adopt a proactive stance on the environment.

Advantages

33.16 Companies should adopt environmental management strategies; by examining their current activities they can identify potential efficiency improvements. Action on energy efficiency, resource use, waste minimisation and recycling

can produce real savings and quick recovery of initial investment. By reducing risk and possible liability, companies are in a better position to attract investment and reduce insurance costs. The Government is fully committed to increasing awareness of the potential benefits of adopting best practice.

33.17 Not all environmental measures have an economic payback. But the development of an appropriate life-cycle approach, and higher expectations of environmental performance among corporate and domestic purchasers, will further highlight the positive link between improved environmental performance and added quality. Trade-offs between environmental action and short term profits may then appear more attractive in long term investment planning.

Reporting and information

33.18 Voluntary reporting on corporate environmental performance is an important development, although one still in its early stages. As the demand for accurate, credible data on environmental performance grows, more companies will come under pressure to produce environmental reports. For such reports to be useful, they will need to contain quantified targets and performance measurements; external verification of the results will increase their credibility still further. The availability of environmental information will increase the pressure for further improvements. Performance so far is encouraging.

Voluntary action

33.19 There are already a number of voluntary schemes to channel environmental action by industry. Participation in these schemes confers a genuine marketing advantage because they are seen as a sign of good practice. They may, in time, become generally required through purchasing specifications. Such schemes build on activities which the most forward-looking companies have already initiated. They provide structured frameworks within which companies can make claims about the environmental credentials of their products; introduce environmental management systems; set targets for continual improved performance, and publish detailed information on their environmental impact.

33.20 The EC Eco-labelling Scheme promotes consumer products which are less damaging to the environment than alternatives. It enables consumers to take environmental considerations into account when making purchases, and provides a real opportunity for manufacturers and retailers of greener products to promote those goods. Criteria have been agreed for the award of labels for washing machines and dishwashers, and other criteria well under way include those for lightbulbs, hairsprays, soil improvers, kitchen rolls and toilet paper. The scheme is administered and promoted in the UK by the UK Eco-labelling Board. The Board awarded the first EC eco-label to Hoover's "New Wave" range of washing machines in November 1993. An increasing range of eco-labelled products should appear in the shops during 1994.

33.21 The Making a Corporate Commitment Campaign encourages Board level commitment to energy efficiency; by November 1993 there were over 1500 signatories. Companies implementing environmental management strategies can demonstrate their commitment to continuous improvement by seeking certification to BS 7750, the new environmental management standard; and, in due course, they will be able to register their sites under the Eco-Management and Audit Scheme, which will come into force in the spring of 1995. Eco-Management and Audit will be particularly valuable in requiring a public statement on environmental performance, which must be validated by an independent third party. Competitions and awards, such as the new Queen's Award for Environmental Achievement, are also valuable as they offer incentives for companies to improve their environmental performance and to develop new, cleaner processes and technologies.

33.22 Many companies are already integrating the environment into their purchasing policies, striking at the heart of business practices. In trying to reduce the environmental impacts of their own products, they are promoting environmentally sound behaviour throughout the supply chain. This kind of initiative is likely to become more widespread.

Dialogue with business

33.23 The Government is committed to a dialogue with business on both general and specific environmental issues. Consultation gives the business community a stake in environmental policy, encouraging the pursuit of best practice. The Advisory Committee on Business and the Environment has proved a valuable forum for high level dialogue between Government and business. Its members include individuals with experience of running both large and small businesses.

33.24 However, it is recognised that businesses, especially small businesses, need assistance to understand how future environmental requirements and opportunities affect them and how they can best respond. The Government is, therefore, providing support, in partnership with the private sector, for

a programme to provide this help and guidance. At the local level this will focus on support for green business clubs; projects in Blackburn, Sheffield, Amber Valley, Dudley, Newcastle, Wearside, Leeds, Hemel Hempstead, and Plymouth are currently being funded as pilot schemes. At the national level, the Government will work with trade associations in specific industrial sectors and through a new environmental technology best practice programme, to disseminate environmental information and examples of best practice in a range of environmental priority areas. The way in which information is presented to small businesses will also be reviewed to ensure that it is easy to comprehend and act on.

33.25 In Northern Ireland, the Government has established an Advisory Committee to promote the messages contained in *Growing a Green Economy*[3], and to encourage local companies to respond positively. *Growing a Green Economy* emphasises that the ability of local companies to meet higher environmental standards cost-effectively is becoming an important determinant of international competitiveness, and highlights the opportunities presented by the developing environmental marketplace. In Wales, industry is provided with expert advice and information through the ARENA/NETWORK campaign.

Business partnerships

33.26 Business-led initiatives have a key role to play in disseminating environmental information. Organisations such as the Confederation of British Industry's (CBI) Environment Business Forum, the Business in the Environment Initiative, the Environment Council's Business and Environment programme, and the growing network of local green business clubs, can all make useful contributions, allowing industrialists to share their practical expertise and experience.

Training

33.27 Industry needs a workforce that is well-informed about environmental issues. Schools have an important role to play (see chapter 32), as do the Further and Higher Education Institutions. The report of the Toyne Committee[4], published in February 1993, made a number of recommendations addressed to institutions and the professions covering specialist environmental courses, other disciplines, training and environmental management. New courses will be needed and, in existing courses, environmental themes arising naturally from the subject must be developed. The Report emphasises the need for employers and professional organisations to advise the educational institutions of the demands of the market place, and the Government strongly supports this approach.

33.28 An environmentally skilled workforce will make a vital contribution to the achievement of sustainable development. Managerial, practical and technical skills will be required. Environmental knowledge and techniques are developing rapidly; both in-service training and open and flexible learning methods will be needed to make environmental training widely available.

33.29 Training and Enterprise Councils (TECs) in England are private sector, employer-led organisations that contract with Government to provide training and enterprise support at local level. TECs have a great deal of flexibility in the way they run programmes, and can include training in environmental awareness and relevant skills as part of Youth Training and Training for Work, depending on their assessment of local training needs. TECs can support businesses with help and advice on environmental issues, and also through individual initiatives. For example, Dudley TEC piloted the "Green IT" project, linking schools and employers in projects designing environmental and amenity improvements to industrial premises with computer technology. This initiative has recently been launched on a national basis. Similar employer-led organisations operate in Scotland as Local Enterprise Companies (LECs).

33.30 Environmental standards have been developed in the wider context of the National Vocational Qualifications (NVQs) and General National Vocational Qualifications (GNVQs) and their Scottish equivalents. NVQs and their Scottish equivalents now cover over 80% of the workforce, with environmental qualifications figuring prominently. NVQs currently cover areas such as waste management and environmental conservation; further qualifications and standards with environmental components are in development. The Government is investigating the feasibility of establishing an Environmental Standards Forum, whose objectives would include providing assistance on the "greening of standards" and helping with the future development of GNVQs. These qualifications and standards will play a much greater part in developing environmental management and enterprise within companies. The Government has launched a publicity campaign to ensure that employers and employees are aware of the new framework of qualifications.

International business action

33.31 The business community played an active part in the preparation for the Earth Summit in Rio, particularly through the Business Council for Sustainable Development (BCSD) and the International Chamber of Commerce (ICC). After the Earth Summit, the ICC established the World Industrial Council for the Environment (WICE). WICE and BCSD are both concerned with providing business input into the international environmental policy debate and promoting sound environmental management at the international level. The UN *Bank Statement on Sustainable Development*[5] commits 30 international banks to take account of environmental assessment in their investment decisions.

33.32 On the technology side, international business cooperation is being actively encouraged through the Technology Partnership Initiative. This aims to promote technology cooperation between businesses in the UK and developing countries (see chapter 28).

REFERENCES AND FURTHER READING

[1] Environmental Protection Act 1990. HMSO. 1990. ISBN 0-10-544390-5.

[2] *Making Markets Work for the Environment*. DOE. HMSO, 1993. ISBN 0–11–752852–8.

[3] *Growing a Green Economy*. DOE Northern Ireland/Department of Economic Development (DED) Northern Ireland, 1993.

[4] *Environmental Responsibility: An Agenda for Further and Higher Education*. Report of a Committee on Environmental Education in Further and Higher Education, appointed by the Department for Education and the Welsh Office (Chairman Peter Toyne). HMSO, 1993. ISBN 0–11–270820–X.

[5] *Statement by Banks on Environment and Sustainable Development*. UNEP Advisory Committee on Banking and the Environment, signed May 1992.

CHAPTER 34

ENVIRONMENTAL ACCOUNTING AND INDICATORS

Current Responses

- Government commitment to developing environmental accounting and environmental indicators.
- UK participation in OECD work on environmental indicators.
- Local Agenda 21 study of sustainability indicators.

The Way Forward

- Building on the experimental work published in 1992, to take forward work on UK environmental accounts.
- New Government working group on environmental indicators.

34.1 For development to be sustainable, environmental considerations must become a central part of the decision-making process within government and industry. For this to happen, better information is needed on the way in which economic development impacts on the environment. The ultimate goal would be the integration of environmental and economic accounting in national accounts, and *Agenda 21* proposed a programme to develop such systems, at least in satellite format, in all countries. This is very ambitious, and in the meantime much more can be done than at present through the development of environmental indicators that measure physical changes in the environment or pressures from economic activity. This chapter looks at these two approaches.

ENVIRONMENTAL ACCOUNTING

Principles

34.2 In the UK, national accounts follow a well-established and internationally agreed system of national accounts standards, which measure the total output of goods and services produced (gross national product, or GNP), representing national income of the country. Traditionally, national accounts are measured on such a gross basis, that is, not netting off (man-made) capital depreciation because of the problems of evaluating depreciation, rather than net national product (NNP).

34.3 The national accounts do not measure, nor claim to measure, national "welfare", nor can they be used to determine whether the country's economic growth is sustainable. Some economists argue that, in order to measure sustainability, capital depreciation (natural and man-

made) needs to be estimated and deducted from GNP. Natural capital covers non-renewable natural resources such as reserves of oil, coal and natural gas, as well as other forms of natural capital such as forests, stocks of fish, wildlife and areas of natural beauty. There is a debate over whether, in sustainability calculations, some natural capital depletion can be regarded as compensated by the substitution of increased man-made capital.

34.4 Some environmental accountants also argue that the cost of environmental degradation (that is, the cost of cleaning up environmental damage) should be deducted from GNP, as well as "defensive expenditure" which is carried out to prevent environmental damage. Both of these types of expenditure add to economic activity, but do not contribute towards sustainable growth because "welfare" remains unchanged.

34.5 Modifying GNP in these ways to take account of capital depreciation, environmental degradation and defensive expenditure would give a measure of the so-called "green NNP", which arguably would be a key indicator of sustainability.

34.6 Some national accountants have argued that it is not feasible to calculate green NNP, however, because of the methodological and practical problems involved, and that work should concentrate on supplementary or satellite accounts, in physical terms, with the main national accounts aggregates remaining unchanged. They also argue that it is not possible to reduce the sustainability debate to one single measure, and that it is dangerous to do so, since a single measure may mask important trends in particular areas.

34.7 The different kinds of environmental accounts, including satellite accounts and green NNP, are summarised (see Box 34.1).

Practice

34.8 The production of any of these environmental accounts is far from straightforward. There are problems because of a lack of suitable data, and there are substantial methodological difficulties.

34.9 For example, natural resource accounts might include not just minerals, metals, and fossil fuels, but commercially exploited flora and fauna, such as timber and fish. Some would argue that all flora and fauna should be included, and that accounts should include values for landscape and other aspects of the environment which people treasure for their own sakes and not just because of their commercial utility.

34.10 Measurement of environmental degradation would need to take account of the impact of a great variety of existing pollutants, and of new ones discovered or produced. In practice, it would only be possible to take account of the most significant, but agreement would be needed about which impacts are significant, how they should be measured, and how such measurements for different pollutants might be combined to give an overall assessment. Views on what constitutes a significant effect may well change over time as knowledge improves and as new substances come into use. For example, chlorofluorocarbons (CFCs) were not known to be harmful when they were first discovered, but are now recognised as being some of the most potent ozone-depleting substances.

34.11 Defining expenditure on environmental defence would require careful definition of scope, particularly since environmentally beneficial features are increasingly built into the design of products.

34.12 The UN Statistical Office has drafted a provisional handbook on integrated environmental and economic accounting which gives concepts and methods for implementing such accounting systems. The UK Central Statistical Office (CSO) published examples of simplified and experimental environmental accounts for this country, generally without quantification, in an article in November 1992[2]. The Department of the Environment (DOE) is anxious to take forward work on constructing environmental accounts, building on the experimental efforts of the CSO. The first step would be to draw together and explore existing sources of data while continuing to work with international bodies on methodological issues.

ENVIRONMENTAL INDICATORS

34.13 There is widespread interest in the international community in the possibility of developing a set of key indicators covering a range of environmental or sustainable

---

BOX 34.1
TYPES OF ENVIRONMENTAL ACCOUNTS

Natural resource accounts
Accounts which give a "balance sheet" showing stocks of natural resources, such as fossil fuels, fish stocks, timber, freshwater. They would also give resource flows showing use of resources over a period, and might also include measures of degradation, or quality of the resource, where appropriate – for example, for freshwater or timber.

Materials balance accounts
Accounts which show balances of potentially environmentally damaging materials such as heavy metals or pesticides. They would show how much the material existed at the start of a period, how much was used up in industrial processes and natural degradation, how much ended up in waste streams, how much was "exported" and how much remained at the end of the period in which media. They are used to estimate the accumulation of potentially harmful materials in the environment.

Satellite accounts
Accounts either in physical or financial terms which are separate from, but can be used in conjunction with, conventional economic accounts, thereby extending their use to include, for example, environmental impacts and use of natural resources. They might include balance and flows of natural resources, estimates of environmental degradation, or defensive expenditure (expenditure which prevents environmental damage). Preparation of these accounts would not affect the main national accounts, but would allow predictive modelling of environmental effects, for example, using such accounts to assess the effect of economic growth on emissions of pollutants.

Modified national accounts – "green NNP"
A modified measure of net national product ("green NNP"), where adjustments are made for the depletion of natural and man-made capital, environmental degradation and defensive expenditure. Monetary values must be assigned to each of these values so that the conventional national accounts measure can be adjusted. Some experts argue that green NNP is the best way to show whether a country is developing sustainably; if so, then green NNP will increase in real terms over time.

development issues. For any country, additional indicators will be needed to meet local circumstances, but there is room for agreement on a number of common definitions and applications. Such indicators would monitor changes in the environment, and pressures on it from economic development, such as the use of energy or road traffic growth. Properly constructed, they could measure performance against agreed targets and objectives, and assist governments and the public to evaluate how well national environmental policies and international commitments are being met.

34.14 There is, as yet, no consensus about what indicators should be included to give a balanced picture of environmental change. Views vary from country to country, depending on the stage of development, the type of economy and the particular environmental problems faced. But some issues are common to all countries, and the Organisation for Economic Co-operation and Development (OECD) published a preliminary set of environmental indicators in 1991. Further work is now being done to refine them and to improve and extend their coverage within an agreed framework. The UK is assisting in this work.

34.15 A set of core environmental indicators, however, are not necessarily indicators of sustainability. Sustainability indicators need to take account of economic linkages, quality of life and perhaps future welfare aspects, as well as environmental quality. Development of environmental indicators is not easy and the development of sustainability indicators raises further and even more complex issues.

34.16 The Government is committed to work on developing indicators for the UK and the DOE will establish a working group to produce a preliminary set within two years. Although much of the data which would be used are already widely available (for example in *The UK Environment*[3], the *Digest of Environmental Protection and Water Statistics*[4], and the *Digest of Energy Statistics*[5]), these publications include too much detail for this purpose. The objective of a key set of indicators is to have a relatively small number, perhaps 20–30, which show the main environmental trends. The challenge is to strike a balance between having a small number so that the main messages are clear, while not oversimplifying the issues or omitting significant areas, or suppressing significant geographical variations.

34.17 While some indicators, for example, those relating to ozone depletion or global warming, have a primarily global or national focus, others have a local dimension. A number of local authorities have already published state of the environment reports, and are keen to develop sets of environmental indicators which will help to show whether, at a local level, policies are leading to environmental improvements.

34.18 The local authority associations' Local Agenda 21 steering group has commissioned a study into local sustainability indicators and is considering with central government how this might fit into a broader framework of national indicators. The aim is to pilot investigations of a sample of local authorities and to make recommendations in 1994.

REFERENCES AND FURTHER READING

1   *Agenda 21* – an action plan for the next century, endorsed at UNCED, 1992.

2   *Economic Trends* (No 469, November 1992). Central Statistical Office. HMSO, 1992.

3   *The UK Environment*. DOE, HMSO, 1992. ISBN 0-11-752420-4

4   *Digest of Environmental Protection and Water Statistics*. DOE. HMSO, annual.

5   *Digest of Energy Statistics*. Department of Trade and Industry. HMSO, annual.

CHAPTER 35

LAND USE PLANNING SYSTEM

Current Responses

- The planning system is a key instrument in delivering land use and development compatible with the aims of sustainable development.
- All local planning authorities must now prepare a development plan taking account of environmental considerations; development control decisions must normally accord with such plans.
- Environmental assessment must be carried out for major development projects.
- Since 1990, the Government has reviewed all planning guidance to reflect environmental priorities.

The Way Forward

- The Government will review the application of sustainable development objectives in the planning system and issue further guidance during 1995.
- The Government will issue further guidance on environmental assessments.
- Local authorities should extend their monitoring of the effectiveness of development plan policies, to cover those relevant to sustainable development.
- The Government will commission further research into public participation in the planning process.

OBJECTIVES

35.1 The planning system provides a combination of:
- guidance, to help people to plan the use of their land confidently and sensibly, and to help local authorities to interpret the public interest wisely and consistently;
- incentive, to enable local authorities to stimulate particular types of development by designating land in their statutory plans;
- control, which ensures that developers cannot ultimately insist for private reasons on development which would be against the public interest;
- involvement, so that people affected by proposals for change can have their views and interests considered.

35.2 The system is well known and generally respected, and will be a key instrument in delivering land use and development objectives that are compatible with the aims of sustainable development. The basis of the system rests in the right of central and local government to control all development (including changes in the use of land). In

practice, many minor developments are permitted automatically, leaving about half a million each year that demand a full planning application. Decisions on most of those applications are taken by local authorities, but there is a right of appeal against a local authority refusal (and in some other cases); appeal decisions are taken by central government. Certain planning applications may also be "called in" for a decision by central government – but in practice this power is exercised rarely, and only when an application raises issues of regional or national significance.

35.3 The system is becoming more proactive. Under the Planning and Compensation Act 1991[1], all local planning authorities must prepare and keep up-to-date a development plan containing policies and proposals relating to the development of the whole of their area. Local planning authorities' decisions on planning applications must accord with their development plan unless material considerations indicate otherwise.

35.4 The preparation of development plans, and the exercise of development control, enable decision-makers to weigh and reconcile priorities in the public interest. They can ensure that the development needed to help the economy grow, and to provide people with jobs and homes, takes place in a way that respects environmental capacity constraints and other conservation interests. Regulations under the 1991 Act require environmental considerations to be taken into account in development plan preparation. Energy, other resource issues and environmental concerns can be relevant to all planning decisions.

PLANNING POLICY GUIDANCE

35.5 Development plans, and hence individual decisions on planning applications, need to reflect national and regional priorities. The Government, therefore, sets out the policies that are to be taken into account by local authorities. Since the 1990 Environment White Paper, *This Common Inheritance*[2], the Government has carried out a comprehensive review of planning guidance; it has issued a series of new national, regional and minerals planning guidance notes for England and Wales (see Box 35.1 and Box 35.2 – minerals planning guidance notes are set out in Box 18.1 in chapter 18). Progress on the review of planning guidance in Scotland is set out in Box 35.3.

35.6 The new notes give guidance on how the planning system can help to secure the objectives of sustainable development. Local authorities must take account of the new

BOX 35.1
PLANNING POLICY GUIDANCE NOTES IN ENGLAND AND WALES

No	Title	1992	1993	1994
1	General Policies & Principles	*		
2	Green Belts			O
3	Land for Housing	*		
4	Industrial & Commercial Development & Small Firms	*		
5	Simplified Planning Zones	*		
6	Major Retail Development		*	
7	Countryside & the Rural Economy	*		
8	Telecommunications	*		
12	Development Plans & Regional Planning Guidance	*		
13	Transport		X	
14	Development of Unstable Land	*		
16	Archaeology & Planning	*		
17	Sport & Recreation	*		
18	Enforcing Planning Control	*		
19	Outdoor Advertisement Control	*		
20	Coastal Planning	*		
21	Tourism	*		
22	Renewable Sources of Energy		*	

NEW PLANNING POLICY GUIDANCE NOTES

No	Title	1992	1993
–	Noise	X	
–	Nature Conservation	X	
–	Planning, Pollution Control & Waste Management	X	
–	Listed Buildings & Conservation Areas (PPG15)		X

* up to date
X consultation draft issued
O expect new consultation draft

BOX 35.2
REGIONAL PLANNING GUIDANCE NOTES (RPGS)

No	Title	1992	1993	1994
1	Tyne and Wear			O
2	West Yorkshire (to be incorporated in future Yorkshire & Humberside RPG)			O
3	London			O
4	Manchester (to be incorporated in future North West RPG)			O
5	South Yorkshire (to be incorporated in future Yorkshire and Humberside RPG)			O
6	East Anglia	*		
7	Northern		*	

NEW REGIONAL PLANNING GUIDANCE NOTES

No	Title	1992	1993	1994
–	East Midlands		X	
–	North West (inc Merseyside – formerly PPG11)			O
–	South East (formerly PPG9)		X	
–	South West	X		
–	West Midlands (formerly PPG10)			O
–	Yorkshire and Humberside			O

* up to date
X consultation draft issued
O expect new consultation draft

guidance as they prepare their development plans. Since development control decisions must accord with the development plan, unless material considerations indicate otherwise, the principles of sustainable development can then be reflected in every planning decision relating to land use, as local planning authorities make progress in their plan preparation. These principles will also be applied by means of the planning system in Scotland, which is described below.

35.7 Starting in 1994, the Government proposes to build on this by further research into ways in which the principles of sustainable development can be applied by planning authorities, and the publication of good practice guidance. That guidance will reflect the new agenda for land use decisions which emerges from the initiatives described in chapter 24.

LAND USE PLANNING SYSTEM IN SCOTLAND

35.8 The planning system in Scotland has to relate effectively to the needs of a densely developed Central Lowlands containing 80% of the 5 million population and of the adjacent Southern Uplands and Highlands which are among the most sparsely populated areas of the European Community. The National Heritage (Scotland) Act 1991[3], which led to the formation, in 1992, of Scottish Natural Heritage combining countryside and nature conservation interests, contained a requirement to have regard to sustainability.

35.9 The Government's proposal for local government reform in Scotland would reduce the number of planning authorities from 49 to 28 but the fundamentals of the planning system would remain the same.

- the national interest in land use is expressed in national policy planning guidelines (NPPGs) which refer to the principles of sustainable development. Emphasis is placed on the importance in development plans of recycling previously developed land and on the protection of natural resources;
- advice on best planning practice is provided in planning advice notes (PANs) and is relevant to the preparation of structure plans which continue to be approved by the Secretary of State for Scotland and to local plans which are adopted by planning authorities; over 80% of Scotland has full development plan coverage;
- development control remains primarily the responsibility of planning authorities. The system of notification will be reinforced by more rigorous requirements when planning authorities propose to approve development contrary to the development plan; the enhanced status of the development plan will be taken into account by planning

BOX 35.3
NATIONAL PLANNING POLICY GUIDELINES (NPPGs) IN SCOTLAND

Published recently or to be published in 1993/94

NPPG 1   The Planning System

NPPG 2   Business and Industry

NPPG 3   Land for Housing

NPPG 4   Land for Mineral Working

NPPG 5   Archaeology and Planning

NPPG –   Renewable Energy

Future topics

Retailing; Green Belts; Transport and Planning; Land for Waste Disposal; Sport and Recreation; Skiing Developments.

Planning Advice Notes (PANs)

Published recently or to be published in 1993/94

PAN 36   Siting and Design of New Housing in the Countryside

PAN 37   Structure Planning

PAN 38   Structure Plan Housing Land Requirements

PAN 39   Farm and Forestry Buildings

PAN 40   Development Control

PAN 41   Development Plan Departures

PAN 42   Archaeology

PAN 43   Golf Course and Associated Development

PAN –   Wind Energy Developments

PAN –   Fit of New Housing in the Landscape

Future topics

Local planning; Renewable Energy Developments.

authorities, by the Secretary of State for Scotland and by the Scottish Office Inquiry Reporters Unit (SOIRU) on appeals and "called in" applications.

35.10 Some of the principles of sustainable development are already well established in Scotland but the planning system can do more to encourage development and investment to take place in ways which will conserve the quality of the environment for the future.

ENVIRONMENTAL CONSIDERATIONS

35.11 The Government is also encouraging all local authorities to integrate environmental considerations properly into development plan preparation. The results of a recent research project have been published in a good practice guide[4]. This should help local planning authorities prepare plans that reflect sustainable development objectives.

35.12 Those plans are then a strong determinant in deciding whether to permit development. Environmental considerations should already be taken into account in considering all planning applications. In deciding planning appeals, central government will respect this approach, as it will in deciding "called in" applications.

35.13 Certain development projects which are likely to have significant environmental effects must also be subject to a separate environmental assessment. The planning application must be accompanied by an environmental statement on which the environmental agencies and the public must be consulted. This helps to ensure that the decision is properly informed. The Government will issue guidance to improve the quality of the environmental statements, and will also publish further guidance on the evaluation of environmental information in reaching decisions.

MONITORING THE EFFECTIVENESS OF PLANS

35.14 As the planning system is a key instrument for helping to deliver sustainable development objectives, it is important to monitor the contribution that it is making. The Government regularly reviews its planning policy guidance and the effectiveness of individual policy initiatives. For example, a current research project is looking at the implementation of the 1992 changes of policy guidance in respect of the countryside and the rural economy.

35.15 The Government also looks to local authorities to monitor the effectiveness of their development plan policies. Planning policy guidance encourages authorities to include policies in their plans which are capable of evaluation. Regular monitoring and review will help to establish the effectiveness of these policies, which again may be significant in helping to deliver sustainable development.

PUBLIC PARTICIPATION

35.16 In all aspects of its approach to sustainable development, the Government is committed to openness and consultation. There are already established ways of involving local people and non-government organisations in decisions on development plans, and in respect of individual planning applications.

35.17 In development plan preparation, the local planning authority must consult widely in the area affected. National agencies such as the Countryside Commission, English Nature and the National Rivers Authority have the right to express their views from the earliest stage of plan preparation, as do their equivalents in Scotland and Wales. In the light of consultation, local authorities publish draft plans, and place them "on deposit". The law gives local people and other interested bodies the right to object to any part of the plan, and to be heard before an independent person who makes a report to the local authority on all objections. Before adopting the final plan, the authority must consider the report, and give reasons if it does not propose to modify its plan in the way recommended. A current research project is looking at ways of making this process more effective and efficient. A future research project will concentrate on ways of enhancing the part that local people can play in development plan preparation.

35.18 The Planning and Compensation Act 1991 has much improved the publicity given to individual applications. The type of publicity depends on the type of development but, in general terms, neighbours will be informed of minor development by either a site notice or a letter and, in addition, on major applications, an advert will be placed in a local newspaper. Parish and community councils and other bodies have a right to be informed. The local planning authority is required to take into account all material comments.

REFERENCES AND FURTHER READING

1   Planning and Compensation Act 1991. HMSO, 1991. ISBN 0–10–543491–4.

2   *This Common Inheritance,* Cm 1200. HMSO, 1990. ISBN 0–10–112002–8.

3   National Heritage (Scotland) Act 1991. ISBN 0–10–542891–4

4   *Environmental Appraisal of Development Plans – A Good Practice Guide.* HMSO 1993. ISBN 0–11–752866–8.

5   *Conservation in Strategic Plans.* Countryside Commission, English Heritage and English Nature, 1993. ISBN 0–85–406626–8.

CHAPTER 36

ENERGY EFFICIENCY

INTRODUCTION

36.1 As described in chapter 19, there are two ways in which sustainability can be encouraged in the energy market:

- reducing the consumption of energy;
- supplying energy in ways which have less environmental impact.

The scope for energy efficiency measures to deliver the first of these, in a cost-effective manner, is considerable. This chapter describes action currently in hand and future prospects, outside the transport sector, which is described in chapter 26.

36.2 The Government believes that improved energy management by consumers, and straightforward investments with a payback of up to three years, could achieve energy savings of around 20% of current energy consumption outside the transport sector, equivalent to carbon dioxide (CO_2) emissions of 24 million tonnes of carbon (MtC) assuming the 1990 fuel mix. The market trends and energy efficiency campaigns already operating late in 1991 could result in just over a third of this potential being achieved by 2000. This is incorporated in the scenarios published in Energy Paper (EP) 59[1].

CURRENT INITIATIVES

36.3 The Department of the Environment's (DOE) programmes include:

- the **Best Practice programme**, which prepares and promotes detailed technical information and guidance on energy efficiency techniques and technologies in industry and all building types. This includes the promotion of Combined Heat and Power (CHP), described in chapter 19, which can increase the efficiency of fuel utilisation in electricity generation from 30–50% to 80–90%;
- the **"Making a Corporate Commitment" campaign**, which aims to increase the priority which businesses give to investment in energy efficiency, and to provide them with targeted information;
- the Energy Efficiency Office's (EEO) **Regional Programme** which aims to promote the economic and environmental benefits of energy efficiency measures through an annual programme of visits targeted at 2,500 energy using organisations in the industrial, commercial and public sectors;
- the **Home Energy Efficiency Scheme** (HEES), which provides grants to low income households, pensioners and disabled people for the installation of basic energy efficiency measures: loft, tank and pipe insulation, draughtproofing and energy advice;
- the **"Helping the Earth Begins at Home"** campaign, which aims to increase awareness of the link between global warming and energy use in the home, in order to encourage take up of domestic energy efficiency measures and behaviour;
- the **"Green House" programme**[2], to demonstrate reduced CO_2 emissions through increased energy efficiency in local authority housing;
- the requirement, from 1993, for local authorities to take fuller account of energy efficiency in their housing investment strategies[3].

36.4 On current projections, the Government's commitment to take measures aimed at returning CO_2 emissions to 1990 levels by 2000 requires an additional improvement of around 10 MtC or 6%, over and above that already projected for 2000 on the above basis. The National Programme to meet this target includes new Government measures, and commitments from many organisations outside Government, to promote energy efficiency. The following paragraphs refer to particular initiatives.

36.5 The independent Energy Saving Trust has been set up by the DOE, Scottish Office, British Gas, the 12 Regional Electricity Companies in England and Wales, ScottishPower and Scottish Hydro-Electric to develop and propose schemes financed by its members, to promote the efficient use of energy, aimed primarily at domestic and small business consumers. The development of the Trust should secure significant amounts of non-Government money to provide consumers with incentives to invest in energy efficiency measures. The Government has also increased the resources devoted to the provision of information and advice to households to reinforce the impact of the Trust.

Together with initiatives on training, these measures should result in CO_2 savings of 2–3.5 MtC by 2000. Many other organisations, including consumer and environmental groups are also providing advice to individuals and households about energy efficiency.

36.6 The Energy Management Assistance Scheme, launched in April 1992, aims to encourage smaller companies to obtain consultancy advice on the design and implementation of energy efficiency projects. The Government is, in particular, strengthening further the EEO's other programmes of advice and information aimed at business, and is working with business groups to ensure the maximum response so that significant additional savings should be achieved in this sector.

36.7 The Government recognises that the public sector should set an example for the country as a whole on energy efficiency. All Government Departments signed up to the Making a Corporate Commitment campaign in 1992 and further targets will be introduced for the Government estate, which should take energy use by central government down to well below 80% of 1990 levels by 2000. The Government is also looking to other public sector bodies to adopt similarly stringent targets. All these measures should result in further savings of about 1 MtC by 2000.

36.8 The proposed strengthening of the energy conservation requirements of the Building Regulations should improve the energy performance for space and hot water heating by 25–35% by comparison with practices complying with current Building Regulation standards. The Government will be working in the EC to agree energy efficiency standards for traded goods, beginning with a directive on standards for domestic refrigerators and freezers which it is hoped will be effective within three years or so. The Government will also be working towards the achievement of 5000 MW (megawatts) of CHP capacity by the year 2000, an increase of 1000 MW

BOX 36.1

CASE STUDY: ENERGY EFFICIENCY IN SCHOOLS

Much has already been done to improve energy efficiency in the schools' estate by both the Energy Efficiency Office (EEO) and the Department for Education, but there is still scope for further savings. Following the introduction of Local Management of Schools (LMS) in 1990, the EEO, together with ESSO, organised a series of energy efficiency seminars targeting the schools sector. The seminars, which began in the Autumn of 1991, aimed to motivate head teachers and governors to adopt energy efficiency measures on their school premises and to provide them with the necessary technical information to help them achieve savings. The information, derived mainly from the EEO's Best Practice programme, comprises comprehensive information on energy auditing of schools, case studies and guidance notes, and includes suggestions for involving pupils in the energy management of schools. The seminars emphasised that under LMS, energy cost savings do not have to be surrendered to the Local Education Authority, but can now be used by the school to purchase, for example, Information Technology equipment or books. Headteachers, therefore, have a real incentive to take action because their school directly benefits, the environment benefits, and the lessons learnt can feed directly into school curriculum activities.

To build on this approach the EEO, with ESSO, has developed the "Schools Turn-key Energy Programme" (STEP). Through STEP practical assistance is being provided by the Building Research Energy Conservation Support Unit (BRECSU), on the EEO's behalf, to help local authorities hold their own energy efficiency seminars aimed at head teachers and governors. This assistance, which is free, includes providing an expert speaker to give talks on various energy efficiency subjects, support material such as 35mm slides, a full information pack for each delegate, posters on energy efficiency, and comprehensive guidance notes on holding seminars. A series of free training days has also been held for potential organisers.

The Government is also funding, jointly with business, the Centre for Research, Education and Training in Energy (CREATE) to help coordinate and promote the teaching of energy efficiency in schools. Funding has been increased to assist with the development of a coherent and integrated approach to the teaching of energy efficiency. Similarly grants are provided under the Environmental Action Fund to support work on materials for teachers by the Council for Environmental Education.

on the previous target, and this should result in additional savings of around 1 MtC.

FUTURE PROGRESS

36.9 The existing energy efficiency programmes and new developments will also have an impact beyond 2000. In addition to the 20% potential outlined above, it is estimated that perhaps another 10% could be saved through take-up of energy efficiency investments with a pay back of three to five years. If all buildings and industrial plant are replaced when necessary by those incorporating the best economic deployment of energy efficiency techniques and technology, an additional 10% could be saved. If energy efficiency were the only consideration, then a further 10% could be saved through the latest technologies; technological advance by 2012 would further increase the potential for savings. As these figures indicate, the potential savings from energy efficiency are very high both in the short and longer term. Much is achievable on a cost-effective basis, more if consumers are prepared to take account of longer term paybacks.

36.10 Progress will, however, depend on the decisions of many millions of individual consumers. Most consumers invest on energy efficiency at a lower rate than economic self-interest would suggest they should, let alone at a level which takes into account long-term environmental considerations. One question that needs to be considered is, therefore, the extent to which continued action by Government, energy industries, and other bodies can secure a significant change in consumers' attitudes to energy efficiency and the relative roles of price signals, financial incentives, advice and regulation in bringing about such a change. As described in chapter 19, attention may need to be given to encouraging companies to develop commercial objectives involving promotion of the more efficient use of energy rather than the use of more energy. The financial regulatory regime under which the gas and electricity companies operate is very important here; and the establishment of the Energy Saving Trust, combined with moves by the electricity and gas regulators to allow certain energy efficiency costs in tariff calculations, form an important first step.

REFERENCES AND FURTHER READING

1   *Energy Paper 59 – Energy Related Carbon Emissions in Possible Future Scenarios for the UK.* Department of Trade and Industry. HMSO, 1992. ISBN 0-11-414157-6.

2   *Green House First Report.* DOE, May 1993 (92 HUG 115).

3   *Energy Efficiency in Council Housing: Interim Guidance for Local Authorities.* DOE, May 1993 (HUG 015A).

CHAPTER 37

SCIENCE, ENGINEERING AND TECHNOLOGY

Current Responses

- Much current research and development in the UK and internationally contributes directly or indirectly to sustainable development.
- Ongoing surveys of the UK's resources.
- Ongoing surveillance of environmental quality.
- The UK possesses sufficient skills in science, engineering and technology.

The Way Forward

- The national Technology Foresight Programme will apply foresight methods systematically to a wide range of market sectors and technologies, taking into account associated environmental impacts and benefits.
- The Government will promote principles of sustainable development and priorities widely among organisations who fund and carry out research and development activities.
- The Government will encourage and participate in relevant programmes of European and international research.
- The Government will encourage the transfer of the UK's acknowledged skills in science, engineering and technology to promote wealth creation and the quality of life in a sustainable manner.

INTRODUCTION

37.1 Science, engineering and technology have vital roles to play in achieving sustainable development. They provide the means to monitor the stock of natural resources passed on to succeeding generations, and to understand the conditions and workings of the environment and society. Research and technological development enable society to prolong the use of non-renewable resources by improving the efficiency by which they are transformed into the next generation's capital, and to ensure the more efficient use of renewable resources. They also provide the means to repair past environmental damage, although increased attention must be given to the detection and deflection of pressures on the environment before they occur. Further, they may provide alternative and improved ways of meeting needs and of sustaining the economy. New ways of promoting skills in science, engineering and technology for sustainable wealth creation, and for improving the quality of life, are now central to Government policy.

37.2 The Government's White Paper, *Realising Our Potential*[1], redraws the boundaries between the Research Councils, creating six Councils spanning engineering and the natural and social sciences, and providing each Council with a clear mission statement. Their objectives, from April 1994, will be to promote and support high quality basic, strategic and applied research and related postgraduate training in their areas of responsibility. The Councils will be expected to place special emphasis on meeting the needs of users of their research and training output, thereby enhancing the UK's industrial competitiveness and quality of life.

37.3 In 1991, expenditure by government and industry on civil research and development (R & D) was estimated at almost £10 billion[2]. Much of this, together with some defence R & D and many environmental monitoring and technology transfer activities which are not classified as research, generates new ideas, information and methods which may assist in making development more sustainable. Such work is carried out by Government Departments, Research Councils, higher education institutions (HEIs) and other public and private institutions. Research has contributed much of relevance already. For example, the National Environment Research Council's (NERC) Institute of Terrestrial Ecology has worked on the impacts of persistent organochlorine pesticides and of polychlorinated biphenyls (PCBs), resulting in controls that have helped affected species, such as sparrowhawks, to recover. Only a limited proportion of R & D is designed explicitly to resolve problems of, and promote, sustainable development. The future research agenda must address the reasons why resources are used in the ways that they are, and how they might best be used to meet longer-term needs. This includes the development of rigorous methodologies to determine the sustainability of a particular resource usage and of environmental capacities and impacts. The UK's Inter-Agency Committee on Global Environmental Change has addressed the key issues involved at the global level and identified priorities for work on the human, environmental and impact dimensions, and on response options[3]. This chapter considers what is being and might be done by the UK, drawing on earlier chapters of this Strategy.

ECONOMY AND THE ENVIRONMENT

37.4 Understanding how the economy, society and the environment work and interact is vital in predicting the nature of change, its consequences and how this may be turned to our advantage.[3,4,5] Such research is multidisciplinary and at the frontiers of knowledge. Technological development should be challenged to demonstrate that it is sustainable as well as beneficial and that it offers an alternative to existing unsustainable practices. Some UK research programmes are beginning to define and address key aspects of sustainable development. For example, the Research Councils are currently supporting work on cities and sustainability, cleaner technology, sustainable farming systems, and rural change and sustainability. However, more work will be required to tackle, for example, problems of transport and air pollution, climate change and clean production. This will require a fully integrated approach to research and to the application of its results. Such research is increasingly international. The UK is an active and often leading participant in relevant international programmes such as:

- the EC LIFE and Framework programmes;
- EUREKA (European high technology initiative), which includes many environmental projects;
- the NATO Committee on the Challenges of Modern Society (CCMS);
- the International Geosphere-Biosphere Programme (IGBP);
- the World Climate Research Programme (WCRP).

R & D underpins many of the UK's aid projects to those developing countries who are concerned to exploit their resources in a sustainable manner.

37.5 If the UK is to contribute usefully to the sustainable development of other nations, this country must have a thorough knowledge of their environmental and economic agendas and recognition of their particular needs. For example, the UK has launched the Technology Partnership Initiative, which aims to encourage greater technology cooperation between businesses in newly industrialising developing countries and those in the UK. Promoting direct access for these overseas companies to information on affordable and appropriate technology, and other knowledge available in the UK, is a positive step in helping developing countries to work towards their own sustainable development.

RESOURCES

37.6 The nation's non-renewable hydrocarbon resources such as oil, gas and coal are under continual survey and reassessment. Thus, research is in hand by industry, Government and the universities to explore ways of locating and best exploiting new hydrocarbon reserves. The rate at which such reserves are prospected and exploited depends not only on the state of scientific knowledge and technological exploitability but also upon economic circumstances and demand. The forces behind these demands and the options for future investment in their responsible use therefore need to be known. For example, research is needed to establish the technological options, economic incentives and infrastructural requirements for encouraging moves from non-renewable to renewable sources of energy, such as alternative fuels from arable

crops. Strategies for reducing the demand for fuel also need to be examined in the wider context of managing demands for travel and communication.

37.7 Renewable energy, including wind power, biofuels and solar power, is an essential element of a broad-based approach to sustainable development, particularly in the medium to long term. Renewable energy has the important additional benefits of helping to ameliorate emissions of pollutants and contributing to the UK's commitments on carbon dioxide (CO_2) targets. Renewables currently supply 2% of the UK's electricity supply, and could supply 5–20% of the current size of the UK's electricity market by 2025 if they can be successfully commercialised.

37.8 The geological, geochemical and geophysical survey, reassessment and exploitation of other resources, such as minerals, aggregates and sand, are governed by a similar combination of economic demand and technological exploitability. Less exploitative approaches to their use are being explored. Further surveys of sand and aggregates for construction and for coastal flood protection are planned by the Ministry of Agriculture, Fisheries and Food (MAFF). Research is indicating more sustainable options for preventing or restraining cliff erosion and managing coastal flood defences, especially where there is no danger to life or valuable property. This work supports a new strategy[6] announced by the Government (see chapter 11).

37.9 Arable crops and forests are renewable potential sources of a wide range of other products including industrial oils and acids, natural pesticides, plastics, starch and fibres provided they can be grown without excessive inputs of energy. Such options for replacing non-renewable sources need to be explored, as do the means of enhancing and extracting natural pharmaceutical products. The potential is already recognised in the priority given to such work in EC, industrial and Government programmes.

37.10 Soil performs a wide range of functions. It is vital for plant and animal communities. It is important not only for food production and forestry, but is also a dominant factor in shaping landscape, in providing habitats for wildlife and in controlling the water cycle (see chapter 10). Knowledge of basic soil structure and the fauna, flora and processes occurring within it is far from complete; soil is known to be renewable only in the very long term. The pressures upon this resource are such that soil protection has been selected as the subject of the next enquiry by the Royal Commission on Environmental Pollution. The aim in the longer term must be to minimise degradation wherever it may be irreversible, especially in respect of contamination by persistent inorganic pollutants[3].

37.11 Chapter 8 highlights current issues of quality and volume of freshwater resources. Surface waters are subject to regular monitoring for research and regulatory purposes. More effort needs to be devoted to assessing and protecting those resources and associated ecology which are currently under threat. Groundwaters are also important resources which, once contaminated, are difficult to clean up. Further surveys of this resource, and research to tackle related pollution problems, are essential.

37.12 Recent droughts and the possibility of climate change, notably global warming, are stimulating new work on crop varieties that can tolerate water stress without recourse to irrigation. This is in addition to ongoing research aimed at optimising the use of water on farms in the context of availability of water in watersheds and catchment areas. A range of projects designed to minimise the risks of soil and freshwater contamination is also under way, including the development of new methods of applying minimum quantities of pesticides and fertilisers. The economic pressures which influence the uses to which land is put may, however, be critical in determining the status of freshwater resources in the longer term.

37.13 The continuing loss of species and habitats is a cause for concern and is addressed in the *Biodiversity Action Plan*[7] and also in the *Sustainable Forestry Programme*[8]. Monitoring of such changes is central to the 1990 Countryside Change survey – funded by the Department of the Environment (DOE), NERC, the British National Space Centre and the Joint Nature Conservation Committee – and in the work of the conservation and countryside agencies. It is important to understand the reasons for such changes and their consequences.

37.14 This applies equally to marine biological resources. Whilst much is known about commercially exploited fish stocks, there are a number of species caught occasionally, especially in deeper waters, about which little is known – including whether they could be exploited. The increasing economic importance of aquaculture in the UK will depend upon exploitation of the coastal zone. There are many concerns about the impacts of such exploitation in waters already under heavy pressure from other activities, such as fishing, aggregates extraction, recreation, industrial and tourist development, and even the demands of conservation. There are special local concerns attached to new demands upon natural resources, such as calcified

merle seaweed, where modern extraction technology has considerable impact upon the structure of marine communities. Information and research to optimise the monitoring, use and conservation of fauna and flora of such waters will be required.

SURVEILLANCE AND MONITORING

37.15 There is inevitable overlap between the assessment and appraisal of available resources and the surveillance and monitoring of their quality. Many bodies are involved in surveying and monitoring the state of the UK environment and these results are reported regularly[9,10]. For example, MAFF and other Government Departments support important programmes of work on both radioactive and non-radioactive contaminants in the marine environment. The National Rivers Authority (NRA) is introducing a General Quality Assessment scheme which will be linked to statutory Water Quality Objectives. NERC sponsors longer-term research-based monitoring in aquatic systems. The need for such work has intensified because of demands for better information on trends in air, soil, freshwater, estuarine and marine pollution levels, in climate change[3] and in changes in the countryside and the natural resources. Such information is an essential input to environmental impact and risk assessment. There is also a significant investment in more strategic operations associated with long-term research (such as the Environmental Change Network, which involves many organisations, including the Research Councils, English Nature, the Ministry of Defence, MAFF, the Scottish Office and universities).

37.16 Many of the advances in knowledge about the environment have been achieved by high quality monitoring and research, and by the successful application of simple but effective new technologies. Advances in automation of sampling and measurement systems have increased the quantity and quality of data on air, soil and water contaminants. On-line measurement systems are being deployed increasingly for a wide range of purposes. Aircraft and satellite remote sensing are also playing an increasingly significant role. The NRA, for example, has project-tested the first European combined air/sea surveillance of coastal waters for water quality and related purposes and the Countryside Change Resurvey 1990 integrates satellite imagery with ground sampled spatial data. The decade to 2000 will see major advances in such technologies, which will vastly improve the volume and quality of environmental knowledge. These must be, and are being, planned now, along with the necessary quality control and interpretation procedures.

OPPORTUNITIES

37.17 Technology is inherently neither good nor bad. However, many environmental problems have arisen by the wilful, ill-informed or misguided application of technology, both in the UK and overseas. There cannot be a return to the pre-technological age, but technology should be applied in a beneficial manner. There are numerous examples of projects designed to mitigate or eliminate past and current environmental problems, such as the reduction of malodorous emissions from agricultural and industrial premises and the development of low input and low leakage farming methods. The next 20 years are likely to witness very significant developments in UK plant and animal science. Advances in the understanding and techniques of genetic manipulation, sensors and computing could produce marked changes in farming systems, both in the range of products produced by farmers and in the inputs required. Some newer varieties of crop plants contain inherent resistance to pests and diseases, so reducing the needs for pesticides. In the future, further developments are possible, such as crops that are more efficient in their use of nutrients and water. The introduction of engine management systems, and possibly of catalytic converters, are examples of the successful introduction of innovative technology to reduce emissions. Techniques are currently being developed in DOE and DTI through ETIS (the Environmental Technology Innovation Scheme), DEMOS (DTI's Environmental Management Options Scheme) and the LINK programmes for the restoration of degraded environments, including biological, chemical and physical methods for treating waste waters and contaminated land.

37.18 Central to many current research and technology programmes are the principles of waste minimisation and more efficient use of raw materials. The more efficient use of resources will bring other benefits, such as reductions in air and water pollution. In many cases, technologies exist or can readily be developed to achieve these ends. Other research programmes have an indirect but, nevertheless, considerable impact on sustainability. A prime example of this is in the field of Information Technology where DTI support for both national and European research programmes promotes the generation of enabling technologies in key areas such as microelectronics, software engineering, performance computing and business systems. These technologies are fundamental to sustainable development – whether applied in the design of environmental satellites, climate modelling, aerodynamic simulation of fuel efficient aircraft, energy efficient systems for the home and factory, or in teleworking. Good design and engineering has a key role to play in achieving better environmental performances. An important task, therefore,

is to provide efficient mechanisms to increase awareness and to optimise the transfer and application of appropriate technologies to potential users, particularly amongst small and medium-sized enterprises. This process is reasonably well developed in areas such as agriculture and food, the DOE Energy Efficiency Office's Best Practice and Green House programmes, certain LINK programmes, and DTI's 'Managing in the 90s' programme. DTI's DEMOS scheme has done much to promote the uptake of environmental technology by industry. Further efforts are being made by Government to promote such transfers. These must include measures to address social and economic barriers to innovation and to technology transfer.

37.19 Adopting an integrated approach to waste and pollution control offers opportunities to look at innovative solutions which address each production process as a whole. This approach is already leading to dramatic decreases in the quantities of resources consumed and of wastes produced, with consequential financial benefits. UK engineers have produced a cost-effective robust machine for recycling unused ready-mix cement, saving millions of tons of aggregates and sand each year. One project funded by regulatory bodies and industry to optimise the use of resources, such as raw materials and energy, has identified over 500 measures to reduce wastes, emissions and operating costs in the Rivers Aire and Calder catchments. Most of the industrial sites examined have the potential to realise annual savings in excess of £50,000, and one claimed £1.6 million. The results of such studies need to be disseminated widely and quickly because they provide important tools for ensuring future economic development of a more beneficial kind, and for making affordable a precautionary approach to potentially hazardous substances and processes.

FUTURE PRIORITIES

37.20 This Strategy seeks to forecast key developments to 2012. Whilst the future environmental agenda may be familiar[4], some major changes could occur. Box 37.1 provides some forecasts derived from science, engineering and technology foresight exercises as exemplars of forward thinking. They underline how different society may be by 2012.

37.21 There is a clear need to apply foresight methods[1,4] systematically to all technological areas and to sectors of the environment and the economy. This is a key aim of the national Technology Foresight Programme announced in the White Paper, *Realising our Potential*. The results will inform the setting of priorities and targets for relevant aspects of science, engineering and technology. In some areas, such as automated sampling and measurement, knowledge and technology are advancing so rapidly that any targets will have to be revised. In others, the time frame is set by external factors, such as the planning and timing of satellite missions for remote sensing (related to climate and countryside change), the effectiveness of technology transfer in promoting waste minimisation, and the rates at which organisations perceive and accept the issues involved in sustainable development.

37.22 Nevertheless, certain priorities for the future can be identified:

- novel application of technologies to product design and manufacture, to waste minimisation and treatment, and to environmental restoration;
- improved methods of risk assessment and of planning for uncertainty, including the evaluation of the sustainability as well as the benefits of exploiting technology;

- development of integrated production and environmental management systems;
- efficient dissemination and transfer of information on best practices and techniques for sustainable activities, including those appropriate to developing countries;
- improved understanding of institutional, corporate, public and consumer attitudes towards sustainability;
- exploration of options for replacing use of non-renewable resources with those renewable ones whose technologies are economically attractive and environmentally acceptable.

37.23 New ways of promoting skills in science, engineering and technology for sustainable wealth creation and for improving the quality of life, are now central to Government policy. The Government will:

- ensure that the basic principles of sustainable development outlined in this Strategy, and the priorities

---

BOX 37.1

SOME FORESIGHT PROJECTIONS TO THE 2012 PERIOD

These are quoted directly from unattributed sources and are in no order of importance or certainty.

- Ecodesign, life cycle analysis, cleaner and leaner production methodologies will be the norm.
- There will be rapid advances in environmental surveillance and monitoring (such as biosensors).
- Advances in communications and related technologies will impact on many areas, including remote sensing and environmental monitoring, reductions in the need to travel to work and reductions in energy consumption. There will be associated major advances in the handling, storage and analysis of the data involved.
- Technologies to exploit non-renewable resources and to exploit alternative renewable resources (for energy, for example) will improve.
- New and improved (for example, biological) techniques for restoring degraded environments, for recycling bulk degradable wastes, and for detoxifying persistent toxic wastes will be developed.
- Improved techniques, data bases and systems (such as advanced Geographic Information Systems – GIS) will be available to assess and predict environmental changes and impacts.
- Chaos theory may be harnessed to create more efficient and flexible production techniques.
- New recycling techniques will reduce domestic and municipal waste by up to half.
- New drugs and techniques for the cure of certain cancers will be introduced.
- It may be possible to produce proteins from atmospheric CO_2 and from ammonia.
- Extremely high energy efficient engines and cleaner fuels for mobile and stationary engines will be introduced. This will be coupled with more extensive use of alternative fuels.
- Biodegradable packaging will find more widespread application.
- Compact separation and treatment systems for the effective removal of insoluble and intractable pollutants in waste streams will be developed.
- It will be possible to eliminate or reduce emissions of many gaseous pollutants on a wide scale.
- Worldwide, CO_2 emissions may be reduced by up to 20% of present day levels, assisted in part by technological methods of absorbing and immobilising.
- Buildings will become much more energy efficient, and the use of self-sufficient energy supply systems may contribute significantly to this.
- Buildings and other artifacts will be designed to be more durable, sustainable and upgradable.
- Transport-related environmental problems will need integrated solutions.

identified, are taken fully into account by public bodies concerned with the promotion, funding and prosecution of science, engineering, technology and design in the UK;

- encourage industry, non-governmental organisations and others to take these principles and priorities into account;
- pursue complementary policies providing appropriate science-based aid to developing countries;
- encourage, and participate in relevant programmes of international research by bilateral agreements, in Europe and in international governmental and non-governmental fora.

37.24 Much of the work necessary to take forward these priorities is in place or requires minor redirection in terms of aims, objectives and dissemination. In others, the need for substantial change will rapidly become apparent as individual programmes and activities are reassessed.

REFERENCES AND FURTHER READING

1   *Realising our Potential: A Strategy for Science, Engineering and Technology.* Cm 2250. HMSO, 1993.

2   *Annual Review of R & D, 1993.* Office of Science and Technology. HMSO, 1993.

3   *Global Environmental Change: The UK Research Framework 1993.* Compiled on behalf of Inter-Agency Committee on Global Environmental Change by the UK Global Environmental Research Office. September 1993.

4   *The UK Environmental Foresight Project.* Volumes I to III. CEST and DOE. HMSO, 1993.

5   *This Common Inheritance. Britain's Environmental Strategy.* Cm 1200. HMSO, 1990. ISBN 0-10-112002-8. And subsequent Anniversary Reports: Cm 1655 (1991) and Cm 2068 (1992).

6   *Strategy for Flood and Coastal Defence in England and Wales.* Ministry of Agriculture, Fisheries and Food and the Welsh Office. PB 1471. MAFF, 1993.

7   *Biodiversity: The UK Action Plan.* Cm 2428. HMSO, 1994. ISBN 0-10-124282-4.

8   *Sustainable Forestry: The UK Programme.* Cm 2429. HMSO, 1994. ISBN 0-10-124292-1.

9   *Digest of Environment Protection and Water Statistics.* Department of the Environment. HMSO, annual.

10 *The UK Environment.* Department of the Environment. HMSO, 1992. ISBN 0-11-752420-4.

CHAPTER 38

WORKING TOGETHER

> **The Way Forward**
> - Government's Panel on Sustainable Development.
> - A UK Round Table on Sustainable Development.
> - A Citizens' Environment Initiative.

INTRODUCTION

38.1 Sustainable development is already being promoted actively in many different ways in the UK, at national and at local level, in business and in people's homes. This chapter proposes new initiatives to strengthen and broaden that work.

38.2 Section 4 has reviewed the UK's existing processes for analysing and discussing environmental and sustainable development issues and for decision-taking. These arrangements are working well. But the Government believes that three new measures are desirable:
- to give authoritative and independent advice;
- to bring together representatives of the main sectors or groups;
- to carry the message to individuals and local communities.

THE GOVERNMENT'S PANEL ON SUSTAINABLE DEVELOPMENT

38.3 The Prime Minister is inviting a small group of individuals, with wide knowledge and practical experience, to advise the Government on strategic issues. They will keep in view general sustainability issues at home and abroad, identify major problems or opportunities likely to arise, monitor progress, and consider questions of priority. The Government will consult them on issues of major importance, and they will be able to offer the Government unsolicited advice.

38.4 They will meet about four times a year. They will have access to all Ministers but will also keep in touch with key people in different sectors of the UK and keep abreast of developments in other countries. They will advise the Government, and Panel members will also be able to express views individually in public. They will not be expected to conduct analytical studies or write detailed reports (which would duplicate the work of many other bodies) but – drawing on their experience and the detailed work of others – they will combine their judgements and offer their collective advice.

A UK ROUND TABLE FOR SUSTAINABLE DEVELOPMENT

38.5 At present there are several different fora that act as channels of communication and advice on sustainable development and environmental issues with different sectors.

38.6 They include the Central and Local Government Environment Forum, in which local government spokesmen meet with Environment Ministers; the Voluntary Sector Environment Forum, in which environmental groups meet the Minister of State for the Environment; the Advisory Committee on Business and the Environment which submits reports to the President of the Board of Trade and the Secretary of State for the Environment; and the Royal Commission on Environmental Pollution. Several non-departmental public bodies also have particular expertise in their own areas, including the National Rivers Authority and the countryside agencies. There is also a panel of environmental economists that advises the Department of the Environment (DOE), and other advisory and consultative groups assist the DOE and other Departments alike.

38.7 The Government proposes to invite some of the members of these fora to meet with Ministers twice a year in a UK Round Table on Sustainable Development, to be chaired by the Secretary of State for the Environment. The Round Table will operate on a UK-wide basis and representatives from England, Wales, Scotland, and Northern Ireland will be included.

38.8 The Round Table will not supplant the work being done by the existing bodies, nor replace any existing channels of communication nor remove the need for consultation with other bodies. Its purpose will be to encourage discussion on major issues of sustainable development between people who approach them from different positions and who have different responsibilities. Members will be able to compare notes on what is being done in different sectors, to develop a better understanding of the problems faced by others, and to see how far a common perspective might be developed on various issues. There will be further consultation about the details of the membership and mode of operation of the Round Table.

CITIZENS AND THE ENVIRONMENT

38.9 Many initiatives are already being taken to work with local communities and individuals. Voluntary groups in the UK have great experience of this. Local government has launched its Local Agenda 21 initiative, promoting round table discussions of local problems and opportunities, running public awareness campaigns and practical projects; some councils have promoted their areas as "Environment Cities". Firms have launched voluntary eco-management and audit schemes, and the EC is promoting eco-labels in the shops.

38.10 Recent UK Government initiatives include the reshaped Environmental Action Fund, the Green Brigade for young people, and Environment Watch; and the Government publishes information and advice for members of the public. The Government proposes to build on all these elements, encouraging each of them to take root in as many local communities as possible. It will therefore continue to work with local authorities, voluntary bodies, church groups and businesses, and will vigorously promote the schemes for which it is directly responsible.

38.11 Community-based activity is only one half of the story, however. There is a key part to be played by individuals in developing a more sustainable world. They may act:

- as green consumers or green householders: people can reduce their consumption of energy, minimise the amount of disposable goods and packaging they purchase, choose environment-friendly goods in the shops, recycle or reuse materials, use their cars less;
- as volunteers: supporting voluntary bodies, becoming active in community or church groups, fund raising, or actively working on conservation projects;
- at work: through supporting drives for energy saving, green purchasing, innovative techniques of management and new technology, that might lead to better products or processes;

- as parents or others involved with children: developing children's interest in environmental issues or responding to the concern that young people and children already express;
- as aware citizens: whether voting, becoming active in political parties, participating in local affairs, or simply exchanging views with friends or writing to newspapers.

38.12 The Government wants to encourage the growth of interest in the issues of sustainable development, and particularly in the things people can do in their own lives. It proposes to stimulate a "Citizens' Environment Initiative".

38.13 The Government will discuss with voluntary bodies, local authorities, the churches and others how this can best be carried forward. The UK will be playing host to World Environment Day on 3 June 1994; it could be useful to link the idea of sustainable development as early as possible with the events surrounding this day, and to emphasise the need for individuals' continuing effort and commitment by launching a national debate. A year of activity could be planned. An umbrella committee might be set up to publicise ideas and advice, to stimulate a local response, and to keep in touch with any local initiatives. The initiative will be supported by a small secretariat, to be funded by the DOE but outside the Department itself.

38.14 The aim will be to increase people's awareness of the part that their personal choices can play in delivering sustainable development, and to enlist their support and commitment in the coming years.

ANNEXES

* Indicates words that can be found elsewhere in the glossary

Abstraction
removal of surface water from lakes, reservoirs, rivers and groundwater from (aquifers) for domestic, commercial and industrial use.

Acid rain
rain, snow, fog and mist which has been acidified by the atmosphere, principally when contaminated by oxides of sulphur and nitrogen. A form of acid deposition.*

Acid deposition
the precipitation of dilute solutions of strong mineral acids (acid rain*), or acidified dry particulate matter from the atmosphere. This acidification is due to the mixing in the atmosphere of various industrial pollutants, for example sulphur dioxide, nitrogen oxides, hydrogen chloride and other minor compounds, with naturally occurring oxygen and water vapour.

Afforestation
the planting of trees on land which has not been under forest or woodland in the recent past.

Agenda 21
action plan for the next century, endorsed at UNCED*.

Aggregate
sand and gravel, and crushed rock.

Agrochemical
chemical substances used in agricultural production including fertilisers, herbicides, fungicides and insecticides.

Algal blooms
rapid growth of algae in marine and freshwater which may colour the water and accumulate on the surface as a green scum. Some blooms, such as certain species of blue-green algae, may produce poisons.

Ambient
with reference to the surroundings, for example, surrounding temperature.

Ammonia
a compound of nitrogen and hydrogen. A colourless, highly soluble gas which is pungent and toxic at high concentration.

Anthropogenic
manmade.

Aquaculture
the cultivation or rearing of aquatic plants or animals.

Aquifer
a porous water-bearing underground formation of permeable rock, sand or gravel capable of yielding significant quantities of water.

Basel Convention on Transboundary Shipments of Waste
agreed in 1989; introduces global controls on waste movements.

Benzene
a carcinogenic* organic* compound which is a component of petrol. It is also produced in trace amounts during combustion of petrol, and hence is emitted from car exhausts.

Bioaccumulation
the accumulation of substances in living organisms. Where the substances are toxic, this can lead to progressive and irreversible harmful effects.

Biochemical oxygen demand
the amount of oxygen used by micro-organisms per unit volume of water at a given temperature, for a given time. It is used as a measure of water pollution by organic* materials.

Biodegradable
capable of being decomposed by bacteria or other biological means.

Biodiversity
the variety of life on earth or any given part of it.

Biomass
the total quantity or weight of organisms in a given area or volume.

Biosphere
that part of the earth and atmosphere in which organisms live.

Biota
see Ecology.

Biotechnology
the application of biological organisms or their products in industrial and chemical processes.

Brown soils
generally free-draining brownish or reddish soils overlying permeable materials.

Bryophyte
a group of primitive, non-vascular plants, for example mosses and liverworts, generally confined to damp locations.

Butadiene
a colourless, gaseous hydrocarbon used in the manufacture of synthetic rubbers.

BS 7750
British Standards Institute Standard for Environmental Management Systems.

Capacity 21
a capacity building programme launched by UNDP in support of Agenda 21.

Carbon cycle
natural circulation of carbon which is exchanged between the large carbon reservoirs in the land and ocean biospheres and the atmosphere.

Carbon dioxide (CO_2)
gas present in the atmosphere and formed during respiration, and by the decomposition and combustion of organic compounds (for example, fossil fuels, wood). A greenhouse* gas.

Carbon monoxide (CO)
a toxic, colourless gas produced by the incomplete combustion of carbon, mainly from combustion of petrol. Cigarette smoking is another important source.

Carcinogenic
producing cancer.

Catalytic converter
a device fitted to the exhausts of motor vehicles which converts carbon monoxide* and nitric oxide to carbon dioxide* and nitrogen respectively, and organic* compounds to carbon dioxide* and water.

Catchment
area from which river systems, lakes and reservoirs collect water.

Cetacean
marine mammal belonging to the order Cetacea, including whales, dolphins and porpoises.

Chlorofluorocarbons (CFCs)
volatile but inert compounds of carbon and (mainly) chlorine and fluorine. Important greenhouse* gases and ozone* layer depletors.

Chlorine loading
the total amount of chlorine in the atmosphere, which is a measure of the potential damage to the ozone* layer.

Coliform
a group of bacteria, often of faecal or environmental origin, and used as indicators in water of the possible presence of disease causing organisms.

Controlled waste
industrial, household and commercial waste, as defined in UK legislation. Controlled waste specifically excludes mine and quarry waste, wastes from premises used for agriculture, some sewage sludge and radioactive waste.

Convention on Biological Diversity
signed at UNCED* in 1992 by over 150 countries. Ratifying countries are required to identify and monitor their genetic resources and to prepare national plans to protect their biodiversity*.

Cost benefit analysis (CBA)
the most comprehensive form of economic appraisal which seeks to quantify in money terms as many of the costs and benefits of a proposal as possible, including items for which the market does not provide a satisfactory measure of economic value.

Critical load
a quantitative estimate of exposure to pollutants below which no significant harmful environmental effects result. Critical load maps can be compared with current deposition maps to show areas where environmental damage occurs.

Crown dependencies
Channel Islands and the Isle of Man. They are not part of the UK, but are self governing dependences of the Crown with their own legislative assemblies and systems of law and administration. They have no representation in the UK parliament, but the UK Government is responsible for their defence and international relations.

Crustacean
organism belonging to the class Crustacea and typically having a thick hard shell including lobster, crabs, shrimps and barnacles.

Cryptosporidium
a microscopic parasite which can cause disease to humans.

DDT
an organochlorine* insecticide widely used from the 1940s to the 1960s.

Dependent Territories
the UK Dependent Territories comprise: Anguilla, Bermuda, British Antarctic Territory, British Indian Ocean, Cayman Islands, Falkland Islands, Gibraltar, Hong Kong, Montserrat, Pitcairn, Henderson, Ducie, Oeno Islands, St Helena, St Helena Dependencies, South Georgia and South Sandwich Islands, Turks and Caicos Islands.

Diffuse pollution
pollution caused by the general use or manufacture of certain substances, which does not readily lend itself to control at the point of use. Examples are the release of solvents into the air through the use of some paints and adhesives, or the discharge of phosphates from washing powders into the sewerage system.

Disinfectant by-products
disinfectants used in waste treatment may react with organic* substances (many of which are naturally present in the environment) and produce chemicals called disinfectant by-products.

Earth Summit
United Nations Conference on Environment and Development*.

EC Directive
a European Community legal instruction, binding on all member states but leaving the method of implementation to national governments, and which must, therefore, generally be transposed into national legislation.

EC Regulation
European Community legislation having immediate and direct legal force in all member states.

Eco-labelling
a scheme of consumer information which awards "labels" to goods which are less harmful to the environment than equivalent brands.

Eco-Management and Audit
voluntary EC scheme to encourage industry to undertake positive environmental management, including regular audits, and to report to the public on their environmental performance.

Ecology
the study of the relationship between living organisms (the biota) and their natural environment.

Ecosystem
a community of interdependent organisms and the environment they inhabit, such as ponds and pond life.

Ecotourism
Environmentally friendly tourism.

Ecotoxicology
the effects of chemical agents on living organisms in the environment, including adverse events that take place in the general ecosystem.

Ecu
European currency unit.

Effluent
liquid waste from industrial, agricultural or sewage plant outlets.

Electrochemistry
the study of chemical change as a result of using energy.

Endemic Species
species of animal or plant confined to a particular region or island and having, so far as is known, originated there.

Environment
external conditions or surroundings in which people, plants and animals live, which tend to influence their development and behaviour. In this Strategy, environment is taken to relate to natural media – air, water, soil, land and natural resources – landscape and the countryside, and man-made developments such as buildings and roads.

Environmental appraisal
the process of defining and examining options, and of weighing costs and benefits before a decision, particularly one having significant environmental costs and/or benefits, is taken.

Environmental capital
the stock of natural (as distinct from man-made) physical assets.

Epidemiology

the branch of medical science concerned with the study of environmental, personal and other factors that determine the incidence of disease.

Eutrophication

the nutrient enrichment of water (especially by compounds of nitrogen and/or phosphorus), causing an accelerated growth of algae and higher forms of plant life, producing an undesirable disturbance in the balance of organisms present and reducing water quality and oxygen content.

Fauna

all animal life.

Fertiliser

any material added to soil to supply nutrients for plant growth.

Flora

all plant life.

Flush

a patch of wet ground, usually on a hillside, where the water flows diffusely and not in a fixed channel.

Framework Convention on Climate Change

signed at UNCED* in 1992 by over 150 countries. Ratifying countries are committed to prepare and report on national strategies to limit emissions of greenhouse gases*.

G7

Group of Seven major industrialised countries: Canada, France, Germany, Italy, Japan, the United Kingdom and the United States.

Genome

all the genetic material contained in a single set of chromosomes of an organism.

Genetically modified organism (GMO)

an organism, for example, a microbe, plant or animal whose genetic make up is modified by molecular techniques in biotechnology*.

Global commons

global natural resources not particular to any one state, such as the atmosphere or the oceans and the fish in them.

Global Environment Facility (GEF)

fund set up in 1992 under management of UN institutions to help developing countries meet the incremental costs of achieving global environmental benefits.

Global warming

the increase in the average temperature of the earth, thought to be caused by build up of greenhouse gases*.

Green Belt

a zone of designated countryside immediately adjacent to a town or city, defined under UK legislation for the purpose of restricting outward expansion of the urban area.

Greenhouse effect

process by which certain gases in the atmosphere behave, in effect, like glass in a greenhouse; glass allows solar radiation in, which heats the interior, but reduces the outward emission of heat radiation.

Greenhouse gases

naturally occurring gases, such as carbon dioxide*, nitrous oxide, methane and ozone*, and man-made gases like chlorofluorocarbons*, which absorb some of the sun's radiation and converts it into heat.

Gross Domestic Product (GDP)

the sum of all incomes derived from the current production of goods and services earned in the economic territory, wherever the earner of the income may reside.

Gross National Product (GNP)

the sum of all incomes earned by citizens of a country. Some of this income arises from abroad but none of it accrues to non-residents.

Ground-level ozone

see ozone.

Groundwater

water held in water-bearing rocks, in pores and fissures underground.

Habitat

the customary dwelling place of a species or community, having particular characteristics, for example, sea shores.

Halons

Volatile but inert compounds of carbon-bromide. Greenhouse gases* and ozone* layer depleters.

Heavy metals

a loose term covering potentially toxic metals used in industrial processes, for example, arsenic, cadmium, chromium, copper, lead, nickel and zinc. Heavy metals may be discharged to the environment and be found as suspended particulate matter in the atmosphere.

High Seas
any fishable waters lying outside all countries' fishing limits.

Hydrocarbons
compounds of hydrogen and carbon which may react in the presence of sunlight and oxides of nitrogen to produce photochemical oxidants.

Hydrochlorofluorocarbons (HCFCs)
used as replacement for CFCs* in refrigeration, foam blowing and aerosols because they are less active ozone-depletors.

Hydrofluorocarbons (HFCs)
halogenated carbons, similar to HCFCs, but not containing chlorine and not, therefore, ozone depletors.

Hydro-electric power
electric power derived from the energy released by water movement.

Insecticide
substance used to kill insects.

Integrated pollution control (IPC)
an approach to pollution control in the UK, which recognises the need to look at the environment as a whole, so that solutions to particular pollution problems take account of potential effects upon all environmental media.

Intensive agriculture
a general term applying to agricultural practices which involve high usage of fertiliser and agrochemicals, mechanisation and so on.

Landfill
waste material used to landscape or reclaim areas of ground; the process of disposing of rubbish in this way.

Leaching
loss of soluble substances from a solid mass by the action of percolating liquid (such as the loss of nitrate from soil into water).

Loam
soil of medium texture composed of roughly equal proportions of clay, silt and sand.

Local Agenda 21
initiative set out in the publication *Agenda 21: a guide for local authorities in the UK* (the Local Government Management Board).

Macrophyte
plants that can be seen by the naked eye.

Man-made soils
soils formed in material modified or created by human activity, for example, soils containing manures or refuse, or resulting from unusually deep cultivation, or soil forming materials for use in land restoration following mining or quarrying.

Marginal land
typically, land of poor quality for agricultural use, due to adverse soil, site or climate.

Minestone
waste rock from collieries.

Monoculture
repeated cultivation of a single crop on a given area of land.

Mutagenicity
the property of a physical, chemical or biological agent to induce mutation in living cells.

Natural resource accounts
accounts showing stocks, flows, inputs, outputs and balances for natural resources such as water, minerals or forests. These may be in physical terms or converted to monetary values. They can be used to help in the management of natural resources which are exploited by man.

Nitrate
a major component of many fertilisers and a natural product of the breakdown of organic matter in soil. It is highly soluble in water and is easily leached from soil.

Nitrogen dioxide (NO_2)
an oxide of nitrogen which mainly arises from fuel combustion in vehicles, boilers and furnaces, which is toxic in high concentrations and contributes to ozone* formation and acid rain*.

Nitrogen oxides (NOx)
a range of compounds formed by the oxidation of atmospheric nitrogen. Some of these oxides contribute to acid rain* and smog, and can affect the stratospheric* ozone* layer.

Nitrous oxide (N_2O)
a relatively inert oxide of nitrogen emitted by soils and during the manufacturing of nylon. This substance is a potent greenhouse gas*.

Nutrient
substance providing nourishment for plants and animals, for example, nitrogen or phosphorus.

Olefine
man-made or naturally occurring chemical compound containing carbon and hydrogen, which is present in petrol.

Organic
describes any substance containing carbon and hydrogen derived from living organisms.

Organochlorine
any organic compound containing chlorine, for example, PCBs* and pesticides* such as DDT and lindane.

Ozone hole
significant depletion in stratospheric ozone* which has been observed over Antarctica.

Ozone
a naturally occurring chemically reactive form of oxygen which is found as a gas throughout the atmosphere. In the lower atmosphere (ground-level or tropospheric* ozone), it is a secondary pollutant and its formation can be enhanced by other pollutants. In the upper atmosphere (the stratosphere*), the ozone layer protects the earth from harmful ultraviolet radiation.

Particulates
fine, solid particles found in the air or emissions.

Peat soils
predominantly organic soils derived from partially decomposed plant remains that accumulate under waterlogged conditions.

pH
the measurer of acidity or alkalinity of a substance. A neutral substance has a pH of 7.0. pHs below 7 are acidic and those above are alkaline.

Photochemical reaction
chemical reaction where the energy is supplied by sunlight.

Photosynthesis
a process, whereby in the presence of sunlight, green plants take in carbon dioxide* from the atmosphere which combines with water to produce simple sugars. Oxygen is released as a by-product.

Plankton
organisms (plant and animal), many of which are microscopic, living in the surface layers of seas or lakes.

Podzolic soils
soils with dark brown, black or ochreous subsurface layers resulting from the accumulation of iron, aluminium or organic matter leached from upper layers. They normally develop as a result of acid weathering conditions.

Polar vortex
a persistently strong westerly wind circulation over the polar regions which, in the Antarctic, prevents the mixing in of air from other latitudes.

"Polluter pays" principle
states that the cost of measures decided by authorities to ensure that the environment is in an acceptable state should be reflected in the cost of goods and services which cause pollution in production and/or consumption.

Pollution from point sources
pollution from specific sources which can be controlled directly, such as power stations whose emissions to the air can be controlled by scrubbing the exhaust gases, or through the use of cleaner fuel.

Pollutant
a substance which is present at concentrations which cause harm or exceed an environmental quality standard.

Polychlorinated biphenyls (PCBs)
a group of very persistent organochlorine compounds manufactured and used in a range of products until the 1970's. They may still be present in some older electrical equipment.

Polycyclic aromatic hydrocarbons (PAH)
a class of hydrocarbons* of high molecular weight emitted by motor vehicles and other processes where there is incomplete combustion. They are toxic in high concentrations, and some are believed to be carcinogenic*.

Precautionary principle
requires that where there are significant risks of damage to the environment, precautionary action to limit the use of potentially dangerous materials or the spread of potentially dangerous pollutants is taken, even where scientific knowledge is not conclusive, if the balance of likely costs and benefits justifies it.

Produced water
the water, with an inevitable oil content, that is drawn from offshore wells along with oil or gas.

Purse seine net
a single panel of netting deployed in a circle around a shoal of fish; the bottom of the net is then pulled together to form a scoop or "purse".

Radioactivity
the spontaneous disintegration of atomic nuclei, with the emission of usually penetrating radiation or particles.

Radon
a natural radioactive gas which forms in the ground indirectly by the radioactive decay of natural uranium and thorium in soils and rocks, and which mixes with air and seeps into the atmosphere. It is particularly prevalent in granite areas.

Ramsar Convention
originally agreed in 1975 to stem the progressive encroachment on, and loss of, wetlands. There are now 77 parties to the Convention from regions throughout the world.

Red List substances
toxic substances, defined by the UK, which cause the greatest potential threat to the aquatic environment. The list includes some heavy metals, certain pesticides, industrial chemicals and solvents.

Run-off
the flow of surface water from snow melt, rainfall or spring seepage which flows directly into streams, rivers and lakes, rather than being absorbed by the soil.

Salting
an area of low ground regularly inundated with salt water; a salt marsh.

Set-aside
the temporary withdrawal of agricultural land from production.

Sewage
liquid waste from communities, conveyed in sewers. Sewage may be a mixture of domestic sewage effluent from residential areas and industrial liquid waste.

Sewage sludge
semi-solid and solid waste matter produced during sewage treatment.

Silage
crop harvested while green for animal fodder and not dried but preserved by excluding air from storage site.

Silviculture
the growing and tending of trees as a branch of forestry.

Slurry
liquid manure.

Smog
smoke fog which contains gaseous pollutants such as sulphur dioxide*, soot and ash; often used as general description for unusually polluted air, irrespective of the pollutants present.

Sovereign bases
Akrotiri and Dhekelia on the island of Cyprus.

Special waste
controlled waste which consists of, or contains, substances which are "dangerous to life" as defined in UK regulations.

Statement of Forest Principles
agreed at UNCED* in 1992. Countries are encouraged to prepare national plans for sustainable forestry.

Stockholm conference
UN Conference on the Human Environment, 1972.

Stratosphere
upper layer of the atmosphere above the troposphere*, approximately 15–50 km above the earth's surface.

Sulphur dioxide (SO$_2$)
a compound of sulphur and oxygen which is emitted into the atmosphere by the combustion of fuels containing sulphur such as coal, diesel oil and fuel oil. It is toxic at high concentration and contributes to acidity in rain.

Sustainable development
development that meets the needs of the present without compromising the ability of future generations to meet their own needs.

Taxa
term for taxonomic groups at any level (such as species, genera and so on).

Technology Partnership Initiative

scheme to encourage greater technology cooperation between UK businesses and those in developing countries through the provision of information on affordable and proven UK technologies and techniques that contribute to sustainable development.

Trace elements

elements which occur in minute quantities as natural constituents of living organisms and tissues. They are, however, generally harmful in large quantities. Trace elements include lead, silver, cobalt, iron, zinc, nickel, selenium and manganese.

Tributyltin compounds (TBT)

an group of substances, extremely toxic to aquatic life, used in marine anti-fouling agents. It is a "Red List" substance.

Troposphere

lowest layer of the atmosphere, extending to approximately 15 km above the earth's surface.

UNCED

1992 UN Conference on Environment and Development, held in Rio de Janeiro (the 'Earth Summit').

UNCSD

UN Commission on Sustainable Development, set up in 1993 under the aegis of the UN to monitor progress in implementing the agreements made at UNCED*.

"User pays" principle

the principle that payment for the use of goods and services ought to reflect the full cost of the resources used. This usually refers to the provision of collective goods and services such as water and roads.

Volatile organic compounds (VOCs)

organic compounds which evaporate readily and contribute to air pollution, mainly through the production of secondary pollutants (for example, ozone).

Water table

the upper surface of permanent groundwater* saturation. The depth of the water table varies according to the season and climatic factors, the overlying topography and the nature of the bedrock.

Western approaches

the part of the Atlantic Ocean to the South of Ireland, to the South and West of Lands End, and to the West of Brittany, which lies within EC member states' 200 mile fishing zones.

ANNEX II: ABBREVIATIONS

Only abbreviations that appear more than once in the text are listed

AFRC
Agricultural and Food Research Council

AONB
Area of Outstanding Natural Beauty

ASSI
Area of Special Scientific Interest (Northern Ireland)

BATNEEC
Best available techniques not entailing excessive cost

BBSRC
Biotechnology and Biological Sciences Research Council

BPEO
Best practicable environmental option

BRE
Building Research Establishment

BRECSU
Building Research Energy Conservation Support Unit

BREEAM
Building Research Establishment Environmental Assessment Method

BW
British Waterways

CAP
EC Common Agricultural Policy

CBA
Cost benefit analysis

CBI
Confederation of British Industry

CCW
Countryside Commission for Wales

CEE
Council for Environmental Education

CFC
Chlorofluorocarbon

CFP
EC Common Fisheries Policy

CHP
Combined Heat and Power

CITES
Convention on International Trade in Endanged Species

CO
Carbon monoxide

CO_2
Carbon dioxide

CSD
UN Commission on Sustainable Development (UNCSD)

DEMOS
DTI's Environmental Management Options Scheme

DFE
Department for Education

DOE
Department of the Environment

DOE(NI)
Department of Environment for Northern Ireland

DOT
Department of Transport

DTI
Department of Trade and Industry

DWI
Drinking Water Inspectorate

EAF
Environmental Action Fund

EEO
Energy Efficiency Office

EC
European Community

EN
English Nature

EPA [1990]
Environmental Protection Act 1990

EQS
Environmental Quality Standard

ESA
Environmentally Sensitive Area

ESRC
Economic and Social Research Council

ETIS
Environmental Technology Innovation Scheme

EUREKA
European high technology programme

FC
Forestry Commission

FCO
Foreign and Commonwealth Office

FGD
Flue-gas desulphurisation

FHE
Further and Higher Education

FPO
Fish Producers' Organisation

FSU
Former Soviet Union

FWAG
Farming and Wildlife Advisory Group

GATT
General Agreement on Tariffs and Trade

GB
Great Britain: England, Scotland and Wales

GDP
Gross Domestic Product

GEF
Global Environment Facility

GMO
Genetically modified organism

GNP
Gross National Product

G7
Group of Seven major industrialised countries

HBFC
Hydrobromofluorocarbon

HEI
Higher education institution

HCFC
Hydrochlorofluorocarbon

HFC
Hydrofluorocarbon

HMIP
Her Majesty's Inspectorate of Pollution

ICC
International Chamber of Commerce

IFIs
International Financial Institutions

IMF
International Monetary Fund

IPC
Integrated pollution control

IPCC
Inter-governmental Panel on Climate Change

IT
Information Technology

ITTO
International Tropical Timber Organisation

JNCC
Joint Nature Conservancy Council

LCP
Large combustion plant

LCPD
Large Combustion Plant Directive

LECs
Local Enterprise Councils

LFA
Less Favoured Areas

MAFF
Ministry of Agriculture, Fisheries and Food

MPA
Mineral Planning Authority (England & Wales)

MPG
Mineral Planning Guidance Note (England & Wales)

NCC
Nature Conservancy Council

NERC
Natural Environmental Research Council

NFFO
Non-Fossil Fuel Obligation

NGO
Non-governmental organisation

NIMBY
"Not in my back yard"

NNP
Net National Product

NNR
National Nature Reserve

NO₂
Nitrogen dioxide

NOₓ
Nitrogen oxides

N₂O
Nitrous oxide

NRA
National Rivers Authority

NPPG
National Planning Policy Guidance (Scotland)

NRTF
National Road Traffic Forcast

NSA
Nitrate Sensitive Area
National Scenic Area (Scotland)

ODA
Overseas Development Administration

OECD
Organisation for Economic Co-operation and Development

OPCS
Office of Population Censuses and Surveys

PAN
Planning Advice Note (Scotland)

PCBs
Polychlorinated biphenyls

PPG
Planning Policy Guidance Note (England & Wales)

PSCs
Polar stratospheric clouds

PWS
Public water supply

R & D
Research and Development

RCEP
Royal Commission on Environmental Pollution

RSNC
Royal Society for Nature Conservation

RSPB
Royal Society for the Protection of Birds

SAC
Special Area of Conservation

SACTRA
Standing Advisory Committee on Trunk Road Assessment

SERC
Science and Engineering Research Council

SNH
Scottish Natural Heritage

SO₂
Sulphur dioxide

SPA
Special Protection Area

SSSI
Site of Special Scientific Interest (Britain)

SWQO
Statutory Water Quality Objective

TACs
Total Allowable Catches

TECs
Training and Enterprise Councils (England)

TPO
Tree Preservation Order

UK
United Kingdom: England, Scotland, Wales & Northern Ireland

UNCED
1992 UN Conference on Environment and Development

UNCSD
UN Commission on Sustainable Development

UNDP
UN Development Programme

UNECE
UN Economic Commission for Europe

UNEP
UN Environmental Programme

UWWT
Urban Waste Water Treatment (EC Directive)

VAT
Value Added Tax

VOC
Volatile organic compound

WGS
Woodland Grants Scheme

WHO
World Health Organisation

WQO
Water Quality Objective

WWF(UK)
World Wide Fund for Nature

INTRODUCTION

1 The Government published a consultation paper on the UK Strategy for Sustainable Development in July 1993. At its launch, the Secretary of State for the Environment invited views from all interested organisations and individuals. The paper itself had built on an earlier round of consultations initiated in November 1992, a seminar held in March 1993 at Oxford for over 100 representatives and ongoing meetings with interested organisations.

2 This Annex summarises the written representations received to the consultation paper from over 500 bodies and individuals. Approximately 35% came from local government, 20% from the voluntary sector, 10% from professional bodies or consultants, 15% from business, 5% from the academic sector, 5% from statutory bodies and 10% from individuals. These representations were taken into account during the preparation of the Strategy. This Annex follows the main subject areas outlined in the consultation paper; the Strategy follows a similar structure.

PRINCIPLES

3 Of those who commented on the scope of the Strategy, about half welcomed the Government's attempt to tackle the subject in a comprehensive; but wide-ranging way and about half considered that the consultation paper did little more than present a review of issues and was a lost opportunity for strong action. A very large proportion of those commenting on the principles of the Strategy felt that the Government should establish a rolling process to set, monitor and act on aims and targets. Many felt that the stated objectives in many areas were vague and sometimes complacent.

4 Responses were almost equally divided over whether the proposed timescale was about right or whether it should be longer, between 30 and 500 years. A number of respondents suggested that a mix of short term and interim plans and a longer-term strategy was required.

5 There was general agreement with the "precautionary principle" among those who responded. Many who commented agreed with the "polluter pays principle"; however, some considered that this became the "consumer pays" in reality, and that identifying the polluter to be held responsible was not always straightforward.

6 About a quarter of the people who replied had comments to make on the definition and principles of sustainable development. Some held that development and economic growth were not compatible with the goal of sustainability at all and that mankind should accept that the carrying capacity of the world with its finite resources is limited. A significant number commented that measures of development should pay heed to notions of alleviating poverty and to social justice and equity as well as environmental issues, and that improvements in the quality of life should not just rest on economic factors. Others also pointed to the disparity between consumption and growth in the West and the needs of developing countries, and asserted that international equity should be a principle of sustainable development.

7 Other views expressed were that economic growth remained essential so that wealth creation could be used to manage and protect the environment; that development could be held to be sustainable where it improved individuals' living standards at little or no cost to future generations and where any costs were compensated for, and that sustainable development, as defined, gave too much weight to trade-offs between economics and the environment.

ENVIRONMENTAL MEDIA AND RESOURCES

8 There were many varied comments on this Section of the consultation paper. On the subject of **population**, the majority of comments focused upon the need for a general reduction in the world population if there is to be an equitable consumption of finite resources, and also on the need to address the question of what upper limit on population can be sustained in the UK. Specific issues raised were the high retirement-age population in the UK; the need to consider how the rising and changing population should be housed; two comments that immigration into the UK should be controlled, and a suggestion that environmental degradation can be associated with a declining population as well as an expanding one.

9 On **health and environment**, comments covered the need to acknowledge that there were strong links between poverty and ill health and the extra vulnerability of children and the elderly; worries that standards relevant to health were not currently being achieved, for example in drinking water and air pollution; that sustainable policies in other areas such as transport and energy would lead to better health, and a proposal that healthier lifestyles should be promoted widely. A number of organisations wanted to see more research and monitoring into various areas, for instance, the links between a poor built environment, traffic, health and the increase in allergic conditions, and the effect of dust from large developments. Better information gathering, with medical data coordinated with environmental quality data, and more information on the chemical risk to health were also proposed.

10 There were many comments relating to the effect of vehicle emissions on **global atmosphere**; these are dealt with in the discussion of the responses on traffic. Other points raised concerning the atmosphere were the need to act internationally against an agreed carbon emissions baseline; a suggestion that there could be a system of tradeable permits to control emissions; that methane gas and ultraviolet light should also be monitored as well as carbon dioxide, and that climate instability was also a factor to be taken into account. A few responses also pointed out that the effect of aircraft pollution on ozone depletion should not be underestimated.

11 In commenting on **air quality**, respondents were equally divided about whether the development of technology would ameliorate the problems of air pollution or could itself have a detrimental effect. It was suggested that targets to reduce pollution should be kept high and that all sources of harmful emissions (not only traffic) should be targeted; also that stronger action should be taken to ban harmful products and enforce flue gas desulphurisation on fossil fuel burning stacks. There was a consensus of opinion among those commenting that there should be an expansion of the national air pollution monitoring scheme, with a standard system of monitoring and improved data. Some commented on the harmful effects of poor air quality on historic buildings and in larger urban areas.

12 There were many comments on the supply and management of **freshwater**. The majority of respondents commented on the need effectively to manage and control the increased demands on water supply by a variety of means, from water metering, a national transfer of surplus water to areas of shortage, the greater use of 'grey water' particularly for non-drinking domestic use, and better management of the distribution and maintenance of water supplies, including stopping leakage. Respondents wanted higher standards of water quality, greater powers for the National Rivers Authority to improve quality, and better protection of groundwater supplies from contamination. Comments on the sea related to the need to treat all sewage before releasing it into seawater; consideration of the effects of dredging; treatment of oil on beaches, and the need for a strategic coastal policy.

13 Most of the comments on **soil** concentrated on the need not to underestimate or sideline the importance of soil erosion or the extent to which it had taken place, and to combat any further erosion. Suggestions were made that soil analysis should be carried out on a long term basis; that soil compaction was as important an issue as erosion; that wind erosion was also a problem, and that alternatives to peat for horticultural use should continue to be investigated. A few responses also referred to the value of hedgerows in reducing soil erosion.

14 Responses on **land use and cover** are summarised in the Section on economic activities, other than responses on the built heritage. Nearly all the comments on the **built heritage** considered that the consultation paper did not place enough emphasis on conserving and protecting this irreplaceable asset; the importance of not losing historic, archaeological and cultural elements of the environment was stressed.

15 There were mixed views concerning **mining, minerals and aggregates**. Most of those involved in the mining or aggregates industries felt that extraction itself was usually environmentally neutral as long as high standards were set in the restoration of sites, and that the benefits of the industry were vital for the functioning of modern society; they generally recommended maximum use of current workings and limiting the development of new sources. They also wanted to avoid the 'sterilisation' of minerals or aggregates sites by other forms of development. On the other hand, a number of people felt that the impact on the environment and the detrimental effect of road transportation of materials

from sites meant that a reduced demand for aggregates should be encouraged. Some pointed out that a change in policy towards road building would reduce substantially both the amount of aggregates needed and the disruption caused by transporting them, and that a greater use of recycled building and other suitable material would also reduce demand for new extractions. A few people were opposed to continued opencast mining because of the blight it caused and the eyesore it constituted whilst in operation.

16 About 10% of those who responded to the paper commented on **wildlife and habitats**. All of them wanted to see a better system of protection against encroachment from development, particularly by roads, and many mentioned stronger powers of designation and instituting the principle of inviolability into decisions affecting wildlife and habitats; Areas of Outstanding Natural Beauty and Sites of Special Scientific Interest (SSSIs) were not thought to provide powerful enough protection. Other comments included the importance of safeguarding and replanting hedgerows as a refuge for wildlife; better conservation of seed and species, especially indigenous trees, and giving wildlife a much higher priority in planning decisions, farming and tourism policies. The possible conflict between SSSI designation, bird protection and water extraction needs was mentioned. A few responses also referred to the need for sites of geological and geomorphological interest to have better protection as these were as irreplaceable as some wildlife sites.

17 Many replies on **environmental indicators** advocated the need for an agreed set of national indicators, and a few recommended that the UK should move towards international environmental standards. Suggestions were made that the indicators should reflect environmental and human welfare, and also reflect progress against targets as well as the critical pathways by which damage occurs. A few responses mentioned the need for sound scientific knowledge to avoid the risk of emotive reactions to unsubstantiated dangers; many referred to the need for better guidance and advice which was objective and could be used in all aspects of decision-making. Mention was made of the use of Tranquil area maps showing the decline in undisturbed countryside. Local monitoring stations were suggested, as was the use of seismic monitoring stations for baseline environmental data, and also the idea that monitoring

should be a joint exercise by the Government and local authorities; but others felt that an independent agency should be set up to monitor standards so that it would be seen to be objective. About 20% of all responses said that the most important task was for the Government to have an agreed programme of aims, targets and priorities that were monitored and acted upon.

ECONOMIC ACTIVITIES AND SUSTAINABILITY

18 A great many comments were received on Section 3 of the consultation paper dealing with economic activities and sustainability. About 15% of all those who replied commented on **agriculture**. Approximately half of those wanted to see a much greater move towards, and Government support for, organic farming as the most sustainable form of agriculture, and a few advocated permaculture as the next stage. Organic methods were not only supported as better for the conservation of wildlife and species and as a factor in better health for the consumer, but also as a lower user of water resources than intensive and chemical methods, and free-range farming as less polluting than battery farms. One response pointed out that not all chemical uses were harmful or all developments in farming detrimental to wildlife.

19 The effect of the EC Common Agricultural Policy on UK farming was generally deplored as too short term in outlook and as a detrimental influence on the quality of the countryside; some also feared similar effects from the GATT talks. A significant proportion of people wanted to see a move away from set-aside land policies towards more productive use of the land, but others pointed out advantages that could accrue from integrating the management of set-aside land with, for instance, conservation policies.

20 Some wanted to see a framework or national plan for farming to allow agriculture to operate sustainably even if this ran counter to market forces; smaller farms and local production for local needs were advocated. Others commented that the potential steady release of surplus farming land should be planned to make the best sustainable use of it; that the wider social and economic value of agricultural land should be recognised and supported, and that a rural strategy, which involved converting redundant buildings to new uses and reversing manpower trends to develop a working countryside, should be investigated.

21 Comments on **forestry and urban trees** covered a number of main areas. A few responses advocated the use of trees as a commercial crop to help in replacing fossil fuels. Some suggested that there should be a target for land coverage by trees; that they could be planted to make use of otherwise redundant set-aside and contaminated land; that as an industry, forestry should be integrated, renewable and more financially-viable; that imports, especially of non-sustainable hardwoods, should be reduced and more of the UK's timber needs should be produced domestically. However, a number of people also commented that forestry for commercial purposes was not necessarily sustainable in itself and affected the yield and quality of water catchment; that ancient and deciduous woodlands were still being lost and should be replaced instead of planting conifers, and that better financing should be available for mixed planting. Some also felt that the privatisation of the Forestry Commission should be halted until the environmental considerations were fully assessed. A number of people commented on the desirability of maintaining a tree-planting programme in urban areas.

22 A variety of responses on **fisheries** pointed to the need to promote more conservation-based fishery techniques; to review UK law; to tackle over-capacity and support voluntary species protection, and to provide safe inshore havens for fish. A few pointed to the many environmental disbenefits in fish farming.

23 **Manufacturing and services** and **voluntary action by industry** attracted comments on a wide range of issues. Many of those involved in manufacturing and commerce commented that there was a gradual move towards more sustainable behaviour and awareness by industry, that there could be commercial advantage from behaving in an environmentally sound way, but that legislative changes should be made gradually to give time to adjust. They emphasised the need to consult and to be allowed to compete on equal terms with companies in other countries. It was pointed out that small firms were less likely to change their unsustainable practices voluntarily because the cost to them was proportionately much greater, and that they often had to scale down and adapt pollution control techniques developed by other sectors, and at a heavier cost. However, some responses queried whether industry was really changing its behaviour without compulsion and pointed out that it is hard to measure the environmental performance of companies locally. Others feared that companies subject to stringent pollution controls in the UK might opt to move their businesses to other countries where controls were less strict.

24 There were very few comments on **biotechnology;** these stressed the vital importance of keeping any developments well-supervised and under control. A system of international agreements was proposed.

25 Over 20% of replies dealt with **energy** issues. About half of these agreed that it was vital to encourage energy conservation through more stringent building regulations, responsibility placed on the building industry to use more efficient materials, better insulation, combined heat and power schemes, and through fiscal and other measures. A significant number suggested alternative energy sources, including utilising solar energy which could be implemented via building regulations and installed in new buildings; wind and tidal energy; biofuels such as sewage sludge and straw; liquefied natural gas and using redundant farmland for growing suitable materials. A plan for better conservation and use of dwindling fossil fuel reserves was recommended, as was the need for a long term national policy based on environmental considerations; some responses pointed out that a sustainable energy policy should not be market led but needed to be directed and promoted actively. Most of the comments on nuclear power were against its continued use and further development. As well as worries about its effect on the environment, disposal of waste, and safety, many felt it was neither cheap nor efficient, although the nuclear power companies recommended its continued use. More research and development into cleaner fuels was also requested.

26 Nearly 20% of those who replied had comments to make about **waste disposal and recycling**. Many responses felt that a waste strategy should concentrate initially on reducing the amount of waste produced, discouraging excess packaging and junk mail. Many supported recycling schemes and made various suggestions about how the rate of recycling could be increased, for instance by way of investing in a proper infrastructure; making sorted waste for recycling part of the routine waste collection system; making greater use of recycled building materials; labelling products at manufacture; selling only returnable bottles, and concentrating on producing useable end products. But many also commented on

the problems of recycled waste; while some products seemed to be successful, such as aluminium recycling and horticultural products, many people felt that the market for recycled material was too uncertain and unreliable and felt that the Government should promote and create better outlets. The costs of recycling, both obvious and concealed, were also a drawback to meeting higher targets, and some felt that more funding and planning of schemes was needed and that recycling should only be part of an integrated national policy for waste disposal which would continue to permit landfill and, as some argued, controlled incineration.

27 There were a number of replies on **chemicals and contaminated land**. Most comments on the latter supported registers of contaminated land, although recognising some of the associated problems. Some respondents felt that there should be higher penalties for the dumping of contaminated waste but others commented that, if the controls were too stringent, it would simply lead to more illegal and dangerous dumping. Some commented that the dangers from the use of chemicals should not be exaggerated and that beneficial uses should be encouraged. Others wanted to see a general reduction in chemical use; it was pointed out that long term disadvantages often outweighed short term benefits, for instance, where pesticides had given rise to resistant pests.

28 Over one third of the responses commented on **transport.** The vast majority of these considered that an unrestrained road-building programme must be halted and that the growth in road traffic must be tackled. Many remarked that the consultation paper appeared simply to accept the projections for increased harmful emissions from traffic without questioning them and that this directly conflicted with any attempt to have a sustainable policy towards the global atmosphere and air quality. Others commented that the road programme was detrimental to conservation and wildlife objectives and took a disproportionate amount of land. However, one response supported the selective building of more town and village bypasses to improve the quality of life for local residents.

29 About half of those who responded on this issue wanted a national integrated transport policy which had much higher environmental priorities and encouraged a shift away from road-building. Most of these people wanted to see a shift towards affordable and sustainable public transport as an alternative to car use. Many proposed greater use of the railways, especially for the movement of freight; some considered that the proposed privatisation of the railways would not be compatible with sustainable objectives. There were also a number of suggestions that the waterways should carry more freight. It was also proposed that an environmentally integrated policy was needed at EC level.

30 Apart from better public transport, other methods suggested to reduce car use were a combination of fiscal disincentives, such as road tolls, a tax on use and fuel taxes, and also the promotion of walking and cycling as healthy alternatives. The motoring organisations and some others argued that cars brought about social benefits and choice, and that road tax paid for road building, but felt that research should be concentrated on making cars cleaner and more fuel efficient. A few responses claimed that the road system in the UK needed to be maintained and improved in order to keep it competitive with Europe and some also pointed out that car use was necessary to provide accessibility for rural areas. One letter welcomed the introduction of increased lorry axle weights as encouraging a better use of large lorries, while another condemned it.

31 A significant proportion of responses mentioned the need to attempt to reduce the demand for mobility, by using planning policies to foster self-sufficient local settlements and reduce the need for transportation of goods and commuting to work.

32 Many people mentioned that transport strategy should be an important part of **development in town and country** and also in **land use planning** which is referred to in the consultation paper as one of the ways of promoting sustainability. As the comments on planning issues (constituting slightly under 10% of the total responses) generally covered both aspects, they are dealt with together in this Annex.

33 Many of the comments, particularly those from local government, suggested that a clearer lead and better advice and guidance should be given on how to put sustainable objectives into practice within the planning system. All felt that environmental priorities should be more important than they appear to be now; some thought that there should be a basic presumption against any new development unless it could be

convincingly proved to be necessary. The principle of carrying out environmental assessments of schemes should be extended and they should be carried out more effectively. A number of respondents felt that stronger powers were needed, including for compulsory purchase.

34 Specific planning issues mentioned included the encouragement of urban green space and open areas; better use of derelict land and historic buildings; restricting the spread of large supermarkets and other out of town developments; better and more sophisticated use of low-energy housing development, with new housing built in the least environmentally damaging places; the concept of Earth Sheltered Development which could be suited to new domestic and industrial sites; and a better recognition of the social and economic needs of rural areas along with strategic planning for the countryside. Consultation with the business community at the outset of development plans was requested, as was a more sensitive treatment of high density urban areas.

35 There were also a significant number of comments about **tourism and recreation** policies. It was suggested that the attractions of both the natural and the built heritage should be regarded as part of the UK's economic capital and treated as such, and that these assets should be the subject of as enthusiastic conservation as other resources. Some considered that National Parks and other attractions should be treated as irreplaceable natural assets and not solely as income generators and that they should be accorded importance in their own right and not just as a recreational resource. A number of people made the point that tourism was beneficial to local communities. However, most agreed that large scale or unrestrained tourism could damage the very environment which was the initial attraction and that it should be properly managed, with more environmentally sustainable tourism encouraged. Local level, integrated tourism management programmes with pilot or demonstration schemes were suggested, as was better and more sensitive management of the National Parks.

36 One response requested that tourism and recreation should not be treated together, as recreation and sporting activity tended to be given lower importance. A plea was made that school playing fields should not be sold since this would curtail sporting opportunities. A few replies wanted land to be set aside for the enjoyment of peace and quiet as an objective in its own right, and commented that inappropriate sporting and other activity in parks and open places should be discouraged.

PUTTING SUSTAINABILITY INTO PRACTICE

37 This Section of the consultation paper concentrated on the processes by which the UK can pursue sustainable development both for itself and as a member of the international community. Many responses were received on **international influences** and also **overseas aid** which are dealt with together in this Annex. Most of the comments referred to the need for the UK to develop its policies towards the environment and sustainable development in conjunction with other nations; some stressed that companies must have a 'level playing field' as regards regulations and requirements; others that any efforts made by the UK would only be effective if they were part of wider action. Many people also referred to the position of developing countries and the Eastern bloc, where ambitions and aspirations for development should be acknowledged but also encouraged to develop in a sustainable way. Some felt that developed countries would have to stop growing to allow others to catch up and a few commented that Third World debt should be written off to the mutual benefit of those countries and the West.

38 Others commented that sustainable technology and the results of research and good practice should be more widely disseminated to developing countries; that small and sustainable projects should be encouraged rather than huge schemes that damaged local habitats and restructured indigenous agriculture; that the World Bank and the International Monetary Fund should reform their practices which overrode national systems and requirements and encouraged a dependence on western industry, and that aid should target environmental problems rather than trade promotion. The effect of the UK economy on other nations and the impact of tourism abroad were also mentioned. A few comments referred to the influence that the UK could have on other countries through the UN Commission on Sustainable Development, and through inter-agency cooperation between officials at working level.

39 Over 15% of all replies commented on the role of **central government** in implementing sustainable

development. The need for the Government to have a clear framework for action with targets and objectives in its strategy was mentioned earlier. A significant proportion of those who responded considered that the Government should better integrate its own policies and avoid giving contradictory messages from different departments; some highlighted the apparent conflict between the policies of the Departments of Transport and Environment. A substantial number of people also wanted the Government to give a much clearer lead in behaving sustainably, with more open decision-making and more participation by informed outside bodies. A few responses commented that the Government should adopt environmental principles in its own procurement and management policies. Some felt that the Government gave the impression of being complacent about the problems, too short term in its view, and not wanting to go beyond what it was forced into doing.

40 While the idea of a 'Green Minister' in each Government Department was welcomed by some, it was suggested that there should also be a Minister with a clear environmental assessment role for all policies. Others wanted to see formal structures to institute appropriate management strategies for sustainability; a 'round table' process with both the public and the private sectors and other agencies; the institution of an Environmental Agency; and, generally, more systems and agencies for handling sustainability issues. One response, however, commented that a strategy for sustainability could not be imposed from the centre but would have to come about by individuals and organisations being motivated. Many responses stressed the need for urgent action, pointing out that irreplaceable assets were slipping away and problems getting out of hand.

41 Nearly 15% of the responses commented on the role of **local government**. Most felt that local government could and should be vital in promoting and enforcing sustainability because it was uniquely placed to liaise with organisations and people at local level as well as with central government. Many referred to the Local Agenda 21 schemes and their place in individual authorities' plans. A large number of authorities remarked that they could operate sustainable development more effectively with better funding; even a minimal level of action had resource implications and many felt hampered from taking more radical action by lack of funds. Many also wanted better and more detailed practical guidance

and targets, and the removal of unnecessary restrictions from the centre. Environmentally sound decisions taken at local level were not necessarily best in the national interest and a number of people sought more guidance on these issues. Some felt that they needed stronger powers to implement effective initiatives. Other suggestions were for less adversarial fora to discuss development issues at local levels; more systems to allow local government to assess its own performance; better dissemination of good practice; and a duty on local government to collect and report on environmental indicators and enforce best practice in all areas, and to act sustainably itself.

42 The role of **voluntary organisations** and the **general public** were the subject of a number of responses. They ranged over the need for better funding for non-profit making organisations to take a wider role in raising awareness of environmental issues; more structures for informal and formal participation in decision-making, and suggestions for ways in which local communities and groups can get involved in voluntary initiatives. Many pointed out that the voluntary sector was uniquely placed to take sustainable development forward in broad and issue-led ways by using a variety of approaches and developing cross-sectoral partnerships.

43 Section 4 of the consultation paper also asked for views on the various instruments which could be used to influence people's behaviour and attitudes. About 20% of the comments received concentrated on the issue of **regulation and economic instruments**. Of these, 75% were opposed to any deregulation in the field of pollution control, arguing that the issue was too important to be market-led; and that there was too much scope for abuse and too much temptation for cost-cutting if a strong regulatory system was weakened. Many people felt that there should be a combination of strong regulations and economic instruments, where appropriate, and that both of these control methods had their place in the Strategy. Those who favoured more deregulation and a greater use of economic instruments argued that positive incentives based on the polluter pays principle were more effective; some said that economic instruments should be applied even-handedly and be fiscally neutral.

44 Comments on **environmental accounting and appraisal** generally favoured greater use of environmental accounting techniques in many areas, and more information about how to use them. The

accountancy profession itself was making moves towards the 'Greening of Accountancy' and the concept of natural capital. The idea of 'whole-life' accounting for a product was also suggested so that the long term gains and disadvantages could be seen. Some felt that current concepts of environmental appraisal were still too dependent on quantifying values and feared that this meant social and other issues would not be properly assessed; it was suggested that this type of appraisal was much more complex and sophisticated than often realised, but that it was a valuable way of getting people to think of long term environmental consequences even if these could not be properly quantified.

45 The role of **education and training** in sustainable development attracted comment in about 12% of the replies; most comments focused on formal education and the generation of publicity as a means of educating the public. Many respondents felt that education was a fundamental aspect of sustainable development, as a change in attitude could not be forced on to respondents, only brought about by education. A number of people commented that schools and colleges should focus on a holistic approach to environmental issues, starting with local problems and working up to global issues and their interrelationship; that schools and colleges should have "ecological areas", and that children's interest in the environment should be stimulated in a moral framework as well as a social and economic one. There were suggestions that companies should participate by educating their workforce in sustainable issues and that the professions, many of which already incorporated environmental awareness into their training, should become more involved.

46 Some felt that the public were still largely unaware of the real issues and that informal education methods were needed to make them aware, for instance,

through further publicity campaigns about energy conservation; more emphasis on the balance between economic and environmental development, and information about the consequences of failure to act sustainably or alternatively, visions of a sustainable future. Others suggested the use of the media, especially television, to incorporate messages and information about the environment into popular programmes.

47 **Environmental technology and research** attracted various comments. Some respondents supported further funding for research into cleaner technology and its use to encourage more sustainable lifestyles; others felt that new technology alone was not the answer to problems which only a fundamental shift in general attitudes would resolve. There were suggestions that research should be more open and better coordinated to avoid duplication of effort; that a distinction should be made between research for commercial purposes and centrally-funded research, and that laboratories, such as Warren Springs, should remain open and be well-funded.

OTHER COMMENTS

48 There were a number of comments from respondents who felt that the Strategy should tackle issues that were not specifically covered in the consultation paper; most of these related to developing alternative lifestyles and priorities. Some people put forward suggestions for self-contained, self-sufficient ways of living whereby production and employment would be on a local basis. Others considered that the current work culture should be reviewed; that flexible working patterns should be tried, including using new technology to encourage much greater working from home, and that opportunities should be provided for people to try alternative sustainable lifestyles without commitment.

ANNEX IV: TECHNICAL ANNEX

This Annex gives for each Figure and Table in the Strategy (and for certain items of text):

* where the information has been published, the published source. If the information has not been published, the Government Department or organisation responsible for providing the information.
* comments about the data (for example explanatory remarks, accuracy of estimates, data limitations, underlying assumptions) and the original data source (if different from the published source).

CHAPTER 5

Figure 5.1
Population trends and projections 1972–2031, UK

Source:
Office of Population Censuses and Surveys, Government Actuary's Department, General Register Office (Scotland), General Register Office (Northern Ireland).

Comments:
Data for 1972 are mid-year estimates of the resident population. Projections for 1992 to 2031 are based on mid-year estimates of the resident population for 1991.

Figure 5.2
Population by age group 1992–2031, UK

Source:
Office of Population Censuses and Surveys, Government Actuary's Department, General Register Office (Scotland), General Register Office (Northern Ireland).

Comments:
Projections for 1992–2031 are based on the 1991 mid- year estimates for resident population.

Figure 5.3
Population change 1982–2012, UK

Source:
Office of Population Censuses and Surveys

Comments:
Data for England are for standard regions. Projections for 1992–2012 are based on 1989 mid-year estimates.

Figure 5.4
Average household size 1972–2012, UK

Source:
Department of the Environment; Welsh Office; Scottish Office Environment Department; Department of the Environment (Northern Ireland).

Comments:
Numbers of households derived from 1989 based OPCS population estimates and projections, marital status projections, and trends in household formation derived from the censuses and the Labour Force Survey. One-person households may share a dwelling.

Figure 5.5
Number of households by marital status 1972–2012, England and Wales

Source:
Department of the Environment; Welsh Office.

Comments:
Numbers of households derived from 1989-based population estimates and projections. Marital status projections and household formation estimates in Labour Force Survey. Lone parent households include one or more never married children of any age.

Figure 5.6
GDP and consumers' expenditure per capita (1990 prices) 1972–92, UK

Source:
Central Statistical Office.

Comments:
Data for GDP and disposable income at 1990 prices. Per capita estimates derived from OPCS 1991 mid-year population estimates.

CHAPTER 6

Figure 6.1
Areas where sea level increases could have a significant impact, GB.

Source:
UK Climate Change Impacts Review Group, (1991). The Potential Effects of Climate Change in the United Kingdom. HMSO.

Figure 6.2
Annual average central England (and global) temperature anomalies, 1660-1990.

Source:
Department of the Environment, (1992). *The UK Environment.* HMSO.

Comments:
Mean annual temperature for four sites in central England recorded over the last three centuries, shown as differences from the 1951–80 average. The recent warming over England is probably a reflection of global changes but other fluctuations may be due to changes in atmospheric circulation. Information provided by the Meteorological Office (Hadley Centre).

Figure 6.3
Historical and possible future trends in carbon dioxide emissions by source and by final energy user, 1970–2000, UK

Source:
National Atmospheric Environmental Inventory and Department of Trade and Industry, (1992). *Energy Related Carbon Emissions in Possible Future Scenarios for the UK*; Energy Paper No 59. DTI.

Comments:
Historical carbon dioxide emissions for a given year are accurate to within +/– 5% but the trend is likely to be more reliable. Uncertainties in estimation arise from using a single carbon content for each fuel source and also because of uncertainties in emissions from non-fuel sources. For final user categories, a simple pro rata method of reallocating estimated emissions from power stations and other fuel processing industries to final energy users has been adopted. Because of this, emissions by final energy user are subject to more uncertainty than those by source. Projections are based on central GDP growth (2.25% pa) and low fuel price assumptions.

Figure 6.4
Historical and possible future trends in carbon dioxide emissions, 1970–2020, UK

Source:
National Atmospheric Environmental Inventory and Department of Trade and Industry, (1992). *Energy Related Carbon Emissions in Possible Future Scenarios for the UK*; Energy Paper No 59. DTI.

Comments:
Scenarios of carbon dioxide emissions are based on a set of interlocking models of the energy market. Major inputs to the model are assumptions about GDP growth (high 2.75% pa, central 2.25% pa, low 1.75% pa) coupled with assumptions concerning trends in fuel prices.

Figure 6.5
Total ozone trends as percentage reductions per decade according to latitude and season

Source:
UK Stratospheric Ozone Review Group, (1991). *Stratospheric Ozone 1991.* HMSO.

Comments:
Based on satellite measurements by the Total Ozone Mapping Spectrometer (TOMS). The TOMS measurements form an internally consistent data set which no longer relies on ground-based instruments for calibration.

Figure 6.6
Chlorine loading 1980–2020

Source:
UK Stratospheric Ozone Review Group, (1991). *Stratospheric Ozone 1991.* HMSO.

Comments:
Current chlorine loading estimates are accurate within +/– 0.2ppb.

Table 6.1
Montreal Protocol and EC target reductions for ozone depleting substances

Source:
Department of the Environment, (1993). *Digest of Environmental Protection and Water Statistics*, No 15. HMSO.

CHAPTER 7

Figure 7.1 Exceedence of critical loads for acidity for UK soils, 1986–1988 data
Source:
UK Critical Loads Mapping Centre, Institute of Terrestrial Ecology, Monkswood.

Figure 7.2

Tropospheric ozone: hourly averages exceeding 100ppb, summer 1990, UK

Source:

Department of the Environment, (1992). *The UK Environment*. HMSO.

Comments:

The number of hours exceeding specified concentrations can vary substantially from year to year. Information provided by Warren Spring Laboratory.

Figure 7.3

Concentrations of sulphur dioxide and smoke at selected sites and EC limit values 1970–1991

Source:

Department of the Environment, (1993). *Digest of Environmental Protection and Water Statistics*, No 15. HMSO.

Comments:

Sites have been chosen to provide a representative UK perspective, and to maximise historic data (ie at least 21 out of 22 years' data available). Information provided by Warren Spring Laboratory.

Figure 7.4

Historical and future trends of carbon monoxide, particulates and VOCs emissions from road transport, 1970–2010, UK

Source:

Warren Spring Laboratory, (1992). *Pollution in the Atmosphere: Future Emissions from the UK*. WSL.

Comments:

Total carbon monoxide and VOC emissions are accurate to +/– 50%, particulate emissions to +/– 20–25%. Uncertainties specific to road transport are not quantified. Projected emissions are based on forecasts of numbers of vehicles and usage last published in 1989. Total traffic is expected to increase by between 85% and 142% by 2015. The main determinant of traffic growth is considered to be growth in GDP, with fuel price having a lesser influence.

Figure 7.5

Consumption of petrol and estimated emissions of lead from petrol-engined vehicles, 1975–1992, UK

Source:

Department of Trade and Industry,(1993). *Digest of United Kingdom Energy Statistics 1992*. Department of the Environment, (1993). *Digest of Environmental Protection and Water Statistics*, No 15. HMSO.

Comments:

The percentage of unleaded petrol consumed has risen from virtually zero in 1987 to over 50% today. Sales are projected to account for around 90% of total sales by 2000 and 100% by 2015. Lead emissions have also decreased because of reductions in the lead content of petrol from 0.45 g/l to 0.40 g/l in 1981, to 0.15 g/l in 1985.

CHAPTER 8

Figure 8.1

Comparison of actual abstractions in 1991 with effective drought rainfall, England and Wales

Source:

National Rivers Authority, (1992) *Water Resources Development Strategy: a Discussion Document*. Department of the Environment, (1993) *Digest of Environmental Protection and Water Statistics*, No 15. HMSO.

Comments:

Figures for effective rainfall are based on the rainfall that would be available during a drought to be expected on average once every 50 years. Actual abstractions exclude abstractions from tidal water and abstractions for fishfarming and watercress growing.

Figure 8.2

Comparison of demand and yield from the developed resources in Scotland, 1991/92

Source:

Scottish Office Environment Department, (1993) *Public Water Resources in Scotland, 1991–2*.

Figure 8.3

Public water supply: present regional surplus of resources as a percentage of 1990 average demand, England and Wales

Source:

National Rivers Authority, (1992) *Water Resources Development Strategy: a Discussion Document*.

Figure 8.4

Public water supply average demand projections for England and Wales to 2021

Source:

National Rivers Authority, (1992) *Water Resources Development Strategy: a Discussion Document.*

Comments:

Baseline demand projections were made for each region and then summed to give an England and Wales figure. Methodology adopted was different in each of the regions, but the main factors used in making each projection were changes in population, per capita consumption, losses in the mains system and at consumers premises and level of economic activity. Upper and lower bounds have been estimated subjectively by assuming decreases or increases in forecasts of unaccounted for water, metered demand and per capital consumption.

Figure 8.5

River and canal water quality by region, 1990, UK

Source:

National Rivers Authority, (1991). *Quality of Rivers, Canals and Estuaries in England and Wales: a Report of the 1990 Survey,* NRA; Scottish Office Environment Department, 1992. *Water Quality Survey of Scotland, 1990*; Department of the Environment (Northern Ireland), (1993). *River and Estuary Quality in Northern Ireland 1991.*

Comments:

Surveys of rivers and canals are carried out in England and Wales and Scotland every 5 years, and more frequently in Northern Ireland. Quality categories used in Scotland differ from those used in the rest of the UK. Categories presented are broadly based on levels of dissolved oxygen, biochemical oxygen demand, and ammoniacal nitrogen in each river length.

Figure 8.6 Annual average concentrations of dissolved oxygen, Biochemical Oxygen Demand, and ammoniacal nitrogen, 1976–1992 GB

Source:

National Rivers Authority and Scottish River Purification Boards

Comments:

Harmonised Monitoring Scheme (HMS) information. Three determinands are shown:

Dissolved Oxygen – the amount of oxygen dissolved in water; a test of the ability of the water to support life.

Biochemical Oxygen Demand (BOD) – measures the amount of oxygen consumed in water, usually by organic pollution.

Ammoniacal Nitrogen – often found in water as a result of the discharge of sewage effluent, widely used to characterise water quality.

The averages shown are based on samples taken at about 230 HMS sites on just over 200 rivers in GB. Most of these sites are situated at tidal limits of major rivers or at points of confluence of significant tributaries. Thus the data are not comparable in coverage to the more extensive river quality surveys carried out every 5 years, which cover the full lengths of each river in the country.

Figure 8.7

Annual average concentrations of certain heavy metals, 1976–1992, GB

Source:

National Rivers Authority and River Purification Boards in Scotland.

Comments:

Harmonised Monitoring Scheme (HMS). The averages for copper, lead, and zinc are based on samples taken at HMS sites on nearly 200 rivers in GB (see also notes for Figure 8.6). The Rivers Red and Carnon in Cornwall and the Ystwyth and Nant Y Fendrod in Wales are excluded because they had very high levels of either zinc, lead or copper which significantly distort the national average.

Table 8.1

Estimated consumption of groundwater and non-tidal surface water abstracted in 1990

Source:

National Rivers Authority, (1992) *Water Resources Development Strategy: a Discussion Document.*

Comments:

Excludes tidal abstractions and those abstractions where 100% of water is returned to source. Data are approximate and are for categories where consumption is likely to be taking place.

Table 8.2
**Public water supply baseline average demand
projections to 2021, surplus resources in 2021 as a
percentage of average demand, England and Wales**

Source:
National Rivers Authority, (1992) *Water Resources
Development Strategy: a Discussion Document.*

Comments:
See comments for Figure 8.4. Figures for surplus resources
assumes present resources continue to be available together
with schemes identified in S.143 of the above report.

CHAPTER 9

Figure 9.1
**Concentration of caesium-137 in the Irish and
North Sea, 1980, 1985 and 1991**

Source:
Department of the Environment, (1993). *Digest of Environmental
Protection and Water Statistics,* No 15. HMSO

Comments:
Data obtained from seawater samples collected on research
vessel cruises by the Directorate of Fisheries Research,
Ministry of Agriculture, Fisheries and Food (MAFF).

Figure 9.2
**Mercury concentrations in fish muscle by species
and area, 1980–1992.**

Source:
Department of the Environment, (1993). *Digest of
Environmental Protection and Water Statistics,* No 15. HMSO

Comments:
Results obtained from the fish monitoring programme
carried out by the Directorate of Fisheries Research, MAFF.

Figure 9.3
Stocks of cod in the North Sea, 1963– 1993

Source:
Department of the Environment, (1993). *Digest of
Environmental Protection and Water Statistics,* No 15. HMSO

Comments:
Information obtained by MAFF from the International
Council for the Exploration of the Sea.

Table 9.1
**Direct and riverine inputs from the UK to saline
waters around the UK, 1985–1991**

Source:
Department of the Environment, (1993). *Digest of
Environmental Protection and Water Statistics* No 15. HMSO.

Comments:
Figures for the two earlier years are likely to be less reliable,
and not entirely comparable with later information. The
results give an approximate indication only of trends since
the mid-1980s. All figures shown are upper estimates; some
samples may contain minute quantities of substances below
the detection limits of the monitoring equipment, and it is
assumed that where samples show no concentrations then
the true concentration is at the limit of detection. Figures
derived from North Sea Conference Reports (1985 and
1988 data) and UK reports to the Paris Commission (1990
and 1991 data).

Table 9.2
**Average concentrations of heavy metals in fish
muscle by species and area, 1980–1992**

Source:
Department of the Environment, (1993). *Digest of
Environmental Protection and Water Statistics,* No 15. HMSO

Comments:
Results obtained from the fish monitoring programme
carried out by the Directorate of Fisheries Research, MAFF.
Samples are not taken every year in all areas.

CHAPTER 10

Figure 10.1
Distribution of the major soil groups, UK

Source:
Soil Survey and Land Research Centre

Comments:
Based on National Soil Map 1983, with 2 or 3 observations
per square kilometre.

Figure 10.2

Organic matter, England and Wales

Source:
Soil Survey and Land Research Centre

Comments:
Based on National Soil Inventory for England and Wales. Aggregate samples of the top 15 cm collected from each intersect of a 5 km grid during 1978–83. Factor of 1.7 used to convert organic carbon content to organic matter.

Figure 10.3

Land at most risk from erosion, England and Wales

Source:
Soil Survey and Land Research Centre

Comments:
Based on data collected during field soil survey for the National Soil Map 1983. Monitored 17 sites with an average area of 30 km². Occurrence of soil erosion by water was related to soil type and the national distribution of these soils was used to map land at risk.

Figure 10.4

Soil buffering capacity, England and Wales

Source:
Soil Survey and Land Research Centre

Comments:
Based on broad classes of soil reclassified on the basis of their acidity and cation exchange capacity.

Figure 10.5

Concentration of zinc in topsoil, England and Wales

Source:
Soil Survey and Land Research Centre

Comments:
Based on information from the National Soil Inventory of England and Wales. Each intersect on a 5 km grid was visited during 1978–83 and an aggregate sample taken from the top 15 cm.

CHAPTER 11

Figure 11.1

Rates of urbanisation 1981–2001, England

Source:
Department of the Environment, (1990). *Rates of Urbanisation in England 1981–2001*. HMSO.

Comments:
The rate of urbanisation is defined as the percentage increase to 2001 in urban areas based on the stock of land in urban use in 1981. Forecasting was based on the relationship between residential construction and urban growth. Housing completions statistics for calendar years and changes in residential rateable hereditaments for financial years were used as measures of housing output. Land Use Change statistics for England were used to assess growth in urban land between 1985 and 1988. Forecasts of urbanisation are also underpinned by 1985 based household projections.

Figure 11.2

Motor vehicle ownership per 1000 population by county 1991, GB

Source:
Department of Transport, (1993). *Transport Statistics GB, 1992*. HMSO.

Comments:
Car ownership data based on records of licensed vehicles at the Driver and Vehicle Licensing Agency (DVLA). Per capita estimates derived from 1989 mid-year population estimates.

Figure 11.3

Major retail developments 1960–1992, UK

Source:
Oxford Institute of Retail Management; British Council of Shopping Centres

Comments:
Results from a comprehensive survey of shopping centres in the UK over 5000m² or 50,000 sq ft.

Figure 11.4
Distance travelled by car per person per annum by purpose 1975/76 and 1988/90, GB

Source:
Department of Transport, (1993). *Transport Statistics GB, 1992*. HMSO.

Comments:
Information derived from 1975/6 and 1988/90 National Travel Surveys. Excludes journeys under 1 mile.

Figure 11.5
Approved Green Belt land, 1991, England, Scotland and Northern Ireland

Source:
Department of the Environment; Scottish Office Environment Department; Department of the Environment (Northern Ireland).

Figure 11.6
Protected areas in the UK

Source:
Countryside Commission

Figure 11.7
Livestock numbers 1972–1992, UK

Source:
Ministry of Agriculture, Fisheries and Food. *Agriculture in the UK* (annual). HMSO.

Comments:
Data derived from annual agriculture censuses of England, Scotland, Wales and Northern Ireland.

Figure 11.8
Total crops, wheat and barley areas 1972–1992, UK

Source:
Ministry of Agriculture, Fisheries and Food. *Agriculture in the UK (annual)*. HMSO.

Comments:
Data derived from annual agricultural censuses.

Figure 11.9
Crop yields 1972–1992, UK

Source:
Ministry of Agriculture, Fisheries and Food. *Agriculture in the UK (annual)*. HMSO.

Comments:
Data on yields derived from gross output (tonnes) divided by cropping areas (hectares). Data on output and crop areas derived from annual agricultural censuses.

Figure 11.10
Forest health surveys: crown density of certain species, 1987–1992, UK

Source:
Department of the Environment, (1993). *Digest of Environmental Protection and Water Statistics*. HMSO.

Comments:
Changes in tree health monitored by annually re-assessing the condition of five species in plots distributed throughout Great Britain. Crown density is used as an index of tree condition and is assessed relative to a tree with full foliage. Based on information supplied by the Forestry Commission.

Table 11.1
Statutory protected areas, November 1993, UK

Source:
Department of the Environment, (1993). *Digest of Environmental Protection and Water Statistics*. HMSO.

Comments:
Some areas may be included in more than one category. SSSIs are for Great Britain only. Areas of Scientific Interest and Areas of Special Scientific Interest are for Northern Ireland only. Based on information supplied by Department of the Environment (Northern Ireland), MAFF, English Nature, Countryside Council for Wales, Scottish Natural Heritage.

CHAPTER 12

Figure 12.1
Primary aggregates consumption and projections, 1961 –2011, GB

Source:
British Geological Survey (Institute of Geological Sciences prior to 1983) Annual Reports. *UK Mineral Statistics*, HMSO (historic data). Department of the Environment (projections).

Comments:
Projections made by ECOTEC Research and Consulting Ltd and Cambridge Econometrics for DOE. (*Forecasting the Demand for Primary Aggregates* – unpublished ECOTEC report, 1992; and *Forecasts of Long-term Economic Growth and Construction Output*– unpublished Cambridge Econometrics report, 1992). Cambridge Econometrics produced forecasts of construction activity using a model of the UK economy which produces forecasts of sectoral economic growth. The model inputs key assumptions such as interest rates, government spending, world output and inflation. It is assumed that there is no change in government policy for construction and related industries. The construction forecasts were used by ECOTEC to forecast the demand for aggregates using a regression model of the relationship between construction investment and primary aggregate consumption. The forecasts give a view of the likely demand over the period; they are not intended to denote demand over a shorter term, nor do they represent production targets.

Figure 12.2
Mineral production, 1960–1991, UK

Source:
British Geological Survey (Institute of Geological Sciences prior to 1983) Annual Reports. *UK Mineral Statistics*. HMSO.

Figure 12.3
Production of coal, oil and gas, 1967–1992, UK

Source:
Department of Trade and Industry, (1993). *Digest of UK Energy Statistics* 1993. HMSO

Table 12.1
Oil and natural gas reserves, 1981–1992, UK

Source:
Department of Trade and Industry, (1993). *Development of the Oil and Gas Resources of the UK*. DTI

Paragraph 12.14
Projections of silica sand and minerals to produce cement

Source:
Department of the Environment

Comments:
Projections made by ECOTEC Research and Consulting Ltd and Cambridge Econometrics for DOE. (*Forecasting the Demand for Silica Sand* – unpublished ECOTEC report, 1992; *A Forecasting Methodology for the Estimation of Demand for Cement and Cement Materials* – unpublished ECOTEC report, 1990; and *Forecasts of Long-term Economic Growth and Construction Output*- unpublished Cambridge Econometrics report). Cambridge Econometrics provided long term forecasts of construction activity using a model of the UK economy, which produces forecasts of sectoral economic growth. The model inputs key assumptions such as interest rates, government spending, world output and inflation. It is assumed that there is no change in government policy for the construction and related industries. The construction forecasts were used by ECOTEC to derive forecasts for demand for silica sand, and minerals to produce cement, based on a regression model of the relationship between construction activity and consumption. In the case of silica sand ECOTEC also made separate projections of car and commercial vehicle production which is also a major determinant of the demand for silica sand. The forecasts give a view of the likely demand over the period; they are not intended to denote demand over a shorter term, nor do they represent production targets.

CHAPTER 13

Figure 13.1
Gross change in mean species number, 1978 and 1990, GB.

Source:
Department of the Environment, (1993). *Countryside Survey 1990*

Comments:
Gross change in species numbers in paired plots surveyed in 1978 and 1990; regardless of whether the plots includes changes within the same habitat type. Thus, gross change includes changes within and between habitat types. Plots are allocated to the habitat type recorded in 1978. The random plots are 200 m^2

Figure 13.2

Change in mean species numbers within habitat types, 1978 and 1990, GB

Source:

Department of the Environment, (1993). *Countryside Survey 1990.*

Comments:

Change in species numbers in paired plots surveyed in 1978 and 1990; analysis restricted to those plots that remained within the same habitat type in both survey years.

Table 13.1

Areas of special scientific interest, 1993, UK

Source:

English Nature, Scottish National Heritage, Countryside Council for Wales, Department of the Environment (Northern Ireland).

Comments:

Figures relate to designated Sites of Special Scientific Interest (SSSIs) in GB and to Areas of Special Scientific Interest (ASSIs) in Northern Ireland in November 1993.

CHAPTER 17

Figure 17.1

Fish landed into the UK by UK vessels, 1962–1992

Source:

Ministry of Agriculture, Fisheries and Food, (annual). *Sea Fisheries Statistical Tables*, HMSO.

CHAPTER 19

Figure 19.1

Comparison of demands for types of fuel between 1973 and 1992, UK

Source:

Department of Trade and Industry.

CHAPTER 23

Figure 23.1

Typical composition of household (dustbin) waste and its potential for recycling

Source:

Warren Spring Laboratory, (1993) *An Overview of the Impact of Source Separation Schemes on the Domestic Waste Stream in the UK and their relevance to the Government's Recycling Target.*

Table 23.1

Estimated total annual waste arisings in the UK, by sector

Source:

Department of the Environment, (1993) *Digest of Environmental Protection and Water Statistics* No. 15. HMSO.

Comments:

Figures for agricultural wastes refer to wastes from housed livestock only and are wet weight. Figures for mining and quarrying wastes excludes wastes from opencast coal mining, but includes wastes from primary aggregate extraction. Figures for sewage sludge arisings are estimated from dry weight figures on the basis of 4% solid content on average. The figure for household waste is an estimated maximum value which includes up to 5 million tonnes from civic amenity sites. The figure for commercial waste is rounded to the nearest 5 million tonnes of which approximately 5 million tonnes is wastes normally collected from retail shops and small commercial premises by Local Authorities. The figure for construction and demolition wastes includes hard materials, for example bricks and concrete and road planings, only.

Table 23.2

Estimated disposal routes for the main elements of controlled waste in the UK

Source:

Department of the Environment, (1991) *Digest of Environmental Protection and Water Statistics* No. 13. HMSO. Department of the Environment, (1992) *The Occurrence and Utilisation of Mineral and Construction Wastes.*

Comments:

All figures are rounded to the nearest 5%.

Table 23.3

Recycling levels achieved by some key industrial sectors

Source:

Department of the Environment, (1993) *Digest of Environmental Protection and Water Statistics* No. 15. HMSO

CHAPTER 26

Figure 26.1
Transport growth 1952–1992, GB

Source:
Department of Transport, (1993). *Transport Statistics GB.* HMSO.

Comments:
Passenger transport – different methods were used for calculating bus and coach travel before and after 1970. The series therefore gives only a broad guide to trends.

Freight transport – figures for water transport from 1972 are not comparable to earlier years; from 1972, water transport includes all UK coastwise and one-port freight movements by sea, and inland waterway traffic. Earlier years include only GB coastwise traffic and internal traffic on British Waterways Board waterways.

Figure 26.2
Transport contribution to emissions, London and national, 1990

Source:
Department of the Environment

Figure 26.3
Transport emissions; actual and target

Source:
Eggleston, H.S., (1992). *Pollution in the Atmosphere: Future Emissions from the UK*, Warren Spring Laboratory.

Comments:
Historical data obtained by Warren Spring Laboratory from the National Atmospheric Emissions Inventory.

Table 26.1
International comparisons passenger and freight transport

Source: Department of Transport, (1993). *Transport Statistics GB.* HMSO.

CHAPTER 31

Table 31.1
Allocation of the Environmental Action Fund, 1993/94

Source:
Department of Environment

CHAPTER 32

Table 32.1
Public concern about the environment and personal "green" actions, 1993, England and Wales

Source:
Department of the Environment. *1993 Survey of Public Attitudes to the Environment*

Comments:
Percentages given are for all respondents except for the last two actions relating to car use given in the table. For these actions the percentages relate only to those respondents with access to a car. The proportions are for respondents who reported taking action mentioned on a regular basis in the previous 12 months.

Table 32.2
Green consumerism and the need for product information, 1993, England and Wales

Source:
Department of the Environment. *1993 Survey of Public Attitudes to the Environment*

Comments:
Percentages for green consumers exclude all respondents who said the question was inappropriate to them, for example non-car users are excluded from the percentage using unleaded petrol. The proportions are for respondents who reported taking the action mentioned on a regular basis in the previous 12 months.

Printed in the United Kingdom for HMSO
Dd 5061972 3/94 C15 51-4162 12521 Ord 278440

PICTURE CREDITS

TOPIC	SOURCE	PHOTOGRAPHER
Countryside	ACE Photo Agency	P.L.I
Housing	Pictures Colour Library	[Not stated]
Traffic	Environmental Picture Library	Martin Bond
Recycling	Environmental Picture Library	Philip Carr
Industry	Image Bank	[Not stated]
Agriculture	Environmental Picture Library	Martin Bond
Environmental	Department of the Environment	Crocodile Photography
Divider Pages "People"	Image Bank	[Not stated]